CLIMBING AND BOULDERING GUIDE

HUECO TANKS

CLIMBING AND BOULDERING GUIDE

HUECO TANKS

SECOND EDITION

John Sherman

Chockstone Press, Inc.
Evergreen, Colorado

HUECO TANKS: Climbing and Bouldering Guide, Second Edition

ISBN 0-934641-87-0

Published and distributed by
Chockstone Press, Inc.
Post Office Box 3505
Evergreen, Colorado 80439

TO THOSE
WHO CLIMB
FOR FUN.

PREFACE

Since the first edition of this guidebook appeared, a lot has happened at Hueco Tanks. Over 200 new boulder problems have been established and the place has transformed from a little known paradise to an international hot spot. Even the Europeans (with the measly exception of the French) have declared Hueco Tanks "the best bouldering area in the world." It's not a bad cragging spot either.

Because the first edition has sold out (relegating it to collector's item status) and there has been so much new route development, I have been coerced through the cajoling of countless people and the promise of making more than 95 cents an hour (like on the first edition) to do a revised second edition.

From the first edition I learned that not even a wet t-shirt photo could entice people to read the text so this edition has far less text and far more photos. I also learned that folks with no sense of humor should steer wide of far West Texas.

I give thanks to the following people for making this second edition possible: Mike Head, James Crump, and Dave Head for cataloging the roped climbing history of the park in the first edition of this guide; everybody else I thanked in the first edition; everybody who provided new route information for this guide, especially Dean Potter, Jim Belcer, Chris Baker and Jim Hurst; and Donny Hardin and Greg Burns for providing dark grainy beverages, inspiration, and spots. For their cooperation and the generous use of many photos, I thank the Texas Parks and Wildlife Department, in particular David Riskind, Warren Watson, and Dave Parker. Last, but not least, I thank the scores of people who told me that the first edition was the best guide they'd ever used, thereby convincing me that guidebook writing, if done right, is not a thankless task.

–**John Sherman**

WARNING: CLIMBING IS A SPORT WHERE YOU MAY BE SERIOUSLY INJURED OR DIE.

READ THIS BEFORE YOU USE THIS BOOK.

This guidebook is a compilation of unverified information gathered from many different climbers. The author cannot assure the accuracy of any of the information in this book, including the topos and route descriptions, the difficulty ratings, and the protection ratings. These may be incorrect or misleading and it is impossible for any one author to climb all the routes to confirm the information about each route. Also, ratings of climbing difficulty and danger are always subjective and depend on the physical characteristics (for example, height), experience, technical ability, confidence and physical fitness of the climber who supplied the rating. Additionally, climbers who achieve first ascents sometimes underrate the difficulty or danger of the climbing route out of fear of being ridiculed if a climb is later down-rated by subsequent ascents. Therefore, be warned that you must exercise your own judgment on where a climbing route goes, its difficulty and your ability to safely protect yourself from the risks of rock climbing. Examples of some of these risks are: falling due to technical difficulty or due to natural hazards such as holds breaking, falling rock, climbing equipment dropped by other climbers, hazards of weather and lightning, your own equipment failure, and failure or absence of fixed protection.

You should not depend on any information gleaned from this book for your personal safety; your safety depends on your own good judgment, based on experience and a realistic assessment of your climbing ability. If you have any doubt as to your ability to safely climb a route described in this book, do not attempt it.

The following are some ways to make your use of this book safer:

1. **CONSULTATION:** You should consult with other climbers about the difficulty and danger of a particular climb prior to attempting it. Most local climbers are glad to give advice on routes in their area and we suggest that you contact locals to confirm ratings and safety of particular routes and to obtain first-hand information about a route chosen from this book.
2. **INSTRUCTION:** Most climbing areas have local climbing instructors and guides available. We recommend that you engage an instructor or guide to learn safety techniques and to become familiar with the routes and hazards of the areas described in this book. Even after you are proficient in climbing safely, occasional use of a guide is a safe way to raise your climbing standard and learn advanced techniques.
3. **FIXED PROTECTION:** Many of the routes in this book use bolts and pitons which are permanently placed in the rock. Because of variances in the manner of placement, weathering, metal fatigue, the quality of the metal used, and many other factors, these fixed protection pieces should always be considered suspect and should always be backed up by equipment that you place yourself. Never depend for your safety on a single piece of fixed protection because you never can tell whether it will hold weight, and in some cases, fixed protection may have been removed or is now absent.

Be aware of the following specific potential hazards which could arise in using this book:

1. **MISDESCRIPTIONS OF ROUTES:** If you climb a route and you have a doubt as to where the route may go, you should not go on unless you are sure that you can go that way safely. Route descriptions and topos in this book may be inaccurate or misleading.
2. **Incorrect Difficulty Rating:** A route may, in fact, be more difficult than the rating indicates. Do not be lulled into a false sense of security by the difficulty rating.
3. **INCORRECT PROTECTION RATING:** If you climb a route and you are unable to arrange adequate protection from the risk of falling through the use of fixed pitons or bolts and by placing your own protection devices, do not assume that there is adequate protection available higher just because the route protection rating indicates the route is not an "X" or an "R" rating. Every route is potentially an "X" (a fall may be deadly), due to the inherent hazards of climbing – including, for example, failure or absence of fixed protection, your own equipment's failure, or improper use of climbing equipment.

THERE ARE NO WARRANTIES, WHETHER EXPRESS OR IMPLIED, THAT THIS GUIDEBOOK IS ACCURATE OR THAT THE INFORMATION CONTAINED IN IT IS RELIABLE. THERE ARE NO WARRANTIES OF FITNESS FOR A PARTICULAR PURPOSE OR THAT THIS GUIDE IS MERCHANTABLE. YOUR USE OF THIS BOOK INDICATES YOUR ASSUMPTION OF THE RISK THAT IT MAY CONTAIN ERRORS AND IS AN ACKNOWLEDGMENT OF YOUR OWN SOLE RESPONSIBILITY FOR YOUR CLIMBING SAFETY.

CONTENTS

INTRODUCTION

Congratulations! You have just purchased the finest climbing and bouldering guide ever written for Hueco Tanks State Park. If you haven't purchased this book and are just browsing through it in a climbing shop memorizing the location of the mega-gnarlies, you're in for a disappointment. Without this guide in your hands, your chances of finding 90% of Hueco's climbs and boulder problems are about as good as Charles Manson's chance of parole and subsequent election as governor of California...maybe worse, they did elect Reagan.

Hueco Tanks is one of the most complex climbing areas in the nation, and other than a few teaser classics on the easily found Mushroom Boulder, the majority of three-star superproblems are well hidden, making it worth hocking your rack to buy this book.

When I think of Hueco Tanks, I think of desert sunshine, haunting Indian paintings, cheap beer, great Mexican food, abysmal dollar movies and sleazy strip joints. But it's more than that – it's a wonderland of boulders bristling with positive microflakes and peppered with gaping huecos; it's enormous roofs, vein-bursting traverses, and pleasant mantle-free topouts; it's joyful jughauls, cerebral sequences, and impossible looking problems that go; it's dirtying your shorts starting a sit-down problem, then filling them committing to the off-the-deck moves. It's quite simply the best bouldering in America.

In addition to its tremendous bouldering reputation, Hueco Tanks is quickly gaining fame as one of the foremost cragging areas in the U.S. It has everything from overbolted faces to devious runout death leads, from 35-foot roof cracks to 250-foot chimneys. If you don't have fun here, you've got problems.

WHAT'S INSIDE

Lead climbs and topropes are listed with Yosemite Decimal Ratings. Boulder problems are listed with V-ratings, an open-ended system explained later in the introduction. Many people have asked me, "Where do you draw the line between bouldering and soloing?" My stock reply has been, "If you fall soloing you die." For the purposes of this guide, however, I've included only problems with a maximum height off the ground of 30 feet.

There are many problems I have left out of the guide as being too obscure, or too difficult to find. I've included all problems I felt to be worth two or more stars, no matter how difficult to find.

Every lead climb and toprope I have information on is included regardless of quality, with the exception of those I couldn't find from the given information.

Climbs and boulder problems which are positively known to have been chiseled or doctored prior to their first ascent have been omitted from the guide.

GETTING THERE

Hueco Tanks State Park is located in far West Texas approximately 30 miles east of El Paso. Look at the map on page 3. Most people will approach the area via I-10 and El Paso. From El Paso, highway 62/180 heads east out of town to Hueco Tanks. Most signs for 62/180 also read Carlsbad.

Getting onto 62/180 from I-10 would seem easy, but the freeway interchange is confusing, especially if you're coming from the west. This is often the case in El Paso; many interchanges take you off the freeway long before you actually reach the street you exited for. In the 62/180 from the west case you will exit the freeway then parallel it through one stoplight (Chelsea Ave – be sure to get out of the left lane before this light or you'll be forced to turn left onto Chelsea) until you reach a second light at Paisano. Turn left (north) on Paisano, which Y's into Montana (Montana and 62/180 are one and the same.) Follow this ugly boulevard (Montana) east past miles of car lots, shopping centers, stoplights, and 7-11s and eventually it will take you out of town and east on 62/180 towards Hueco.

Once you're on Montana Blvd heading east from El Paso, Hueco Tanks is easy to find. The turnoff for Hueco Tanks is Farm Road 2775, but is more easily identified by the land sales office for Hueco Tanks Estates. This building looks like the Jupiter 2 spacecraft from "Lost In Space." It's right on the corner of 62/180 and Farm Road 2775. Turn north on 2775 (the only way you can turn onto it) and follow it eight miles to the park.

Another way to get to 62/180 from I-10 (a way that is shorter from the east and less confusing from the west) is to take the Zaragosa Rd (Farm Rd 659) exit off of I-10. This exit is on the eastern outskirts of town, where the development currently thins out. Turn north at the interchange (the sign will tell you you're on George Dieter, but don't panic, Zaragosa reappears) and get into the right lane as soon as possible.

At 0.3 mile, you will reach an intersection where Zaragosa angles off of George Dieter to the right. (Signs for the Tony Lama factory outlet will also direct you north off of I-10, along George Dieter, then onto Zaragosa.) Take Zaragosa to the right and follow it 8.5 miles to 62/180.(Zaragosa takes a potentially confusing jog across Farm Road 359 at 3.2 miles; be sure to follow the Farm Road 659 signs.) Turn right (east) on 62/180 and follow it 8.0 miles to the Jupiter 2 Hueco Tanks exit.

ENTERING THE PARK

As you approach Hueco Tanks from the south, your first glimpse of the rocks will be disappointing, unless you're from Stoney Point. The park appears to be nothing more than a couple of enormous brown lumps. If Paul Bunyon had made it this far south, the lack of trees would be attributed to him and the lumps credited to his ox Babe. Fortunately, Pecos Bill has a lock on the legend stuff around these parts. Don't be put off by initial appearances, the southern aspects of the Hueco rock are usually the least sound. As you drive along the western perimeter of the park the multitude of boulders on the Frontside will be visible, begging you to mount them. First, however, you must get through the entrance station.

The daily entry fee is $2.00 per person ages 13 and up. Between ages six and 12 the fee is $1.00 per person. Children under six are admitted free. Students with a currently valid student ID (any school in the country)get in for $1.00. An annual pass, called the Conservation Passport, costs $25.00.

In addition to the entry fee, each person entering the park to go rock climbing or bouldering must pay a climbing activity fee. This fee is $2.00 per person per day. If you have a Conservation Passport, the fee is $1.00 per person per day.

CAMPING/ACCOMMODATIONS

The campground facilities at Hueco Tanks State Park are outstanding. The heads are heated, the showers are hot, and each site sports electric outlets and a cold water faucet. It can't be beat. Unfortunately, it doesn't come cheap. The 17 standard campsites, with water and electricity currently cost $11.00 per night. You can have up to eight people in the site

and two cars. An additional $2.00 parking fee is charged if you have a third vehicle. Be sure all wheels of all vehicles are on the pavement or risk the wrath of the rangers.

If you didn't bring any electrical appliances, like a heater for your tent, reading lamps, toaster oven, Cuisanart, or Vacujac, then I suggest you go for one of the three undeveloped sites. They have no electricity and currently cost $8.00 per night.

Campfires are no longer allowed in the park. You must cook on gas or propane stoves (no charcoal).

During climbing season the campground is nearly always full. To ensure getting a site you should make reservations by calling (512) 389-8900 (in Austin, Tx). You can make reservations from 48 hours to one year in advance.

You can receive mail at the park. Address it:

(your name)
c/o Hueco Tanks State Park
6900 Hueco Tanks Road #1
El Paso, Tx 79938

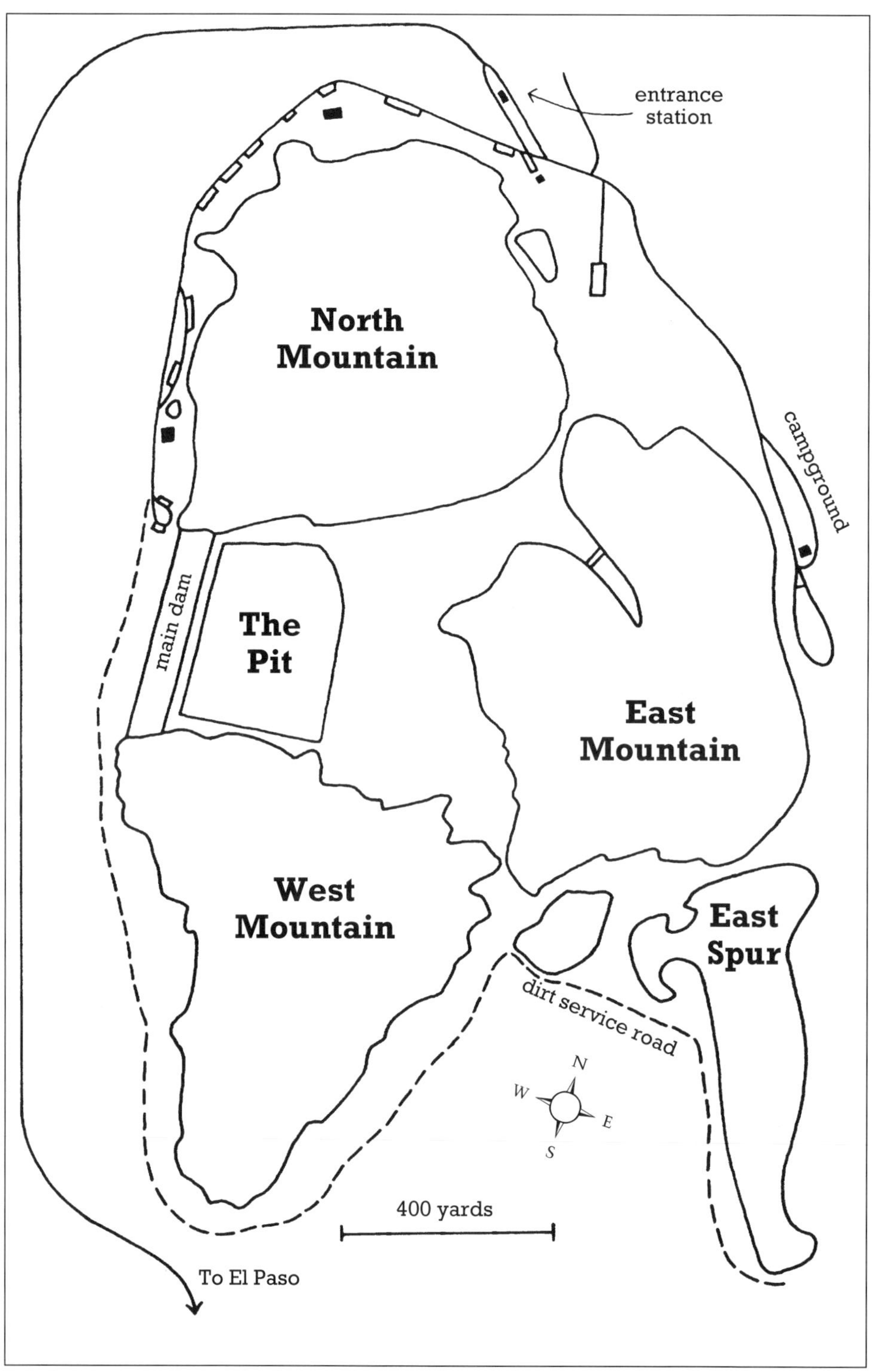
entrance
station
North
Mountain
campground
main dam
The
Pit
East
Mountain
West
Mountain
East
Spur
dirt service road
N
W
E
S
400 yards
To El Paso

The phone number for Hueco Tanks State Park is (915) 857-1135. **Do not** use this number for campground reservations.

You may still use the showers even if you aren't a registered camper or your mom isn't forcing you. You may not, however, park in the campground to do so. Park at the East Parking Lot and take the five minute stroll.

If you're cheap, adventuresome, or just hate Good Sam Clubbers, then Pete's is the place for you. Also known as the Hueco Tanks Country Store, Pete's is the quonset hut located outside the park three miles from the entrance station. Pete will let you camp outside the hut. Pete and his wife Queta are famous worldwide for taking care of visiting climbers. If you stay with Pete, you can arrange with him to have your mail or UPS packages delivered there. When at Pete's, take care not to disturb his neighbor Willy to the north (in the camouflaged compound). Do not park on Willy's property. Respect Willy's privacy.

For the more intrepid (read lowest budget) expeditions there are many dirt roads leading out into the desert around the park. Camping in the desert is strictly at your own risk. All of the land surrounding the park is privately owned. Watch out for land owners, coyotes, snakes, rough roads, illegal aliens, and evil dwarfs with chainsaws.

RANGER RICK TALK

Hueco Tanks bustles with biology, from the two-dimensional bunnies adorning Farm Road 2775 to freshwater shrimp in the intermittently water-filled huecos atop the mountains. Most of the fauna is well hidden, however, the flora is unavoidable. Nearly all of the plants have spines, hooks, or thorns. Below I've ranked the plants in order from those you'd least like to fall into to those you can walk through with relative impunity.

Heinous	**Jingus**	**Casual**
Cactus	Sotol	Cresosote
Mesquite	Goathead burrs	Oak tree
Catclaw	Ocotillo	Lichen
Banana yucca	Most grasses	Ferns
Lechuguilla		

It's worth learning to identify these, not just to avoid them, but also to locate the boulder problems (some problems are located by marker plants, e.g. starts just right of then traverses left over the bloodstained yucca.) See the cartoon at right. As far as fauna goes, the things to look out for are snakes, mosquitoes and scorpions. Rattlers hibernate in the chilly months when conditions are best for bouldering. The mosquitoes also disappear at this time. Scorpions hide under rocks, so be careful when you're removing a cheater stone left by some short-on-talent climber. Kick it over first before you slide your fingers under it. Scorpions also like to cozy up in shoes. If your shoes smell like mine and you leave them outside the tent at night, be sure to shake them out before you slip the digits in.

GEOLOGY

A long time ago, before the advent of Bosch drills, before TCUs, even before EBs, The Hueco Mountains were just so much flat-lying limestone. Then, 34 million years ago, a big glob of molten rock rose from the depths of the earth and nearly made it to the surface before it quickly cooled and solidified. In essence, it formed a giant embarrassing blackhead under the earth's skin. The overlying skin eventually eroded away, exposing the crusty plug of syenite porphyry. In time this plug will wash away too, but for now it's still with us and known as Hueco Tanks.

Hueco Tanks is famous for its narrow-necked spherical pocket holds; so famous, that the term hueco is now used worldwide to refer to such holds. How do huecos form? Scientists know little more than you do. Although theories abound, mostly calling upon wind, water, or salt weathering, there has never been any quantitative research on this phenomenon. Why spend money researching this oft-asked question when it could be spent on countless artillery shells with which nearby Fort Bliss can deliver your 6 AM wake up call?

Another geologic phenomenon of interest to climbers at Hueco Tanks is what the locals call "ironrock." This is the hard, dark brown rock upon which most of the problems in this guide are found. Ironrock coatings form where water runs down the faces. The ironrock coating case hardens the rock, making microholds unbelievably solid, and sharp. Be wary of ironrock plates stuck to tan colored rock. Pick on one of these "scabs" and you'll be a long time healing. To test one, rap it with your knuckles – if it sounds hollow, don't trust it to hold body weight. These scabs are frequently found at the tops of ironrock overhangs, where the angle kicks back to under vertical.

The tan rock is softer than the iron rock and usually crumbly. There are notable exceptions (the rock at Blood and Gore comes to mind), and these areas are the last to get wet when it rains or snows.

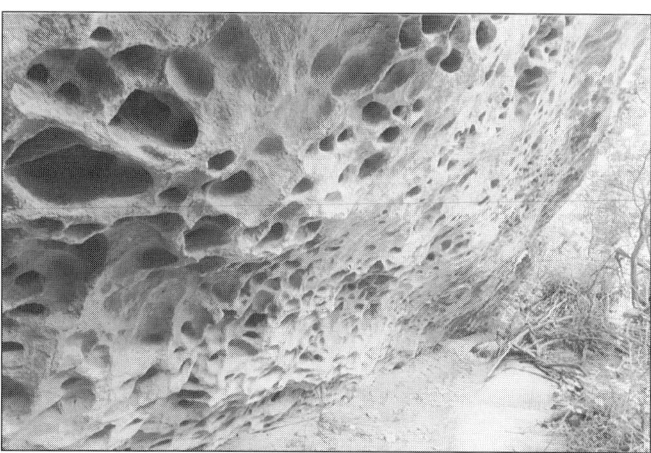

WEATHER

West Texas is justifiably famous for its sunshine. It's equally infamous for its winds and dust storms. Rainfall is minimal. El Paso averages about eight inches of precipitation a year, most of it coming in the hot summer months.

Hueco Tanks' reputation is as a winter area and there is no other U.S. area with better climbing and better weather in the winter. Despite all the sunshine, winter can be cold. There are usually two or three days each winter when it snows. Hueco Tanks is over 4000 feet in elevation. Nevertheless, a pleasant day of bouldering can be had if one stays out of the wind and close to the sun. The rock here warms up quickly. At night, temperatures can drop drastically. A 40-degree difference between daily high and low temperatures is not uncommon. Bring a good sleeping bag.

The combination of high elevation and desert sunshine can wreak havoc on human skin. Imagine crimson blisters raising on your forehead, leaking thin, clear pus into your eyes. Don't forget sunscreen, lip balm, and a sombrero. Drink lots of water; dehydration can transform tendons from healthy kevlar licorice whips into fragile candy canes.

The most popular months to visit Hueco Tanks are November through March. October and April are also good, but hot for some folks' tastes (70's and 80's). May can be boulderable as well, if one avoids the heat of midday. One of the hardest problems in this guide, Bad Judgement, was done in May on a 90 degree day. The grease factor was minimal because the humidity was only 8%. In June, temperatures hit the triple digits and conditions remain prohibitively hot through September. Only the hardiest locals brave the summer heat.

RULES

In the previous edition of this guide I gave a recipe on how one can piss off the rangers, get arrested and possibly close the park to climbing altogether (hop the fence, bring your unleashed dog, etc.). Either some climbers didn't get the joke or they truly have their heads up their asses.

Hueco Tanks is a state historical park. The park's primary mission is to preserve the historical and natural resources of the park. Recreational use is secondary. In other words, Hueco Tanks is not an amusement park created for climbers.

As climbers, we share the park with other user groups such as birdwatchers and picnickers. We also share it with each other as climbers. If we wish to retain the privilege of climbing at Hueco Tanks we must show each other respect. Maybe the birdwatchers would rather listen to a songbird than to your Dokken CD. How would you like it if they cranked Donny and Marie at volume ten?

Get a clue, don't leave your carpets or sketchpads fixed out in the park. The last time I cleaned up the East Spur Maze it looked like a homeless hideout. This shit will get us kicked out of the park. Selfish climbers have gotten the park closed to climbing before, they can do it again. If you find fixed rugs, remove them. They might get YOU and every other climber kicked out of the park. Ditto with picking up tape wads, butts, and chalk and Powerbar wrappers.

Climbers used to have a reputation as the most responsible user group at Hueco Tanks. We are rapidly losing that reputation. Anyone who reads the letters to the El Paso newspapers knows that public sentiment is against us. The people who write to the newspapers also write to the parks department, the governor and their congresspersons – in other words, the people who can and will kick us out if we don't stop acting like spoiled brats.

EMERGENCIES

In case of emergency, contact the rangers at the entrance station. After hours you might find them at either of the two small houses east of the entrance station. If you can't find the rangers then contact Montana Vista Volunteer Fire Dept. at 857- 0999 (24 hours) for accidents and injuries. For police emergencies call El Paso County Sheriff Eastside Substation at 546-2280.

BOLTING

Until 1989, placing fixed gear (bolts or pitons) on routes at Hueco Tanks was illegal. Thanks to the efforts of the El Paso Climbers Club and others, bolting is now legal, but only in adherence to the park's bolting policy. Placement of unauthorized bolts will endanger the future of climbing in the park, not to mention the violator's own future in the climbing community. Illegal bolting has closed the park to all roped climbing before (in 1988). Needless to say, the selfish climbers whose actions closed the park are not very popular anymore.

If you want to put up a new route that requires fixed protection you fill out an application available at the ranger station. The rules for bolting are covered in depth on the application. Read it carefully. The application goes through two approval steps—first through the El Paso Climber's Club, then through the Texas Parks and Wildlife Department. The application process is time consuming; allow at least a month for approval or denial.

The following are rules you may want to know before requesting an application.

- All routes, lead or toprope, that require fixed protection must be applied for.
- Only one application per applicant can be submitted during a review period (one month).
- Only the applicant will be eligible to place the fixed gear on the route, if approved.
- Applicant with an approved route is ineligible to submit another application until the previous one is lead by applicant.
- All gear (ropes, quickdraws, etc.) left on climbs more than 24 hours is subject to confiscation by the park.
- All routes under 40 feet will be considered as top-rope problems only.
- All fixed gear will be painted brown to match the rock color.
- Applications will be processed on a first come, first through basis.

UNNATURAL HISTORY

Due to the presence of water and game at Hueco Tanks, the area has attracted humans for over 10,000 years. Since pre-historic times, people have left their mark on Hueco Tanks in the form of pictographs (rock paintings). Over 3000 pictographs adorn the walls of Hueco Tanks (not including 20th century graffiti), making the park one of the greatest rock art sites in North America. The different styles of paintings–the Archaic, the Jornada Mogollon, and the Historic (Apache)–are described in the booklet "Rock paintings At Hueco Tanks State Historical Park," available at the entrance station. This booklet is recommended reading for all visitors to Hueco Tanks. A knowledge of the park's history, both cultural and natural, adds greatly to one's enjoyment of the park. If one looks at Hueco Tanks and sees only an enormous climbing gym, they are missing out big time.

(Learning to recognize the paintings, sometimes only a faded brushstroke or two, helps us to avoid climbing in areas where we shouldn't. The Indians at Hueco Tanks generally painted on smooth surfaces and us climbers need textured surfaces, i.e. holds, to climb on, so conflicts are rare. Nevertheless, there are a few areas, such as spots along the Nuclear Arms wall where climbers, if not careful, could come in contact with the paintings. An ability to discern these areas and the willingness to avoid them are skills to take pride in.)

In the 1600's Spaniards arrived in the region and in the mid-1800's the first Anglo settlers showed up. Many of the Historic Period paintings depict the Apache's contact with European culture (horses, European dress, rifles). Names and dates painted on the rock date back to 1849 and continue to the present. Gang tagging has been a big problem in the last few years.

One interesting period of Hueco Tanks history is not covered in the literature available at the office. In 1959, Hueco Tanks was acquired by Gerald P. O'Leary, president of Mt. Franklin Homes, Inc. For just $237.50 you could buy one of 90,000 60 x 110 foot lots in this budding resort. Imagine putting out on the eighteenth green, where now lies the shower block, then retiring for cocktails in the Space Needle restaurant atop the main buttress. Plenty of folks did.

They also imagined slaloming around the Dam Boulders on waterskis, while the kids were entertained at the Frontier Town theme park. The dams were built and The Pit flooded for long enough to snap a photo of the refreshing lake, upon which a swimsuited waterskiing nymph was superimposed. Soon thereafter, the water all drained out through the abundant fissures in the rock.

Not much later O'Leary was convicted of fraud. The subsequent owners of Hueco Tanks "donated" the land to El Paso County for a park (in exchange for a rumored $80,000). Eventually, the State of Texas acquired the land and Hueco Tanks State Park opened in June 1970

LEAD CLIMBING HISTORY

The history of lead climbing at Hueco Tanks can be summed up in one name – Mike Head. Mike first ascended over two-thirds of the lead climbs in this guide, usually in very bold style. Imagine leading *Window Pain* or *Head Fox* with only two bolts apiece as Mike first did. Or free soloing the first ascent of *Sea Of Holes,* before the loose rock had been cleaned off. Mike placed the majority of retrobolts in Hueco Tanks, changing his routes from sporty climbs into sportclimbs.

BOULDERING HISTORY

Dozens of boulderers have left their mark on the rocks of Hueco Tanks, but three climbers stand out as the main movers of Hueco Tanks bouldering. These three are Mike Head, Bob Murray, and myself. Mike Head is responsible for scores of moderate classics, as well as such desperates as The Bucket Roof (Dynamic Tension), Dragonfly, and The Mushroom Roof.

Bob Murray has done more to develop hard bouldering in the southwest than anyone else. His testpieces can be found throughout the park, the most prominent being the three El Murrays on the North Face of the Mushroom Boulder. The hardest topropes in this guide are also the work of Bob Murray. A wrist injury in 1984 ended Murray's days as a force at Hueco Tanks.

After Murray's departure, I was one of the only serious boulderers visiting the park in the mid- to late-80's. At one point there were over 1000 known boulder problems in the park that I had ascended, and fewer than 10 that I hadn't. It looked like I might be able to say I had done every problem at Hueco Tanks, but this never came to be. Nevertheless, I put up about 500 first ascents out of the estimated 1400 problems now established in the park. My favorite first ascents include Mother Of The Future, Double Boiler, Sex After Death, Splatter High, The Tall Cool Red One, Sign Of The Cross, Crash Dummy, Complete Dummy, High Ideals, and The Best Of The Best.

Since the publication of the first edition of this guide, bouldering has become the favored style of climbing at Hueco Tanks. Strong climbers from throughout the world have visited Hueco and left their mark on the boulders. Swiss climber Fred Nicole has done a number of impressive first ascents lately, including Crown of Aragorn, currently touted as Hueco's hardest.

ETHICS

Good style or bad style, however you choose to climb a route is your own business, until it threatens the climbing privileges of others. The types of behavior discussed below have been cited as potential reasons to close the park to climbing.

Tick Marks

Tick marks are chalk lines, dots, arrows, crosshairs, bullseyes, etc. drawn on the rock to point out holds. Ninety-nine percent of the time they are unnecessary, the other one percent of the time they are overdone. Tick marks show a blatant disrespect for the natural environment, other climbers' abilities, and other user groups.

Whereas most chalk marks can be mistaken as guano or other natural staining, tick marks are obviously unnatural and constitute little more than climbers' grafitti. Instead of relying on these "rookie stripes" to point out holds, develop an eye for the subtleties of the stone. Know that the crux foothold lies three inches left of that quarter-sized patch of lichen. Zero in on the hairline seam that intersects a handhold right where you want your ring finger to land. Rely on your sense of feel to tell you how your hand should settle onto each hold, not somebody else's stripes. If they're ticking every hold, the problem must be beyond their ability, so why depend on some wannabe's beta?

Furthermore, by keying into nature's varied clues you develop a more agile memory for moves and the ability to read the rock quickly. Who knows when you'll be looking at a lengthy groundfall, have no tick marks to bail you out, and need these skills to survive?

If you absolutely can't see a hold without ticking it, make your marks subtilely. Don't draw with a block of chalk. Instead leave a faint thumbprint. Your eyes will be drawn to the hold just as well. Brush the marks off when you're done. When you come upon tick marks, brush them off. It's a small price to pay to climb here.

Doctored Holds

A doctored hold is the signature of a coward. If you can't do a problem with the holds Mother Nature provided, then you're in over your head and don't belong on the problem.

When I wrote the first edition of this guide in 1990, I knew of only four holds chiseled in Hueco's boulders. In just one day this last fall I found six newly doctored problems. All six had been climbed before, ranging from V0 to V11 originally.

Some people don't get it that by filing, chipping, gluing, "enhancing," "comfortizing," doctoring, chiseling, and beating on the holds with other rocks that *they aren't doing the problem.* I don't care whether it's been done or not, the challenge wasn't met, the ascent (if there was one) wasn't valid and the problem has been destroyed for all future generations.

Granted, I'm pissed that many of my favorite problems like Moonshine Roof, Double Boiler, and Sex After Death have been violated, but at least I got to do those problems in their original condition. Those of you who weren't so lucky should be twice as pissed as I. Some sniveling talent-free dickweed has ripped you off of the opportunity to feel the same elation myself and others had when doing these climbs and the many others that have been bludgeoned.

If you see someone chiseling, filing, or otherwise doctoring holds, stop them, report them to the rangers, get them kicked out of the park. They are stealing your future. If the bad eggs aren't removed from the park, the park will be closed to all climbers.

Doctoring of holds is considered defacement of the rock, just as spraypainting is, and could lead to the park being closed to climbing.

Glue

About 15 years ago, glue was dripped behind the lip hold of Bucket Roof to reinforce it. It created a god-awful mess and was considered a mistake to be learned from and not repeated. It was proved that this tactic was unnecessary to put up quality problems at Hueco Tanks as nearly a thousand new boulder problems were put up after this with no glue.

Furthermore, the tactic didn't work as the hold just broke off anyway. Hueco has a strong tradition of boulder problems put up with respect for the rock. Lately a few individuals have turned their backs on this proud tradition and once again created a mess. And once again the glue has proven ineffective as many of these doctored holds have broken off anyway. (Doug Reed's Long Dong Roof comes to mind as an example of both.) If you can't cope with loose holds then your technique is defective, not the rock.

When confronted with loose rock, don't reach for the glue gun, rather use the opportunity to develop your ability to climb on shaky stone. Learn the right way to pull on loose holds (pull down and push in; don't pull out) and how to adjust your weight distribution to catch yourself should a hold fail. Learn how to use holds that will only support a fraction of your body weight. By practicing these techniques, you can stack the odds in your favor, a good thing should you one day find yourself very run out on loose holds.

Trash

Littering is as definitive a sign of low moral standing as doctoring holds. If you litter, don't be surprised when a crucial hold snaps, sending you into a thick patch of Prickly Pear Cactus.

OUTSIDE THE PARK

The following road log lists the distances from the park entrance station to facilities of interest to climbers, the nearest gas, the nearest food, the cheapest beer, the closest XXX drive-in, etc. Also see the map for locations of key facilities in East El Paso. Many of the places listed in the road log lie between the State Park and the area covered by the map. George Dieter Rd, the furthest east N-S road on the map lies 21.2 miles from the entrance station. (Note – it is local custom for slow cars to pull onto the wide shoulder of Montana to let others pass.)

Road Log

All distances are in miles from the entrance station along Farm Rd 2775 and 62/180 aka Montana Boulevard towards town. N, S refer to north or south side of Montana.

Miles	What you'll find
0.0	Nearest Coke machine and public phone (no incoming calls; collect or calling cards calls only) – the entrance station
2.9	Nearest food, beer, wine, cafe, coin-accepting pay phone – Hueco Tanks Country Store (Pete's) Hours: 9AM to 10 PM
11.4N	Nearest dragstrip – El Paso Speedway
13.3 N	J & R Supermarket
13.8S	Nearest gas – Pete and Bros. (also food, beer, wine, auto mechanic) Hours: 6AM – 10PM M-Sat, 7AM – 10PM Sun.
14.0N	Nearest laundromat – Eastwind Trailer Park
14.5S	Montana Vista Grocery (and bakery)
14.5N	Best Mexican restaurant in East El Paso – El Rancho Escondido
15.2S	Sheriff/Fire Dept. (and Papagayo store – gas, food, beer, wine)
15.6S	Nearest XXX drive-in – Fiesta drive-in, new films each Wednesday.
16.4N	Breakfast and lunch – Palmera Cafe
18.5S	Nearest cemetery (you never know when you'll have to dig up a date)

The following is on the East El Paso map:

22.5S	nearest 24 hr gas (also convenience store) – 7-11 at Montana and Lee Trevino

By now you are in East El Paso and the map and key on the facing page should guide you to other facilities you might need.

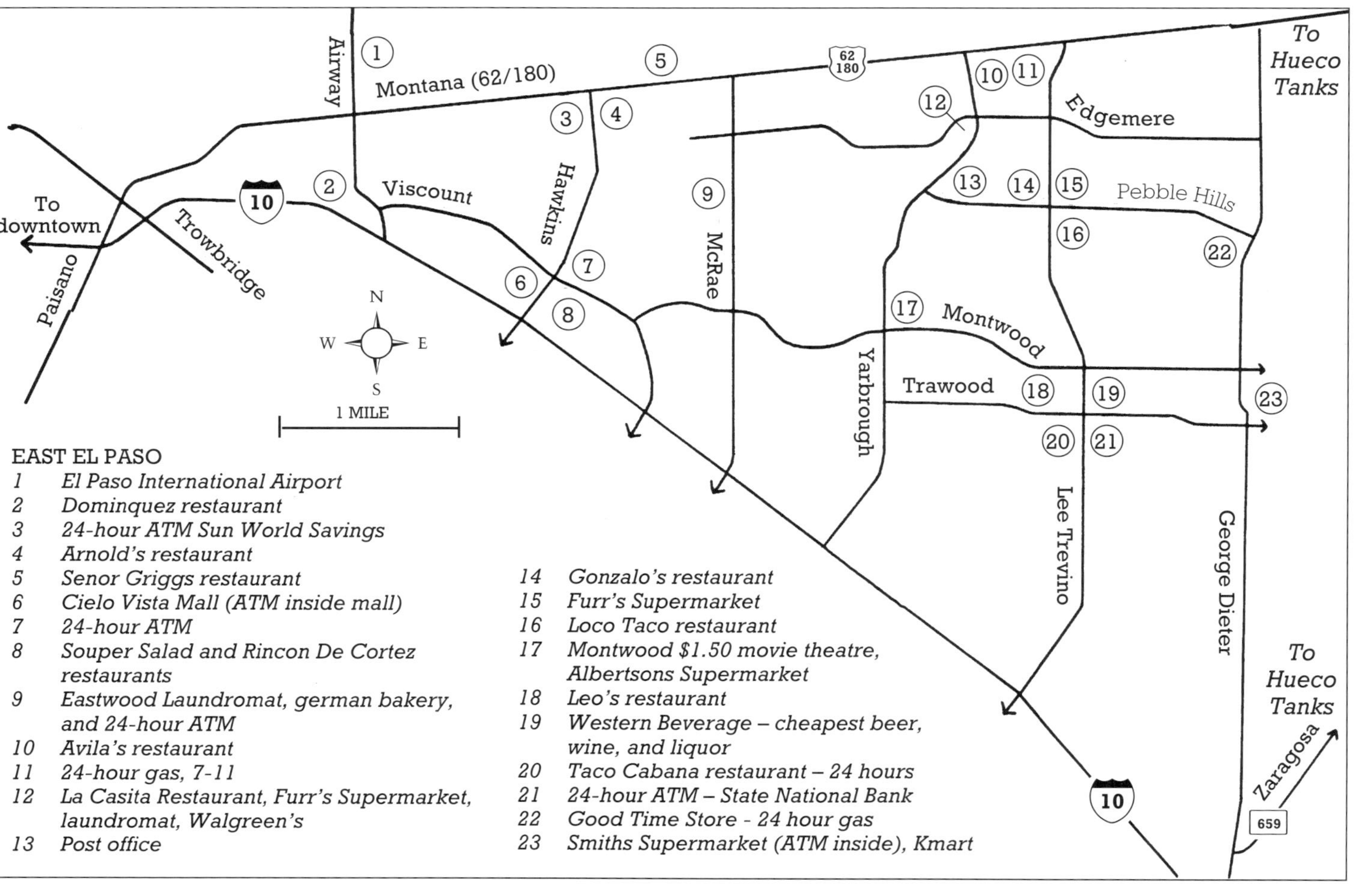
Airway
Montana (62/180)
62 180
To Hueco Tanks
Edgemere
Pebble Hills
Viscount
Hawkins
McRae
To downtown
Trowbridge
Paisano
10
N
W
E
S
1 MILE
Montwood
Trawood
Yarbrough
Lee Trevino
George Dieter
To Hueco Tanks
Zaragosa
659
EAST EL PASO
1 El Paso International Airport
2 Dominquez restaurant
3 24-hour ATM Sun World Savings
4 Arnold's restaurant
5 Senor Griggs restaurant
6 Cielo Vista Mall (ATM inside mall)
7 24-hour ATM
8 Souper Salad and Rincon De Cortez restaurants
9 Eastwood Laundromat, german bakery, and 24-hour ATM
10 Avila's restaurant
11 24-hour gas, 7-11
12 La Casita Restaurant, Furr's Supermarket, laundromat, Walgreen's
13 Post office
14 Gonzalo's restaurant
15 Furr's Supermarket
16 Loco Taco restaurant
17 Montwood $1.50 movie theatre, Albertsons Supermarket
18 Leo's restaurant
19 Western Beverage – cheapest beer, wine, and liquor
20 Taco Cabana restaurant – 24 hours
21 24-hour ATM – State National Bank
22 Good Time Store - 24 hour gas
23 Smiths Supermarket (ATM inside), Kmart

EATING IN EL PASO

A guidebook should not only direct the user towards the best climbs to do and coolest places to go; it should also direct one away from places certain to cause discomfort, financial ruin, and everlasting embarrassment. Below are my ratings of Mexican restaurants and all-you-can-eat restaurants frequented by visiting climbers.

Mexican Food

Note: many of the Mexican restaurant owners are practicing Catholics, therefore some of these establishments are closed on Sundays. Lots of them change hours as frequently as tablecloths, so I've opted not to include this data.

El Rancho Escondido, 14549 Montana
Great food, good margaritas, good service, expensive ($5-8/plate), but you'll save the difference in gas. ★★★

Leo's, 2285 Trawood
Good, costly food. ★★

Senor Griggs, 9007 Montana
Pathetic beans, but the rest of the food is quite good. As expensive, but not as good as El Rancho Escondido. ★★

Taco Cabana 1777 N. Lee Trevino
A chain restaurant you wish would open in your town. Surprisingly good for fast food. ($3- $4.50/plate.) Way cheap breakfasts ($2 Huevos Rancheros), open 24hrs a day. ★★★

Gonzalos, 10801 Pebble Hills
Cheap ($3-4/plate), especially on Tuesday's dollar off nights. Good service, huge-looking servings, but actually just a big plate thinly spread, lots of free chips with tasty salsa mild enough to chug. ★★★

La Casita, 3333 N. Yarbrough
Velveeta enchiladas smothered in American cheese, toxic waste salsa, no stars.

Avilas, 10600 Montana
Good food at the $4-5/plate range, but inconsistent service. ★★

La Salsa (next to Montana Vista Grocery)
No margaritas, so-so food.

Loco Taco, 3008 N. Lee Trevino
So authentic I can't understand the menu. Cheap. ★

Palmera, 13515 Montana
Between town and Hueco Tanks. Not the hole-in-the-wall it appears to be from outside. A menu as extensive as their postcard collection, all at bargain prices ($3-$3.50/plate). Breakfast and lunch only. ★★

Dominguez, 1201 Airway
Great when they're open (not Sundays), about $4 a plate. ★★

El Rincon De Cortez, 8900+ Viscount
(located a few doors left of Souper Salad) Chile rellenos the size of Ninjas. Most plates are about $3. The best in it's price rang. ★★

Arnold's, 1550 Hawkins
The best and worst service I've had in El Paso. Tasty food, $4-6 plate. ★★

All-you-can-eat

Panchos, McRae and Sims
The all-you-can-eat Mexican buffet that should be spelled with a "u." The food acquisition system is complex, but the guacamole is good and the other food better than it looks.

Souper Salad, 8900 Viscount
The eatery of choice amongst Hueco Tanks climbers. Possibly the world's best salad bar, awesome selection, reasonable price – Silly decor, but lots of unkempt climbers give it atmosphere. ★★★

Part of the allure of the climbing lifestyle is the aspect of exploration. There are quite a few all-you-can-stand marshmallow salad and fried mystery meat joints in East El Paso. Go for it.

LOCAL LIQUOR LAWS

Convenience stores and supermarkets can only sell beer and wine. Liquor stores have no sales after midnight, before 7 AM, or on Sundays. Beer and wine can be bought after noon on Sundays at markets and convenience stores. The legal age is 21. It is no longer legal to drink and drive in Texas (several years ago you could swill in your car as long as you weren't yet legally drunk. Now there is an open container law.) BAC for DUI is .10%.

THE DOPE ON DOPE

El Paso is the headquarters of the government's war on drugs. All major roads out of El Paso have Customs checkpoints manned by dope-sniffing dogs.

JUAREZ

Across the border from Texas officially lies the Third World. In actuality, the Third World begins about half a mile into El Paso. Unless you're a Deadhead and enjoy spending hours in line, don't drive over to Juarez, walk. When you get on the bridge over the Rio Grande and see all the cars waiting to pass US customs, you'll know why. I suggest forking the two or three bills to park in an attended lot near the walkover bridge. The street is not a safe place to park unless your car is filled with rabid pit bulls. "Importing" cars to Mexico is big business, with over a hundred cars a week immigrating from El Paso.

If your pocket isn't first picked by some tousle-haired street urchin, then you'll have a chance to buy all kinds of groovy crap in Juarez. Bargaining is expected. The merchant will usually ask for at least four times the price he'll finally settle on. Shake your head a lot, look hurt, and start walking out if he won't meet your price. If he pursues you out the door, you've got him. Just be sure to give in the tiniest bit to salve his ego and you've got a deal.

Must Buys – Don't leave Juarez without a velvet painting featuring either a cantaloupe breasted woman or Elvis Presley. If Texas has proved colder than you planned for, then Juarez is the place to pick up a good, cheap blanket and a serape – one of those cool wool ponchos Clint Eastwood hides his six-shooter behind. Devout Christians will want a Jesus of the Smokes dashboard ashtray in addition to an 8X10 3-D Winking Jesus. It's illegal to bring back the really cute stuffed frogs, but you can return with an armadillo handbag.

You may bring back one liter of booze or a case of beer per person free of US customs duty, but you must pay a Texas state tax ($1.10 per quart, $.94 per case of beer). Certain prescription medicines such as anti-inflammatories and antibiotics (but not weight loss pills) can be bought over the counter in Juarez Pharmacias and legally brought back into the US. They are much cheaper than their US equivalents. Of course taking these without a doctor's supervision is like soloing on loose rock, if you fuck up you'll know it. Also, the

Customs officer may ask to see your prescription. Not all Mexican pharmacists are fluent in English.

Drinking water in Mexico is foolish if you don't first purify it yourself. Stick with beer or soda. The food ranges from good to debilitating. Liability prevents me from recommending any particular Juarez eateries – you're on your own.

Night life – not only does liability prevent me from making suggestions, but my long hair (touching the shirt collar) has made me ineligible to enter the finer Juarez establishments. Once again, you're on your own.

Getting back over the border – All you have to do is state your nationality (e.g. "US citizen") and if you have any purchases to declare tell the officer what they are. The officers don't take kindly to jokes. Their idea of fun is to snap on a latex glove and strip search you. If they're in a good mood and think you're cute, they might even grease the mitt. You're better off keeping your nose clean.

The Texas booze tax is collected at a small building just past the customs building.

CLIMBING GEAR

Commercial Sales, 520 West San Antonio (downtown) has a very limited, but pricey selection of climbing gear. 542-1721. The old standby, Gardenswartz Sports, has recently been bought out by another company and may no longer carry climbing gear.

Pete's sometimes has softwear and chalk for sale.

Resoling

Wilson's Eastside Sports, 206 Main, Bishop, CA 93514, (619) 873-7520, does a state-of-the-art job of resoling climbing shoes. Tony has personally resoled over 20,000 pairs of rock boots.

HOW TO USE THIS BOOK

First, show it to all your friends, tell them how great it is, then force them to buy a copy.

Seriously, all numbered routes are shown on a topo or photograph. The topos are organized in counterclockwise order around each mountain with side trips up approach paths to boulders above ground level. The lead climb descriptions follow the same order. Use the maps at the beginning of each chapter and follow the dashed approach lines and sequential page numbers around the mountains.

The individual topos are all birds-eye-views. The problems are numbered counterclockwise around each boulder (left to right across each face). All topos have a 30 foot scale and a north arrow. If you're confused finding north, remember that the large earthen Main Dam between North and West Mountains runs north-south.

The lead climbing topos are of two types, birds-eye views and tourist-eye views. Not all of the lead climbs are on topos; many have just written descriptions.

New route information should be sent to the author care of Chockstone Press, Post Office Box 3505, Evergreen, Colorado 80439.

LITERACY AND BOULDERING

The text is chock-full of goodies: distances from trees to problems, which picnic table is next to which boulder, which holds the problem generally starts from (is it a sit down start?), loose hold warnings, bad landing cautions, fear factors, and high crux alerts.

Unfortunately, many problems can be identified by the graffiti next to them. Graffiti is given in quotation marks; for example "AC/DC Rules" or "Peter loves Muffy."

Judging distances

Counting one's paces is an easy way to judge distances. To figure the length of your pace, walk along a known distance. The back wall (east face) of Outhouse 2 (the one next to the Mushroom Boulder) is a hair over 10 yards long.

Topropes, bad landings, loose rock and scary problems

Every boulder problem in this guide has been done by at least one climber as a boulder problem without prior toprope rehearsal. Some of the problems listed were toproped on the first ascent, but later bouldered by another climber.

The 45 Degree Wall is an example of a climb that was originally toproped then later gained popularity as a boulder problem. Just because all the boulder problems in this book have been done without ropes is no reason you can't use a rope on one of these problems if you feel like it. Of course, if you do use a rope we'll all think you're light and won't party with you unless you're buying.

Many of the boulder problems at Hueco Tanks have landings a yogi couldn't sleep on. If you fall on a problem listed as having a bad landing, expect to get hurt. Even if the problem isn't listed as having a bad landing, you may still get hurt if you fall and land poorly. Use your judgement; if you're short on that, use a rope. The suffix **BL** after a problem's rating indicates that the problem has a bad landing; **SD** stands for a sit-down start; **TR** is for toprope.

Just because a boulder problem isn't listed as loose doesn't mean the holds on it will never break. The problems listed as loose are ones on which a climber must pull on hollow sounding holds or carefully avoid them. Solid sounding holds, especially thin ironrock flakes, have been known to snap at Hueco Tanks. This is more often a problem on climbs with few ascents than on the established classics. Beware when attempting what you might think is a first ascent.

The rock at Hueco Tanks becomes friable when wet; allow the rock to dry for 24 hours after it rains before pulling on any flakes. Ninety percent of the holds that break on established problems do so the day after a rain. If you must climb the day after a storm, stick to problems that never get wet in the first place: routes like Martini Roof and the lines at the Aircraft Carrier. Looseness is mentioned only for boulder problems; expect loose holds on most leads of any length at Hueco Tanks.

Any boulder problem listed as scary is one that I was scared on when climbing it. Maybe it had a bad landing, maybe it was off the deck or maybe I thought I'd fall in front of a crowd. Anyway, it's my personal opinion, nobody else's, printed here for what benefit it might offer the user. No judgement is printed as to the scariness of lead climbs in this book.

YOSEMITE DECIMAL RATINGS

These are so standardized in the U.S. now as to need no explanation. At Hueco Tanks the postscripts R and X mean the following: R – a fall will result in serious injury, X – a fall will end your climbing career, if not your life.

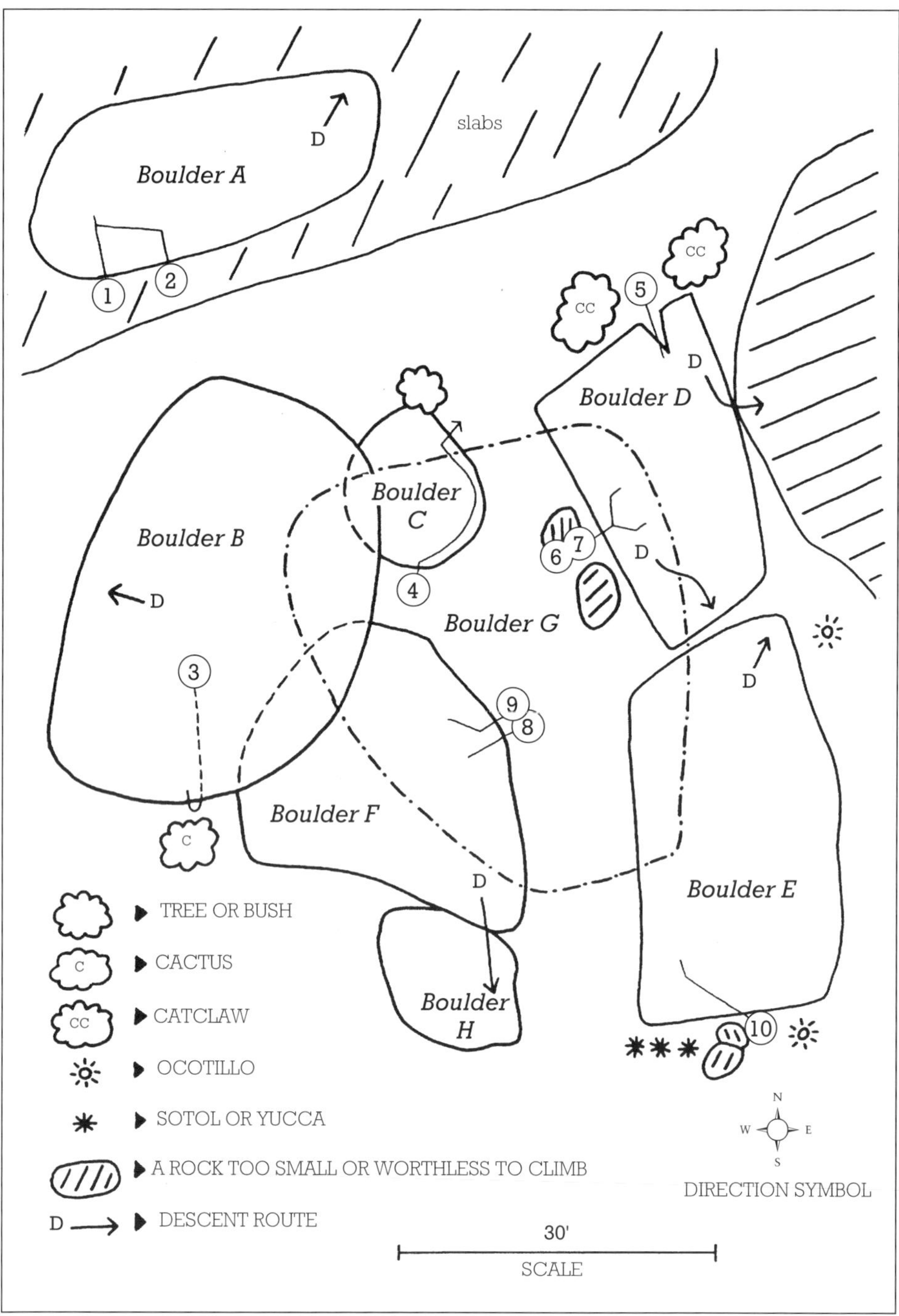
slabs
Boulder A
D
1
2
5
CC
CC
D
Boulder D
Boulder C
Boulder B
D
4
6
7
D
Boulder G
D
3
9
8
C
Boulder F
D
Boulder E
Boulder H
10
TREE OR BUSH
CACTUS
CATCLAW
OCOTILLO
SOTOL OR YUCCA
A ROCK TOO SMALL OR WORTHLESS TO CLIMB
DESCENT ROUTE
N
W
E
S
DIRECTION SYMBOL
30'
SCALE

THE SAMPLE BOULDERING TOPO

Boulders

Boulder A is just over 30 feet wide along its northwest- southeast axis (from comparison with the scale at the bottom of the topo). It lies atop a large expanse of slabby rock. Problems 1 and 2 have a rock slab landing.

Boulder B extends over or lies atop parts of Boulders C and F. The outlines of Boulders C and F are dashed in cartoon X-ray style where Boulder B overlies them.

Boulder G, with the dashed and dotted outline, is a huge caprock lying over Boulders B, C, D, E, and F. There are no problems on Boulder G. Problems 4, 6, 7, 8, and 9 usually stay dry because Boulder G forms a roof above them. Boulders D and E come close, but do not touch each other.

Boulder D has a large, hatched rock contacting D's east side. This hatched rock is either too low to boulder on, too loose to boulder on, or in some other way worthless enough that a climber would tend to ignore it.

Boulders F and H contact each other.

Problems

Problem 1 goes straight up.

Problem 2 starts about 7 feet right of Problem 1. At first it goes straight up, then it angles left to finish on the same moves as Problem 1. The descent for Boulder A is off the northwest end.

Problem 3, with the dashed line that starts inside the boulder's outline, then hooks around the outline, is a long roof problem. A large number of the problems in this guide overhang severely; only the biggest roofs are marked in this fashion. A climber pumped at the lip of Problem 3 might fall into the patch of cactus shown.

Problem 4 traverses Boulder C from left to right then steps off instead of topping out. The arrowhead pointing back outside of the boulder's outline indicates stepping off or climbing down from a problem's end.

Problem 5 starts between two catclaw bushes, then climbs a wide crack.

Problems 6 and 7 start between two small rocks. The huge capstone is above. 6 and 7 have joined number circles because they both start on the same holds. Problem 6 goes up and left. Problem 7 goes up and right.

The number circles of Problems 8 and 9 overlap. This means the problems start close to each other, but on separate holds. Consult the text for a detailed description of the start of any problem. The descent from Boulder F involves crossing to Boulder H, then descending Boulder H's south side.

Problem 10 starts between rocks to the left and an ocotillo to the right. It trends up and left over the small stones and some sotols or yuccas. The text for this problem would mention the bad landing. Ditto for Problem 3.

The heights of problems given in the text are distances climbed on a given problem, this is not always the same as the height of the lip. For example, if a problem traverses ten feet before going straight up another fifteen feet, then it is listed as 25' long, although the lip may only be fifteen feet up.

V RATINGS

The V rating system is an open-ended system for grading boulder problems. It originated at Hueco Tanks. The standard problems for each grade are here so nobody can complain that Hueco Tanks problems are over or under rated. It currently extends from V0– to V13.

As with all rating systems for climbing, the larger a number you tick, the bigger a stud you are and the more excuse you have for acting like an arrogant twit. Whether a problem is intimidating, scary, loose, or has a bad landing has no effect on the V grade – only the physical difficulty counts – that is, the technicality of the moves combined with the demands on one's power and endurance. Therefore the rating would remain the same whether it was toproped or bouldered. Hence, a scary V2 may be more difficult for some to boulder than a safe V5. It may be tougher to do a V6 without beta than a V7 with the moves shown to you. The ratings are a consensus of opinions of expert boulderers in excellent shape, or when lacking a consensus, the opinion of the first ascensionist and/or author.

Sample V ratings

The following ratings are the standard problems at each V grade in Hueco Tanks. Comparable problems from other well known areas are also given with the area in parentheses.

V0–	*The Round Room Traverse, Home Of The D-Cups, Beginner's Crack* (Indian Rock)
V0	*Blast-Off, Split Crack, The Melon Patch,* Southwest Corner of Beer Barrel Rock (Flagstaff, CO)
V0+	*Left Wannabe, Right Wannabe, Legal High, Wonderhole, Watercourse Right* (Indian Rock)
V1	*Thunderbird, Blood And Gore, Orifice Affair, King Conquer* (Flagstaff, CO)
V2	*What's Left of Les, Local Flakes, Breashears Roof* at the Black Hole (Morrison), *Jaws* (Mt. Woodson)
V3	*Sign Of The Cross, Warm Up Roof, Standard Route* on the Mental Block (Ft. Collins), *Bachar Cracker* (Yosemite)
V4	*Left El Sherman, Michael Kenyon, Artist's Opposition, Milton* (Eldorado), *Right Eliminator* (Ft. Collins), *Blue Suede Shoes* (Yosemite)
V5	*Left Donkey Show, Right Donkey Show, 45 Degree Wall, The Morgue, Germ Free Adolescence* (Eldorado), *Left Eliminator* (Ft. Collins)
V6	*Left El Murray, Center El Murray, Bucket Roof, High Plains Drifter* (Buttermilks), *Pinch Route* on the Mental Block (Ft. Collins)
V7	*Left El Murray* or *Center El Murray* from the sit down start, *Babyface, Crash Dummy, Caveman Traverse* (Joshua Tree), *Jungle Fever* (Indian Rock), *Nat's Traverse* (Indian Rock), *Cytogrinder* (Morrison)
V8	*Mushroom Roof, The Devil In Chris Jones, Micropope, Pumping Monzonite* (Joshua Tree), *Midnight Lightning* (Yosemite), *Bill* (Gloria's, Flagstaff, AZ), *Air Lupus* (Morrison)
V9	*Sex After Death, Nachoman, Bad Judgement*
V10	*Full Service, Martini Roof*
V11	*Full Monty, A.H.R.* (Flagstaff, CO)
V12	*Right Martini, The Dominator* (Yosemite), *Slapshot* (Dinosaur Mountain, Colorado)
V13	*Crown of Aragorn*

No Sandbag Ratings Guarantee

Every rating in this guide is guaranteed to be 100% accurate as of the time of writing. If you feel you have been sandbagged, just return the unused portion of the guide to Chockstone Press and your money will be grudgingly refunded. Some restrictions do apply .*

*V ratings are only guaranteed at 55°f, 20% humidity, for 6' 11/2" tall climbers weighing 160 lbs with below average flexibility, above average strength, minor finger arthritis, a bad left hip, size 101/2 feet crammed into size 8 Fires, perfectly even ape index, a hand size that precisely matches the author's and no beta.

QUALITY RATINGS KEY

no ★s	Anywhere from worth doing if you're in the area to less fun than a dulfersitz rappel.
★	An awesome route
★★	An awesome scary route with a bad landing
★★★	An awesome scary route with a bad landing first ascended by the author.

There may be exceptions to this scheme, but I'm told this is how it works. If it looks good, do it.

HINTS FOR HAPPY BOULDERING

The heart of bouldering is the search for maximum gymnastic difficulty and the limits of one's personal ability. In this respect it's a lot like its poorer relation sportclimbing except there are no ropes for a belayer to winch you past the hard moves. Hence, it's a sport plagued with honesty that demands the best from its participants. Don't be put off however, the hints below will make bouldering more enjoyable if you're one of the uninitiated.

Bouldering gear

Since every bouldering fall is a ground fall, I recommend high top boots over low tops because they have more ankle support. Slippers are great for desperate smears, thin toe jams, strengthening foot muscles, and looking Euro, but they suck for landing. Save them for showing off on problems you have wired.

Clean soles stick better than dirty soles. A square of carpet is useful for brushing dirt off your shoes at the base of problems. Carpet stores will usually sell their sample squares of discontinued lines for a few bucks each. To get soles cleaner than rubbing them on a carpet, wipe them with a hand moistened with spit or water. Anal retentives insist alcohol works even better.

Sketchpads have become standard issue at Hueco Tanks. These are carpet and foam sandwiches used to land on when falling or jumping off of boulder problems. You can make them yourself or buy swank, high-tech ones from better climbing stores. (For serious bouldering, I recommend the one made by Kinnaloa.)

The most obvious benefit of sketchpad use is the prevention of bruised and broken heels and tailbones. The greater benefit is the reduced wear on your spine and joints. The cumulative effect of thousands of falls and jumps, even just tiny ones, can be degenerative joint disease (arthritis). When using Sketchpads, position them where you will most likely fall, which is often not right at the base. They do no good if you miss them.

Dogs love lounging on sketchpads and more than one pup has earned the nickname "Spot" from doing just that. For their safety and yours, keep them tied up away from the problem (regulations say they must always be on leash anyway).

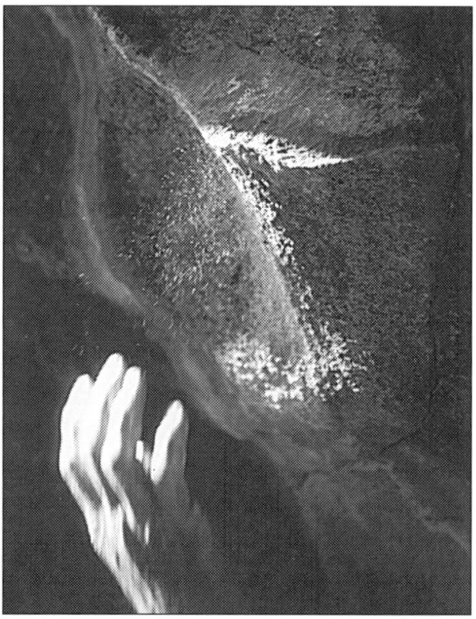

Clean holds are easier to grip than dirty ones. On established problems, a toothbrush is all that's needed to brush chalk off. Some first ascents will benefit from a scrubbing with a wire brush to remove stubborn dirt and birdcrap. Paint removal brushes are commonly used and easily found. Pipe cleaning brushes work well in crevices and pockets. They look like a test tube brush, but are made of wire and can be found in the plumbing section of most hardware stores.

The "Bubbabrush", a long handled brush for cleaning distant holds is also a popular tool. It's a homemade contraption and if constructed properly can score you extra style points. Mine features a MacGregor Response II golf club shaft (3 wood length), Griptite handle and Colgate Adult Firm toothbrush. It's very lightweight and features a blow tube for maximum cleaning power.

The thing to keep in mind when making a Bubbabrush is to never put a big brush on the end. This implies an inability on the owner's part to hang on large holds unless they're spotless. In other words, it labels the owner as "a complete bumbly." Better to take the few extra swipes to clean the big holds with an undersized brush.

Chalk

White chalk is the only chalk currently legal at Hueco Tanks State Park. Colored chalk was found to stain the rock. Not that white chalk looks any better, but the El Paso Climber's Club does wash the boulders several times a year in agreement with the State Parks. Experiments with non-staining colored chalks are underway and in the future we may be required to use it instead of white chalk.

On desperate problems, you may not want to lug the extra weight of a full chalk bag up with you. Chalkbags with collapsible midsections tend to spill less when left on the ground.

Rosin

NO POF. POF VERBOTEN. Rosin use is prohibited at Hueco Tanks and is unwelcome anywhere else in the United States. On some of the big name testpieces like Serves You Right (Full Service) and Martini Roof, rosin-packing Euros have made a mess of the holds.

If you see someone using rosin (look for their pof rag, a tied-up dishtowel that looks like a miniature halloween ghost being whacked on the rocks and their shoes) confiscate their pof rag immediately before they do more damage to the rock. Rosin forms an insoluble coating on the rock which is nearly impossible to grip without more rosin. Rosin is very hard to clean off. Park officials request that those climbers using rosin be reported to the rangers.

Euros are fond of arguing that rosin is not destructive, but it boils down to the fact that its use is a violation of park regulations and as such could get the park closed to climbing if we don't put a stop to its use. Tell them you're sorry, but they'll have to climb with chalk like everyone else.

Skin Kit

The bloody flapper is the official injury of Hueco Tanks. Few other rock types are as adept at snagging a rough spot in one's finger pad and peeling back a flap of callous. In many cases, the ironrock scalpels will dig deep enough to draw blood. To patch up these injuries and/or hopefully avoid them, many Hueco boulderers carry a skin kit consisting of a roll of tape, nail clippers, emery board or pad, and a tube of Krazy Glue™ (get this brand name, not Super Glue™ which is toxic). The nail clippers are used to cut away flaps of dead skin, the emery pad helps to bevel the edges of the newly formed crater in the skin.

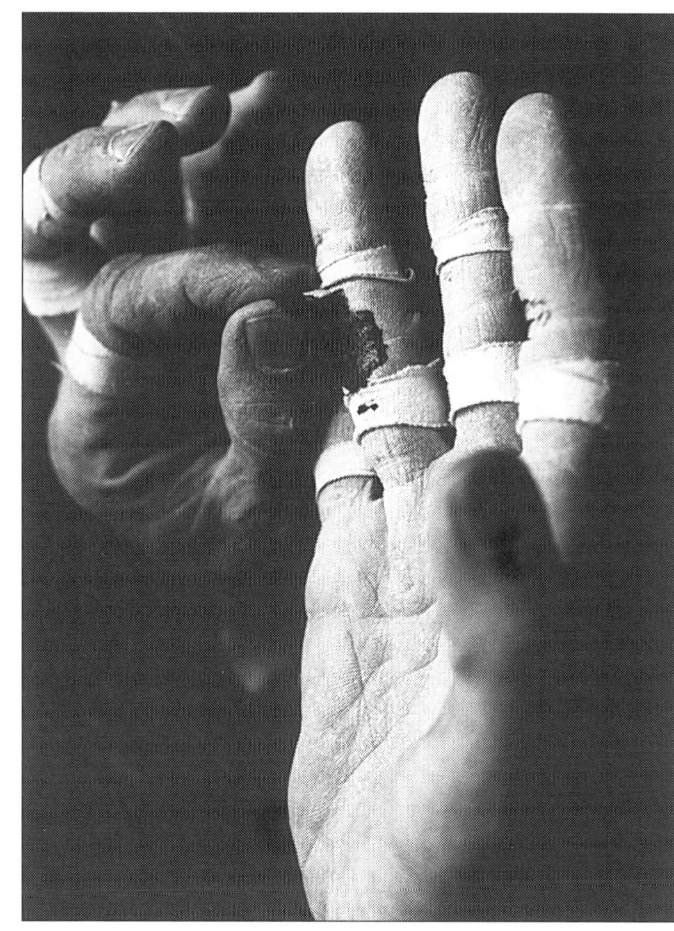

The pad is also used to remove small ridges and shreds of skin that might hook on sharp holds and initiate the peeling of a flapper. The Krazy Glue™ helps keep tape from rolling off of fingertips. In extreme cases, I've used it to glue the flapper itself back down, but it's usually best to trim the flapper off then tape over it. When gluing tape on, apply the Krazy Glue™ to the skin first, then wrap the tape over it. Be careful not to glue your fingers together.

After bouldering, to heal a flapper quickly, do the following. Trim away the dead skin, clean the wound, then apply an antibiotic ointment, Neosporin™ works well, and bandage the wound. If you are bouldering within the next three days, keep the cut taped while climbing. On the fourth day, if treated right, the finger should be ready for climbing without tape.

To prevent finger pads from drying out and flaking away, rub petroleum jelly on them before going to sleep each night. This keeps the skin healthy and pliable. It also helps prevent skin splitting. Since starting this treatment, my incidence of flappers decreased by at least 75%.

Spotting

The function of the spotter is to protect the falling climber's head, break his fall, and guide his body to the best available landing. Usually this is best accomplished by grabbing the falling climber's hips and steering his fall towards a convenient predetermined landing spot. Breaking his fall does not mean catching him like a football.

On roofs and other severely overhung problems, the spotter should grab the falling climber, grasping the bulging lats just below the fetid armpits, thus putting the climber's center of gravity below the spotter's hands. This will cause the feet to swing down and reduce the chance of the climber splitting his melon. When spotting, watch the climber's center of gravity (on men a spot about five inches up the spine from the waist belt, on women at the waist belt). When you see the center of gravity drop quickly, you can be assured that the climber is falling off and it is time to break their fall.

Don't watch the hands, arms, feet, or legs as these can flail about giving the impression that the climber is coming off, when actually they may still hold on. The spotter should not touch the climber unless the climber falls – none of that touchy feely stuff. Any weight bearing by the spotter, even one gram, invalidates an ascent.

Stretching

The extreme moves and frequent groundfalls associated with bouldering make flexibility essential. In addition to the all around stretching one would do for roped climbing, the boulderer should give extra attention to stretching and strengthining the ankles, wrists, and shoulders as these are the most commonly injured joints in bouldering. One thing a true boulderer prefers not to stretch is the truth. Leave that for the roped climbers.

Warming-up

Bouldering without warming-up is like bedding a Ugandan prostitute without putting a condom on – it can easily be done, but you risk serious injury. To reduce the risk of injury, stretch thoroughly, squeeze Power Putty or a rubber donut for 15 to 20 minutes, then do a dozen or more easy problems until you feel loose and powerful. Doing a hard problem you have wired can help you judge if you're warmed-up enough to try an unfamiliar desperate.

Bouldering with style

As with most endeavors in life, the more you put into climbing, the more you get out of it. There are two basic ways to approach bouldering: you can be at war with the rock, or you can be at one with the rock. By far, the more lasting rewards are obtained by following the latter approach. Here are some hints as how to become at one with the rock.

Approach every boulder problem as a challenge set before you by nature, not by other climbers. Bring yourself up to the level of the problem, don't bring it down to your level. By raising your own level you constantly improve.

Endeavor to figure problems out for yourself. Puzzling out sequences is one of the great joys of bouldering. You learn more this way. The path toward mastery is upward. You can not side-step it by begging beta.

Liberate your mind. Pursue the qualitative aspects of the sport, not the quantitative. Once you say, "Fuck the numbers" and mean it, you will feel an enormous release. Your mind is free to pursue the moves, not other climbers or some artificial standard by which they compare themselves. When I divorced myself from ratings (not an easy process, especially since I helped develop the V-system) I started climbing much better because my energy was focused on actually climbing. Fat, old, arthritic me was sending problems the anorexic, ten times stronger, hate-your-way-up-the-rock-meisters were struggling on. I had to chuckle. Numbers are only standards set for the masses. Climb for the joy of the moves, the aesthetics of the line, the intensity of the experience. Forget the numbers and you will go beyond them.

Prior to lift off

Before getting on any boulder problem, be sure to locate the descent. Next check the landing for potential hazards in case you fall. If it looks bad take out a life insurance policy and/or recruit a spotter. Step back if you can to check out the holds, lots of jugs turn into sloping butter dishes when you do this. Some huecos might contain broken glass, courtesy of would be Nolan Ryans. Don't wait until you're up there to find this out. Try to pre-visualize a sequence of moves that will get you to the top. Clean the hand and foot holds if necessary and wipe the dirt off your boots. Take the natural aggressiveness that society tries to suppress and cut it loose. Feel the adrenalin jolt through your chest. Let the spittle foam through your lips. Promise yourself you won't let go then...

Crank it.

John Sherman

A Last Minute Reminder:

Several areas covered in the text are currently closed to climbing. These are marked as closed in the text. Hueco Tanks State Park is currently reviewing their management plan, particularly as it relates to visitor-resource conflicts. Some of the currently closed areas may be reopened in the future. Other areas now open may be closed.

As a climber visiting Hueco Tanks State Park, you have an investment in the park, not just through the fees you pay, but through your efforts on the rocks, your picking up of trash, and policing of the area to prevent vandalism. Let Park officials know that you want access to climbs that do not endanger archaeological sites, such as those on the Kiva Cave Wall. Support and respect closure of routes that pose a threat to rock art, such as *The Forbidden.* Do not climb in the rock art zones marked on certain photos with crosshatches. Through our input and cooperation we can work with the TPWD to create a route closure policy that protects Hueco's archeological heritage and allows maximum freedom for us to climb.

Remember, Hueco Tanks is a State Archaeological Landmark. If in doubt whether the climb or boulder problem you wish to attempt might adversely affect the park's archaeology, pick another climb; there are more than 1,000 in the park to choose from. Have fun.

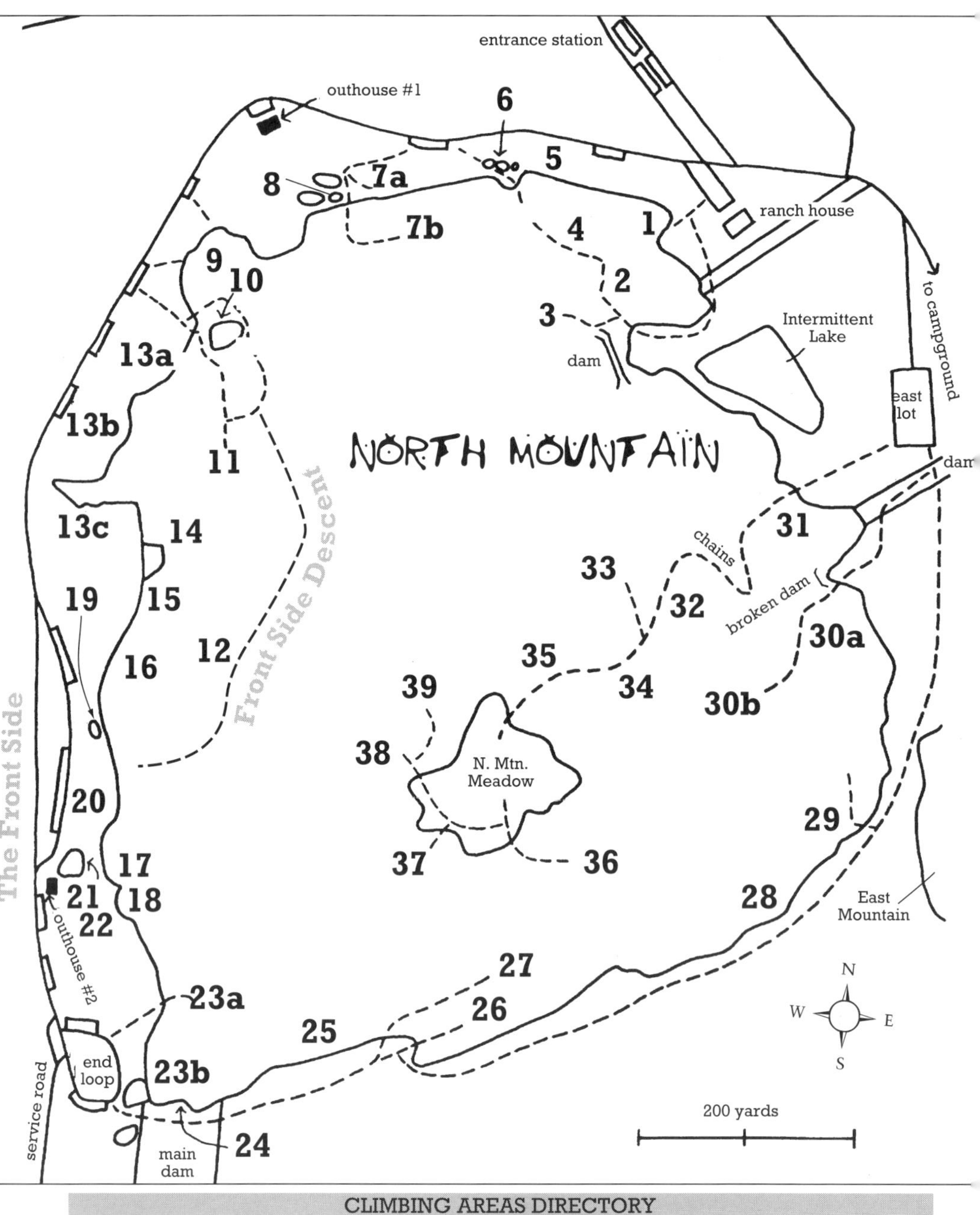

CLIMBING AREAS DIRECTORY

NORTH MOUNTAIN

Descriptions go counterclockwise around the mountain, and counterclockwise around each boulder (i.e. left to right on each boulder face). North Mountain descriptions start at the Escontrias Ranch House. From the entrance station, this is the white house 200 yards to the southeast. The road in points straight towards it.

Map, p. 26

ESCONTRIAS RANCH HOUSE

The Kitchen

The following problems are located uphill (west) from the Escontrias Ranch House parking lot.

Approach from the swing sets south of the parking lot.

1 *Garbage Disposal 10 feet V1 BL*

2 *The Butcher Block 10 feet V3 BL*
Start on white fingertip flake.

3 *A Woman's Place 11 feet V4 ★ SD BL without spot*

4 *Poppin' Fresh 11 feet V2 BL without spot, watch head on rock behind.*

5 *Gulp 'n Blow 15 feet V5 ★ BL scary*
Start 1 foot left of shelf on big jug 8 feet up. Up and left to basketball-sized hueco at lip.

The Kitchen

1 *Garbage Disposal 10 feet V1 BL*

2 *The Butcher Block 10 feet V3 BL*

3 *A Woman's Place 11 feet V4 ★ SD BL*

4 *Poppin' Fresh 11 feet V2 BL without spot,*

5 *Gulp 'n Blow 15 feet V5 ★ BL scary*

6 *Deep Fryer 20 feet V2*

9 *Corner Crack 30 feet 5.10TR*

10 *Unnamed Unrated TR*

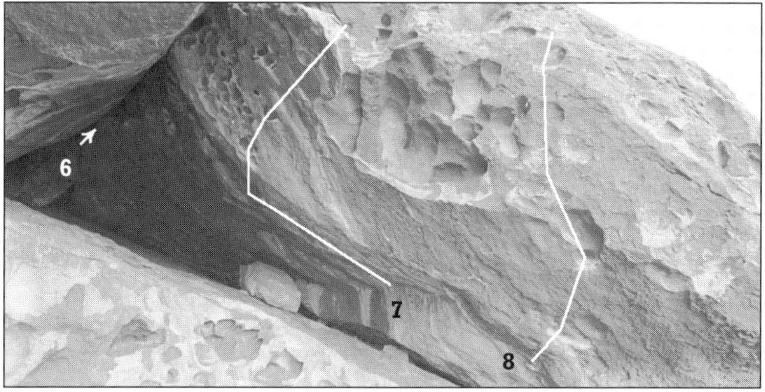

The Kitchen

6 *Deep Fryer 20 feet V2*
7 *Rear Burner 17 feet V6 ★★ SD*
8 *Short Order Cook 15 feet V6 ★ SD*

Problems 6-10 are pictured on pages 27 and 28.

6 *Deep Fryer 20 feet V2*
From the back of the A-frame traverse right out the overhanging right (southeast-facing) wall. The left wall is off-route.

7 *Rear Burner 17 feet V6 ★★ SD*
Start in undercling at base of roof.

8 *Short Order Cook 15 feet V6 ★ SD*
Start from an undercling hueco 2 feet off the ground.

9 *Corner Crack 30 feet 5.10 TR*

10 *Unnamed Unrated TR 30 feet*

THE GUMS AREA

To find the Gums area, start at the southwest end of the earthen dam (where it meets the rocks) behind the Escontrias Ranch House. Drop down south into the usually empty reservoir (marked on the North Mountain map as intermittent lake). Walk 120 yards west and northwest alongside the base of the mountain to where a 4- to 5-foot deep drainage chute exits the slabby rocks to the northeast. (A big tree with a four-forked trunk marks the chute's exit. 35 yards southeast is a stone dam used as a marker to find Sign Of The Cross.) Walk through the chute and 60 yards

Approach to Gums, Sign Of The Cross and Lamo Rocks

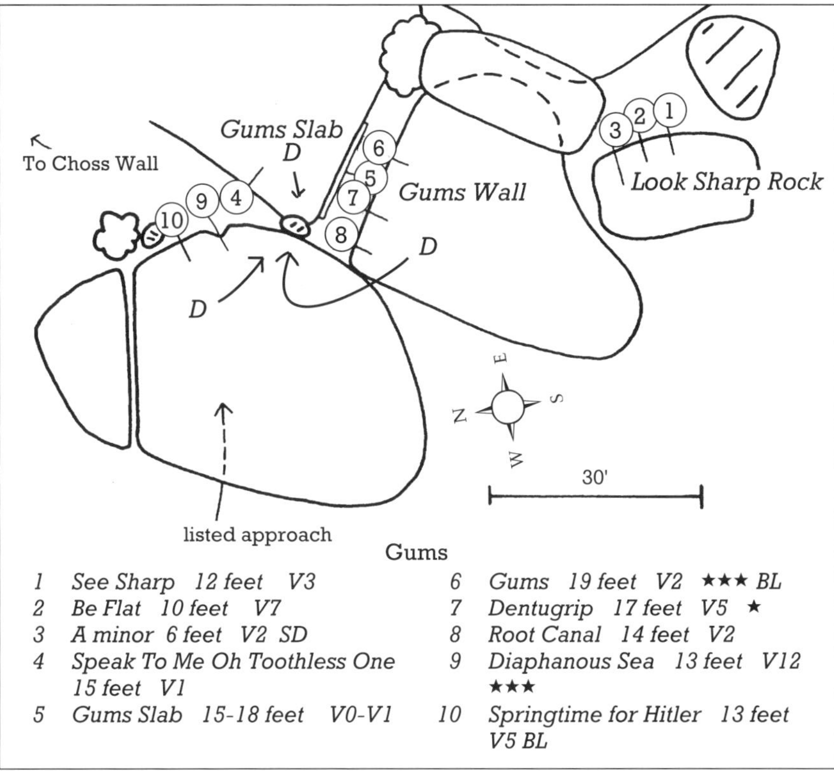

northeast up the drainage to a 10- by 30-foot grassy patch. A black water streak descending the low-angled slab to the north drains into the grassy patch. Walk 19 yards up this streak to the huge suspended boulder. Duck through the tunnel under this boulder to enter the Gums area. Gums itself is in the corridor 15 feet to the south.

Look Sharp Rock

Look Sharp Rock is the first boulder south of Gums Boulder. Photo on p.30.

1 *See Sharp 12 feet V3*
Start in the dirt 2 feet right of slabby rock at the base. A catclaw is behind the start. Follow the tan streak up.

2 *Be Flat 10 feet V7*
Start 1 foot left of slabby rock at the base. Up and right to a golf ball size horn at the lip (if it hasn't snapped yet). The top out is the crux.

3 *A Minor 6 feet V2 SD*

Gums Slab

Gums Slab is the low-angled southwest face in the Gums corridor.

4 *Speak To Me Oh Toothless One 15 feet V1*
Around the corner north of *Gums Slab,* on the same rock is a 15 foot problem on thin flakes, some of which flex. Start at a left angling seam 4 feet left of "GUTY".

5 *Gums Slab 15-18 feet V0 to V1*
Many friction possibilities here, tending to get harder the further right you start. The hardest one starts 10 feet left of the oak tree and tops out through the tips of the branches.

Look Sharp Rock (right)

1 *See Sharp 12 feet V3*
2 *Be Flat 10 feet V7*
3 *A minor 6 feet V2 SD*

Gums Wall

View from atop Gums Slab.

6 *Gums 19 feet V2 ★★★ BL*
7 *Dentugrip 17 feet V5 ★*
8 *Root Canal 14 feet V2*

Springtime Boulder

9 *Diaphanous Sea 13 feet V12 ★★★*
10 *Springtime for Hitler 13 feet V5 BL*

Gums Wall

Topo, page 29.

6 *Gums 19 feet V2 ★★★ BL*
7 *Dentugrip 17 feet V5 ★*
8 *Root Canal 14 feet V2*

Springtime Boulder

Topo, page 29.

9 *Diaphanous Sea 13 feet V12 ★★★*
10 *Springtime for Hitler 13 feet V5 BL*

SIGN OF THE CROSS

To get to Sign Of The Cross, start at the stone dam mentioned in the Gums approach directions. Sign Of The Cross is well hidden in a triangular room between the low-looking boulders 35 yards northwest of the stone dam's northwest end. Gums is across the gully, 100 yards to the north. All three entrances to the triangular room involve ducking through low gaps, or squeezing through chimneys.

1 *Whatsa Matter Baby 11 feet V4*
Do a long stretch or grim jump to start, then throw to the small left-facing flake/horn on the lip. Start 6 feet left of *Sign of the Cross.*

2 *Sign of the Cross 18 feet V3 ★★★*
The standard for V3. Starting low on an undercling from the white stained hueco is V4.

3 *Thin White Line 11 feet V3*
Contrived. Up the streak on the left of the boulder. The left arête is off-route, so is anything that feels good to the right.

4 *Lughead 11 feet V0–*

Sign Of The Cross
1 *Whatsa Matter Baby 11 feet V4*
2 *Sign of the Cross 18 feet V3 ★★★*
3 *Thin White Line 11 feet V3*
4 *Lughead 11 feet V0–*

Lamo Rocks

Twenty yards uphill (west) atop the slope is a cluster of big attractive looking boulders. Unfortunately, the climbing on them sucks. Nothing done yet deserves repeating. Your time is better spent elsewhere.

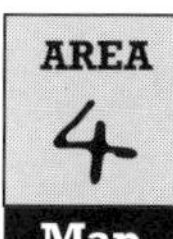

CHOSS AREA

Choss Wall

Choss Wall is located 55 yards northwest of Gums area. Descend these two problems by walking 35 yards to the east.

1 *Sign of the Choss 17 feet + 8 foot escape traverse V4* ★
Some faint, illegible chiseled initials at the 5 foot level adorn the start.

2 *Choss Training 14 feet V3*
Start 4 feet left of the big catclaw, 10 feet right of *Sign Of The Choss.*

Choss Chimneys

Ten yards left of *Sign Of The Choss* is a chimney between the Choss Wall and a huge boulder. Don't enter the chimney. Instead, skirt the west side of the 20 yard long boulder and enter the corridor at the west end of the boulder.

Flake Magnet 14 feet V4
Climb the overhanging right (NW-facing) wall of the corridor. Start on a two hand flake 6.5 feet up and 6 feet left of the right end of the wall. The arête to the right is off route.

Mexican Toprope 30 feet 5.12-
To get to *Mexican Toprope*, slip through the gap at the right rear of the *Flake Magnet* corridor to get to another corridor which contains the route. Climb the west-facing wall starting 6 feet right of a tree. Thin edges lead to a large, elongated hueco 20 feet up.

Choss Wall

1 *Sign of the Choss 17 feet + 8 foot escape traverse V4* ★
2 *Choss Training 14 feet V3*

RANGER STATION ROCKS

This is the closest group of rocks to the ranger station. The first two routes described are on a 35 foot tall north–facing wall at the left side of Ranger Station Rocks. This wall is 20 yards south of the first parking pullout past (west of) the frontside road gate. *Blue Balls,* et. al., lie at the right (northwest) end of Ranger Station Rocks, on the wall above table #2.

Ranger Station Rocks, Left Side

1 *Citation Face 35 feet 5.9 TR*
2 *Regulation Crack 35 feet 5.10*

Ranger Station, Michael Kenyon areas

Ranger Station Right Side

1 *Death Dyno 35 feet 5.9*
2 *Cal Gal 40 feet 5.12 TR ★★*
3 *Blue Balls 40 feet 5.12– TR ★★*
4 *Chip Shot 40 feet 5.12+ TR ★★*

Mission Impossible Rock

5 *Mission Impossible*

Michael Kenyon Boulder

15 *Chocolate Thunder 20 feet V1 ★★*
16 *Tralfaz 18 feet V0*
17 *Midriff Bulge 23 feet V0*
18 *Michael Kenyon (aka The Illinois Enema Bandit) 20 feet V4 ★★*

Left Side and Right Side problems are pictured on page 33.

Left Side

1 *Citation Face 35 feet 5.9 TR*

2 *Regulation Crack 35 feet 5.10*

Right Side

1 *Death Dyno 35 feet 5.9*
Most of the few ascents this has seen have been free solo efforts. Halfway along the wall between tables #1 and #2 is an overhang above a tree. From the slab, do a hazardous leap for the 2-foot diameter hueco 4 feet up and left of "MIK." Romp to the top.

2 *Cal Gal 40 feet 5.12 TR ★★*
Start between "1973 Isela and J Ortega" and "Margaret W." Straight up.

3 *Blue Balls 40 feet 5.12– TR ★★*

4 *Chip Shot 40 feet 5.12+ TR ★★*

Map, p. 26

MICHAEL KENYON AREA

The boulders in this area surround picnic table #3 (uncovered). Overview photo, page 33.

Mission Impossible Rock

5 *Mission Impossible 13 feet V0+*
Start between the shrubs. Angle right via a flared jam to top out 2 to 3 feet right of "Pete Graves" chiseled name. Photo, p. 33.

Problems 6 and 7 are inside the corridor on the south face of Mission Impossible Rock.

6 *IM Force 14 feet V0 BL*
Up the seam above "JUDR."

7 *Ah-So 14 feet V0 BL*
Hollow flakes above "KIM."

Donkey Head Rock.

Uphill from Mission Impossible rock, this forms the other side of the corridor on Mission Impossible Rock's south side. The descriptions start in the corridor.

8 *What's Left of Lloyd 17 feet V0+ BL*
The line just left of "Lloyd Johnson."

Donkey Head Rock

8 *What's Left of Lloyd 17 feet V0+ BL*

9 *What's Right of Lloyd 19 feet V1 BL*

10 *African Head Charge 19 feet V1*

11 *Alias Mig 19 feet V1 ★*

12 *Donkey Head 24 feet V4 ★*

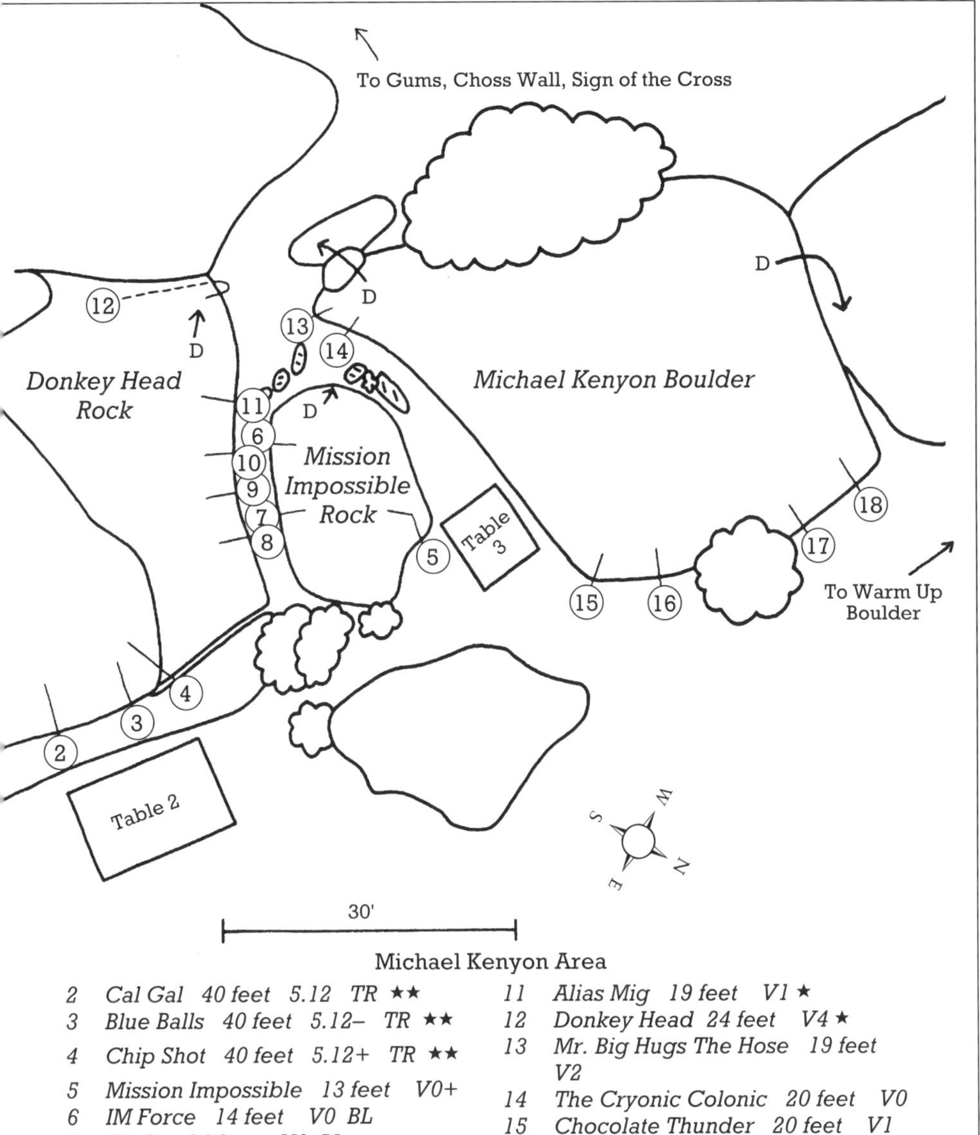

Michael Kenyon Area

2 *Cal Gal 40 feet 5.12 TR* ★★
3 *Blue Balls 40 feet 5.12– TR* ★★
4 *Chip Shot 40 feet 5.12+ TR* ★★
5 *Mission Impossible 13 feet V0+*
6 *IM Force 14 feet V0 BL*
7 *Ah-So 14 feet V0 BL*
8 *What's Left of Lloyd 17 feet V0+ BL*
9 *What's Right of Lloyd 19 feet V1 BL*
10 *African Head Charge 19 feet V1*
11 *Alias Mig 19 feet V1* ★
12 *Donkey Head 24 feet V4* ★
13 *Mr. Big Hugs The Hose 19 feet V2*
14 *The Cryonic Colonic 20 feet V0*
15 *Chocolate Thunder 20 feet V1* ★★
16 *Tralfaz 18 feet V0*
17 *Midriff Bulge 23 feet V0*
18 *Michael Kenyon (aka The Illinois Enema Bandit) 20 feet V4* ★★

Problems 9-12 are pictured on page 34; topo, p. 35.

9 *What's Right of Lloyd 19 feet V1 BL*
Via the small ledge just right of "Lloyd Johnson."

10 *African Head Charge 19 feet V1*
Directly across corridor from *IM Force*.

11 *Alias Mig 19 feet V1 ★*
Starts using the fingertip flake next to "Luis Sanchez."

12 *Donkey Head 24 feet V4 ★*
From as far back as possible, traverse out the left wall of the cave, avoiding the right wall. Exit the cave and finish up overhanging jugs.

Michael Kenyon Boulder

This boulder overhangs the table faintly marked 3. Photo, p. 33; topo, p. 35.

13 *Mr. Big Hugs The Hose 19 feet V2*
Climb the arête above "Sylvia + Bert." Watch for loose flakes.

14 *The Cryonic Colonic 20 feet V0*
The left-angling crack 5 feet right of *Mr. Big Hugs The Hose.*

15 *Chocolate Thunder 20 feet V1 ★★*
6 feet right of picnic table platform #3 is a white wall with a line of brown huecos.

16 *Tralfaz 18 feet V0*
12 feet right of *Chocolate Thunder.* The bulging flake with a small bush growing on it.

17 *Midriff Bulge 23 feet V0*
6 feet right of the tree. Over the bulge and up the slab.

18 *Michael Kenyon (aka The Illinois Enema Bandit) 20 feet V4 ★★*
"7-22-23 TD Mohat" marks the start. "At the time of these robberies, Michael decided to give his female victims a little enema. Apparently there was no law against that." – Γ. Zappa.

MAMMARY LANE AND THE MORGUE

Mammary Lane and The Morgue are located south of the Warm Up Boulder, hence are listed before it in this guide. Mammary Lane is the five foot wide gully to the south of table #5 (uncovered and very faintly marked). To find The Morgue it is easiest to first locate the Warm Up boulder and approach from there. The Warm Up boulder is behind the tree 5 yards south of picnic table #6 (uncovered). Photos, pages 38 and 47.

Mammary Lane

1 *Pearl Necklace 17 feet V4 ★*
Start 2 feet right of a rock blocking the gully. "2TF" is just under the first hold hueco. Tricky moves get one to the flake crack on the right. Follow this up.
Photo on page 39.

Mammary Lane and The Morgue (topo at right)

1 *Pearl Necklace 17 feet V4 ★*
2 *Inverted Nipples 17 feet V2 ★*
3 *Full Figure 17 feet V2 ★ scary*
4 *Big Mama Jama 15 feet V2*
5 *Home Of The D-Cups 12 feet V0– ★★*
6 *T-Bone Shuffle 20 feet V4 ★ BL*
7 *The Slash 24 feet V4 ★ BL*
8 *The Morgue 36 feet V5 ★★★ BL*
9 *World's Shortest Man 12 feet V0*
10 *Another Nigga In The Morgue 19 feet V4 ★★ BL scary*
11 *Larry 12 feet V1 ★*
12 *Curly 10 feet V0+*
13 *Moe 9 feet V0+*
14 *Roll Over Beethoven 16 feet V1*
15 *Playtex Husband 18 feet V0*
16 *Evelyn Rainbird 20 feet V1 ★*
17 *Zippermouth 20 feet V0 ★★*

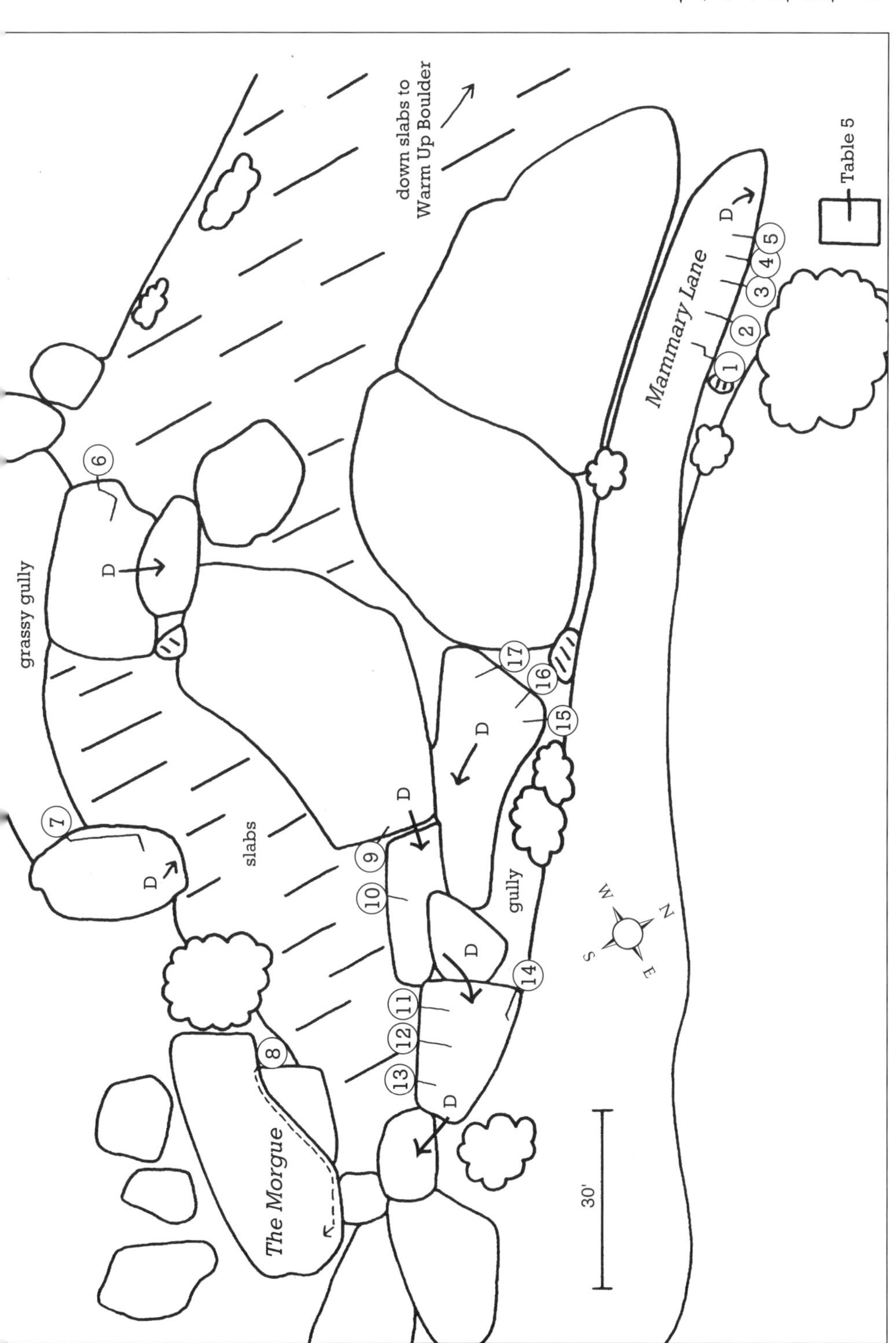

down slabs to
Warm Up Boulder
Table 5
Mammary Lane
grassy gully
slabs
gully
The Morgue
30'
N
E
S
W
D
1
2
3
4
5
6
7
8
9
10
11
12
13
14
15
16
17

Overview of Michael Kenyon to Mammary Lane areas

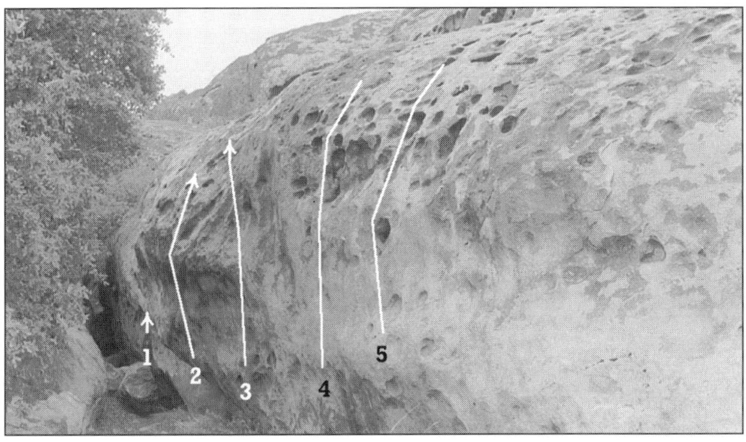

Mammary Lane

1 *Pearl Necklace 17 feet V4 ★*
2 *Inverted Nipples 17 feet V2 ★*
3 *Full Figure 17 feet V2 ★ scary*
4 *Big Mama Jama 15 feet V2*
5 *Home Of The D-Cups 12 feet V0– ★★*

Topos for problems 2-5 are on page 35.

2 *Inverted Nipples 17 feet V2 ★*

10 feet right of the gully-blocking boulder and 9 feet left of the chicken wire and concrete erosion control dam is a right angling pitted seam line and a slightly left angling pitted flake. Climb straight up the "V" between these.

3 *Full Figure 17 feet V2 ★ scary*
4 *Big Mama Jama 15 feet V2*
5 *Home Of The D-Cups 12 feet V0– ★★*

The Morgue

To find The Morgue, start at the Warm Up Boulder. Walk up the slab to the southeast, keeping the Warm Up Wall on your right. You'll pass *Nice Girls Do* then the wall becomes a series of blocks worthless for bouldering. After 60 yards of walking along the Warm Up Wall, you'll be able to drop down another 10 yards into a grassy gully that trends SE-NW. Just before dropping down

T-Bone Shuffle Boulder

6 *T-Bone Shuffle 20 feet V4 ★ BL*

through the rocky gap into this gully you may notice the T-Bone Shuffle Boulder (marked with "WC") bounding the east (left) side of the gap. Once in the grassy gully turn left on a trail through the grass and walk southeast. After 20 yards you'll run into a boulder with a prominent 18-foot finger crack angling up and left under the rim of the boulder. This is *The Slash.* Skirt the Slash Boulder to the right, then follow the indistinct rocky trail that trends left behind this boulder. Head towards the big tree and bush cluster on the left. Hidden behind this tree is the Morgue Boulder which is 20 yards southeast of *The Slash.* Topo, p. 35; overview photo, p. 38.

6 *T-Bone Shuffle 20 feet V4 ★ BL*
This starts as a sit-down problem grabbing a hueco on the prow 9 feet down and right of the "WC" inscription. Photo on page 39.

7 *The Slash 24 feet V4 ★ BL*
All holds above the crack are off-route.

8 *The Morgue 36 feet V5 ★★★ BL*
One of the best roof crack problems anywhere. Every size from big flared fingers to off-width, but mostly juicy hand jams. Start at the northwest end of the boulder 9 feet southeast of the tree trunk. Either climb down the lieback crack from above, pull into it from the ground, or stem across to it from the wall to the north. After gaining the crack this wall to the north is off-route. Drop under the roof and jam the 27-foot roof crack to where it butts into another boulder. Either exit the notch between the boulders, the pansy lightweight variant that degrades the problem to V4, or continue jamming the flare between the rocks to finish in a manly V5 fashion.

9 *World's Shortest Man 12 feet V0*
The easy corner crack in a left-facing dihedral up the slab north of the Slash Boulder.

The Morgue Area
7 *The Slash 24 feet V4 ★ BL*

10 *Another Nigga In The Morgue 19 feet V4 ★★ BL scary*
Double-decker fall potential from up high. Killer.

11 *Larry 12 feet V1 ★*

12 *Curly 10 feet V0+*

13 *Moe 9 feet V0+*
Start low.

The following problems listed are in the gully between The Morgue and Mammary Lane.

14 *Roll Over Beethoven 16 feet V1*
Climb the arête with your body on the right (north) side. Rock over the arête to top out.

15 *Playtex Husband 18 feet V0*
Climb huecos above the fork in the tree trunk.

16 *Evelyn Rainbird 20 feet V1 ★*
Climb straight up the delicate face above "Irene and Dick Filleman 10-26-24."

17 *Zippermouth 20 feet V0 ★★*
Climb the enjoyable face above "Mike Caldarella".

The Morgue Area

View looking north from atop the Morgue Boulder.

9 *World's Shortest Man 12 feet V0*
10 *Another Nigga In The Morgue 19 feet V4 ★★ BL scary*
11 *Larry 12 feet V1 ★*
12 *Curly 10 feet V0+*
13 *Moe 9 feet V0+*

AREA 6

WARM UP WALL, WARM UP BOULDER, AND OUTHOUSE ROCK

Map, p. 26

These areas are located southeast of outhouse #1. Outhouse Rock's southeast end overhangs picnic table #6 (uncovered).

The Warm Up Boulder is behind a tree 5 yards southwest of table #6. The Warm Up Wall is west and south of the Warm Up Boulder. Topo on page 42.

Warm Up Wall

Problems 1-5 are pictured on page 43; topo, p. 42.

1 *Nice Boys Can't 16 feet V3 BL*
On the way up The Morgue approach slabs, 10 feet left of the biggest oak tree on the right, is a 5 foot wide break in the wall with a giant flake pointing up from the floor. Start in the pit left (south) of the flake. Climb the wall above off-routing the arête on the left.

2 *Nice Girls Do 16 feet V5 ★★ BL*
Start low at a great undercling below the roof. Move right along the lip to avoid bumping into the wall behind. Also pictured on page 47.
Variation: ***Nice Girls Do Donny 24 feet V7 ★★ BL***
Start 8 feet left of *Nice Girls Do* on two huecos in the narrow chimney around the corner. Undercling out right under the roof to join *Nice Girls Do* at its start.

3 *First Degree Burns 12 feet V1*
4 *The Backscratcher 17 feet V1*
5 *Bad Influence 15 feet V0*

6 *Juju Wall 15 feet V0 to V0+*
The whole wall right of the crack can be climbed anywhere. It's hardest straight above "Bud Minnie" without using the big hueco on the left.

7 *Rumble In The Jungle 10 feet V0*
Start right of the tree. Up the slab through the branches.

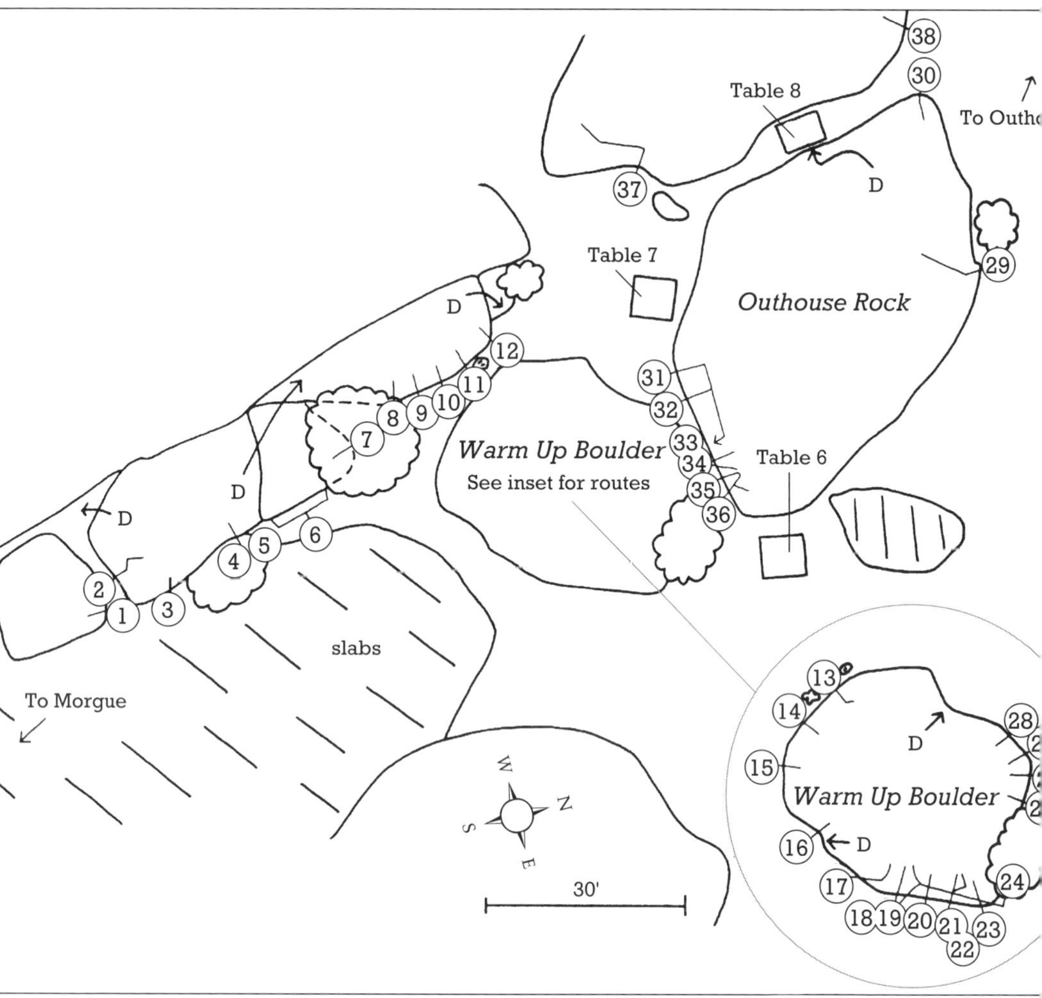

Warm Up Wall Area

1	*Nice Boys Can't 16 feet V3 BL*	10	*Young Man Blues 12 feet V0+*
2	*Nice Girls Do 16 feet V5 ★★ BL*	11	*Elder Statesman 12 feet V0–*
3	*First Degree Burns 12 feet V1*	12	*Loopzilla 11 feet V0–*
4	*The Backscratcher 17 feet V1*	13	*No Contest 14 feet V1*
5	*Bad Influence 15 feet V0*	14	*Stranded In L.A. 14 feet V0+*
6	*Juju Wall 15 feet V0 to V0+*	15	*Mud Shark 17 feet V0*
7	*Rumble In The Jungle 10 feet V0*	16	*Lonesome Electric... 12 feet V0+*
8	*Bitch Magnet 14 feet V0 ★*	17	*Namedropper 18 feet V3*
9	*Dumbo 14 feet V0–*	18	*Murray Lunge 15 feet V6 ★★*

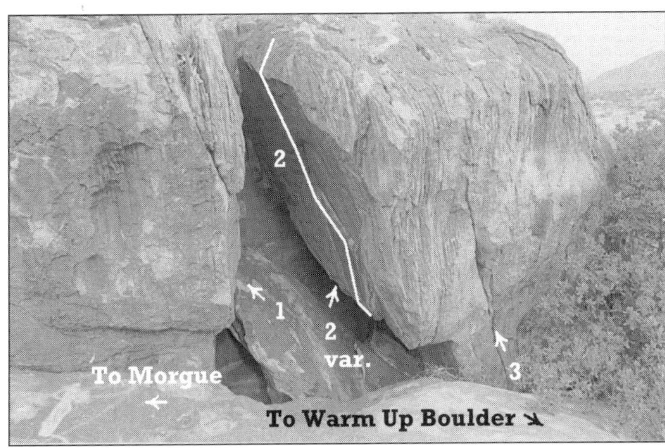

Warm Up Wall

Left:

1 *Nice Boys Can't 16 feet V3 BL*

2 *Nice Girls Do 16 feet V5 ★★ BL*

3 *First Degree Burns 12 feet V1*

Below:

4 *The Backscratcher 17 feet V1*

5 *Bad Influence 15 feet V0*

Problems 8-11 are pictured on page 44.

8 *Bitch Magnet 14 feet V0 ★*

9 *Dumbo 14 feet V0–*

10 *Young Man Blues 12 feet V0+*
Mantle 3 feet right of "Chilo B."

11 *Elder Statesman 12 feet V0–*
Above and right of "John W. Elder", climb the huecos just right of *Young Man Blues.*

12 *Loopzilla 11 feet V0–*
The rounded arête at the Warm Up Wall's right end; descent is just to the right.

---

19 *Barnstormer 16 feet V1 ★★*
20 *Thunderbird 15 feet V1 ★★*
21 *The Butter Dish 14 feet V2 ★★*
22 *Big Shot 15 feet V0+ ★*
23 *Noh Bada Wid It 16 feet V0+*
24 *Pounding System 25 feet V4 ★★*
25 *Stinking Jesus 17 feet V6 ★★*
26 *Winking Jesus 14 feet V7 ★*
27 *Black Napkins 14 feet V2 ★*
29 *Terminal Football 30 feet V0+*
30 *Padilla Prow 11 feet V0+*
31 *The Hens From Hell 16 feet + escape V2 ★*
32 *Set Loose 16 feet V1*
33 *Fat Burner 14 feet V0+*
34 *Fatty Fatty 11 feet V0+*
35 *Double Dribble 11 feet V0*
36 *Why? 11 feet V0*
37 *Jump For Joy 32 feet 5.9+*
38 *Tailfeather 25 feet 5.11*

Warm Up Wall and Warm Up Boulder

8 *Bitch Magnet 14 feet V0* ★
9 *Dumbo 14 feet V0–*
10 *Young Man Blues 12 feet V0+*
11 *Elder Statesman 12 feet V0–*
14 *Stranded In L.A. 14 feet V0+*
15 *Mud Shark 17 feet V0*

Warm Up Boulder

This popular boulder gets the morning sun. Topo, p. 42. Photos, pp. 44-46.

13 *No Contest 14 feet V1*
Just left of a small tree is a right angling crack topped by ugly blocks.

14 *Stranded In L.A. 14 feet V0+*
Climb the wall right of the midget tree. A three foot crack splits the summit block.

15 *Mud Shark 17 feet V0*
Climb the ramp above "BMA."

16 *Lonesome Electric Turkey 12 feet V0+*
Climb the wall just left of the bottom of the east face descent ramp. "May 11-1-4" is 4 feet up.

17 *Namedropper 18 feet V3 SD*
Sit down start from an incut 3 feet right of "JLB" and 3 feet above the ground. Traverse up and right along the lipline topping out 3 feet left of "Bob, Ethel, Gladys and Ralph."

18 *Murray Lunge 15 feet V6* ★★
4 feet right of "Harry R. Barnes" is a good flake. Lunge from this 5 feet up to the flake straight above. Everything right of the starter flake is off-route.

19 *Barnstormer 16 feet V1* ★★
Start on the *Murray Lunge* flake. Zig right then zag left along the flake line to the top.

20 *Thunderbird 15 feet V1* ★★
Climb the crack up the shallow corner. The V1 standard.

21 *The Butter Dish 14 feet V2* ★★

22 *Big Shot 15 feet V0+* ★

23 *Noh Bada Wid It 16 feet V0+*
Climb the prow through the branches.

Warm Up Boulder

17 *Namedropper 18 feet V3 SD*

18 *Murray Lunge 15 feet V6* ★★

19 *Barnstormer 16 feet V1* ★★

20 *Thunderbird 15 feet V1* ★★

21 *The Butter Dish 14 feet V2* ★★

22 *Big Shot 15 feet V0+* ★

23 *Noh Bada Wid It 16 feet V0+*

24 *Pounding System 25 feet V4 SD* ★★

Warm Up Boulder

25 *Stinking Jesus 17 feet V6* ★★

26 *Winking Jesus 14 feet V7* ★

24 *Pounding System 25 feet V4 SD* ★★
Start sitting down behind the tree on the northeast face. Traverse left around the corner, undercling the arch, then finish up *Barnstormer.*

25 *Stinking Jesus 17 feet V6* ★★
Photo above.

26 *Winking Jesus 14 feet V7* ★
Find "The Burnett Party" graffiti at 8 foot level. A polished scoop 1 foot right of this is on route. Everything else on the polished prow and to its right is off-route. Work up sharp flakes above the "Burnett Party" to the top. Photo above.

27 *Black Napkins 14 feet V2* ★
Start on incut first digit flakes just right of the prow. Straight up. Photo, p. 46.

28 *Easy Skanking 11 feet V0*
Up the middle of the short sand-blasted slab. Photo, p. 46.

Outhouse Rock

On the northwest end of this rock is a prow pointing toward the outhouse. "R. Padilla 4-27-58" is at the top of the prow. The first route described is 30 feet left of this prow. The descent wanders down from left at the top to right at the bottom along the face above picnic table #8 (right of *Padilla Prow*). An alternative descent is to hang off the lip of *Padilla Prow* and drop off. Topo, p. 42.

29 *Terminal Football 30 feet V0+*
5 feet left of the tree trunk is a tongue of rock pointing towards the toilet block. Climb the tongue then wander up loose rock to the top. More of a solo than a boulder problem, although the crux is low.

30 *Padilla Prow 11 feet V0+*
Climb the prow via crumbly rock on its right side.

The following routes are in the gap next to the Warm Up Boulder. They climb only partway up the face.

31 *The Hens From Hell 16 feet + escape V2 ★*
The spare tire-sized rock just left of the start is off-route. Climb 15 feet straight past 2 horizontal seams then traverse right on loose holds until you can step or jump across to the Warm Up Boulder. An alternative to the loose escape traverse is to downclimb.

32 *Set Loose 16 feet V1*
Pass the upper horizontal seam at its right end. The descent alternatives are the same as for *The Hens From Hell.*

33 *Fat Burner 14 feet V0+*
Start where Outhouse Rock comes closest to the Warm Up Boulder at a grapefruit size hueco 4 feet above ground. Angle up and left. Step across to Warm Up Boulder.

Outhouse Rock

27 *Black Napkins 14 feet V2 ★*
28 *Easy Skanking 11 feet V0*
31 *The Hens From Hell 16 feet + escape V2 ★*
32 *Set Loose 16 feet V1*
33 *Fat Burner 14 feet V0+*

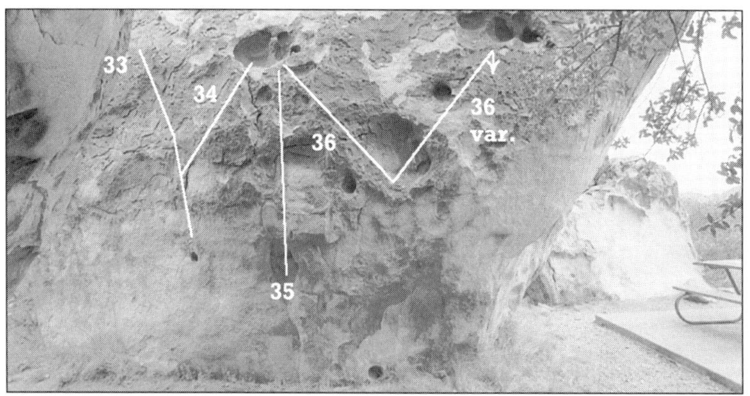

Outhouse Rock

33 *Fat Burner 14 feet V0+*
34 *Fatty Fatty 11 feet V0+*
35 *Double Dribble 11 feet V0*
36 *Why? 11 feet V0*

Overview of the *Mopboys* to Asylum areas

Problems 34-36 are pictured on page 46; topo, p. 42.

34 *Fatty Fatty 11 feet V0+*
The same start as *Fat Burner*, but angle right to the big hueco atop *Double Dribble.*

35 *Double Dribble 11 feet V0*
Start in a basketball size hueco 3 feet right of *Fatty Fatty.* Straight up to the big hueco.

36 *Why? 11 feet V0*
Start 3 feet right of *Double Dribble* in two huecos at 6 foot level. Up and left to big hueco on *Double Dribble* or (stupid variation) right to nowhere and jump off.

Hawkbill Rock

This is the 30 foot tall boulder 5 yards east of Outhouse Rock. The projection at the south end of the rock looks like a Hawk's beak. Topo, p. 42; photos, pp. 45 and 47.

37 *Jump For Joy 32 feet 5.9+*
On the left end of the east face, climb up the easy ramp then left along the horizontal crack to within 3 feet of its end. Angle up and left from there to the top of the bill.

38 *Tailfeather 25 feet 5.11*
On the right end of the east face, start 8 feet right of the small chicken wire and rock erosion control structure. Climb the bulge with the thick left pointing flake halfway up.

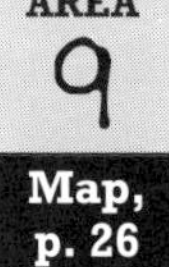

Map, p. 26

ASYLUM

This the big rock formation 130 yards southwest of Outhouse #1. It is home to several 50-70 foot top-rope problems as well as the following boulder prob-lems. The descent from the top is tricky and hard to find. No two parties walk down the same way. Walk south and zig-zag around boulders and short walls, eventually descending the ramp 20 yards southeast of table 18. Photos, pp. 47, 48.

Electro Shock 20 feet V3 ★
On the same rock as *Mojo Risin'* (See below), but 15 yards to the left and facing southeast, stands an obvious short , left-facing dihedral. The dihedral starts 5 feet off the ground and is capped by a small roof. Stem and lie-back up the dihedral to the roof and pull over.

Electric Aunt Jemima 20 feet V2 ★
Between *Electro Shock* and *Mojo Risin'* is a steep east-facing wall. Start 10 feet right of *Electro Shock,* 4 feet right of the arête. Climb the wall on small holds to a baseball-sized hueco and continue to the top.

The Asylum

1 *Mojo Risin' 26 feet 5.11 TR ★★*
2 *Jail Break 75 feet 5.8 TR*
3 *After Burn 70 feet 5.10+*
4 *Zumi 70 feet 5.11*
5 *Zombi 70 feet 5.11*
6 *Battle Scar 70 feet 5.11 TR*
7 *Battle Star 5.11+*
8 *So Cal Route 70 feet 5.12 TR*
9 *Whimper Roof 70 feet 5.12 TR*
10 *Short Crack 50 feet 5.8*

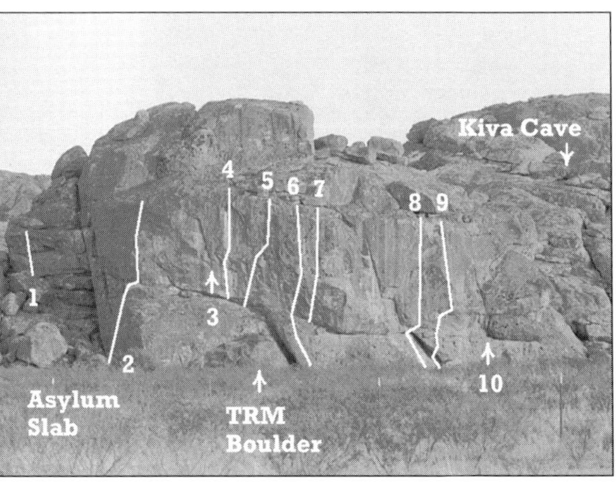

1 *Mojo Risin' 26 feet 5.11 TR ★★*
This wall starts 40 feet above ground level, 30 yards uphill from the Asylum Slab boulder. Toprope the severely overhanging dark brown streak 10 feet right of the arête on the left end of the wall.
Variation: Climb the start of *Mojo Risin',* then climb left to a crack that leads to the top of the arête.
Still Crazy 70 feet 5.10 TR
This route is up the hill, 15 yards to the left of *Jail Break,* and starts off a 6'x6'x10' boulder halfway up the gully. Climb up the huecos to a sloping ledge. Instead of following corners up and left, climb up and right.
2 *Jail Break 75 feet 5.8 TR*
Step from the southeast end of Asylum Slab boulder to a prow and climb moderate rock to the left end of a block ledge (marked "Natalie Shaw" on its right end). Climb a steep section to an upsidedown V-shaped flake. Climb up on the flake and continue on good rock to the top

Asylum Slab

Below the left side of the Asylum formation's north face is this boulder sitting next to picnic table #15. An 11-foot hand and fist crack splits the boulder on it's right side (V0–). One can climb this boulder virtually anywhere. The hardest problem (V1) is just left of the crack straight above the sandblasted patches. Problems get progressively easier to the left.

3 *After Burn 70 feet 5.10+*
A dogleg crack starts 20 feet above a sloping ledge on the left side of the north face. Reach up to a large hueco, clip a bolt, then climb difficult moves to the crack. Follow the crack to the top.
4 *Zumi 70 feet 5.11*
A large white water streak runs down the north face. Start at the base of the white water streak and climb good rock to the top. Halfway up is an old bolt.
5 *Zombi 70 feet 5.11*
Start on good holds 10 feet to the right of *Zumi* and climb up and right to the top. A toprope can be rigged with two ropes.

TRM Boulder

TRM Boulder is located next to a water faucet 30 yards west of table #15. A 30 foot tall left angling chimney bounds the right side of the boulder. Behind the water faucet is a bulge with "TRM" inscribed at 11-foot height.

Glazed Old Fashion 15 feet V1
Climb the polished blocks. The lowest block sounds hollow.
Bory Samory 15 feet V1
Just left of "Lole y Maye 47", off-routing the polished blocks to the left.
TRM 16 feet V3 ★
The Tough, Rough Mother. Start directly below "TRM". Fire straight up.
6 *Battle Scar 70 feet 5.11 TR*
25 feet to the right of the white water streak is a long overhanging hueco wall. Start on the slab 10 feet right (across the chimney) of TRM Boulder.
7 *Battle Star 5.11+*
A toprope at the time of writing, but will probably have lead bolts soon.
8 *So Cal Route 70 feet 5.12 TR*
The climb 12 feet left from *Whimper Roof.* Up the green lichen streak.
9 *Whimper Roof 70 feet 5.12 TR*
10 *Short Crack 50 feet 5.8*
Above table #17 is a short hand crack that splits a bulge. Climb the crack through the bulge and belay on a good ledge.

What's Left of Les, V3 lunge variant, Mushroom Boulder

Asylum Amphitheater

Located on the south side of Asylum Rock, at the dry east end of Laguna Prieta, is a large southeast-facing amphitheater. The amphitheater is is formed by two walls: an east-facing and a south-facing wall. This area is protected from wind, making it good for climbing on cold, windy mornings, and is in the sun in the afternoons. A top rope in this area requires two ropes: one for the anchor and one for the toprope. The east-facing wall has five hueco lines: three on the vertical section and two on the overhanging left side. The south-facing wall has one route described.

EAST-FACING WALL

Windy Days 33 feet 5.11 TR

Toprope the overhanging center of the east-facing wall, directly above a large ledge. Climb to the biggest hueco on the face then straight up to small holds near the top.

Crazy Days 30 feet 5.11 TR

Toprope the wall 8 feet right of Windy Days.

Left Route 40 feet 5.7

A conspicuous black water streak marks the route on the left side of the wall. Climb on good holds, in the water streak, to the top.

Center Route 40 feet 5.10 R

In the center of the east wall is a steep line of good huecos. Climb up 10 feet, then traverse right 15 feet to a vertical line of huecos. This climb is best top-roped if you don't have a rack of Big Bros.

Right Route 40 feet 5.7

Climb up the black water streak on the right side of the east-facing wall.

SOUTH-FACING WALL

Center Route 35 feet 5.8

Climb good huecos to a small roof. Pull over the roof to a small tree. An easy gully is 10 feet left of this line.

LAGUNA PRIETA

To the south of the Asylum formation is Laguna Prieta, The Black Lagoon. This stagnant sump is sometimes dry, sometimes full.

Gold Star Roof 20 feet V2 ★ CLOSED TO CLIMBING – STAY OFF.

On the north side of this lake is a 20-foot crack arching out a roof to a lip about 15 feet above the lake bed or a lesser distance above the water if present. Don't touch the paintings on the wall next to the crack, i.e. if you can't jam it straight in with both hands and feet, don't get on it.

KIVA CAVE

The Kiva Cave is hard to find. It's 200 yards uphill to the SSE of Laguna Prieta. The best approach scrambles up slabs above table #19 (very faintly marked, the only table east of Laguna Prieta in the same depression). Inside the cave are some of Hueco Tanks' best Indian paintings. Outside the cave are some of Hueco Tanks' most fearsome classics. The Kiva Cave entrance is marked by a tiny white squared-off "Q." Overview photos, pp. 47, 52 and 60.

THIS AREA IS CURRENTLY OFF LIMITS TO CLIMBING.

The climbing ban was enacted to combat vandalism to the paintings underneath the boulder. As the vandalism was the product of non-climbing El Paso youths, this ban is unfair to climbers and unjustified. Let the Texas Parks and Wildlife Department know that climbing activities in this area cannot possibly damage the paintings and that the presence of climbers in the area can serve as a deterent to future vandals. If enough voices are heard, then the Kiva Cave Wall may someday be reopened to climbing. In the hope that this will be the case, the following route descriptions are given:

1 *Loaf 'N Jug 12 feet V0 SD*

2 *The Ceremony 15 feet V4 ★ SD*

3 *Clitorectomy 15 feet V3 ★ SD*
Sit down start 7 feet right of the "Q" at the lone hueco 4 feet above the ground.

4 *A Pleasant Lashing 23 feet V2 ★*
10 feet right of "Q" is a left-facing flake starting 6 feet up. Climb the flake then traverse right to the top of Splatter High.

5 *Splatter High 22 feet V7 ★★★ BL scary*
The awesome vertical seam line 20 feet right of "Q". It overhangs a gnarly bad landing on a boulder behind it. Fortunately, this boulder can be friend as well as foe as it's close enough to chicken off to.

6 *Montana Crack 15 feet 5.11+ TR ★*
This is the fingercrack on the right side of the wall, starting off the boulder behind it. Starting from the ground would add 10 feet and much difficulty and pain.

Overview of *Mopboys* and Kiva Cave
View from near the top of the approach slabs.

Kiva Cave

1 *Loaf 'N Jug 12 feet V0 SD*

2 *The Ceremony 15 feet V4 ★ SD*

3 *Clitorectomy 15 feet V3 ★ SD*

4 *A Pleasant Lashing 23 feet V2 ★*

5 *Splatter High 22 feet V7 ★★★ BL*

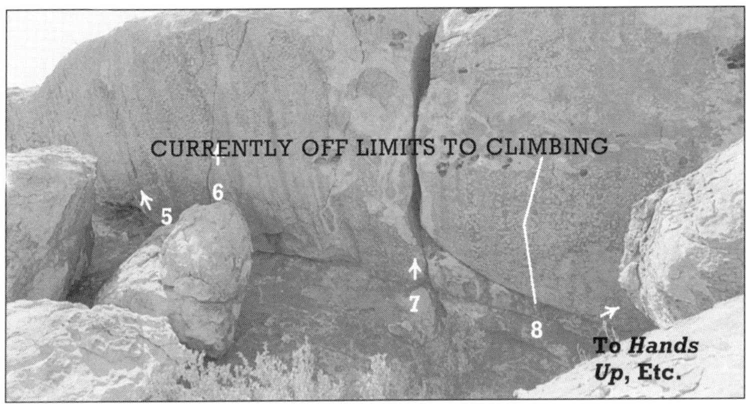

Kiva Cave

5 *Splatter High 22 feet V7 ★★★ BL*
6 *Montana Crack 15 feet 5.11+ TR ★*
7 *Highlands' Manhood Ritual 16 feet V0+*
8 *Velvet Elvis 16 feet V7 ★★*

7 *Highlands' Manhood Ritual 16 feet V0+*

8 *Velvet Elvis 16 feet V7 ★★*
Shralper on the tips.

The following climbs are inside a corridor between boulders.

9 *Hands Up 18 feet V1*
Climb the bombay to handcrack.

10 *Frisco Thin Crack 20 feet V0 ★*
Climb the fist crack. Hey, don't call it Frisco.

11 *When Legends Lie 18 feet V4 ★*
Start 12 feet right of the fist crack at a well incut plate. Footholds are microscopic. Climb straight up past a poorly incut plate to the hueco above. Finish up the blunt arete.

12 *Carbide Tips 18 feet V4 ★*
Grab holds just left of the fresh white C-shaped patch and climb straight up razors to easy huecos.

13 *Dial Direct 19 feet V2 ★ scary*
Climb directly up the wall above the sotol 5 feet right of *Carbide Tips.* Move slightly right to meet *911* at the top. Escape right or left at the horizontal top crack.

14 *911 20 feet V1 ★ scary*
Climb up left along the vague ramp to a scary top-out directly above the bush. Escape left or right along the horizontal top crack.

Kiva Cave

8 *Velvet Elvis 16 feet V7 ★★*
9 *Hands Up 18 feet V1*
10 *Frisco Thin Crack 20 feet V0 ★*
16 *Trenchtown Mix Up 14 feet V0+ ★*
17 *Fire Code 14 feet V0+*

15 976 15 feet V0 ★

The descent for problems 11-14 is 10 feet right of 976. Problems 16-17 are pictured on page 53.

16 Trenchtown Mix Up 14 feet V0+ ★
The blunt prow opposite the fist crack.

17 Fire Code 14 feet V0+
5 feet right of Trenchtown Mix Up.

Mopboys 55 feet V6 ★★★
This east-facing pump traverse is found 75 yards southeast of the Kiva Cave. Commonly done from right to left, this low level traverse goes either way. Numerous straight up problems of poor quality go up the same wall. The Mopboys wall is currently open to climbing and gets ample morning sun. Photos, pages 47 and 52.

Squirm 14 feet V4 SD
70 yards east of *Mopboys* is a low cave that also faces east (not to be confused with the bigger west-facing cave 50 yards east of *Mopboys,* the *Squirm* cave is behind and to the right of the west-facing cave). Start very low on the right and angle over to top out at the left side of the semi-circular lip.

Kiva Cave

11 When Legends Lie 18 feet V4 ★
12 Carbide Tips 18 feet V4 ★
13 Dial Direct 19 feet V2 ★
14 911 20 feet V1 ★ scary
15 976 15 feet V0 ★

THE FRONT SIDE

The Front Side is the imposing west face of North Mountain which extends from the south end of Laguna Prieta to the Fox Tower. It includes Lunch Rock Wall, The Perverted Sanctuary, Cakewalk Wall, The Central Wall, Indecent Exposure Buttress (aka Main Buttress) and Fox Tower. Most of the Front Side climbs are from 200 to 350 feet long and don't get sun until almost noon. Great bouldering lines the base of the Front Side. Described first is the descent from the Front Side and the associated bouldering found atop the Front Side. Next, Lunch Rocks bouldering is described, followed by lead climbs from Lunch Rock Wall to Fox Tower. Lastly, the bouldering beneath the main faces south of Lunch Rocks is described.

THE FRONT SIDE DESCENT

The accompanying map (page 56) of the Front Side Descent is for routes from Cakewalk Wall to Indecent Exposure (Main) Buttress. Descending from Cakewalk Wall is trickier than from the other Front Side routes and involves either a very exposed 3rd or 4th class climbing across a natural chockstone bridge (many climbers will rope up for this), a balls-out one-chance-only jump across the same gap, or a short rappel into the gully below and 2nd class slabs out of the gully. All other Front Side descents should involve few or no 3rd class moves. If you find yourself downclimbing more than one or two moves, you are not on the best route. For routes from *All The Nasties* to *Pink Adrenaline,* walk along the top of the Main Wall until atop the route *Desperado* (marked by the Super Bowl – a 40-foot-wide, 20-foot-deep pit on top of the wall). Then walk east until across a 20-yard wide grassy gully. Head north, walking parallel to the gully on its east side until large boulders force you to the right (The Groupie Alert Wall, et.al.). From here pass the See-Thru Hueco Boulder (*The Laughing Sutra*) on its

The Front Side

A. *Lunch Rocks, p. 60*
B. *Hueco Walk, p. 67*
C. *Perverted Sancturary, p. 67*
D. *Split Boulder, p. 82*
E. *Scary Boulder, p. 89*
F. *Mushroom Boulder, p. 91.*
G. *End Loop. , p. 100*
H. *Cakewalk Wall, p. 70*
I. *Central Wall, p. 73*
J. *Indecent Exposure Buttress, p. 76*
K. *Fox Tower, p. 82*

FRONT SIDE DESCENT

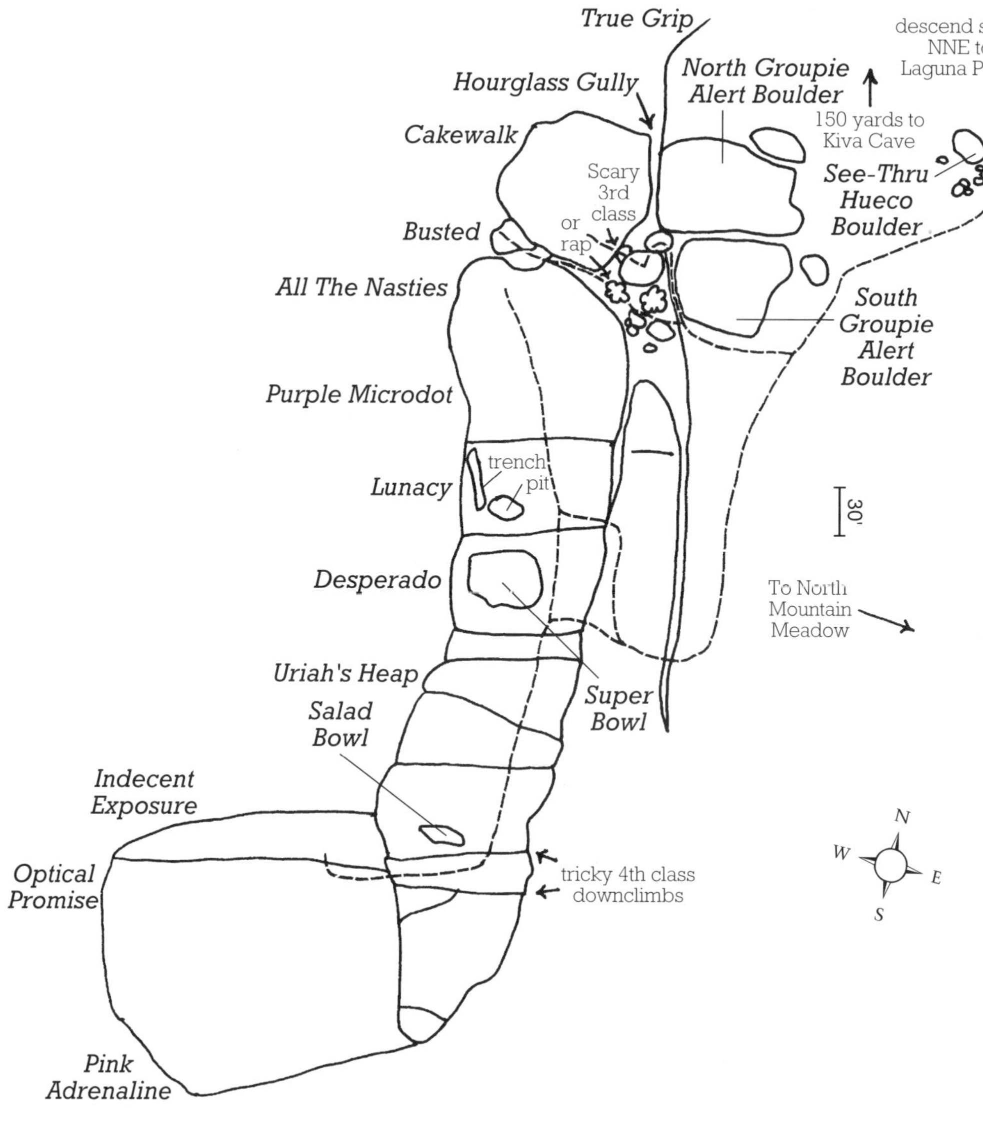

right then head north-northeast down slabs to Laguna Prieta at ground level. Forty feet above ground level a short 3rd class section may be encountered.

Descent Boulders

GROUPIE ALERT BOULDERS

NORTH GROUPIE ALERT BOULDER

1 *Groupie Alert 20 feet V2 ★★ scary*

2 *The Power of Negative Thinking 22 feet V1 ★★ scary*
Via the "negative plate" 14 feet up.

3 *Stretch And Fetch 22 feet V0 ★*
3 feet right of the "negative plate." Reachy. Powerful forthe grade.

4 *Jugular 22 feet V0 ★*

SOUTH GROUPIE ALERT BOULDER

Problems 5-10 are pictured on page 58.

5 *Navajo Bubba 22 feet V0-*

6 *The Colonel's Secret Recipe 20 feet V0*

7 *The Grey Look 20 feet V1 BL scary*

8 *Easy Dilater 20 feet V0 BL*

9 *Potato Bud 19 feet V0+ BL*

10 *D-Cell Delight 17 feet V0+ BL*

North Groupie Alert Boulder

1 *Groupie Alert 20 feet V2 ★★ scary*

2 *The Power of Negative Thinking 22 feet V1 ★★ scary*

3 *Stretch And Fetch 22 feet V0 ★*

4 *Jugular 22 feet V0 ★*

Groupie Alert Boulders

1 *Groupie Alert 20 feet V2 ★★ scary*
5 *Navajo Bubba 22 feet V0-*
6 *The Colonel's Secret Recipe 20 feet V0*

South Groupie Alert Boulder

6 *The Colonel's Secret Recipe 20 feet V0*
7 *The Grey Look 20 feet V1 BL scary*
8 *Easy Dilater 20 feet V0 BL*
9 *Potato Bud 19 feet V0+ BL*
10 *D-Cell Delight 17 feet V0+ BL*

See-Thru Hueco Boulder

11 The Laughing Sutra 17 feet V0 ★

SEE-THRU HUECO BOULDER

This unusual rock is found 50 yards northeast of the Groupie Alert Walls. Map, page 56.

11 The Laughing Sutra 17 feet V0 ★

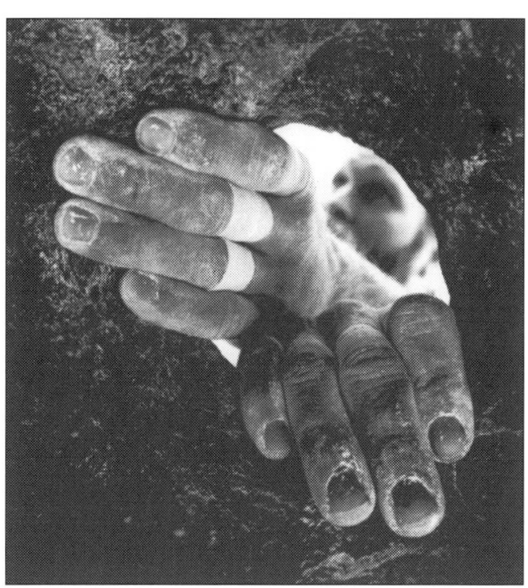

LUNCH ROCKS AREA

The Lunch Rocks complex is located at the far left (north) end of the Front Side. The Lunch Rocks nearly reach the road at their west end.

The Nachoman and Smooth Moves boulders are located north of Lunch Rocks and are not on the topo. Overview photo, p. 55. Route descriptions begin on page 62.

Lunch Rocks (topo at right)

1 *Feel Like Shit... Deja Vu 9 feet V1*
2 *Roughage 18 feet V7 ★★★ BL*
3 *Slip It In 9 feet V7 ★★*
4 *Another Dick Face 10 feet V5*
5 *Wonderhole 10 feet V0+ ★★*
6 *No Wonder 11 feet V7 SD*
7 *Turtle Wax 15 feet V0–*
8 *Armor All 18 feet V1*
9 *Orifice Affair 11 feet V1 ★*
10 *Tell Mama 16 feet V1*
11 *Hard Again 16 feet V3*
12 *Hungry Belly... 16 feet V2*
13 *Potbelly 16 feet V1 BL*
14 *RBI 16 feet V1 BL*
15 *Pedro Drives One In 16 feet V1 ★★ BL scary*
16 *Culture 18 feet V0+ BL*
17 *Just Another Pretty Face 14 feet V2*
18 *The Dripping Gash 12 feet V0*
19 *The Thighburner 14 feet V1*
20 *Swinging Single 11 feet V3*
21 *Jingomo 12 feet V4 BL*
22 *Scarface 20 feet V2*
23 *Daily Grind 16 feet V2*
24 *Another Day, Another... 14 feet V2*
25 *How Cilley Can You Get 15 feet V6*
26 *Present Arms 15 feet V2 ★*
27 *The Lazy Cowgirls 17 feet V2*
28 *Thingfish 15 feet V4*
29 *The Torture Never Stops 15 feet V3*

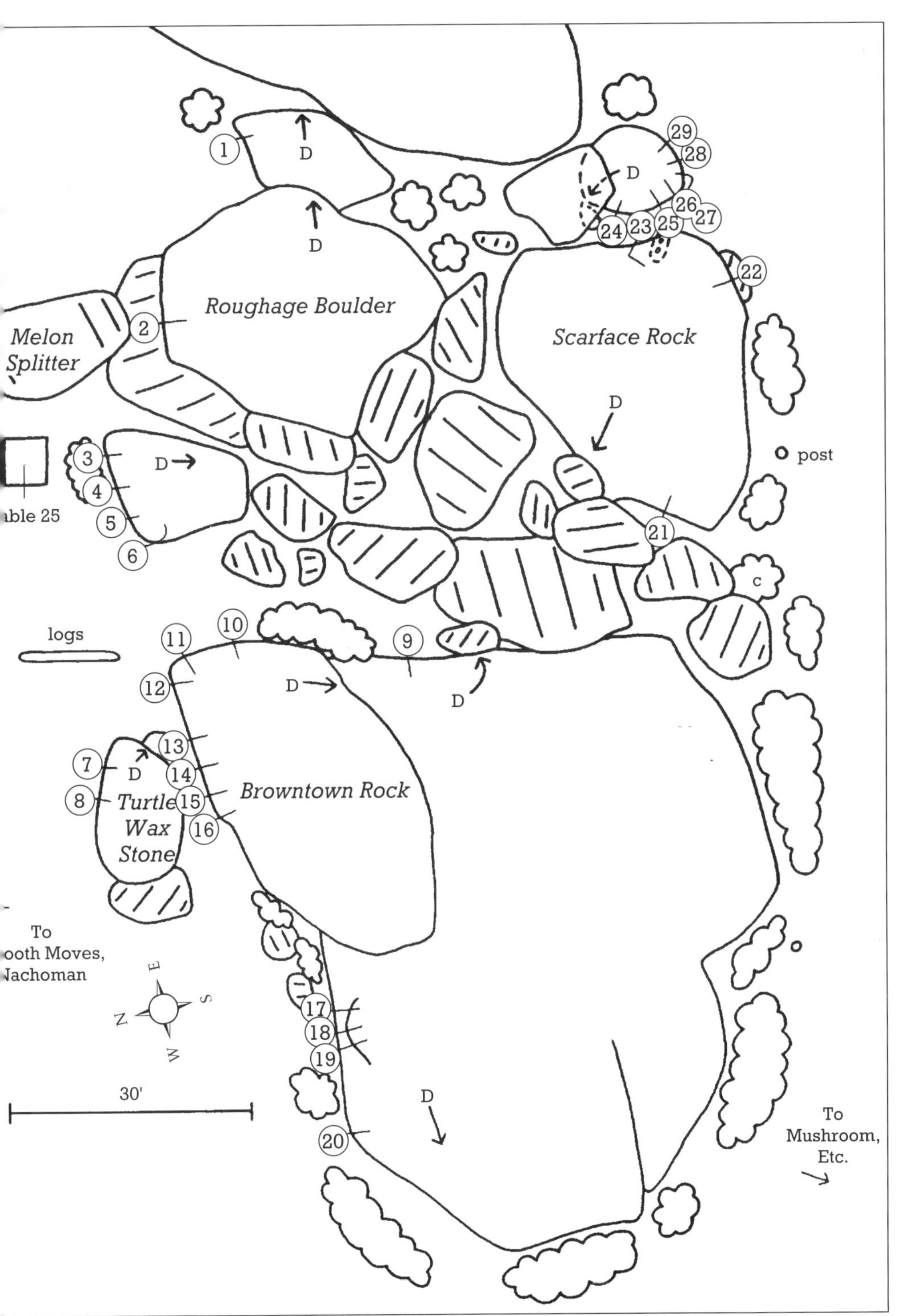

Roughage Boulder
Melon Splitter
Scarface Rock
post
able 25
logs
Browntown Rock
Turtle Wax Stone
To
ooth Moves,
Jachoman
30'
To
Mushroom,
Etc.

Nachoman Boulder
1 *Nachoman 13 feet V9 ★*
2 *Coffee Achiever 17 feet V5 ★★*

Nachoman Boulder

The Nachoman Boulder is immediately south of covered picnic table #23. These problems face the table (north). Descend the backside. Overview photo, p. 60.

1 *Nachoman 13 feet V9 ★*
2 *Coffee Achiever 17 feet V5 ★★*

Smooth Moves Boulder

Smooth Moves Boulder is located 18 yards northwest of table #25 (uncovered). Descend the southeast side. Overview photo, p. 60.

Slick Watts 12 feet V5 ★
Easy if you jump from the ground. The trick is to get both feet on the rock before lunging. The wickedly polished northeast arête marked by "Jack, Chris, Bev, Cinda."

Vanilla Smoothie 11 feet V0+ ★
The white scoop in the center of the north face. Better than it looks.

Lunch Rocks

The Lunch Rocks topo is on page 61.

1 *Feel Like Shit... Deja Vu 9 feet V1*
Pull the lip of the overhang right of the bush and left of the *Roughage* boulder.

2 *Roughage 18 feet V7 ★★★ BL scary*
Climbs the overhang's middle, tempting bad landings below the first moves and a melon-splitting block behind the lip. Terrifying, technical.

Variation: ***Purple Panty Eater 10 feet V3.*** From atop the melon splitter grab the lip of *Roughage* and climb the moves to the top. Scary. Bad landing.

The next three problems are on the short boulder just south of table #25 (uncovered).

3 *Slip It In (aka Chong Li) 9 feet V7 ★★*
Start sitting down at a made to order 4 finger pocket 3½ feet above the ground. Crank the major lock off with or without an intermediate to the twin finger pockets above.

4 *Another Dick Face 10 feet V5*
Start halfway between *Slip It In* and *Wonderhole*. Climb sick blades to the top.

5 *Wonderhole 10 feet V0+ ★★*

6 *No Wonder 11 feet V7 SD*

Lunch Rocks

Left:

2 *Roughage 18 feet V7 ★★★*
BL scary

4 *Another Dick Face 10 feet V5*

5 *Wonderhole 10 feet V0+ ★★*

6 *No Wonder 11 feet V7 SD*

Below:

View from atop *Melon Splitter* and next to *Roughage*.

3 *Slip It In (aka Chong Li) 9 feet V7 ★★*

9 *Orifice Affair 11 feet V1 ★*

10 *Tell Mama 16 feet V1*

11 *Hard Again 16 feet V3*

12 *Hungry Belly A De New Stylee 16 feet V2*

Turtle Wax Stone

This is the rock two yards north of Browntown Rock. Topo, p. 61.

7 *Turtle Wax 15 feet V0–*
Climb the polished jigsaw puzzle plates.

8 *Armor All 18 feet V1*
6 feet right of *Turtle Wax.*

Browntown Rock.

Descend problems 6-13 to the south of *Orifice Affair.* Topo, p. 61.

9 *Orifice Affair 11 feet V1 ★*
Start 2 feet left of a catclaw. Do all three holes up the slightly overhung wall.

10 *Tell Mama 16 feet V1*
6 feet left of the arête, climb the ironrock face via huecos and loose lip holds. A saner top out goes to the right.

11 *Hard Again 16 feet V3*
Climb the wall forming the left side of the arête. Tricky.

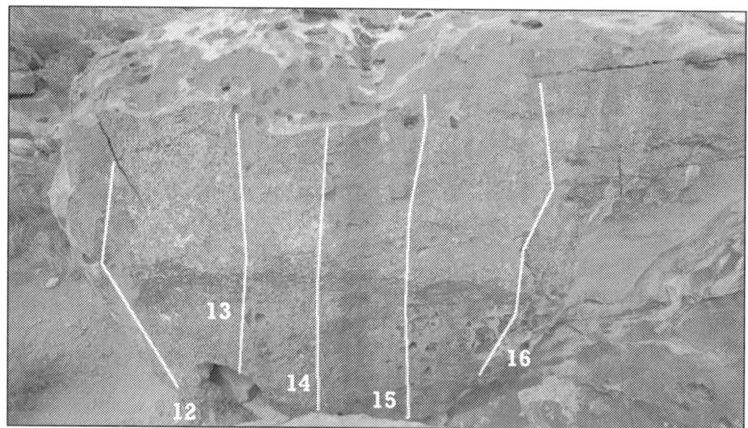

Browntown Rock as viewed from atop Turtle Wax Stone

12 Hungry Belly A De New Stylee 16 feet V2
13 Potbelly 16 feet V1 BL
14 RBI 16 feet V1 BL
15 Pedro Drives One In 16 feet V1 ★★ BL scary
16 Culture 18 feet V0+ BL

Topo for problems 12-20 is on page 61.

12 Hungry Belly A De New Stylee 16 feet V2
Climb the right side of the arête. Photos above and on page 63.

13 Potbelly 16 feet V1 BL

14 RBI 16 feet V1 BL

15 Pedro Drives One In 16 feet V1 ★★ BL scary
Committing moves up high.

16 Culture 18 feet V0+ BL

Problems 17-20 lie approximately 15 yards to the right of *Culture,* in between bushes at the right end of the north-facing wall.

17 Just Another Pretty Face 14 feet V2
This is the thin slab 4 feet left of *The Dripping Gash.*

18 The Dripping Gash 12 feet V0

19 The Thighburner 14 feet V1

20 Swinging Single 11 feet V3
Six feet right of the bush is this smooth bulge. Swing from the ground to the lip and grovel over. The swing hold borders the right side of a two tone brown and cream streak at 8 foot level. A tall man's start unless you're Spud Webb. No longer a problem a few feet to the right.

The following problems are on the south side of Lunch Rocks near picnic table #28 (covered). 15 feet north of table 28 is a wooden post with a small concrete pad in front of it where a water faucet once was. Behind this is a big suspended boulder with a cave under it. Problems 21-23 are on this rock.

Scarface Boulder

21 Jingomo 12 feet V4 BL
Jingomo is located at the west entrance to the cave 20 feet north of the wood post. Climb the undercut ironrock overhang. Topo, p. 61.

22 Scarface 20 feet V2
The original and still the worst. Start on the small rock that holds the big one up. Climb crappy flakes up the scoop to the top. Topo, p. 61.

Browntown Rock (left)

17 *Just Another Pretty Face 14 feet V2*
18 *The Dripping Gash 12 feet V0*
19 *The Thighburner 14 feet V1*
20 *Swinging Single 11 feet V3*

Scarface, Present Arms from inside boulder cluster (below)

23 *Daily Grind 16 feet V2*
24 *Another Day, Another Dollar 14 feet V2*

23 *Daily Grind 16 feet V2*
Start right of the stone with the 3 deep grinding holes. Climb up and right to the diagonal crack. Go as high as you dare before stepping back to the rock behind. Topo, p. 61.

Present Arms Boulder

Problems 24-29 are on the next rock to the east of Scarface Rock; topo, p. 61.

24 *Another Day, Another Dollar 14 feet V2*
On the boulder behind *Daily Grind* is an inscription ("SJL") that looks like a dollar sign "$." Climb the face left of this. The boulder to the left is off-route.

25 *How Cilley Can You Get 15 feet V6*
Climb sharp fragile flakes right of "Fermin." No fun. Photo, p. 66.

26 *Present Arms 15 feet V2* ★
Start at the leftmost jug in the horizontal crack, then go straight up. Photo, p. 66.

27 *The Lazy Cowgirls 17 feet V2*
The same start as Present Arms, but reel right along the crack to its high point and top out there. Photo, p. 66.

28 *Thingfish 15 feet V4*
Start at the other (right) end of the horizontal crack on the last fullhand jug (at 7-foot level). Straight up, sharp and loose. Photo, p. 66.

Present Arms Boulder

23 *Daily Grind 16 feet V2*
24 *Another Day, Another Dollar 14 feet V2*
25 *How Cilley Can You Get 15 feet V6*
26 *Present Arms 15 feet V2* ★
27 *The Lazy Cowgirls 17 feet V2*
28 *Thingfish 15 feet V4*
29 *The Torture Never Stops 15 feet V3*

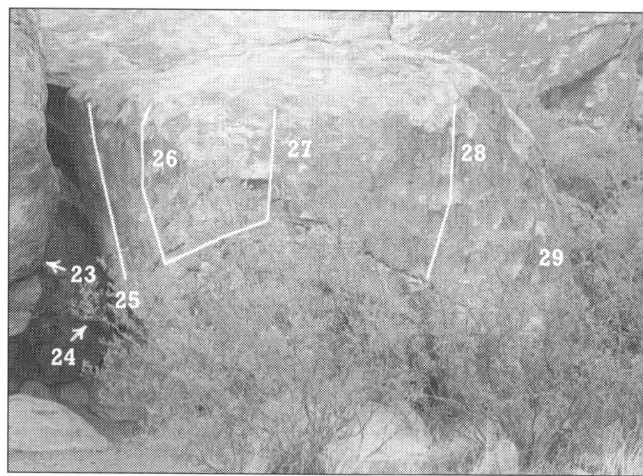

29 *The Torture Never Stops 15 feet V3*
A chest level, 8"x2" jug, the only jug on this problem, is the first hold. Beware of loose holds. Topo, p. 61.

Lunch Rock Wall

Located on the north end of The Front Side 65 yards northeast of table 28 is a 100-foot west-facing wall with two cracks that meet 75 feet up to form a single left-leaning crack. One pitch routes follow each of these cracks.

1 *Lunch Rock Indirect 100 feet 5.9*
Climb the face 12 feet left and up the hill from *Lunch Rock Direct.*

2 *Lunch Rock Direct 10 feet 5.7* ★
This route climbs the left crack. Begin on moderate face moves and climb to a finger and hand crack which leads to a small roof 60 feet up. Pull over and climb the obvious left-leaning crack system. To descend, walk north and scramble down.

3 *Lunch Rock 100 feet 5.8* ★
Climb the short, left-facing dihedral capped by a small roof 45 feet up. Follow the wide crack up and left to the left-leaning crack system.

4 *Luther 60 feet 5.11* ★
This spectacular hand to finger crack is hidden in a large cave near the base of Lunch Rock. Walk through trees to the hidden entrance of the cave. This entrance is 10 yards right of the *Lunch Rock* route. Proceed, in the cave, to a large open room. Climb the obvious finger crack on a bulging, south-facing wall for sixty feet.

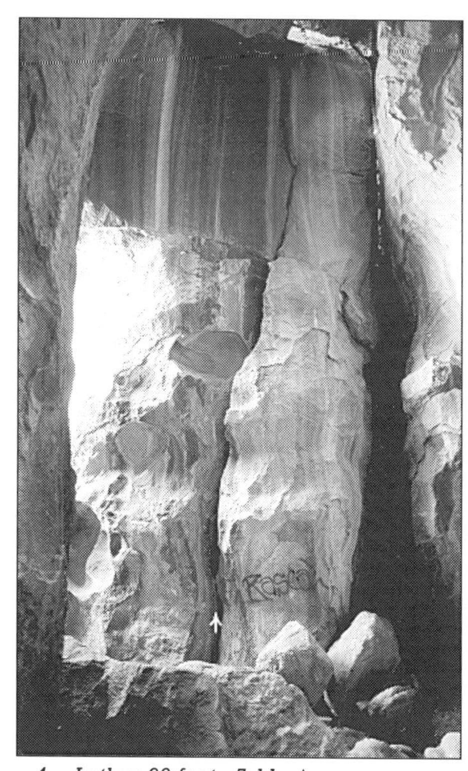

4 *Luther 60 feet 5.11* ★

5 *Cave Exit 100 feet 5.6*
This route ascends a right-facing dihedral on the right side of the cave mouth.

6 *Looking for Mars Bars 40 feet 5.4*
This line follows the right-facing dihedral capped by a large roof. Start on top of a group of boulders and climb on good holds to the base of the roof. Escape right around the roof. Photo, p. 71.

7 *Hueco Walk 80 feet 5.6 R ★★*
Hueco Walk starts to the left of the group of 2 to 5 foot tall boulders at the base of the wall. Climb spectacular huecos on steep rock to a wide left–angling crack near the top. This is a nice route with classic holds. Photos, pages 55 and 71.

THE PERVERTED SANCTUARY

The Perverted Sanctuary is the raised area left of Cakewalk Wall. This small amphitheater contains several one and two pitch climbs.
See topo on page 66. Photo below; additional photo on page 55.

8 *Left Hand Perverts 40 feet 5.11+TR ★*
Nut anchor.

9 *Pervert's Delight 40 feet 5.11+ ★*
On the left side of the sanctuary, climb the steep south-facing wall past two bolts to a two bolt anchor.

10 *Right Hand Perverts 40 feet 5.12-TR ★*

11 *K-Y Ridge 80 feet 5.10*
To the right of *Pervert's Delight* is a west-facing wall at the entrance of a cave. This cave leads to *Luther* (see Lunch Rock Area). Begin on the right side below the huge overhang and step left onto the route. 30 feet up is a bolt. Climb a bulge on small holds and continue up on steep rock.

12 *Gravy Train 55 feet 5.12 ★*

The Perverted Sanctuary

8 *Left Hand Perverts 40 feet 5.11+TR ★*
9 *Pervert's Delight 40 feet 5.11+ ★*
10 *Right Hand Perverts 40 feet 5.12-TR ★*
11 *K-Y Ridge 80 feet 5.10*
12 *Gravy Train 55 feet 5.12 ★*
13 *S-Crack 50 feet 5.10*

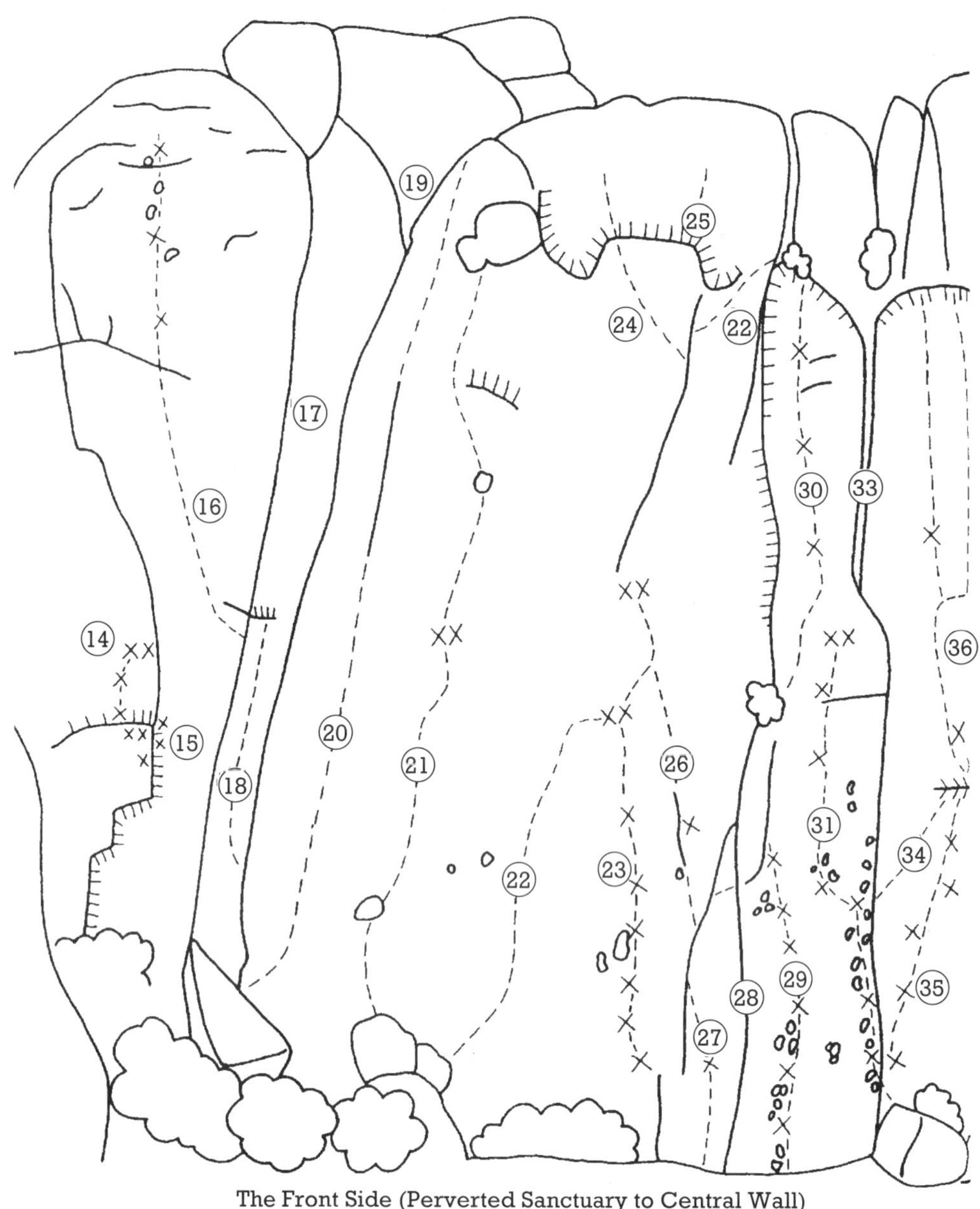

The Front Side (Perverted Sanctuary to Central Wall)

14 *Flake Roof 55 feet 5.11* ★★★
15 *Flake Roof Indirect 55 feet 5.11–* ★
16 *True Grip 180 feet 5.10–* ★★
17 *Left Side 200 feet 5.6*
18 *Center 200 feet 5.7 X*
19 *Right Side 200 feet 5.6*
20 *Son of Cakewalk 250 feet 5.6*
21 *Return of Cakewalk 280 feet 5.7* ★
22 *Cakewalk 300 feet 5.6* ★★★
23 *Cakewalk Direct 100 feet 5.9* ★
24 *Let Them Eat Cake 20 feet 5.10 R*
25 *Peasant's Revolt 30 feet 5.8* ★
26 *Banana Cake 300 feet 5.10 R*
27 *Banana Patch 300 feet 5.10* ★
28 *Bitchin Chimney 300 feet 5.9*
29 *Alice In Banana Land 105 feet 5.10–* ★
30 *Busted 300 feet 5.9* ★
31 *Malice in Bucket Land 125 feet 5.9-* ★★
33 *Paul Bunyon Chimney 275 feet 5.7*
34 *All The Nasty Urinals 260 feet 5.9 R*
35 *Divine Wind 100 feet 5.7*
36 *All The Nasties 260 feet 5.10* ★★

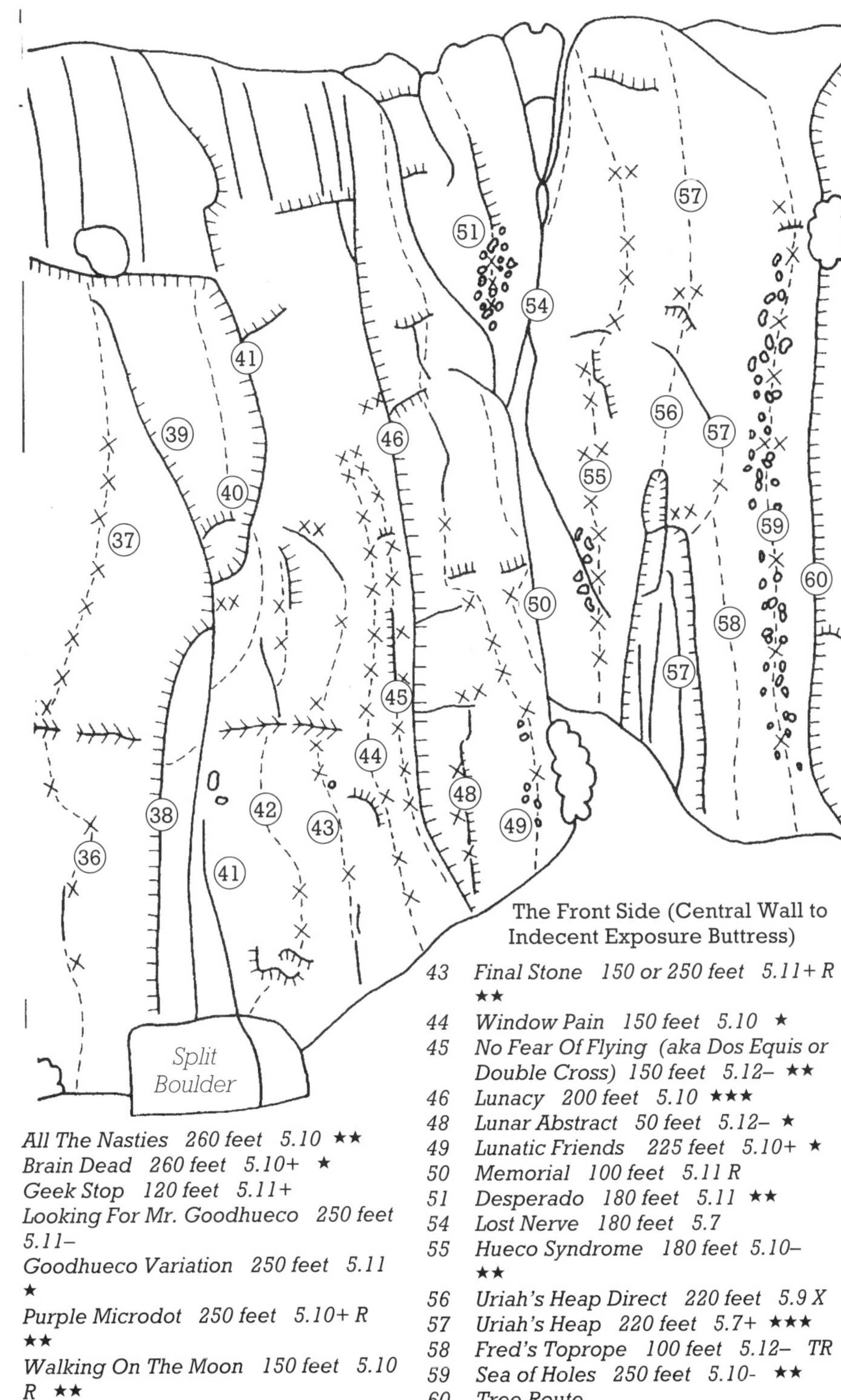

The Front Side (Central Wall to Indecent Exposure Buttress)

36 *All The Nasties 260 feet 5.10* ★★
37 *Brain Dead 260 feet 5.10+* ★
38 *Geek Stop 120 feet 5.11+*
39 *Looking For Mr. Goodhueco 250 feet 5.11–*
40 *Goodhueco Variation 250 feet 5.11* ★
41 *Purple Microdot 250 feet 5.10+ R* ★★
42 *Walking On The Moon 150 feet 5.10 R* ★★
43 *Final Stone 150 or 250 feet 5.11+ R* ★★
44 *Window Pain 150 feet 5.10* ★
45 *No Fear Of Flying (aka Dos Equis or Double Cross) 150 feet 5.12–* ★★
46 *Lunacy 200 feet 5.10* ★★★
48 *Lunar Abstract 50 feet 5.12–* ★
49 *Lunatic Friends 225 feet 5.10+* ★
50 *Memorial 100 feet 5.11 R*
51 *Desperado 180 feet 5.11* ★★
54 *Lost Nerve 180 feet 5.7*
55 *Hueco Syndrome 180 feet 5.10–* ★★
56 *Uriah's Heap Direct 220 feet 5.9 X*
57 *Uriah's Heap 220 feet 5.7+* ★★★
58 *Fred's Toprope 100 feet 5.12– TR*
59 *Sea of Holes 250 feet 5.10-* ★★
60 *Tree Route*

13 *S-Crack 50 feet 5.10*

This route follows the S-shape crack in the back of the Sanctuary. This crack is 30 feet left of the sloped ledge below *Flake Roof.* Photo, p. 67.

14 *Flake Roof 55 feet 5.11* ★★★

The Flake Roof is one of the classic roofs at Hueco Tanks. On the west–facing wall of the amphitheater, scramble up to a square, sloping ledge at the base of a left-facing dihedral. Stem up the dihedral to the right side of a large roof, and climb left 10 feet to good holds. Climb the roof using good holds to the lip and grunt over. Belay at 2 bolts over the roof. An excellent finish is the last pitch of *True Grip* (see below), the steep headwall 150 feet above the *Flake Roof.* 5 bolts, 2-bolt anchor. Topo, p. 68. Photo, p.71.

15 *Flake Roof Indirect 55 feet 5.11–* ★

This route starts on the smooth face to the right of *Flake Roof,* and climbs straight up to the roof. Climb the thin crack out the right side of the roof. 4 bolts, 2 bolt anchor. Topo, p. 68.

16 *True Grip 180 feet 5.10–* ★★

This fine two-pitch route begins immediately to the right of *Flake Roof,* on the *Left Side* of The Hour Glass (See below). The route climbs the steep headwall above *Flake Roof.* Start at a wide crack and face-climb 120 feet to a miniscule roof. Follow a thin crack left out of the chimney system, (5.7). The second pitch climbs a beautiful section of sweeping rock to a steep headwall with big huecos. Descend by following the slabs north towards the Asylum Rocks. Topo, p. 68. Photo, p.71.

The Hour Glass

This 200-foot double chimney system is in the southeast corner of the Perverted Sanctuary, right of *Flake Roof.* Several routes access this chimney system. Topo, p. 68.

17 *Left Side 200 feet 5.6*

Start at a wide crack and face climb past a bulge to a good belay, (80 Ft.). The second pitch follows the left chimney past a roof and to the top. This is sometimes used as an alternative Front Side descent by expert climbers.

18 *Center 200 feet 5.7 X*

Start at the right side of the Hour Glass, climb up 5 feet then traverse left 10 feet to a prow. Climb straight up on huecos to easier ground and an obvious belay. This route can the join the *Left Side* or *Right Side* of The Hour Glass.

19 *Right Side 200 feet 5.6*

Begin on the right side of the Hour Glass in a large chimney with a hand-sized crack. Climb 80 feet to a comfortable belay; last pitch climbs crack system on the right side.

CAKEWALK WALL

To the right of The Hour Glass is a 250-foot hueco wall with infinite route possibilities. Cakewalk Wall is incredibly climbable, and no two teams go the same way. The descent is a little tricky. At the top of the routes, walk south until the way is barred by a crevasse. A natural chockstone bridges the crevasse on the east side. Scramble down to the bridge and climb across, jump across, or make one short rappel into the crevice. Follow the Front Side Descent to Laguna Prieta. Overview photo, p. 55; topo, p. 68. Photo, p. 71.

20 *Son of Cakewalk 250 feet 5.6*

Begin 10 feet to the right of The Hour Glass and climb 10 feet up to a small roof with a left-facing dihedral. Pull over the roof at the dihedral and climb straight up, on good holds, to a crack that begins 150 feet above the ground, and belay. The second pitch climbs the crack to a short headwall.

21 *Return of Cakewalk 280 feet 5.7* ★

Start this climb on top of the highest boulder at the base of Cakewalk Wall. Step off the left side of the boulder and climb up to an umbrella–size hueco 20 feet above the

Perverted Sanctuary, Cakewalk Wall

6 *Looking for Mars Bars* 40 feet 5.4
7 *Hueco Walk* 80 feet 5.6 R ★★
14 *Flake Roof* 55 feet 5.11 ★★★
16 *True Grip* 180 feet 5.10– ★★
17 *Left Side* 200 feet 5.6
18 *Center* 200 feet 5.7 X
19 *Right Side* 200 feet 5.6
20 *Son of Cakewalk* 250 feet 5.6
21 *Return of Cakewalk* 280 feet 5.7 ★
22 *Cakewalk* 300 feet 5.6 ★★★
23 *Cakewalk Direct* 100 feet 5.9 ★
24 *Let Them Eat Cake* 20 feet 5.10 R
25 *Peasant's Revolt* 30 feet 5.8 ★

boulder. Step up and right from the hueco, and climb a steep section, on small holds, to easier ground. Climb beautiful rock to a belay 150 feet up the wall. The second pitch follows good holds to the left and top bypassing a large white roof on its left.

22 ***Cakewalk* 300 feet 5.6 ★★★**
This classic route starts 15 feet to the right of the boulder at the base of *Return of Cakewalk* (p. 70). Climb a black water trough with good holds until the angle decreases. Traverse up and right to a hand-size crack and belay. On the second pitch, climb the crack to the top. Topo, p. 68; photos, pp. 71 and 74.

23 ***Cakewalk Direct* 100 feet 5.9 ★**
From the ground behind trees next to table #37, climb up and right to a black water streak leading to huecos and a bulge. Climb the bulge on the right side up to easier ground; belay at a hidden crack with two bolts. The second pitch follows *Cakewalk* to the top. A more popular variant start is just right of the trees; climb the first 15-foot thin crack of *Banana Patch* listed below (nuts are handy), then move up and left past a bolt to the black streak. 5 bolts, 2-bolt anchor. Topo, p. 68; photos, pp. 71 and 74.

Marie Antoinette Roof

At the top of Cakewalk is a large roof with a hand-size crack. There are two routes over the roof. Topo, p. 68. Routes 25-31 are pictured on page 74.

24 ***Let Them Eat Cake* 20 feet 5.10 R**
Climb the left side of the roof with long reaches and no protection. Photo, p. 71.

25 ***Peasant's Revolt* 30 feet 5.8 ★**
Climb the hand crack on the right side of the roof. Photo, p. 71.

26 ***Banana Cake* 300 feet 5.10 R**
Climb the first 40 feet of *Banana Patch* to the thin crack. Climb above and to the right of the black water streaked trough which leads to *Cakewalk*.

27 ***Banana Patch* 300 feet 5.10 ★**
Start in a thin crack 15 feet left of a squeeze chimney or climb the face 4 feet left of the chimney past a bolt. Either way (both 5.10) join a thin crack that starts 20 feet above the ground. Climb this crack for 35 feet until you can step over the chimney and join a thin crack on its right side. Follow this crack to a two bolt belay next to a tree in the chimney. Finish up the chimney or do Busted.

28 ***Bitchin' Chimney* 300 feet 5.9**
This is the squeeze chimney to the right of *Banana Patch*. As far as we know it has only been climbed once by a skinny and lanky person who said it was tight. Use natural chockstones for protection.

29 ***Alice In Banana Land* 105 feet 5.10– ★**
An inconspicuous line of huecos 13 feet to the right of the squeeze chimney leads to a vertical thin crack 60 feet above the ground (the same crack as *Banana Patch*). 6 bolts, 2 bolt anchor, nuts for top crack or run it out.

30 ***Busted* 300 feet 5.9 ★**
Climb the first pitch of *Banana Patch* or *Alice in Bananaland* to the two bolt anchor. Climb up and right from the belay to a steep buttress. Follow the steep buttress 100 feet to the top.

31 ***Malice in Bucket Land* 125 feet 5.9- ★★**
This spectacular route climbs the rounded outside corner between *Bitchin' Chimney* and *Paul Bunyon Chimney*. Start atop a 15 foot tall boulder (Malice Boulder) at the base of the chimney. Follow a line of good huecos, first on the outside corner, then to the left of the corner, past seven bolts to a thin horizontal crack 120 feet above the ground. Belay at two bolts above the horizontal crack. 8 bolts, 2-bolt anchor.

32 ***Cowboyography* 140 feet 5.13 ★★★**
Photo, page 80.

33 ***Paul Bunyon Chimney* 275 feet 5.7**
This is the 15-foot-wide chimney to the right of the Cakewalk Wall. There is a large chockstone in the chimney about 25 feet above the ground. Climb directly above the chockstone, veering slightly to the left using the right (south) side of the chimney for 2 pitches.

AREA 16

Map, p. 26

THE CENTRAL WALL

The Central Wall starts at the *Paul Bunyon Chimney* and includes all the climbs to *The Tree Route.* Topos, pages 68 and 69; photos, pages 74 and 80.

34 ***All The Nasty Urinals 260 feet 5.9 R***
Start inside *Paul Bunyon Chimney* below a large chockstone. Climb to the top of the chockstone, then up and right to Urinal Ledge, (the belay ledge for *All The Nasties*). The second pitch starts on the left side of the ledge. Climb to a steep headwall and traverse left back to *Paul Bunyon Chimney.*
Variation: 5.10 Climb straight over the headwall on the second pitch.

35 ***Divine Wind 100 feet 5.7 ★***
To the right of *All The Nasty Urinals,* a rib of rock leads to Urinal Ledge. Climb this rib past 5 bolts to Urinal Ledge. The second pitch follows *All The Nasties.* Photo, p. 74.

36 ***All The Nasties 260 feet 5.10 ★★***
This classic two-pitch route ascends the center of the steep face to the right of *Paul Bunyon Chimney.* Climb good holds past a bolt to a thin crack 35 feet up the wall. Climb the short crack. Next, step right to good holds on deteriorating rock (2 bolts), then traverse left (1 bolt) to a comfortable belay ledge (Urinal Ledge, 2 bolt anchor). On the second pitch, step left off Urinal Ledge and climb up to a steep headwall and good protection. From here, either climb straight up past a bolt or traverse right along a break in the wall for 20 feet, then climb straight up on beautiful rock to the top. Photo, p. 74.

37 ***Brain Dead 260 feet 5.10+ ★***
Climb *All The Nasties* to Urinal Ledge. From Urinal Ledge climb right, eventually getting to steep dark rock. Traverse on difficult rock and then angle up left through a shallow trough to easier climbing. (2nd pitch, 7 bolts) Photo, p. 74.

38 ***Geek Stop 120 feet 5.11+***
Climb the thin obvious crack left of *Purple Microdot* for 80 feet then traverse right into *Purple Microdot.* Photo, p. 80.

39 ***Looking For Mr. Goodhueco 250 feet 5.11–***
After *Geek Stop* or the first pitch of *Purple Microdot,* climb the left Y-crack. Photos, pages 74 and 80.

40 ***Goodhueco Variation 250 feet 5.11 ★***
After 25 feet of *Looking For Mr. Goodhueco,* climb out the right-angling roof crack/hand traverse. Continue up on bulging face moves.

41 ***Purple Microdot 250 feet 5.10+ R ★★***
Behind Split Boulder are three crack lines on the wall. *Purple Microdot* begins in the right crack. Climb to a two bolt belay beneath the upper Y–cracks. Undercling to the right under the roof to a large right-facing dihedral. Climb the dihedral passing a small roof on its left side to gain a large ledge. From here, either climb one of the cracks above the ledge or follow the ledge left. Photos, pp. 74 and 80.
Variation: 5.10 – Start with the center crack (between *Geek Stop* and the leaning crack on *Purple Microdot*).

42 ***Walking On The Moon 150 feet 5.10 R ★★***
This hair-raising route begins at the tree right of *Purple Microdot.* Start next to the large juniper tree and climb a short overhang to a tiered ledge with a bolt. Ten feet up is another bolt. Veer left and up to a small vertical crack 100 feet off the ground (will take a wired nut). From here angle up and right toward the small left-facing dihedral; climb up and over it to the right and belay on *Final Stone.* From here, either traverse left to the upper dihedral on *Purple Microdot* or rappel down. Photo, p. 74.

43 ***Final Stone 150 or 250 feet 5.11+ R ★★***
This strenuous, thin face climb will probably become more difficult as micro-holds peel off. Start up a shallow right leaning dihedral then follow the 6 bolts straight up the face towards the crescent flake system on *Walking on the Moon.* When you pull over the horizontal rib after the crux, you will have earned the no-hands rest. Take a good

Cakewalk, Central walls

22 *Cakewalk 300 feet 5.6* ★★★
23 *Cakewalk Direct 100 feet 5.9* ★
25 *Peasant's Revolt 30 feet 5.8* ★
26 *Banana Cake 300 feet 5.10 R*
27 *Banana Patch 300 feet 5.10* ★
28 *Bitchin Chimney 300 feet 5.9*
29 *Alice In Banana Land 105 feet 5.10–* ★
30 *Busted 300 feet 5.9* ★
31 *Malice in Bucket Land 125 feet 5.9-* ★★
35 *Divine Wind 100 feet 5.7*
36 *All The Nasties 260 feet 5.10* ★★
37 *Brain Dead 260 feet 5.10+* ★
39 *Looking For Mr. Goodhueco 250 feet 5.11–*
41 *Purple Microdot 250 feet 5.10+ R* ★★
42 *Walking On The Moon 150 feet 5.10 R* ★★
43 *Final Stone 150 or 250 feet 5.11+ R* ★★
44 *Window Pain 150 feet 5.10* ★★
46 *Lunacy 200 feet 5.10* ★★★
48 *Lunar Abstract 50 feet 5.12–* ★
49 *Lunatic Friends 225 feet 5.10+* ★
51 *Desperado 180 feet 5.11* ★★
54 *Lost Nerve 180 feet 5.7*
55 *Hueco Syndrome 180 feet 5.10–* ★★
56 *Uriah's Heap Direct 220 feet 5.9 X*
57 *Uriah's Heap 220 feet 5.7+* ★★★
58 *Fred's Toprope 100 feet 5.12– TR*
59 *Sea of Holes 250 feet 5.10-* ★★

one – the next 35 feet consists of runout 5.10+ moves to the last bolt. Continue up to the crescent crack; belay at it's top (2 bolts). Two ropes (150 Ft.) will get you to the ground, or continue up unprotected 5.9 rock for a long way to the top. Photo, p. 74.

The topo for routes 44-51, and 54 is on page 69.

44 Window Pain 150 feet 5.10 ★★
Begin on a ramp to the left of *Lunacy* and climb up and left to a stance above a small roof. Continue on steep rock past many bolts to a nice belay ledge. From here, rappel down (two ropes required) or continue on bad rock up and right to the roof on *Lunacy.* 11 bolts, 2 bolt anchor.

45 No Fear Of Flying (aka Dos Equis or Double Cross) 150 feet 5.12– ★★
Climb the wall 10 to 12 feet left of *Lunacy.* Anchor at the *Window Pain* belay.

46 Lunacy 200 feet 5.10 ★★★
This obvious left-facing dihedral with a wide crack is a beautiful and sustained stem problem. Stem 75 feet to a small roof, pull over and continue to a finger crack section. Belay on a ledge above the finger crack (2-bolt anchor). Climb the second pitch to a large roof with a wide crack. Squeeze through the roof and continue up the chimney to the top.

47 (unnamed) 150 feet 5.13 TR ★★
The wall between *Lunacy* and *Lunar Abstract* has been topropped from the anchors atop the first pitch of *Lunacy.*

48 Lunar Abstract 50 feet 5.12– ★
Climb the thin, overhanging crack/seam in the right wall of the *Lunacy* dihedral. Come down from the 2-bolt anchor or join *Lunatic Friends.*

49 Lunatic Friends 225 feet 5.10+ ★
Lunatic Friends is on the buttress to the right of *Lunacy.* Start 10 feet left of a bushy tree and climb to a difficult bulge. After the bulge, continue to a steep headwall and traverse left around the corner. From here, climb steep, well protected rock to the *Lunacy* belay ledge. Belay at the right side to avoid running out of rope. The first pitch is 165 feet long. On the second pitch, climb right under a small roof and continue on easier ground to the top. This climb makes a nice start to *Desperado* (See below). To reach *Desperado,* traverse right above the roof on the second pitch. Belay on a small stance below *Desperado.*

50 Memorial 100 feet 5.11 R
Start at the tree right of *Lunatic Friends* and climb up a brown trough to a bolt 5 feet below the left end of a small roof. Undercling the roof to the right and pull over. Traverse back left into a bowl, and belay. First ascent party recommended double ropes and a 2 Friend.

51 Desperado 180 feet 5.11 ★★
This amazing route climbs a line of huecos up the left side of a shield between the upper pitches of *Lunatic Friends* and *Uriah's Heap.* Chimney up 70 feet to an awkward roof slot. Climb the roof to a small belay stance below an overhanging hueco-wall. Step over a chimney to the start of the overhanging hueco-wall. Climb straight up on huecos for 80 feet to a thin crack in a dihedral. Follow the crack to the top.

52 Desperado Direct 85 feet 5.10 TR (no topo)
Toprope the smooth slab to the right of the first pitch of *Desperado.*

53 Pegasus 180 feet 5.9 R (no topo)
Start on *Lost Nerve* and climb to the belay alcove. *Pegasus* begins here. Climb a left-facing dihedral on the left wall of the alcove. After passing a small bulge, follow easy ramps right to the top.

54 Lost Nerve 180 feet 5.7
Begin in an easy groove and climb to a chimney above a small bulge 35 feet up. Belay in an alcove at the top of the chimney. On the second pitch, climb the right wall of the alcove. Continue on good rock, with sparse protection to the top. Photo, p. 77.

Variation: 5.7 – Climb a 30-foot hand crack in an acute dihedral to the right of the start of *Lost Nerve.* This variation joins *Lost Nerve* at the small bulge on the first pitch.

The topo for problems 55-59 is on page 69.

55 ***Hueco Syndrome 180 feet 5.10– ★★***
Walk uphill along the left side of the *Uriah's Heap* pillars. Start 6 feet left of the pillars and follow 5 bolts straight up to a 2 bolt belay. On the second pitch, climb the shallow left-facing dihedral above and follow bolts to the top. Traverse right 15 feet to easy ground and climb good holds to the top. Two toprope routes climb the face left of the first pitch. The 5.12 toprope is just right of the *Lost Nerve* crack. Ten feet further right is a 5.11+ line. Photo, p. 74.
Variation 5.9: Start at the top of the first pitch at the base of the dihedral. Traverse right, via a crack, to the second pitch of *Uriah's Heap.*

56 ***Uriah's Heap Direct 220 feet 5.9 X***
At the top of the highest pillar of *Uriah's Heap,* climb straight up to overhanging rock, then traverse right to the crack on *Uriah's Heap.* Continue up on *Uriah's Heap.*

57 ***Uriah's Heap 220 feet 5.7+ ★★★***
This spectacular route starts on the obvious pillars 40 feet to the left of the *Tree Route.* There are several ways to reach the top of the pillars. The right side of the pillars is longer and technically harder then the left side. Belay on a comfortable ledge just below the highest pillar. The second pitch traverses right from the pillars to a light brown water streak. Climb straight up past one bolt to the base of a left-leaning crack. Climb up to the end of the crack, then step up and right to a small white belay stance with two bolts. The third pitch climbs easy rock bypassing a roof and loose plates on the right side. Photo, p. 74.
Variation 5.8: On the second pitch, traverse around right at the base of the left-leaning crack to the belay on *Sea Of Holes.*

58 ***Fred's Toprope 100 feet 5.12– TR***
Toprope a line 5 feet right of the right side of *Uriah's Heap's* pillars. Climb straight up to the right end of the left-angling crack on *Uriah's Heap's* second pitch. Photo, p. 74.
M & M Sex Toy (continuation of Fred's Toprope) 250 feet 5.12- ★
Originally a toprope route between the first pitches of *Uriah's Heap* and *Sea of Holes,* a second pitch (5.11-) has been added on the right side of the rounded prow. Bolts have been applied for (5 on first pitch, 3 on second), but at the time of writing not placed.

59 ***Sea of Holes 250 feet 5.10- ★★***
This follows a two-pitch hueco line through steep and overhanging rock. The first pitch starts 10 feet to the left of the *Tree Route.* Climb steep, overhanging rock past three bolts to a two bolt belay (140 feet 5.9). The second pitch (4 bolts) climbs up and right to the base of an overhanging headwall, and continues straight up the wall 15 feet left of the tree. Photo, p. 74.

THE INDECENT EXPOSURE BUTTRESS

This huge overhanging buttress dominates The Front Side and includes all routes starting with the *Tree Route* and ending at *Pink Adrenaline.* The Indecent Esposure Buttress has some of the finest routes at Hueco Tanks, including *Indecent Exposure* and *Rainbow Bridge.* Overview photo, p. 55; photo, p. 77.topo, p. 78.

60 ***Tree Route 250 feet 5.9 ★★***
The obvious huge dihedral with the bushy tree at the top. Begin at a fist-sized crack in a dihedral and follow the crack for two spectacular pitches to the top. Topo, p. 69.

61 ***Eternal Apples 250 feet 5.11+ ★★***
10 feet to the right of the Tree Route is an obvious hueco line leading to a right-leaning arch. Climb the huecos to the arch (2 bolts) then step left and pull over the arch at a

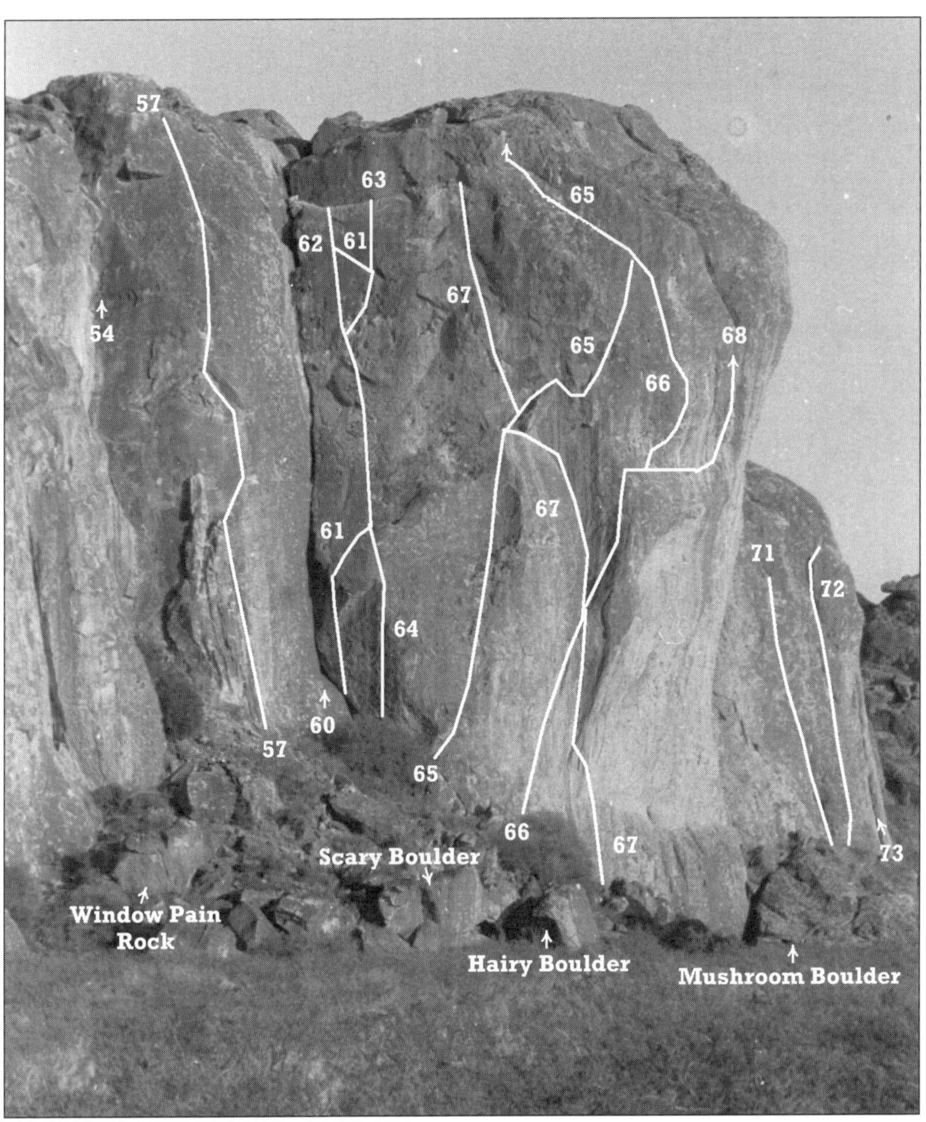

Central Wall, Indecent Exposure Buttress and Fox Tower

Central Wall
54 Lost Nerve 180 feet 5.7
57 Uriah's Heap 220 feet 5.7+ ★★★

Indecent Exposure Buttress
60 Tree Route 250 feet 5.9 ★★
61 Eternal Apples 250 feet 5.11+ ★★
62 Amplified Apples 110 feet 5.10+ ★★★
63 Eternal Heat 110 feet 5.11 ★
64 Amplified Heat 260 feet 5.11+ ★★
65 Indecent Exposure 300 feet 5.9+ ★★★
66 Rainbow Bridge 330 feet 5.11 R ★★★
67 Deliverance 350 feet 5.12– ★★
68 Optical Promise 350 feet 5.11+ ★★★

Fox Tower
71 Head Fox 150 feet 5.10 ★
72 Fox Trot 165 feet 5.9+ ★
73 Fox Tower Indirect 200 feet 5.9

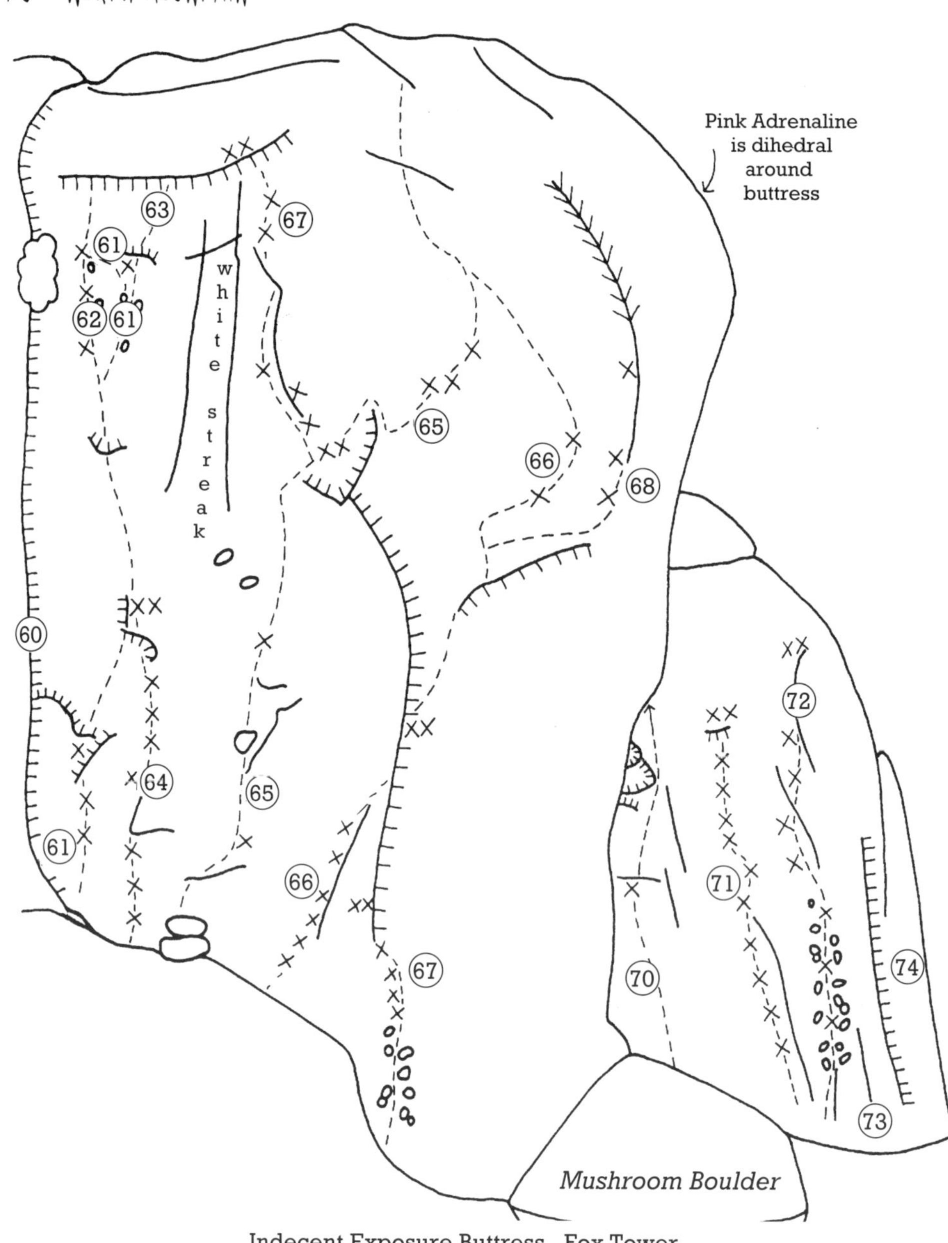

Indecent Exposure Buttress, Fox Tower

Indecent Exposure Buttress

61 *Eternal Apples 250 feet 5.11+* ★★

62 *Amplified Apples 110 feet 5.10+* ★★★

63 *Eternal Heat 110 feet 5.11* ★

64 *Amplified Heat 260 feet 5.11+* ★★

65 *Indecent Exposure 300 feet 5.9+* ★★★

66 *Rainbow Bridge 330 feet 5.11 R* ★★★

67 *Deliverance 350 feet 5.12–* ★★

68 *Optical Promise 350 feet 5.11+* ★★★

Fox Tower

70 *Buttless Goulies 200 feet 5.10 X*

71 *Head Fox 150 feet 5.10* ★

72 *Fox Trot 165 feet 5.9+* ★

73 *Fox Tower Indirect 200 feet 5.9*

74 *Fox Tower 200 feet 5.8*

third bolt. Continue to the roof (friend slot) and pull over. Climb easy rock up and right to a good ledge with a two bolt anchor. The second pitch climbs the outrageous headwall 30 feet to the right of the last pitch of *Tree Route.* Climb up on excellent huecos to the base of a small roof and a hidden bolt. From here, traverse the left-angling crack to the top.

62 ***Amplified Apples 110 feet 5.10+ ★★★***
As a second pitch to either *Eternal Apples* or *Amplified Heat,* climb the huge huecos in the steep iron rock wall in between *Tree Route* and the last pitch of *Eternal Apples,* 10 to 15 feet right of the tree. 3 bolts. Photo, p. 77.

63 ***Eternal Heat 110 feet 5.11 ★***
This is a variation to the second pitch of *Eternal Apples.* From the small roof step right to a right leaning crack/seam and continue straight up. Photo, p. 77.

64 ***Amplified Heat 260 feet 5.11+ ★★***
Start at the very bottom of *Tree Crack* Climb straight up a green streak to a short leaning crack. Climb straight up the thin face above the crack to a two bolt belay. The second pitch climbs the impressive headwall to the right of the *Tree Route* following either the last pitch of *Eternal Apples* or *Amplified Apples.* Photo, p. 77.

65 ***Indecent Exposure 300 feet 5.9+ ★★★***
This two-pitch route climbs the formidable buttress to the right of the *Tree Route. Indecent Exposure* is the Hueco Tanks classic that everyone should make an effort to climb. The imfamous second pitch traverses right on steep rock above the severely overhanging big buttress on The Front Side. The first ascent party found the second pitch so intimidating that they retreated after the first pitch to re-evaluate the route. After a week of reassuring each other that the second pitch would go, the first ascent party showed up at the base hungover and ready for another attempt. In this state, a successful ascent was a sure thing. The strategy worked, and the route was completed with minimal pain. This ascent widened the scope of climbing at Hueco Tanks, and showed that intimidating rock can be climbed.
The first pitch starts 10 yards to the right of the tree at the base of *Tree Route.* Start atop stacked boulders. Climb 20 feet up and right from the top of the boulder stack to the first bolt. Continue straight up on easy rock to a short moderate section directly below the belay ledge. Climb this section, past a bolt and memorial plaque, then traverse 15 feet right to the belay ledge. The intimidating second pitch steps off the right end of the belay ledge into space to a right-facing dihedral. It continues right to the obvious flake-pillar. At the pillar climb up 10 feet then traverse right on amazing holds and intimidating exposure. After the angle lessens, climb up a few moves and then traverse right, staying on moderate rock to a thin crack. At the top of the thin crack, climb straight up to good holds and the belay. Photo, p. 77.
Variation 5.11 X: After traversing to the obvious pillar on the second pitch, climb up left on a flake-crack system to a steep difficult headwall. Climb straight up on hard, unprotected moves to the top of the headwall.

66 ***Rainbow Bridge 330 feet 5.11 R ★★★***
The first pitch (5.10+) of *Rainbow Bridge* climbs a right-leaning, left-facing flake system to the big arching dihedral on *Deliverance* (See below). A thin face section leads up and right to the base of the flake system which starts 50 feet above the ground. At the top of the flake system, step right into the *Deliverance* dihedral and climb the 5.9 crack to the belay. On the second pitch, (5.8) step right from the belay to a black rib, and climb 50 feet straight up good holds to a large scooped ledge area and belay here. The last pitch is one of the wildest pitches at Hueco Tanks. It climbs the overhanging buttress to the right of *Indecent Exposure.* Start by stepping right from the belay and climbing straight up to a bolt. From here, climb right then step up to a no-hands rest and a second bolt. After resting at the stance climb up to a small bulge and traverse left under the bulge, bypassing the bulge on the left side. From here, climb straight up to the top on easier rock (150 feet 5.11 R). Photo, p. 77.

Cakewalk and Central walls, Indecent Exposure Buttress, Fox Tower

32	*Cowboyography 140 feet 5.13 ★★★*	67	*Deliverance*
38	*Geek Stop 120 feet 5.11+*	68	*Optical Promise*
39	*Looking For Mr. Goodhueco 250 feet 5.11–*	69	*Pink Adrenaline*
41	*Purple Microdot 250 feet 5.10+ R ★★*	70	*Buttless Goulies*
		74	*Fox Tower*
		75	*Brain Death Gully*

Routes 67-69 are pictured above and on page 77; topo for problems 67 and 68 on page 78.

67 *Deliverance 350 feet 5.12– ★★*

This three-pitch route climbs the large curving dihedral to the right of *Indecent Exposure.* Start on easy huecos and continue on difficult thin moves up and left past three bolts to attain the dihedral and a fourth bolt. Either lower off the two bolt sportclimber convenience anchor or continue up the 5.9 crack to the real belay. The second pitch climbs the remaining section of the dihedral to the belay at the top of the first pitch of *Indecent Exposure.* The third pitch climbs left off the belay ledge, and follows a left–angling seam 15 feet right of a large white water streak. Belay on a grassy ledge 15 feet from the top.

The Snake 330 feet 5.10+ ★★

Climb the first pitch of *Rainbow Bridge* and finish up the last 2 pitches of *Deliverance.*

68 *Optical Promise 350 feet 5.11+ ★★★*

This amazing route climbs a severely overhanging crack 35 feet right of the last pitch of *Rainbow Bridge.* Start by climbing the first two pitches of *Rainbow Bridge,* or the first pitch of *Deliverance* to the second pitch of *Rainbow Bridge,* then traverse right on the sloping ledge to the belay below *Optical Promise.* From here there is 200 feet of overhanging rock below and 150 feet of overhanging climbing above. The last pitch follows a line of holds up and right to a crack which leads to the top. The anchor (nuts) is a long way back the groove over the lip. 3 bolts, 1 pin, bring Friends.

69 *Pink Adrenaline 140 feet 5.11+ ★★★ (no topo)*

70 feet to the right of *Optical Promise,* and 200 feet above the ground, is a right-facing, J-shaped crack in a huge dihedral. This is *Pink Adrenaline.* To approach the climb, rappel from the top over the lip to the hanging belay. This is the most stimulating approach at Hueco Tanks. *Brain Death Gully* provides a convenient walk up. 5 pins, 2 bolts. Testing the pins on the way down would be a good idea; you have to clip some of them anyway to remain close enough to the rock to reach the belay.

Fox Tower

70	*Buttless Goulies 200 feet 5.10 X*	*73*	*Fox Tower Indirect 200 feet 5.9*
71	*Head Fox 150 feet 5.10 ★*	*74*	*Fox Tower 200 feet 5.8*
72	*Fox Trot 165 feet 5.9+ ★*		

FOX TOWER

This 200-foot buttress is to the right of the tall overhanging buttress (Indecent Exposure Buttress) on the Front Side. Fox Tower contains five climbs. Overview photo, p. 55; photo p. 81; topo, p. 78.

70 *Buttless Goulies 200 feet 5.10 X*
This route ascends 10 to 15 feet to the right of gully next to the right-side of the Indecent Exposure Buttress. Climb the face using the most obvious handholds toward the leaning cracks and ledges. Clip a bolt below a horizontal crack; continue up scooped steps toward an overhanging block. The 30-foot run-out crux section below this block maybe protected by a shaky small nut. Continue on easier rock to an excellent cave belay. Scramble up 4th class rock to the top. Photos, pp. 80 and 81.

71 *Head Fox 150 feet 5.10 ★*
Climb alongside the left angling crack until it ends. Continue straight up past many bolts to a two bolt belay. 10 bolts, 2 bolt anchor. Photos, pages 77 and 81.

72 *Fox Trot 165 feet 5.9+ ★*
This route climbs 80 feet up huecos to the two discontinuous cracks on the west face of Fox Tower. Start 6 feet right of the *Head Fox* crack. Bring nuts for the top crack. 7 bolts, 2 bolt anchor. Photos, pages 77 and 81.

73 *Fox Tower Indirect 200 feet 5.9*
To the right of *Fox Trot* are two crack systems. This route follows the left crack, which forms a left-facing dihedral, for 75 feet then traverses right into the right crack system. Photos, pages 77 and 81.

74 *Fox Tower 200 feet 5.8*
This is the easiest route on Fox Tower. It climbs the right crack which turns into a chimney 100 feet above the ground. Photos, pages 80 and 81.

75 *Brain Death Gully 240 feet 5.2*
Climb the gully system to the south of Fox Tower. This place has a habit of collecting broken tourists, hence the name. Photo, p. 80.

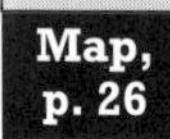

SPLIT AND MALICE BOULDERS

Malice Boulder

Thirteen yards east of table #39 (covered) is a boulder directly below the popular lead climb *Malice in Bucketland.* The boulder is cleaved by a severely overhung crack, *Ricardo Cracker.* Descend to the right, stepping off onto a tree. Topo, p. 83; photo, p. 84.

1 *Baby Snakes 14 feet V2*
Stretch or jump to a flake at the lip 5 feet left of the crack. Crank over. The boulder to the left is off-route.

2 *Ricardo Cracker 16 feet V4 ★★ SD*
Start sitting down with feet at the back and hands palming the slope or fist jamming against it.

3 *The A-Cup Team 13 feet V3 ★*
Start on 2 shallow, sloping huecos at the lip 8 feet right of the crack. The rock to the left is off-route (start with feet in the dirt).

Split Boulder

Photos on pages 55 and 84.

4 *Split Second 13 feet V0–*
The face left of the descent starting 4 feet right of a tree. One of the easiest problems in this guide.

5 *Split Crack Jr. 13 feet V0–*
The east side of Split Crack.

6 *Splitting Hairs 16 feet V0*
Start on a horizontal crack between two vertical cracks; go straight up through the branches.

7 *7-10 Split 17 feet V0*

8 *Splitter Splatter 19 feet V1 ★*
Intimidating for the grade.

9 *Split Level 19 feet V0+ BL*
Either top out straight up, hard if you're short, or step right on the ledge then up.

10 *Split Personality 20 feet V0+ BL*
Start low, below the boulders then angle left over the rocky landing to the right end of the Split Level ledge.

11 *Split Infinitive 20 feet V2 ★*
Same start as *Split Personality,* but then straight up the north face reaching right for the arête at the top.

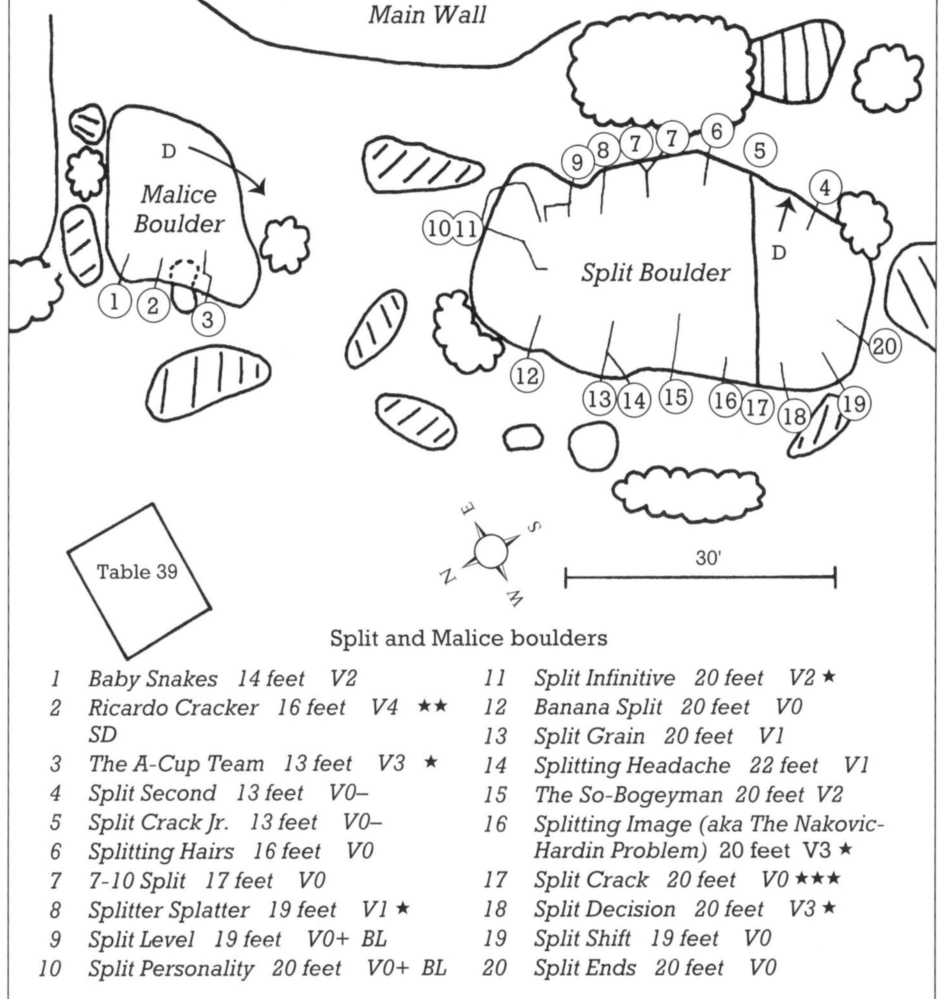

Split and Malice boulders

Malice Boulder

(Top photo)

1 *Baby Snakes 14 feet V2*

2 *Ricardo Cracker 16 feet V4 ★★ SD*

3 *The A-Cup Team 13 feet V3 ★*

Split Boulder

(Middle photo)

7 *7-10 Split 17 feet V0*

8 *Splitter Splatter 19 feet V1 ★*

9 *Split Level 19 feet V0+ BL*

10 *Split Personality 20 feet V0+ BL*

11 *Split Infinitive 20 feet V2 ★*

(Bottom photo)

11 *Split Infinitive 20 feet V2 ★*

12 *Banana Split 20 feet V0*

13 *Split Grain 20 feet V1*

14 *Splitting Headache 22 feet V1*

15 *The So-Bogeyman 20 feet V2*

16 *Splitting Image (aka The Nakovic-Hardin Problem) 20 feet V3 ★*

17 *Split Crack 20 feet V0 ★★★*

18 *Split Decision 20 feet V3 ★*

19 *Split Shift 19 feet V0*

The topo for problems 12-20 is on page 83.

12 *Banana Split 20 feet V0*
On the left side of the north face is a 9 foot high body width white scoop. Start left of this and finish up the ironrock groove above it.

13 *Split Grain 20 feet V1*
Loose and lousy.

14 *Splitting Headache 22 feet V1*
Loose and lousy.

15 *The So-Bogeyman 20 feet V2*

16 *Splitting Image (aka The Nakovic-Hardin Problem) 20 feet V3* ★

17 *Split Crack 20 feet V0* ★★★

18 *Split Decision 20 feet V3* ★

19 *Split Shift 19 feet V0*
The rounded arête joining the west and south faces.

20 *Split Ends 20 feet V0*
The white and brown trough on the south face.

BETWEEN SPLIT BOULDER AND MUSHROOM BOULDER

Windowpain Rock

This rock lies 20 yards uphill (south) of Split Boulder and just west of the lead climb *Windowpain.* A left-angling crack splits its northwest face. Photos below and on page 77; topo, p. 86.

1 *The Window Washer 18 feet 5.13 TR* ★★
Most people trying this will quickly decide they don't do windows.

2 *Glass Plus 20 feet 5.13- TR* ★★
The smooth face 7 feet left of *Graphic Jam.*

3 *Graphic Jam 20 feet V1* ★

Windowpain Rock, Pyramid

1 *The Window Washer 18 feet 5.13 TR* ★★
2 *Glass Plus 20 feet 5.13- TR* ★★
3 *Graphic Jam 20 feet V1* ★
9 *Tobacco-chewing Gut-chomping Kinfolk From Hell 15 feet V0*

The Pyramid

Fifteen yards south of Split Boulder and 10 yards east of The Three Stack is a pyramidal boulder cracked on its north face. On its east face are several sit down problems beneath a small roof. Topo, p. 86; photo, p. 87.

4 *Flesh Tuxedo 12 feet V2 SD*

5 *Tiny Rubber Love 20 feet V2 SD*
Start sitting down at the right most jug in the horizontal crack.

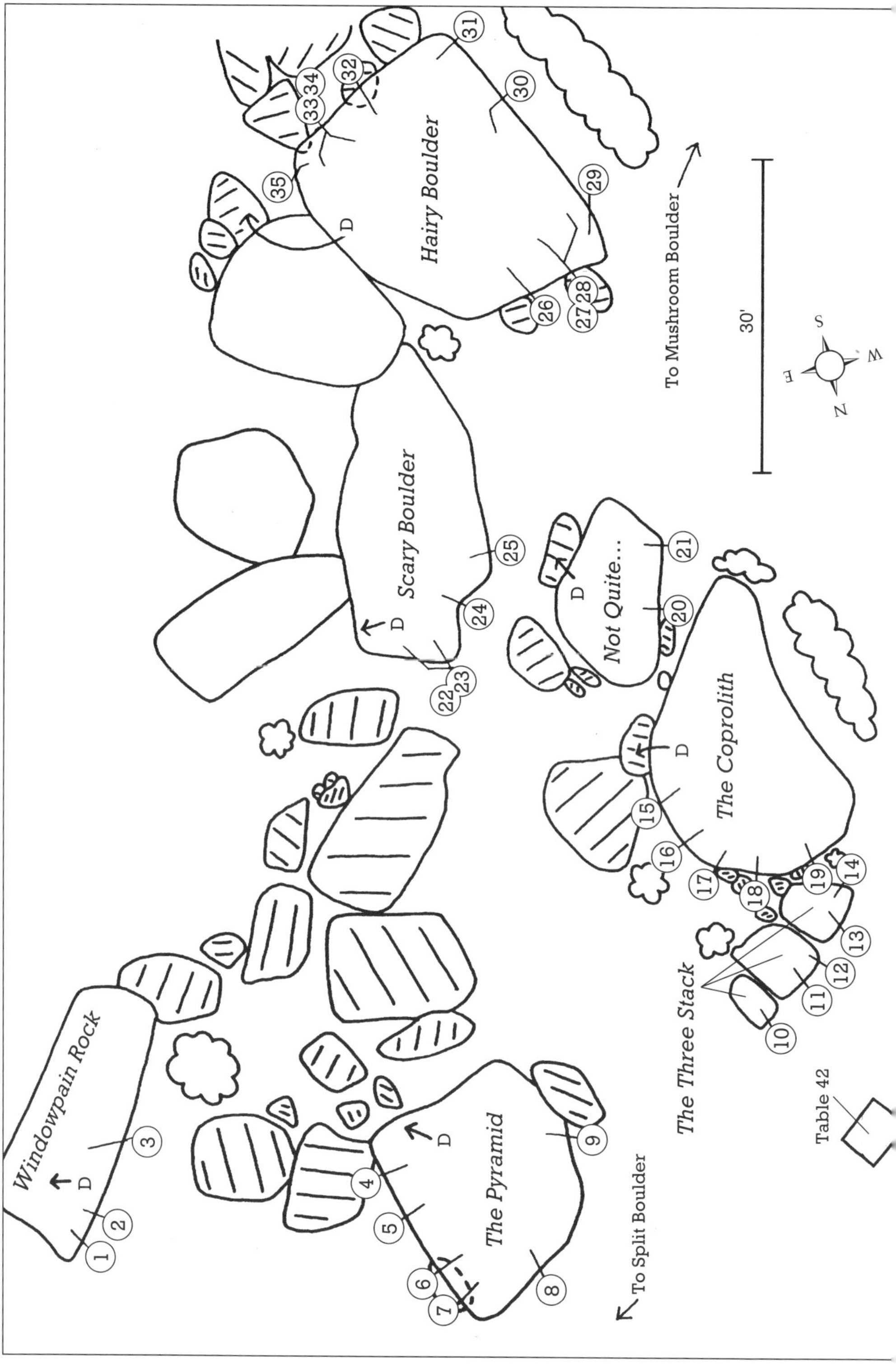

Hairy Boulder

To Mushroom Boulder

30'

S
W
E
N

Scary Boulder

Not Quite...

The Coprolith

Windowpain Rock

The Pyramid

The Three Stack

Table 42

To Split Boulder

The Pyramid

4 *Flesh Tuxedo 12 feet V2 SD*

5 *Tiny Rubber Love 20 feet V2 SD*

6 *Secret Weapon 12 feet V2 SD*

7 *Buzz Bomb 6 feet V1 SD*

8 *Indians Lying On Dawn's Highway Bleeding 20 feet V0–*

6 *Secret Weapon 12 feet V2 SD*
Sit down on a rock to start with hands 2 feet over the roof on a smile-shaped hold. Straight up.

7 *Buzz Bomb 6 feet V1 SD*
Sit down on same rock as *Secret Weapon*, but on the rock's north end. Start with hands at a lip incut, then crank up to the arête. The shortest problem in the guide.

8 *Indians Lying On Dawn's Highway Bleeding 20 feet V0–*
Anywhere up the cracked north face.

9 *Tobacco-chewing Gut-chomping Kinfolk From Hell* 15 feet V0
Up the west face left of the white rock. Photo, p. 85.

Between Split and Mushroom boulders (topo at left)

1 *The Window Washer 18 feet 5.13 TR ★★*
2 *Glass Plus 20 feet 5.13- TR ★★*
3 *Graphic Jam 20 feet V1 ★*
4 *Flesh Tuxedo 12 feet V2*
5 *Tiny Rubber Love 20 feet V2*
6 *Secret Weapon 12 feet V2*
7 *Buzz Bomb 6 feet V1*
8 *Indians Lying On Dawn's Highway Bleeding 20 feet V0–*
9 *Tobacco-chewing Gut-chomping Kinfolk From Hell* 15 feet V0
10 *Butt Buddy 7 feet V0*
11 *Lucky Pierre 12 feet V2*
12 *Saxon Tactics 12 feet V0*
13 *Top Guy 1 1 feet V0–*
14 *Gay Abandon 11 feet V0–*
15 *The Sphincter 12 feet V0*
16 *Dingleberry Jones And The Lost Crusade 13 feet V0*
17 *Hard Wipe 13 feet V0–*
18 *The Hashmarker 12 feet V0– BL*
19 *Feces Of The Ages 13 feet V0 BL*
20 *Boo 16 feet V0*
21 *Eek-A-Mouse 15 feet V0–*
22 *The Bonetender 12 feet V2*
23 *Scary Arete 15 feet V3 ★*
24 *Scary Dihedral 25 feet 5.12 TR ★★*
25 *The Melon Patch 24 feet V0 ★★★*
26 *Proud To Be An, Uh Merkin 18 feet V0+ ★ BL*
27 *Gherkin In A Merkin 20 feet V1 ★★ BL*
28 *The Sideburn 19 feet V2 ★ BL*
29 *Eczema 20 feet V0*
30 *Seborrhea 25 feet V0+*
31 *Psoriasis 25 feet V0+*
32 *Epilady 18 feet V0+ ★ BL*
33 *Shaved Pits 15 feet V1 ★★ BL*
34 *Five O'Clock Shadow 15 feet V2 ★ BL*
35 *Nair 13 feet V0–*

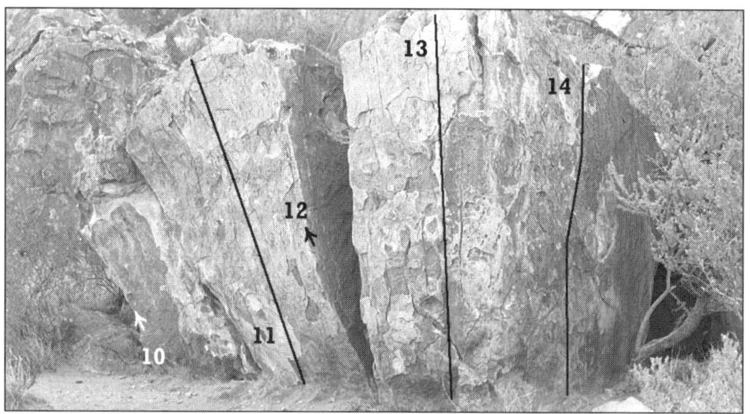

The Three Stack

10 Butt Buddy 7 feet V0
11 Lucky Pierre 12 feet V2
12 Saxon Tactics 12 feet V0
13 Top Guy 1 1 feet V0–
14 Gay Abandon 11 feet V0–

The Three Stack

7 yards south of table #42 (uncovered) is this short boulder split into three leaning hunks. Topo, p. 86.

10 Butt Buddy 7 feet V0
Start sitting down and climb the fin on the left side of the left boulder.

11 Lucky Pierre 12 feet V2
The arête on the right is off-route.

12 Saxon Tactics 12 feet V0

13 Top Guy 1 1 feet V0–
Both arêtes are off-route.

14 Gay Abandon 11 feet V0–

The Coprolith

15 The Sphincter 12 feet V0
16 Dingleberry... 13 feet V0
17 Hard Wipe 13 feet V0–
18 Hashmarker 12 feet V0– BL
19 Feces Of The Ages 13 feet V0 BL

The Coprolith

Just south of The Three Stack is a good beginner boulder. The east face is climbable anywhere, the following lines are suggested. Topo, p. 86.

15 *The Sphincter 12 feet V0*
Start in the notch between rocks on the left side of the east face. A one-finger hueco at the 6-foot level marks the start.

16 *Dingleberry Jones And The Lost Crusade 13 feet V0*
A seam with two V notches one at the 5 foot level, one at the 6 foot level marks the start. Holds right of the seam are off-route.

17 *Hard Wipe 13 feet V0–*
The wall right of the *Dingleberry Jones* seam; start in the dirt left of a small rock.

18 *The Hashmarker 12 feet V0– BL*

19 *Feces Of The Ages 13 feet V0 BL*
Start just left (south) of a catclaw in the notch between The Three Stack and The Coprolith. Straight up. This problem is separated from the other Coprolith problems by chockstones between the two boulders.

Not Quite As Scary Boulder

Not Quite As Scary Boulder is 6 yards northwest of Scary Boulder. The following two problems are on it's northwest face. Topo, p. 86.

20 *Boo 16 feet V0*
Start three feet right of low stacked blocks. Climb straight up the face topping out at its highest point.

21 *Eek-A-Mouse 15 feet V0–*
Climb the arête on the right side of the northwest face.

Scary Boulder

25 yards uphill (east) from table #44 (covered) is this 25 foot tall boulder with a brilliant hueco line up it's west face and an overhanging northwest facing dihedral left of this hueco line. Overview photos, pages 55 and 77; topo, p. 86.

22 *The Bonetender 12 feet V2*
Start as per *Scary Arête* then climb the face on the left.

23 *Scary Arête 15 feet V3 ★*
Climb the north arête of the boulder 15 feet left of the dihedral. A top rope version climbs the wall to the right (5.12).

Scary Boulder

23 *Scary Arete 15 feet V3 ★*

24 *Scary Dihedral 25 feet 5.12 TR ★★*

25 *The Melon Patch 24 feet V0 ★★★*

24 *Scary Dihedral 25 feet 5.12 TR* ★★
Topo, p. 86; photo, p. 89.

25 *The Melon Patch 24 feet V0* ★★★
Front Side's classic jug haul. Look out – loose hold up high. Topo, p. 86; photo, p. 89.

Hairy Boulder (aka Picnic Boulder)

This is the next boulder downhill (west) from Scary Boulder. Route descriptions start on the north face. Overview photo, p. 77; topo, p. 86.

26 *Proud To Be An, Uh Merkin 18 feet V0+* ★ *BL*
Start on the ground immediately right of a small boulder Hairy Boulder leans on.

27 *Gherkin In A Merkin 20 feet V1* ★★ *BL*
Climb the center of the face starting on the rock beneath it.

28 *The Sideburn 19 feet V2* ★ *BL*
Same start as *Gherkin In A Merkin,* but launch out right to top out at a flat spot atop the arête.

29 *Eczema 20 feet V0*

30 *Seborrhea 25 feet V0+*
Climb loose flakes 8 feet left of the right end of the west face, then left along a diagonal crack to the top. Usually toproped for it's looseness. Continuous.

Hairy Boulder

26 *Proud To Be An, Uh Merkin 18 feet V0+* ★ *BL*
27 *Gherkin In A Merkin 20 feet V1* ★★ *BL*
28 *The Sideburn 19 feet V2* ★ *BL*
29 *Eczema 20 feet V0*
30 *Seborrhea 25 feet V0+*
31 *Psoriasis 25 feet V0+*

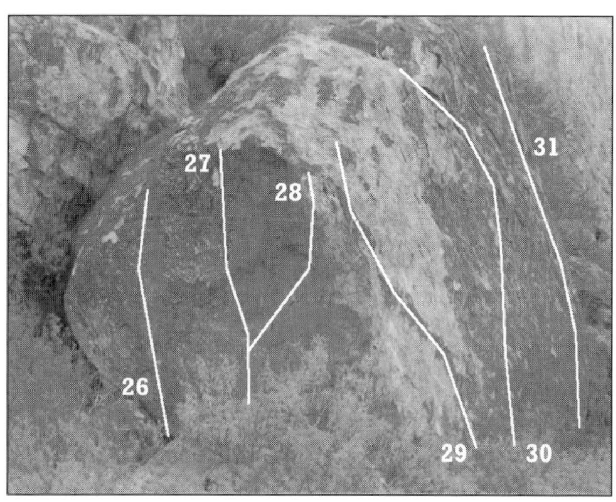

Hairy Boulder

South Face (below)
32 *Epilady 18 feet V0+* ★ *BL*
33 *Shaved Pits 15 feet V1* ★★ *BL*
34 *Five O'Clock Shadow 15 feet V2* ★ *BL*
35 *Nair 13 feet V0–*

31 *Psoriasis 25 feet V0+*
Start where right side of the west face meets the ground.

32 *Epilady 18 feet V0+ ★ BL*

33 *Shaved Pits 15 feet V1 ★★ BL*

34 *Five O'Clock Shadow 15 feet V2 ★ BL*

35 *Nair 13 feet V0–*
Start around the corner right of the overhang. Angle up and left across the face with the medicine ball sized hueco.

MUSHROOM BOULDER & SATELLITES

Mushroom Satellites

The Mushroom Satellites are the three small boulders flanking the east side of the Mushroom Boulder. Overview photos, pages 55 and 77; topo, p. 92.

SATELLITE 1

The southernmost of the three.

1 *Captain Satellite 12 feet V0*
Climb the center of the southwest face.

2 *Challenger 8 feet V0+*
Start low with hands below the 6-foot level. Climb sharp flakes up the right side of the face.

SATELLITE 2

The middle of the satellites.

3 *Craterface 11 feet V0– ★*
Climb the huecoed north face above "Jenny 85."

SATELLITE 3

The northernmost of the three satellites. Problems 5-7 are pictured on page 94.

4 *Uranus Probe 10 feet V1*
Climb sharp flexers on the south face.

5 *The Gantry 15 feet V0– ★*
The easy arête left of the northwest face; also used as an alternate descent.

6 *Blast-Off 14 feet V0 ★★*

7 *Collision Course 15 feet V0+ ★*
Take care not to scrape against the Mushroom Boulder.

Mushroom Boulder

The Mushroom Boulder is the huge rock north of Outhouse #2. The North Face is perhaps the best single bouldering face in the United States. Descriptions start at the descent ramp for the south face problems. This ramp runs down the west side of the boulder. Topo, p. 92.

8 *Ascent of Man 15 feet V0*
Where the descent ramp meets the ground on the west side of the Mushroom there is a line of huecos going straight up. This is the route. Photo, p. 97..

9 *Descent of Man 30 feet V0+*
Starting halfway up the descent ramp, pull onto huecos on the wall above the ramp then descend by traversing them down and left until *Ascent of Man* can be downclimbed.

Problems 10-14 are on the South Face. See photo on page 93.

10 *Family Size 14 feet V0 ★*

11 Busted 15 feet V0+ ★
12 Legal High 19 feet V0+ ★
13 Twisted 19 feet V3 ★
14 Hueco Cranks 29 feet 5.12 TR ★★★
Hueco Cranks Start 15 feet V4
This is the start to the popular *Hueco Cranks* toprope problem. "Tanka y Lola 65" marks the start. Do hard, greasy moves up and right to a big hueco. Drop from the hueco to descend.

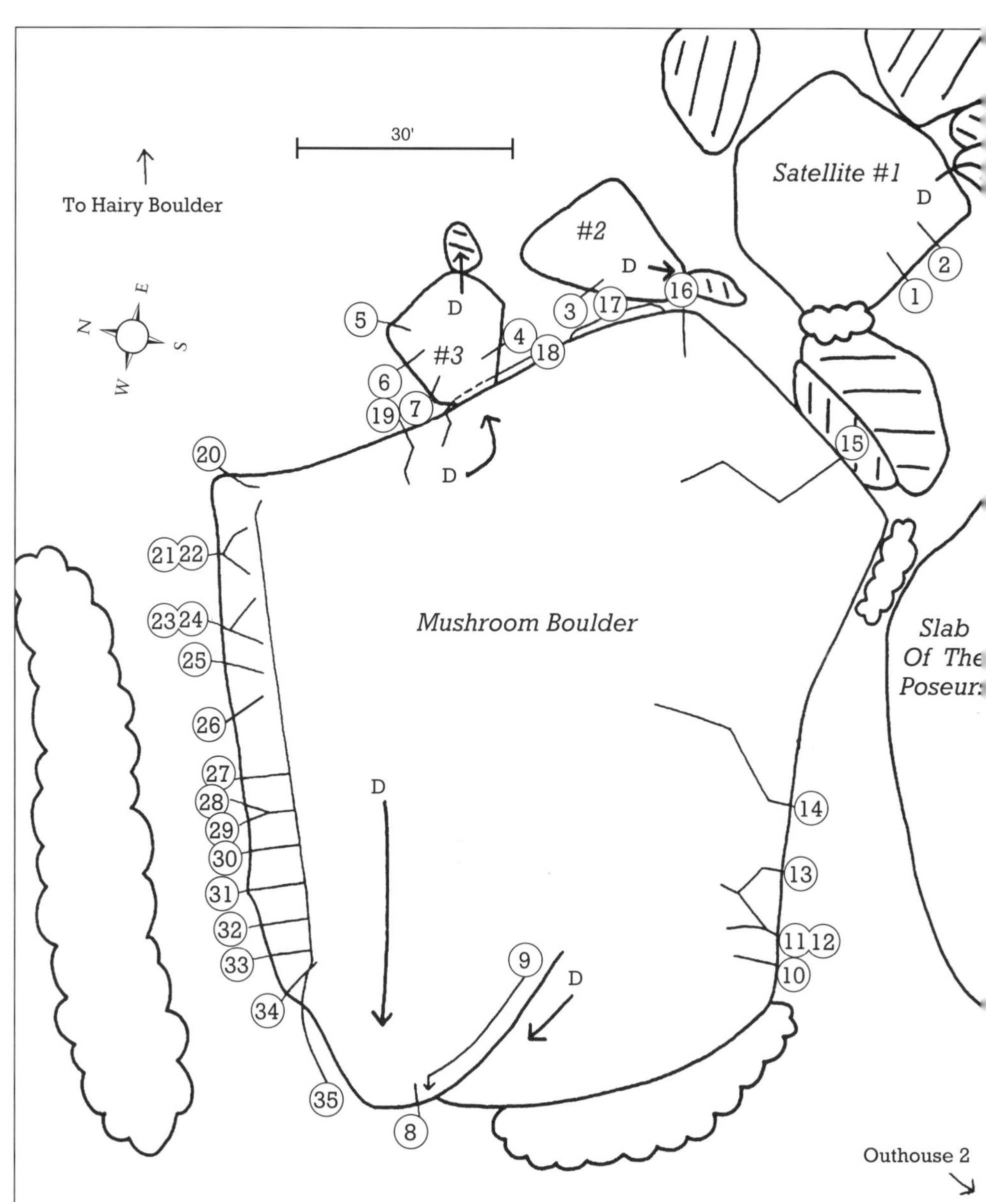

15 *New Chautauqua 40 feet 5.10+ ★*
Begin 4 feet right of the southeast corner of the Mushroom Boulder. Climb past 3 bolts then move right into a dihedral. Climb to a bolt, then left out of the dihedral to the top. Toprope variation: 5.11 – Instead of moving right into the dihedral, continue straight up the face.

16 *The East Arête 25 feet 5.9 BL*
The two bolt arête on the left edge of the east face.

17 *East Face 20-25 feet V0 ★★ SD*
Numerous lines have been bouldered up the face right of *The East Arête.*

The Mushroom Boulder South Face

10 *Family Size 14 feet V0 ★*
11 *Busted 15 feet V0+ ★*
12 *Legal High 19 feet V0+ ★*
13 *Twisted 19 feet V3 ★*
14 *Hueco Cranks 29 feet 5.12 TR ★★★*
15 *New Chautauqua 40 feet 5.10+ ★*

The Mushroom Boulder and Satellites (topo at left)

1 *Captain Satellite 12 feet V0*
2 *Challenger 8 feet V0+*
3 *Craterface 11 feet V0– ★*
4 *Uranus Probe 10 feet V1*
5 *The Gantry 15 feet V0– ★*
6 *Blast-Off 14 feet V0 ★★*
7 *Collision Course 15 feet V0+ ★*
8 *Ascent of Man 15 feet V0*
9 *Descent of Man 30 feet V0+*
10 *Family Size 14 feet V0 ★*
11 *Busted 15 feet V0+ ★*
12 *Legal High 19 feet V0+ ★*
13 *Twisted 19 feet V3 ★*
14 *Hueco Cranks 29 feet 5.12 TR ★★★*
15 *New Chautauqua 40 feet 5.10+ ★*
16 *The East Arete 25 feet 5.9*
17 *East Face 20-25 feet V0 ★★*
18 *That's Entertainment 18 feet V6 ★★*
19 *Mushroom Roof 18 feet V8 ★★★*
20 *Crap Arete (aka Dynamo Hum) 18 feet V4*
21 *Left El Sherman (aka What's Left Of Les Left) 18 feet V4 ★★*
22 *What's Left of Les (aka Right El Sherman) 18 feet V2 ★★★*
23 *Stuck Inside of Baltimore (aka Left El Murray) 17 feet V6 ★★★*
24 *Texas Medicine (aka Center El Murray) 17 feet V6 ★★★*
25 *Railroad Gin (aka Right El Murray) 17 feet V8 ★★★*
26 *The Woman With... 16 feet V10 ★★*
27 *My Fifteen Minutes 15 feet V7 ★*
28 *The Local Flakes 14 feet V2 ★★*
29 *Local Flakes Direct 24 feet V4 ★*
30 *Micropope 15 feet V8 ★★*
31 *Left Wannabe 15 feet V0+ ★★*
32 *Right Wannabe 15 feet V0+ ★★*
33 *Gotta Want It 12 feet V6 ★*
34 *Frankie's 12 feet V4 ★*
35 *Lip Traverse 85 feet V5 ★*

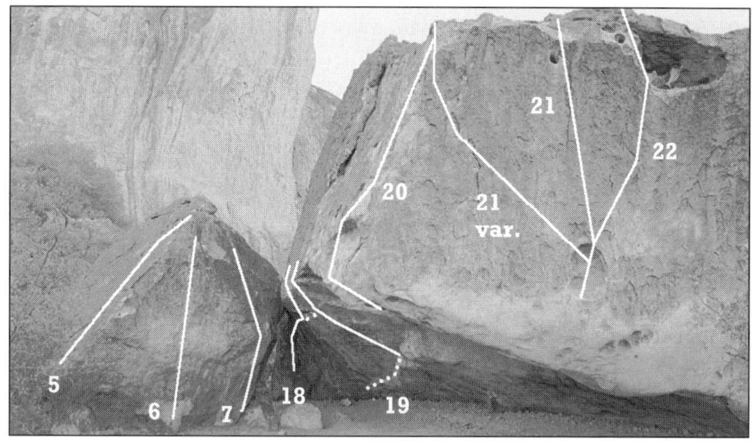

Satellite 3, left, and North Face of the Mushroom

5 *The Gantry 15 feet V0– ★*
6 *Blast-Off 14 feet V0 ★★*
7 *Collision Course 15 feet V0+ ★*
18 *That's Entertainment*
19 *Mushroom Roof*
20 *Crap Arete (aka Dynamo Hum)*
21 *Left El Sherman (aka What's Left Of Les Left)*
22 *What's Left of Les (aka Right El Sherman)*

18 *That's Entertainment 18 feet V6 ★★*
Start between satellites 2 & 3, sitting in the sand next to a small rock. The hands are at the 3 foot level at the leftmost incut of a series of incut overlaps that trend right under the gap between Satellite 3 & the Mushroom. 8 feet left and slightly up of this starting incut, Holgar Woltrand inscribed his name. Traverse the incuts right under the gap, being sure not to touch Satellite 3. After making it through the gap, conquer the lip at your first convenience. Bad landing in spots. Topo, page 92.

19 *Mushroom Roof 18 feet V8 ★★★*
The megaclassic line out the roof next to satellite 3. It represents the standard for V8. It used to be harder before some wanking, shithead dicksmoker enlarged one of the fingerslots. Start on the 9-inch-thick hueco-pitted flake at the back of the roof. Climb flakes out the roof topping out either left or right. This problem has also been started on the far left end of the hueco pitted flake, adding 8 feet of butt-dragging moves and increasing the pump at the lip. Topo, page 92.

North Face of the Mushroom

Topo, page 92.

20 *Crap Arête (aka Dynamo Hum) 18 feet V4*

21 *Left El Sherman (aka What's Left Of Les Left) 18 feet V4 ★★*
The first time I saw this problem "El Sherman" had been written next to the big hueco, but that graffiti has fortunately been removed. Head left from the hole via small flakes or a big lunge to an obvious one hand hueco just under the lip.
Variation: V5 – Traverse left from the big hole to the *Crap Arête.*

22 *What's Left of Les (aka Right El Sherman) 18 feet V2 ★★★*
The same start as Left El Sherman, but then out right on small holds (V2) or a big lunge (V3) to the 3 foot wide U-shaped summit bowl. Along with *The Local Flakes,* this is the V2 standard.

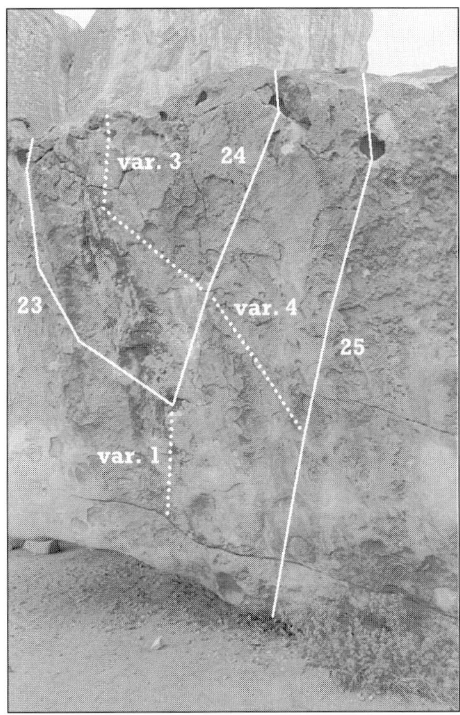

The El Murrays

23 *Stuck Inside of Baltimore (aka Left El Murray) 17 feet V6 ★★★*

24 *Texas Medicine (aka Center El Murray) 17 feet V6 ★★★*

25 *Railroad Gin (aka Right El Murray) 17 feet V8 ★★★*

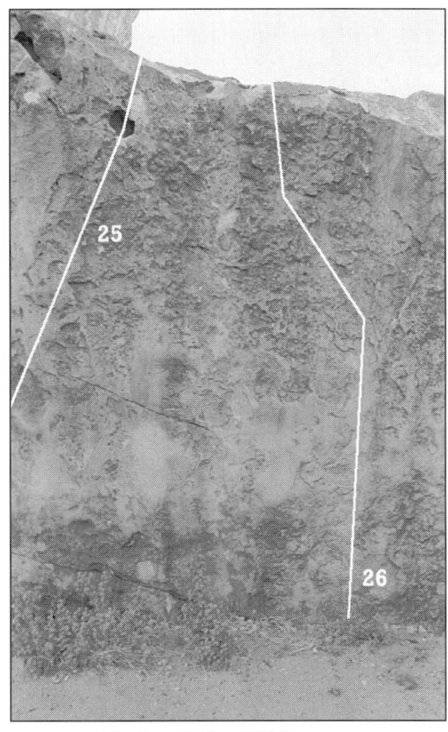

Right of The El Murrays

25 *Railroad Gin (aka Right El Murray) 17 feet V8 ★★★*

26 *The Woman With The Hueco In Her Head 16 feet V10 ★★*

THE EL MURRAYS

While researching a book on US bouldering, I came across some old Hueco Tanks topos Bob Murray had sent to a friend in Tucson. On the topos, Bob named a small percentage of his problems, including the El Murrays. The names were lost to his and everyone else's memory until these topos were discovered. Here are the original names. Topo, page 92.

23 *Stuck Inside of Baltimore (aka Left El Murray) 17 feet V6 ★★★*

24 *Texas Medicine (aka Center El Murray) 17 feet V6 ★★★*
The classic problem on the classic face.

25 *Railroad Gin (aka Right El Murray) 17 feet V8 ★★★*
Easier if you have a long reach.

Numerous variations have been done on this wall. Four of the more significant follow:

Variation 1: The sit down start to the Left and Center routes is a three-star classic. V7 either way.

Variation 2: Double lunge from the start of *Center El Murray* to the "inverted-V hold" 12 feet up. Murray's way.

Variation 3: Climb the Center route to the "inverted-V hold" then finish between the Left and Center routes (V7).

Variation 4: Start on *Right El Murray*, finish on *Center* (V7).

26 *The Woman With The Hueco In Her Head 16 feet V10 ★★*

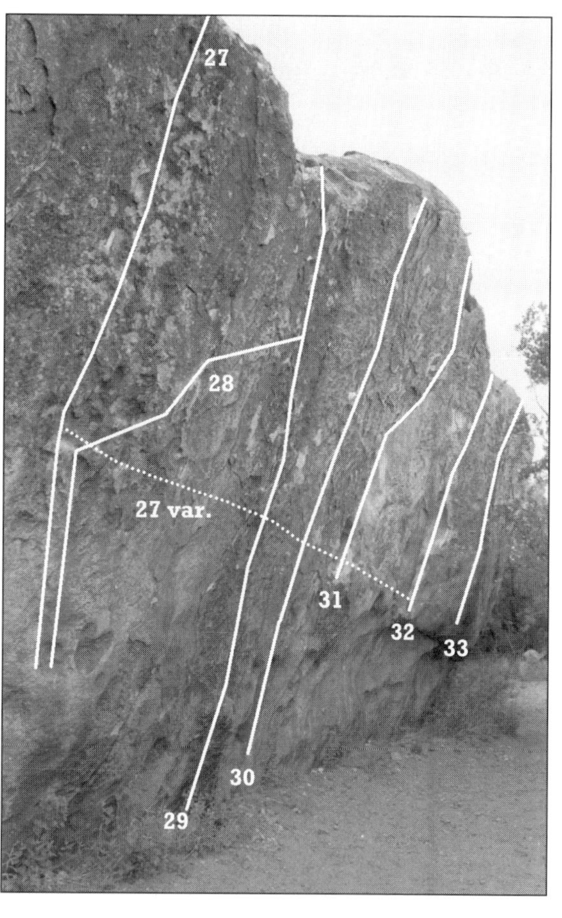

Mushroom Boulder

27 *My Fifteen Minutes 15 feet V7* ★
28 *The Local Flakes 14 feet V2* ★★
29 *Local Flakes Direct 24 feet V4* ★
30 *Micropope 15 feet V8* ★★
31 *Left Wannabe 15 feet V0+* ★★
32 *Right Wannabe 15 feet V0+* ★★
33 *Gotta Want It 12 feet V6* ★

The topo for problems 27-32 is on page 92.

27 *My Fifteen Minutes 15 feet V7* ★

Starts on the same holds as *The Local Flakes* but goes straight up on small sharp holds in a faint black streak. In the future all boulder problems will be famous for fifteen minutes. Variation: ***Microdick 27 feet V8*** ★★ Starts between the *Wannabes,* traverse left to *My Fifteen Minutes* and finishes up that.

28 *The Local Flakes 14 feet V2* ★★

29 *Local Flakes Direct 24 feet V4* ★

Up and left to *The Local Flakes* top out. The right angling flake on *The Local Flakes* is off-route. The upper holds are on.

30 *Micropope 15 feet V8* ★★

Climb the wall between *The Local Flakes* direct and *Left Wannabe*. The left foot uses holds on *Local Flakes Direct* which are off-route for the hands. All other holds used are exclusively on *Micropope*. This was one of Hueco Tanks thinnest, sharpest faces until one of its largest holds snapped off, raising doubts if it could be repeated. It still goes and now the resurrected *Micropope* is gnarlier than ever.

31 *Left Wannabe 15 feet V0+* ★★

32 *Right Wannabe 15 feet V0+* ★★

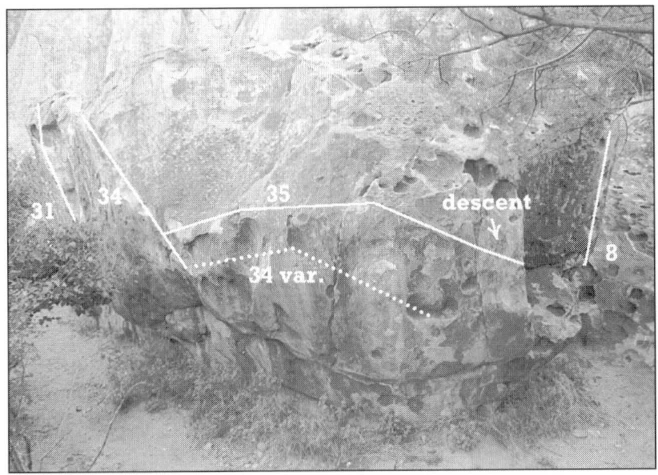

Mushroom Boulder West end.

8 *Ascent of Man 15 feet V0*

31 *Left Wannabe 15 feet V0+* ★★

34 *Frankie's 12 feet V4* ★

35 *Lip Traverse 85 feet V5* ★

33 *Gotta Want It 12 feet V6* ★
Topo, page 92.

34 *Frankie's 12 feet V4* ★
Climb the vague arête above "Frank Ramirez" (variation: this has been started sitting down 10 feet to the right from a jug 3 feet right of and below "Oscar Perez" off-routing the sloping lip in the middle of the traverse. Way contrived. The hole above "Oscar Perez" is on route.) Topo, page 92.

35 *Lip Traverse 85 feet V5* ★
Descending from the north face involves a short downclimb off the west side to the ground. Starting at this downclimb traverse the entire lip of the North Face to the *Crap Arête*. The crux is doing *Frankie's* along the way. Topo, page 92.

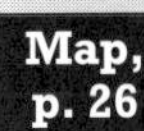

AREA 22 Map, p. 26

DELIVERANCE BOULDERS

The Deliverance Boulders lie southeast of the Mushroom Boulder. They both have excellent vertical faces facing the 300-foot Main Buttress.

Slab Of The Poseurs.
This is the shoe-up slab below the South Face of the Mushroom Boulder. Topo, page 98.

1 *The Affectation 9 feet V1*
Immediately left of the polished bulge facing Outhouse #2.

2 *To-Bo Or Not To Be 10 feet V0–*
Climb the left side of the southeast face nearly in the catclaw.

3 *Jellyroll Jamboree 13 feet V0–*
Climb the southeast face directly to its highest point.

The Scruple
The next boulder east of the Slab Of The Poseurs. Topo, page 98.

4 *Sir Nose D'Voidoffunk 10 feet V0–*
Just east of Slab Of The Poseurs is a short, squat boulder. Climb the northwest face just right of a super easy arête.

5 *No Scruples 10 feet V0–*
Start at this boulder's closest point to Slab of the Poseurs. Up then diagonally left along the seam.

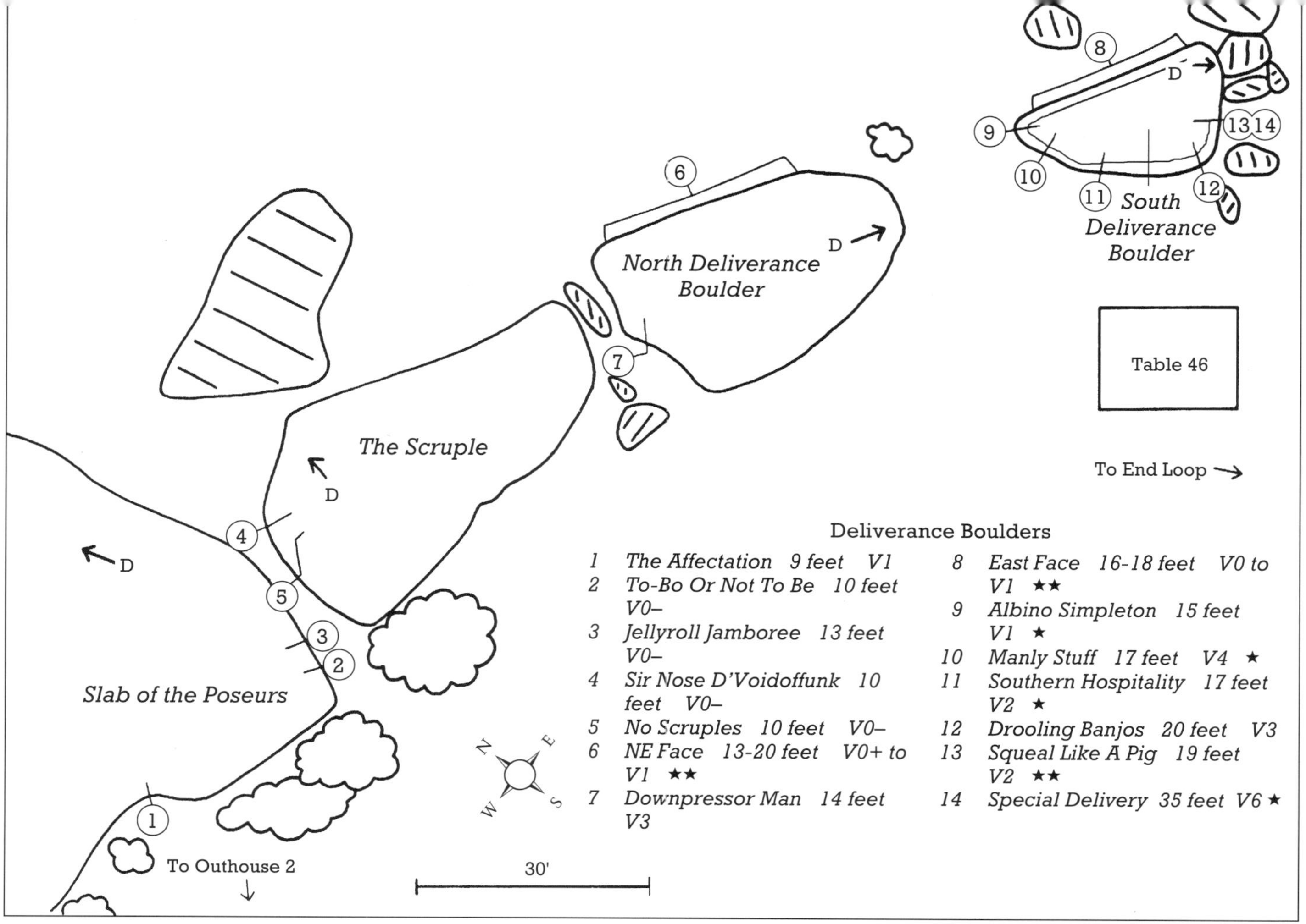

Slab of the Poseurs

The Scruple

North Deliverance Boulder

South Deliverance Boulder

Table 46

To End Loop →

To Outhouse 2 ↓

30'

N E S W

D

Deliverance Boulders

1 *The Affectation 9 feet V1*
2 *To-Bo Or Not To Be 10 feet V0–*
3 *Jellyroll Jamboree 13 feet V0–*
4 *Sir Nose D'Voidoffunk 10 feet V0–*
5 *No Scruples 10 feet V0–*
6 *NE Face 13-20 feet V0+ to V1 ★★*
7 *Downpressor Man 14 feet V3*
8 *East Face 16-18 feet V0 to V1 ★★*
9 *Albino Simpleton 15 feet V1 ★*
10 *Manly Stuff 17 feet V4 ★*
11 *Southern Hospitality 17 feet V2 ★*
12 *Drooling Banjos 20 feet V3*
13 *Squeal Like A Pig 19 feet V2 ★★*
14 *Special Delivery 35 feet V6 ★*

North Deliverance Boulder

The North Deliverance Boulder lies 10 yards north of table #46 (covered). The South Deliverance Boulder lies 6 yards to table 46's east.

6 *Northeast Face 13-20 feet V0+ to V1 ★★*
The northeast face can be climbed anywhere. The tallest line up the center is the hardest.

7 *Downpressor Man 14 feet V3*
On the northwest face lunge out and right to grab the lip of the roof then traverse left and mantle the roof's point. Loose.

South Deliverance Boulder

8 *East Face 16-18 feet V0 to V1 ★★*
This classic ironrock face is, like its twin on North Deliverance Boulder, climbable anywhere. The left line up the waterstreak is the hardest.

9 *Albino Simpleton 15 feet V1 ★*
Climb the north pointing prow.

10 *Manly Stuff 17 feet V4 ★*

11 *Southern Hospitality 17 feet V2 ★*

12 *Drooling Banjos 20 feet V3*

13 *Squeal Like A Pig 19 feet V2 ★★*

14 *Special Delivery 35 feet V6 ★*
Start at *Squeal Like A Pig* and traverse left around the boulder until you run into the descent route.

Deliverance Boulders

Above:
10 *Manly Stuff 17 feet V4 ★*
11 *Southern Hospitality 17 feet V2 ★*
12 *Drooling Banjos 20 feet V3*
14 *Special Delivery 35 feet V6 ★*

Right:
13 *Squeal Like A Pig 19 feet V2 ★★*
14 *Special Delivery 35 feet V6 ★*

THE END LOOP AREA

Located at the south end of the Front Side road where it loops around. Approach Mussypotamia from the north end of the loop; it is located 100 feet above ground level. All other End Loop Area climbs and boulder problems start at ground level. Photos, pp. 55, 102.

AREA 23A

Map, p. 26

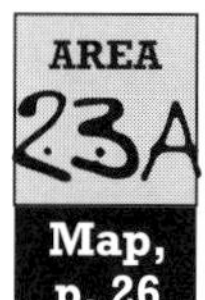

Mussypotamia

East of table #55 is a deep recess in the rocks forming the cliff. The crack systems that form this recess also form Mussypotamia, 100 feet higher. Approach in the gully north (left) of the recess.

Climb the slab in the gully then trend southeast along the line of least resistance towards the top of North Mountain. 40 feet shy of the top is Mussypotamia, a

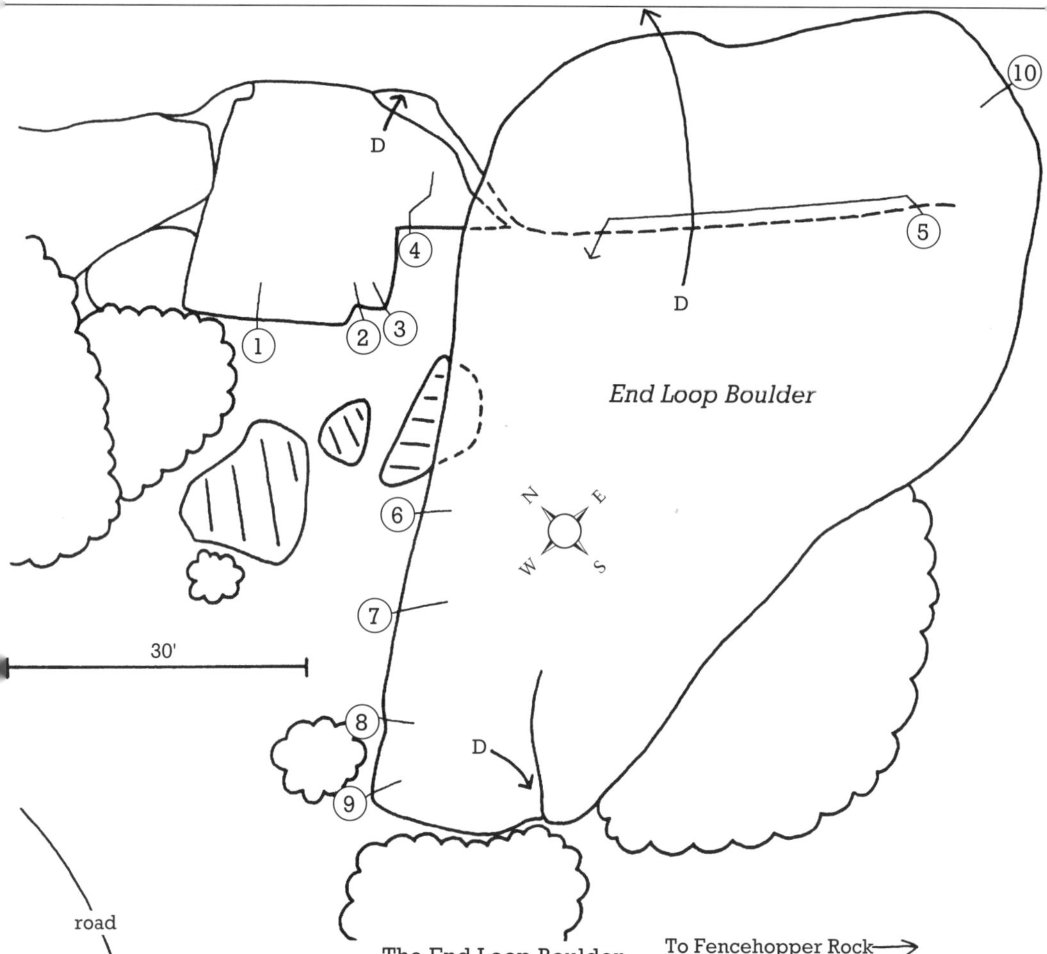
D
4
D
5
10
1
2
3
End Loop Boulder
N
E
W
S
6
7
30'
8
D
9
road
To Fencehopper Rock

The End Loop Boulder

1 *Holy Cow 16 feet V0– ★*
2 *High Protein Snack 11 feet V0 ★*
3 *Napoleon Complex 11 feet V7*
4 *Artist's Opposition 13 feet V4 ★★*
5 *Piss Traverse 27 feet V2*
6 *Wyoming Cowgirl 35 feet 5.12– TR*
7 *The End 30 feet 5.10 TR*
8 *Slam Dip 13 feet V0*
9 *Aretey Or Not 11 feet V0*
10 *Back Side 30 feet 5.12 TR*

dark cleft between rocks with a large oak tree in it. The south facing wall of the Mussypotamia trench contains 2 problems, *Dick Almighty* and *El Mussy.*

Dick Almighty 16 feet V5 ★
Climbs up to the rotting scoop on the left side of the face. Reach right from the scoop to an undercling flake, crank to the top and mantle. The mantle is easier to the left.

El Mussy 16 feet V5 ★
Starts in huecos under *Dick Almighty's* undercling flake. This flake is off-route for *El Mussy.* From the top hueco fire up for a flake under a tiny hueco half a foot below the lip. Go left on the lip to *Dick Almighty's* sick mantle.

End Loop Wall

1 *Cave Exit 60 feet 5.7*
Start in the canyon 15 yards east of table 55. Climb up a well¬huecoed right-facing dihedral on the right side of the right wall. At the large sloping ledge, step over left and climb up a black water streak on good holds.

2 *Short Hands 40 feet 5.7* ★
Climb a right-facing dihedral with a hand/fist crack to a ledge with a 2-bolt rap anchor.

3 *Fast Foods 40 feet 5.8*
Climb the face 10 feet right of *Short Hands.*

Skewed Reality 40 feet 5.10
Climb the overhanging discontinuous flakes 6 to 10 feet left of *Eclipse.* Belay on *Eclipse* or *Fast Foods.*

4 *Eclipse 110 feet 5.9*
Climb 15 feet to an overhanging fist crack. Pull over and continue up the crack (easier) to the top.

5 *Show Me 90 feet 5.9* ★
15 yards to the right of *Eclipse* is a right-leaning crack/ramp. Climb the moderate ramp to a steep headwall with a crack. Climb the headwall on good holds disguised as a crack.

Map, p. 26

End Loop Boulder

At the end loop of the Front Side road is a huge boulder with two popular 30-foot toprope climbs on its north face; this is End Loop Boulder. Problems 1-5 are on rocks under the left end of the toprope face; 6, 7 are on the boulder.

1 *Holy Cow 16 feet V0–* ★
2 *High Protein Snack 11 feet V0* ★

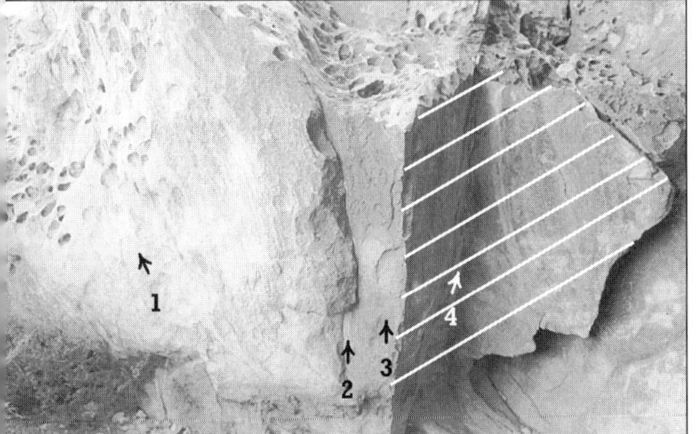

Left of The End Loop Boulder
1 *Holy Cow 16 feet V0–* ★
2 *High Protein Snack 11 feet V0* ★
3 *Napoleon Complex 11 feet V7*
4 *Artist's Opposition* CLOSED – STAY OFF HATCHED AREA

End Loop
Boulder
Mussypotamia
approach
1
2
3
4
5
Fencehopper
Rock

End Loop

The topo for problems 3-10 is on page 100.

3 *Napoleon Complex 11 feet V7*
The short man's problem, grim if you have long legs. Climb the arête. The dihedral left of it is off-route as is anything left of that.

4 *Artist's Opposition 13 feet V4* CLOSED TO CLIMBING – STAY OFF.
Intermingled with the copious graffiti in the dihedral are several faint Indian paintings, hence this dihedral is off limits to climbing. Please respect this ban.

5 *Piss Traverse 27 feet V2*
Traverse the dirty wall from the back of the cave left to "Metal Shop 41".

6 *Wyoming Cowgirl 35 feet 5.12– TR*
Top-rope the face 11 feet to the left of the crack on the northwest face. This has also been led. Variations exist on either side of this line: to the left 5.11+, to the right 5.12-.

7 *The End 30 feet 5.10 TR*

8 *Slam Dip 13 feet V0*

9 *Arêtey Or Not 11 feet V0*

10 *Back Side 30 feet 5.12 TR*
Toprope the southeast corner of the End Loop Boulder.

The End Loop Boulder

6 *Wyoming Cowgirl 35 feet 5.12– TR*
7 *The End 30 feet 5.10 TR*
8 *Slam Dip 13 feet V0*
9 *Arêtey Or Not 11 feet V0*

Fencehopper Rock

An east-west aligned barbed wire fence lies 10 yards south of the looping road and butts into this boulder.

Dynamo To Heaven 13 feet V2 ★
8 feet right of the fence are two huecos 8 feet up a smooth wall. Jump to these then directly up.

Overview of theSouth Side of North Mountain

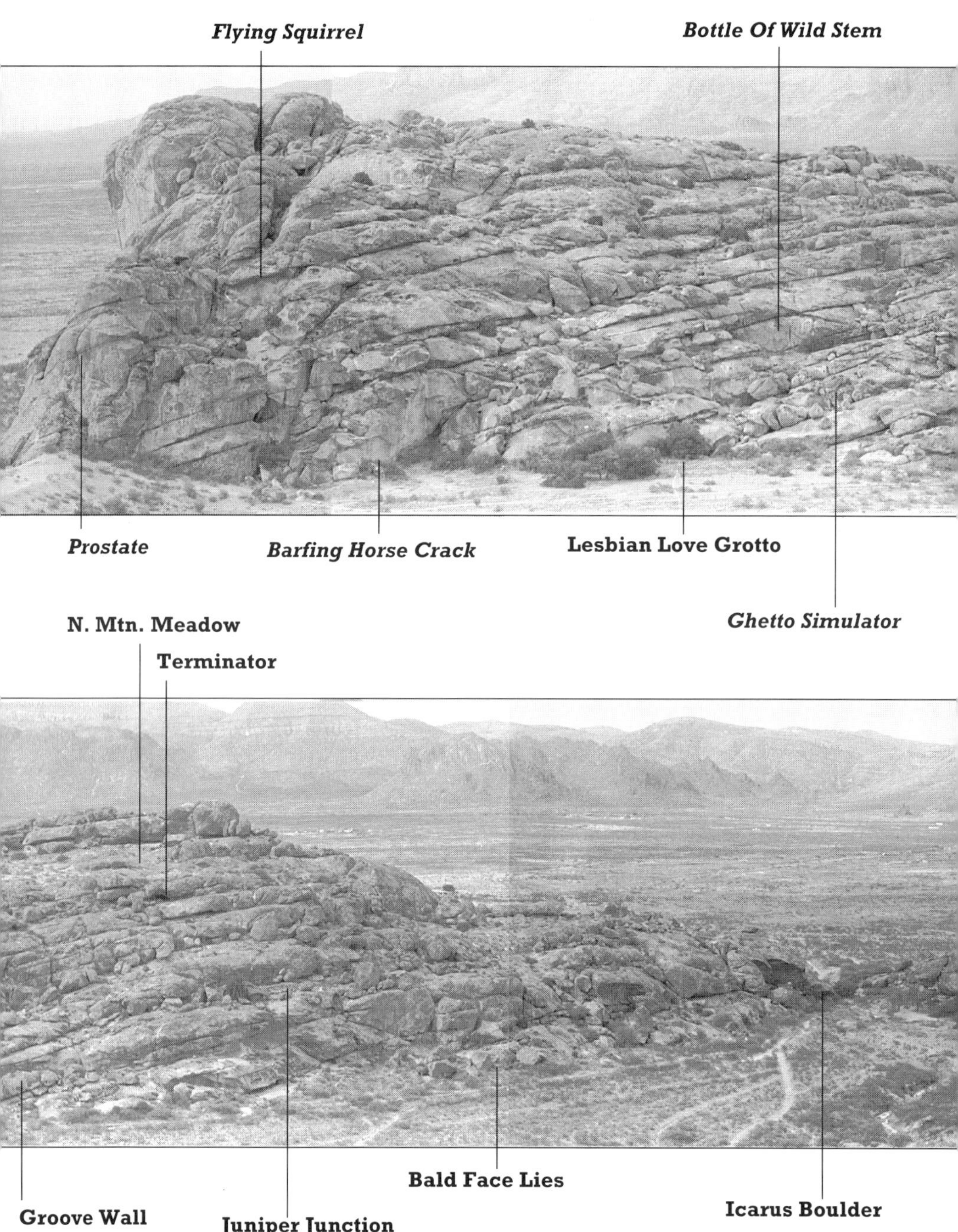

SOUTH SIDE OF NORTH MOUNTAIN

PROSTATE AREA

***Prostate* 50 feet 5.11**

On the south-facing wall above the north end of the Front Side Dam is an obvious crack that penetrates a large bulge. Climb the crack to the top.

***Flying Squirrel* 40 feet 5.10+**

50 yards right from the top of the Prostate is a large, vegetated ledge system/hollow just below the top of the mountain. Climb the south-facing 15-foot roof above the ledge system. A good vantage point to spot this from is midway along the Main Dam looking north to northeast. All approach lines look grievous.

***Barfing Horse Crack* 40 feet 5.12+**

This route is located about a 110 yards east of the dam, at the base of North Mountain. Hard face moves lead to a thin, difficult to protect, slightly overhanging crack on a southeast facing wall. 6 feet right of the base is the Barfing Horse painting; it is currently covered with El Paso gang graffiti.

Center El Murray, Mushroom Boulder

THE LESBIAN LOVE GROTTO

120 yards east of the top of the dam is a grove of oak trees dubbed The Lesbian Love Grotto after a ranger witnessed enlightening acts of female passion unfolding there. Overview photo, p. 104.

To descend problems 1,3, and 4 walk east until you can descend the ramp that touches ground 5 yards east of *Groove Thang.*

1 *Tongue-In-Groove 28 feet V0* ★★★
A couple of good lip pulls and you've earned the juicy stem box above. The deep water groove hidden in the bushes east of the main grove of oaks.
Variation: ***Strap-on Tools 28 feet V1*** Climbs the crack on the right side of the groove, finishing up the wall right of the groove.

2 *Box Lunge 13 feet V3* ★
Surmount the rounded bulge right of the diagonal seam.

3 *Dutch Boy (aka Fingers in the Dyke) 25 feet V0+* ★★
20 yards east of the main oak grove is a lone oak. To the left on the wall behind it is this diagonal fingercrack traverse below a roof. Start as low as you can on the left. Downclimb easy huecos at the right end to get off.

4 *The Vagitarian 18 feet V0+*
Thrash through much vegetation while working up the bulging fingercrack.

5 *Ziplock Liplock 18 feet V2* ★
Six yards right (east) of the lone oak is a black water groove. Climb the face 5 feet to the left of it, off-routing the groove.

6 *Groove Thang 18 feet V0* ★
The black groove 6 yards right of the lone oak. "K Troop 4th" marks the bottom.

20 yards up the *Groove Thang* descent ramp are 3 big ugly boulders in a row.

Lesbian Love Grotto

1 *Tongue-In-Groove 28 feet V0* ★★★
2 *Box Lunge 13 feet V3* ★
3 *Dutch Boy (aka Fingers in the Dyke) 25 feet V0+* ★★
4 *The Vagitarian 18 feet V0+*
5 *Ziplock Liplock 18 feet V2* ★
6 *Groove Thang 18 feet V0* ★

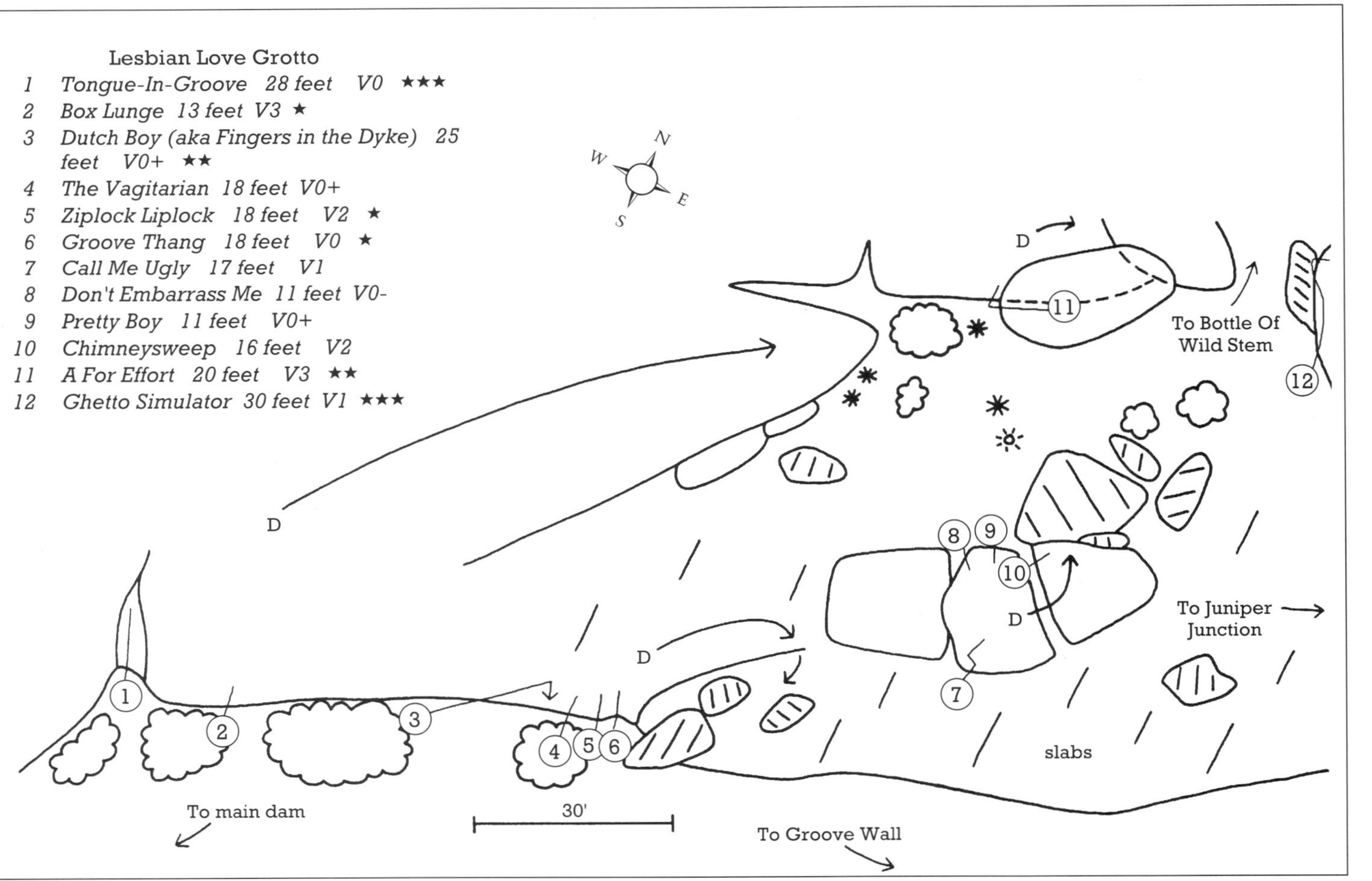
Lesbian Love Grotto
1 Tongue-In-Groove 28 feet V0 ★★★
2 Box Lunge 13 feet V3 ★
3 Dutch Boy (aka Fingers in the Dyke) 25 feet V0+ ★★
4 The Vagitarian 18 feet V0+
5 Ziplock Liplock 18 feet V2 ★
6 Groove Thang 18 feet V0 ★
7 Call Me Ugly 17 feet V1
8 Don't Embarrass Me 11 feet V0-
9 Pretty Boy 11 feet V0+
10 Chimneysweep 16 feet V2
11 A For Effort 20 feet V3 ★★
12 Ghetto Simulator 30 feet V1 ★★★
N
W
E
S
D
To Bottle Of Wild Stem
To Juniper Junction
slabs
To main dam
30'
To Groove Wall

The topo for problems 7-12 is on page 107.

7 ***Call Me Ugly 17 feet V1***
On the middle boulder jump to a hueco 8½ feet up the southwest face, then haul huecos and loose flakes to the top.

8 ***Don't Embarrass Me 11 feet V0- BL***
This easy, huecoed arête right of *Pretty Boy* awaits a hard low start over the bad landing.

9 ***Pretty Boy 11 feet V0+***
One thin move on the north face of the *Call Me Ugly* boulder.

10 ***Chimneysweep 16 feet V2 BL***
Climb the boulder east of *Call Me Ugly* starting at the north end of the chimney between the two with feet on the base of the undercut rock, not the ground. Vaguely right-facing shallow corners mark this line on the left of the face. The actual moves go right of these corners. Bad landing.

20 yards north of *Call Me Ugly* is a boulder leaning against the south-facing wall forming an A-frame. A small oak and occasional water pool is to its left. The A-frame faces west.

11 ***A For Effort 20 feet V3 ★★ SD BL***
Start sitting down on the polished floor of the A-frame. A well incut flake at the 3 foot height is the first hold. Traverse left using jams, face holds and the occasional heel hook until you can pull the lip. Increasingly terrifying the further you go. Bad landing.

12 ***Ghetto Simulator 30 feet V1 ★★★***
One of the best overhanging jugfests in the park. The slab paralleling the wall 4 feet behind it provides a safe opportunity to step off from any move. Usually done as a sit down problem. Overview photos, pp. 104, 106.

Bottle Of Wild Stem 25 feet 5.11– TR
40 yards uphill (north) from *A For Effort* is a water chute shaped like a long neck bottle. The chute is white on the sides with a black streak down the middle and has been stemmed both facing inwards and outwards. Overview photo, page 104.

Lesbian Love Grotto
11 *A For Effort 20 feet V3 ★★*
12 *Ghetto Simulator 30 feet V1 ★★★*

THE GROOVE WALL

AREA 26

Map, p. 26

The Groove Wall area starts 80 yards east of the L.L. Grotto's main oak tree cluster. Two huge boulders leaning against each other, the Head Stones, guard it's west entrance. A smaller block has fallen out between the Head Stones' west sides.

Overview photo, page 104; topo, page 110.

1 *Little Head 8 feet V0*

Mantle the highest point on the west edge of the small block mentioned above.

2 *Head Problem 30 feet V2 ★★*

Start at ground level below the left end of the bigger rock's north face, hand traverse the right angling crack until you can pull onto the face above. A menacing block should be right below you. Climb the gradually easing face above. Scary. Bad landing.

The Groove Wall is the south-facing wall north of the Head Stones. The groove problems start 20 yards east of the Head Stones.

3 *Left Groove 18 feet V0 ★ BL*

4 *Mud Flaps 16 feet V0 BL*

Climb the wall between *Left Groove* and *Center Groove.*

5 *Center Groove 16 feet V0 BL*

6 *Right Groove 19 feet V0+ ★ BL*

The Groove Wall

3 *Left Groove 18 feet V0 ★ BL*

4 *Mud Flaps 16 feet V0 BL*

5 *Center Groove 16 feet V0 BL*

6 *Right Groove 19 feet V0+ ★ BL*

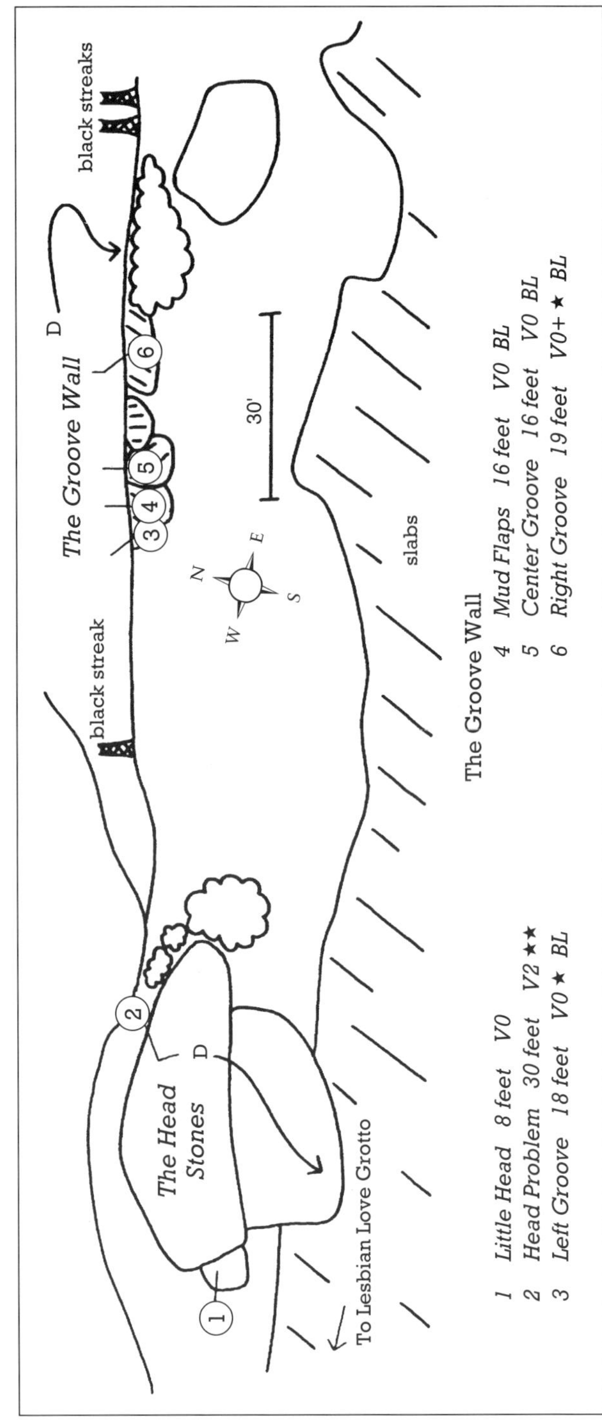
The Groove Wall
black streaks
black streak
D
30'
slabs
N
E
S
W
The Head Stones
To Lesbian Love Grotto
1
2
3
4
5
6
1 Little Head 8 feet V0
2 Head Problem 30 feet V2 ★★
3 Left Groove 18 feet V0 ★ BL
The Groove Wall
4 Mud Flaps 16 feet V0 BL
5 Center Groove 16 feet V0 BL
6 Right Groove 19 feet V0+ ★ BL

Juniper Junction

1 *Gin And Vodka 16 feet V4 ★*
2 *Pimpin' 16 feet V5 ★*
3 *The William's Arete 17 feet V2*
4 *Juniper Slab 14-18 feet V0– to V0 ★*

JUNIPER JUNCTION

This area provides a pleasant setting for beginners to practice without the constant scrutiny of scumbag elitist hardboys. Juniper Junction is located on the level above The Groove Wall 70 yards to the east of the top of the Groove routes. To get there start at the descent for routes at the Lesbian Love Grotto. From the ground, ascend this descent ramp (past Chimneysweep Rocks) to the next level up. Walk east along this level (110 yards to the top of the Groove routes) until you run into Juniper Junction after 180 yards. A 20 foot tall juniper identifies the rocks. This juniper can be seen from the trail at ground level between Bald Face Lies and The Groove Wall. Overview photo, page 104; topo, page 112.

1 *Gin And Vodka 16 feet V4 ★*

2 *Pimpin' 16 feet V5 ★*

3 *The William's Arête 17 feet V2*
The arête 7 feet right of *Gin And Vodka*. Stay on the left side of the arête.

4 *Juniper Slab 14-18 feet V0– to V0 ★*
This north facing slab with the ferns at it's base has many good beginner problems. It's easiest in the middle, harder on the ends.

5 *The Free Salathe 13 feet V0*
The big difference is, this one has had verified ascents. The loose twin cracks on the west face.

6 *The Mick Face 8-9 feet V0– to V0*
This northwest face can be ascended anywhere. It's a good face to practice mantles on. The hardest line is up the center.

7 *Slab Of The Crabs 18 feet V0– ★ BL*
Up the pitted slab 7 feet right of the left arête.

8 *Dungeness 19 feet V0–*
The right side of Slab Of The Crabs, climbing the outside of the 5-inch-thick hollow flake.

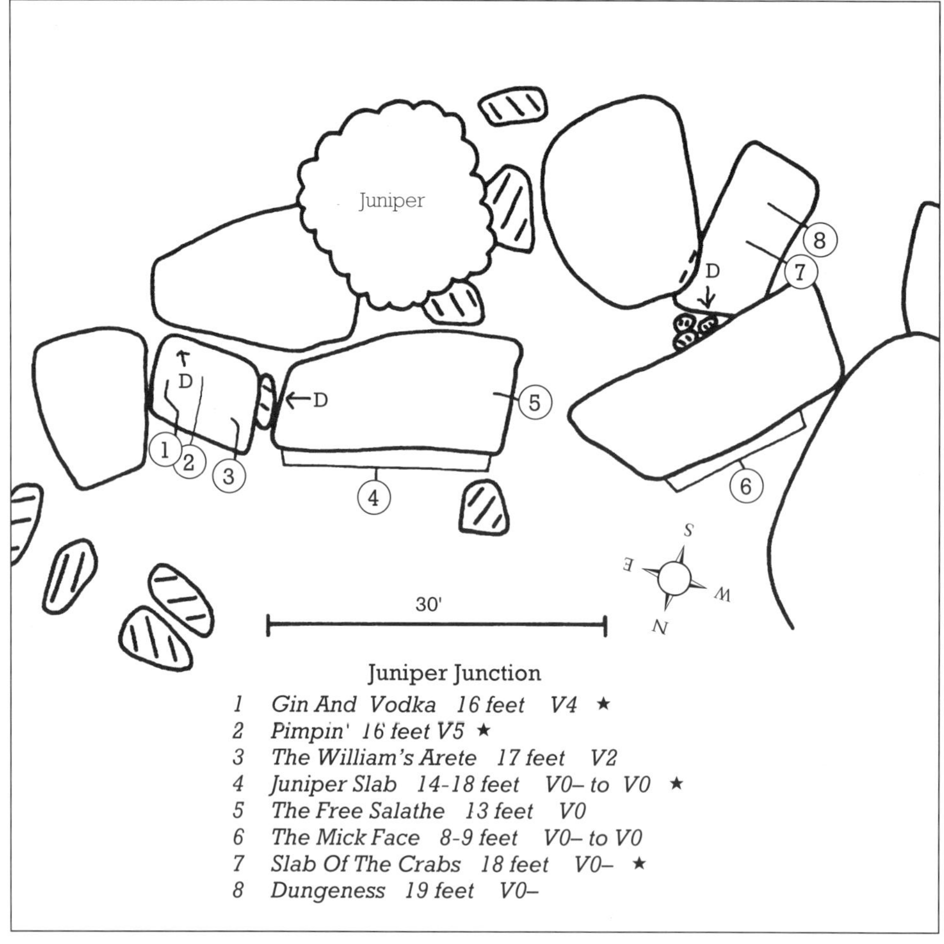

Juniper Junction

1 *Gin And Vodka 16 feet V4* ★
2 *Pimpin' 16 feet V5* ★
3 *The William's Arete 17 feet V2*
4 *Juniper Slab 14-18 feet V0– to V0* ★
5 *The Free Salathe 13 feet V0*
6 *The Mick Face 8-9 feet V0– to V0*
7 *Slab Of The Crabs 18 feet V0–* ★
8 *Dungeness 19 feet V0–*

BALD FACED LIES AREA

The Bald Faced Lies Area is located midway along the southern base of North Mountain. The main cliff behind Perched Boulder and Bald Face Lies Boulder has an easily distinguishable 60-foot crack angling severely to the right. Overview photo, p. 104.

Perched Rock

Perched Rock is the big boulder perched on three stones and not touching the ground. Its south face is well polished.

Same Old Grind 16 feet V1
Climb the west face above the grinding hole in the boulder below.

Hands Off Slab

Hands Off Slab 12 feet V0–
This rock 10 yards north of Perched Rock has an easy 12 foot ironrock north face well suited for no hands problems.

Bald Face Lies Boulder

Bald Face Lies Rock has an unusually light grey to white south face easily seen from the trail. The color suggests freshly broken soft rock, but in reality this face is quite solid. Descend the east face. Photo on p. 104.

1 *Mummy's Boy 11 feet V0–*
The easy left side of the white face starting off the biggest rock on the left. Bad landing.

2 *Bald Faced Lies 15 feet V1 ★★*
The centerline up the face, starting off a short flat rock. Bad landing.

3 *Truth Or Consequences 16 feet V0 ★*
Start 4 feet right of Bald Faced Lies. Climb the wall angling slightly right above the prickly pear. Start left of the cactus.

4 *Standing On The Verge Of Getting It On 16 feet V1 ★*
Start 5 feet right of *Truth Or Consequences.* Mantle the lip 5 feet above a yucca hidden in the grass next to a foot-high stone. Climb the top just inches from *Truth....*

5 *Drastic Season 14 feet V1 ★*
Climb the prow on the right end of the white wall.

Some lowly-recommended problems have been done on the north face. (15 feet, V0)

Bald Faced Lies

1 *Mummy's Boy 11 feet V0–*
2 *Bald Faced Lies 15 feet V1 ★★*
3 *Truth Or Consequences 16 feet V0 ★*
4 *Standing On The Verge Of Getting It On 16 feet V1 ★*
5 *Drastic Season 14 feet V1 ★*

Icarus Area viewed from near bench in gap between East and North Mountains.

ICARUS BOULDER AND THE WALL OF THE EARLY MORNING FRIGHT

Icarus Boulder is the furthest large boulder right (east) on the south side of North Mountain. At first glance it may not appear to be a boulder separate from the main cliffs. It is located 30 yards northwest of the bench and trash can found between East Mountain and North Mountain. Overview photo, p. 104.

Rhonda's Crack 50 feet 5.10

80 yards left of Icarus is this left hand of two prominent corners. There is a tree halfway up the corner. Climb 20 feet to the tree then follow the corner to an exit through the slot in the roof.

Icarus Boulder

Topo, p. 116.

1 *The Face That Launched A Thousand Slips 15 feet V1*

2 *Helen 14 feet V0+ ★*

3 *Hephaestus 15 feet V0–*

4 *Zeus On The Loose 12 feet V0*

5 *The Minitaur 12 feet V0–*

6 *Medusa 12 feet V0–*

7 *Hector 13 feet V0*

8 *Daedalus 20 feet V1*

9 *Athena 20 feet V1*
Climb the blunt prow 4 feet right of the crack without using the big flake on the right side of the prow 9 feet up.

10 *Aphrodite 20 feet V0 ★ BL*
Climb the face immediately right around the corner from the east face. Watch out for the rock behind you.

11 *Hot Wax 22 feet V2 ★★ BL*
Climb the left side of the north face; start 2-3 feet left of a vertical seam.

Icarus Boulder

1 *The Face That Launched A Thousand Slips 15 feet V1*

2 *Helen 14 feet V0+ ★*

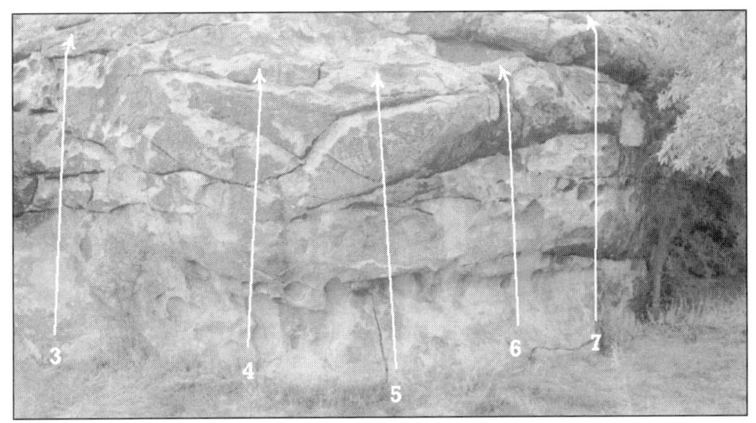

Icarus Boulder

3 *Hephaestus 15 feet V0–*
4 *Zeus On The Loose 12 feet V0*
5 *The Minitaur 12 feet V0–*
6 *Medusa 12 feet V0–*
7 *Hector 13 feet V0*

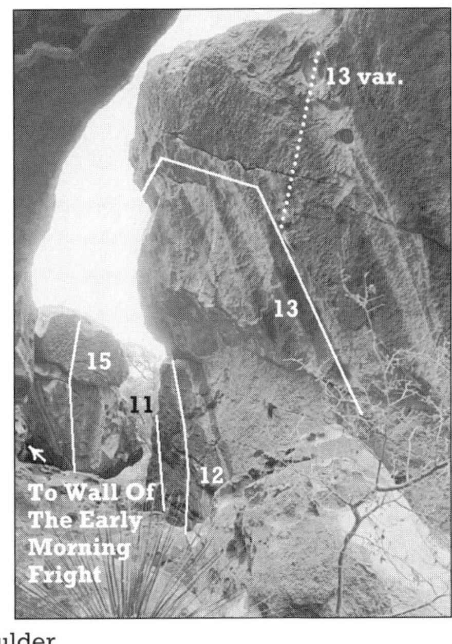

Icarus Boulder

Left:
8 *Daedalus 20 feet V1*
9 *Athena 20 feet V1*

Right:
11 *Hot Wax 22 feet V2 ★★ BL*
12 *The Berserker 20 feet V6 ★★★ BL scary*
13 *Icarus 30 feet 5.11+ ★★*
15 *Greek Fire 11 feet V1*

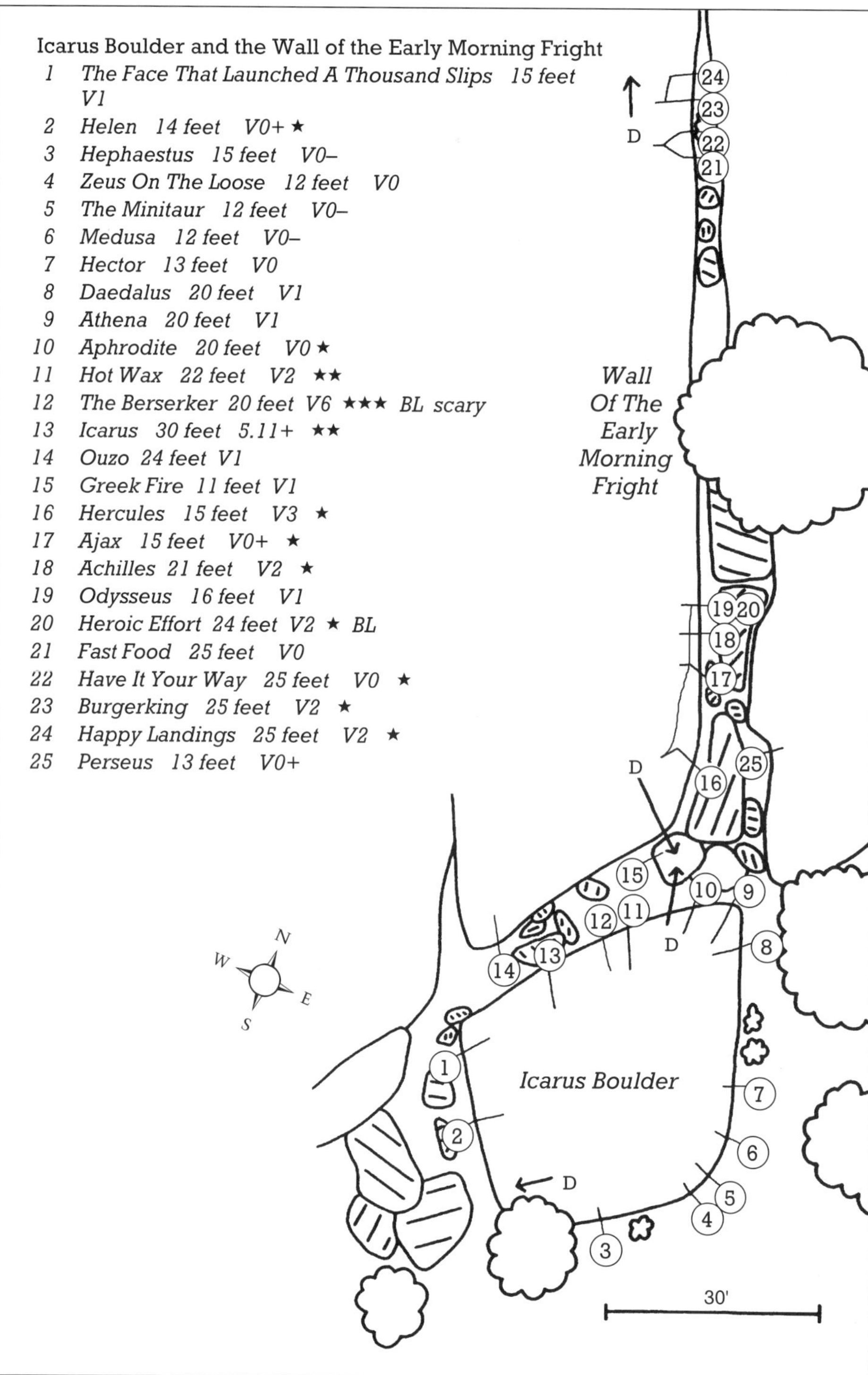

Icarus Boulder and the Wall of the Early Morning Fright
1 The Face That Launched A Thousand Slips 15 feet V1
2 Helen 14 feet V0+ ★
3 Hephaestus 15 feet V0–
4 Zeus On The Loose 12 feet V0
5 The Minitaur 12 feet V0–
6 Medusa 12 feet V0–
7 Hector 13 feet V0
8 Daedalus 20 feet V1
9 Athena 20 feet V1
10 Aphrodite 20 feet V0 ★
11 Hot Wax 22 feet V2 ★★
12 The Berserker 20 feet V6 ★★★ BL scary
13 Icarus 30 feet 5.11+ ★★
14 Ouzo 24 feet V1
15 Greek Fire 11 feet V1
16 Hercules 15 feet V3 ★
17 Ajax 15 feet V0+ ★
18 Achilles 21 feet V2 ★
19 Odysseus 16 feet V1
20 Heroic Effort 24 feet V2 ★ BL
21 Fast Food 25 feet V0
22 Have It Your Way 25 feet V0 ★
23 Burgerking 25 feet V2 ★
24 Happy Landings 25 feet V2 ★
25 Perseus 13 feet V0+
Wall Of The Early Morning Fright
Icarus Boulder
D
N
W
E
S
30'

12 The Berserker 20 feet V6 ★★★ BL scary
Start 6 feet right of *Hot Wax* on the flat spot between boulders. Follow the zigzag seam. Photo, p. 115.

13 Icarus 30 feet 5.11+ ★★
Start on a boulder and reach up to a good flake leading to a left-angling finger crack with a fixed pin. Climb the crack left to the corner and to easy ground. Photo, p. 115.
Variation: Top-rope the huecos straight up from crack above the flake.

14 Ouzo 24 feet V1

15 Greek Fire 11 feet V1
Photo, p. 115.

Wall Of The Early Morning Fright

The Wall Of The Early Morning Fright lies north of the east end of Icarus Boulder. It is an east facing wall with several good problems and is one of the warmer spots on winter mornings. Two large rocks with a smaller rock between them line the base. Overview photo, p. 114.

16 Hercules 15 feet V3 ★

17 Ajax 15 feet V0+ ★
Start off the middle rock or the one to it's right.

18 Achilles 21 feet V2 ★
Start 6 feet right of the small middle rock with your feet on the ground. The huecos to the right (on *Odysseus*) are off-route.

19 Odysseus 16 feet V1
Start on the right hand (north) rock or low.

20 Heroic Effort 24 feet V2 ★ BL
Start at *Odysseus,* finish up *Hercules.*

Further north up the gully, past a big tree, are more problems, reminiscent of the Gymnasium, but with bad landings. The gully at this point is a wide chimney with a rock strewn floor and a small tree in it. Watch for broken glass in the huecos.

21 Fast Food 25 feet V0 BL
Start at the left side of the small tree. A long stretch between huecos is involved.

22 Have It Your Way 25 feet V0 ★
Start at the middle of the tree. Climb up jugs then left

Wall Of The Early Morning Fright

16 Hercules 15 feet V3 ★
17 Ajax 15 feet V0+ ★
18 Achilles 21 feet V2 ★
19 Odysseus 16 feet V1
20 Heroic Effort 24 feet V2 ★ BL

23 *Burgerking 25 feet V2 ★*
Thin moves up to an angling 4 finger slot start the route. Bad landing. Start just right of the small tree. Topo, p. 116.

24 *Happy Landings 25 feet V2 ★*
A hard undercling to a jug romp. The chimney pinches to a squeeze just north of this climb. Topo, p. 116.

25 *Perseus 13 feet V0+*
12 feet east of *Hercules* is this south facing problem climbing out of the cave between boulders. Topo, p. 116.

LOST BOULDERS

The Lost Boulders are found on the east side of North Mountain atop the slabs between Icarus and the Little Itty Bitty Adolescent Titties Area. From the lowest of the Lost Boulders, Rattlesnake Rock, the East Parking Lot is 150 yards to the north, across an earthen dam. The Upper and Lower Lost Boulders are divided by a drainage that was once dammed. The Lower Lost Boulders lie on the south and east side of the drainage. Little Itty Bitty... Area (p. 128) lies to their north across the broken dam. The Upper Lost Boulders lie west and north of the drainage. One of the greatest days in Hueco Tanks history occurred amid these boulders when they became the photo location for one of *Playboy*'s Girls of Texas.

Lost Boulders (from East Parking Lot)

Rattlesnake Rock

Rattlesnake Rock is located below the broken dam, where the Lost Boulders drainage reaches the ground. A large oak flanks the south side of Rattlesnake Rock. An 18-foot painting of a rattlesnake is under an overhang 10 yards northeast of this rock's north face.

This rock is at ground level.

1 *Rattlesnake Left 16 feet V4 ★*
2 *Rattlesnake Right 16 feet V5*

Rattlesnake Rock

1 *Rattlesnake Left 16 feet V4 ★*
2 *Rattlesnake Right 16 feet V5*

The Mayo Clinic Boulder
3 *Hold The Mayo 10 feet V2*
4 *Sir Richard Pump-A-Loaf 17 feet V0+ BL scary*

Lower Lost Boulders

The topo for the Lower Lost Boulders is on page 120.

THE MAYO CLINIC BOULDER

3 *Hold The Mayo 10 feet V2*
Climb the north face starting in the hueco above "Mayo."

4 *Sir Richard Pump-A-Loaf 17 feet V0+ BL scary*
Start from atop boulder.

ORANGUTAN ROCK

5 *Any Which Way You Can 18 feet V3*
Hidden in the corridors between boulders is this arête between north and east faces. Climb the left side starting with a hard move.

DAMBUSTER ROCK

Dambuster Rock has the remains of a dam built against it's north side. The west face is in a chimney. Mortared rocks fill the gap between boulders at the right end of this face.

6 *Dambuster 11 feet V2*
Climb the left side of the face 5 feet from the left end.

7 *Ballbuster 11 feet V3*
Start 6 feet left of the mortared rocks. Stretch or jump to the horizontal hold below a broken patch 8 feet up. Minimal footholds make the move to the summit hard.

LOST KITTEN BOULDER

8 *Pussy Route 10 feet V1 ★ SD*
Start sitting down on a block under the left end of the south face. Crank the horizontal slots to the loose lip moves.

Lost Kitten Boulder
8 *Pussy Route 10 feet V1 ★ SD*
13 *The Bore 11 feet V0+*

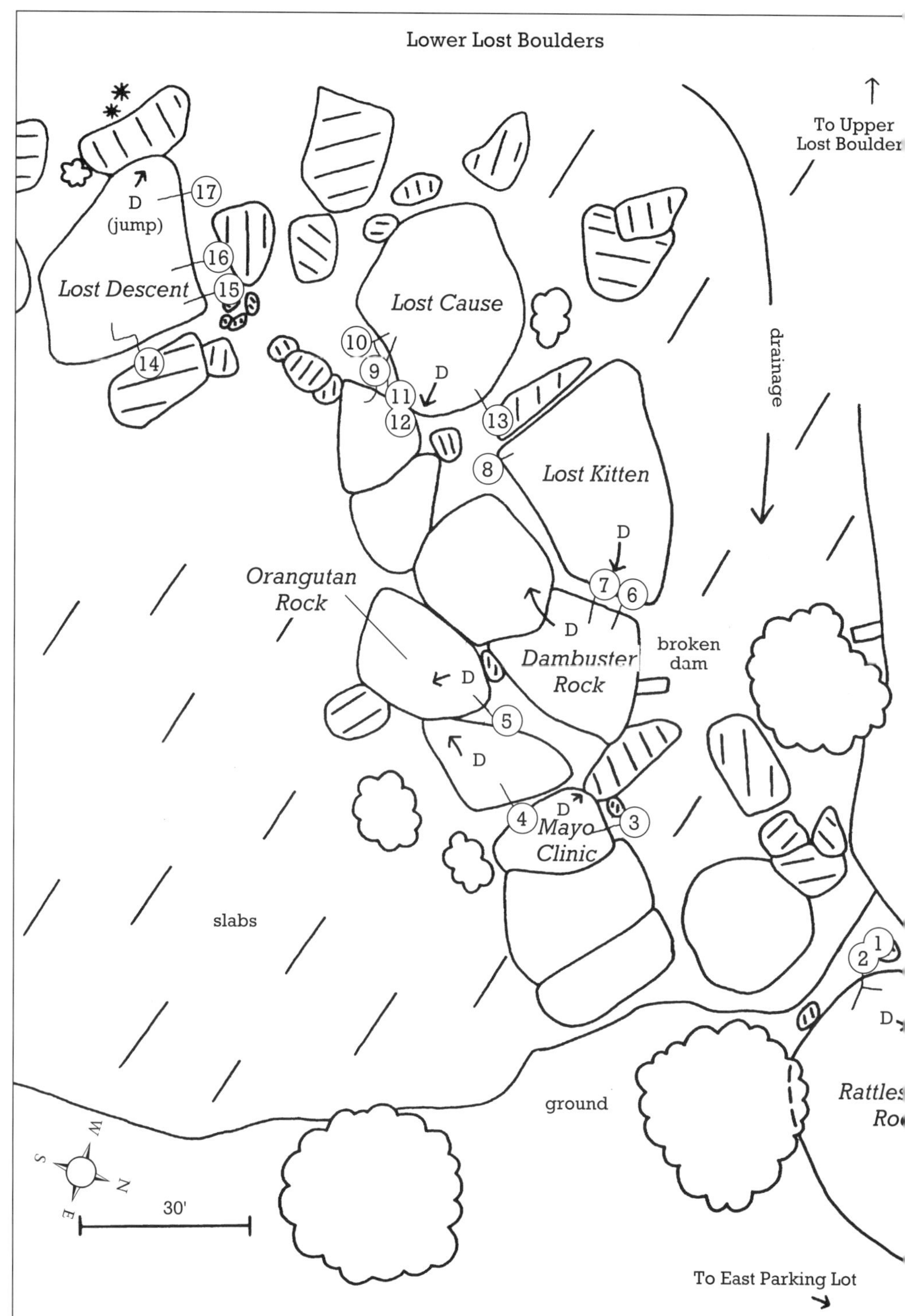
Lower Lost Boulders
To Upper
Lost Boulder
17
D
(jump)
16
Lost Descent
15
14
Lost Cause
10
9
D
11
12
13
8
Lost Kitten
drainage
D
7
6
Orangutan
Rock
D
Dambuster
Rock
broken
dam
D
5
D
D
4
3
Mayo
Clinic
slabs
1
2
D
ground
Rattles
Ro
W
S
N
E
30'
To East Parking Lot

Lost Cause Boulder

9 *Gloria 10 feet V9*
10 *Bloody Flapper 15 feet V4 ★★*
11 *Lip Sync 25 feet V3 ★★*
12 *Banana Juice (aka Bloody Flapper Traverse) 30 feet V9 ★★*

LOST CAUSE BOULDER

9 *Gloria 10 feet V9*
Start 4 feet left of "Geo L." Up and right.

10 *Bloody Flapper 15 feet V4 ★★*
Climb the left brown streak in the center of the south face. A big flake graces the lip.

11 *Lip Sync 25 feet V3 ★★*
Start on the south face's extreme right end. Traverse to the left on sharp flakes and good incuts. Follow the lip to the top of *Bloody Flapper.*

12 *Banana Juice (aka Bloody Flapper Traverse) 30 feet V9 ★★*
Same as *Lip Sync,* but instead of following the lip at the end, drop down and left to finish up *Bloody Flapper.*

13 *The Bore 11 feet V0+*
Climb easy ironrock up the north face to a low angle crack with bushes in it.. See photo, p. 119.

Lower Lost Boulders (topo at left)

1 *Rattlesnake Left 16 feet V4 ★*
2 *Rattlesnake Right 16 feet V5*
3 *Hold The Mayo 10 feet V2*
4 *Sir Richard Pump-a-loaf 17 feet V0+ BL scary*
5 *Any Which Way You Can 18 feet V3*
6 *Dambuster 11 feet V2*
7 *Ballbuster 11 feet V3*
8 *Pussy Route 10 feet V1 ★ SD*
9 *Gloria 10 feet V9*
10 *Bloody Flapper 15 feet V4 ★★*
11 *Lip Sync 25 feet V3 ★★*
12 *Banana Juice (aka Bloody Flapper Traverse) 30 feet V9 ★★*
13 *The Bore 11 feet V0+*
14 *Tension Deficit Disorder 16 feet V0 BL scary*
15 *The Proposition 24 feet V0+ ★★★*
16 *Safe Sects 22 feet V0+ ★★*
17 *Texas Friendly 18 feet V3 ★★ scary*

Lost Descent Boulder

14 *Tension Deficit Disorder 16 feet V0 BL scary*
15 *The Proposition 24 feet V0+ ★★★*
16 *Safe Sects 22 feet V0+ ★★*
17 *Texas Friendly 18 feet V3 ★★ scary*

LOST DESCENT BOULDER

Topo, p. 120.

14 *Tension Deficit Disorder 16 feet V0 BL scary*
This was used as a descent until descending was found to be easier if one jumps off the west end of the boulder.

15 *The Proposition 24 feet V0+ ★★★*
Hey Fella, looking for a good time? Climb the left side of the north face, starting with a big hueco under the roof. Stay 2-3 feet right of the arête.

16 *Safe Sects 22 feet V0+ ★★*

17 *Texas Friendly 18 feet V3 ★★ scary*
A key hold over the lip flexes.

AREA 30B Map, p. 26

Upper Lost Boulders

The topo for the Upper Lost Boulders is on page 124.

WISH IT WERE STILL LOST BOULDER

This rock lies right next to the drainage. A juniper is 20 feet southeast across the drainage.

1 *Gangrene Seam 15 feet V0*

2 *Not Again 17 feet V1*

3 *El Rauncho 19 feet V1*
Climb the right side of the northeast face via a triangular shaped hueco at 12-foot height.

LOST PUPPY BOULDER

Lost Puppy Boulder lies 5 yards north of Wish it Were Still Lost Boulder. Topo, p. 124.

4 *Cheapskate 11 feet V0+*
Climb the right angling seam on the left side of the south face. Start low.

5 *The French Route 10 feet V0+*
Start at the horizontal incut line 5 feet up the right side of south face. Inferior jug hauling to the top.

6 *Fast Break 9 feet V1*
Start sitting down, climb the left side of the north face, just before it rounds around the corner to it's left. Good ironrock flakes make this the only worthwhile crank on this boulder.

7 *El Marko 9 feet V2*
Climb the middle of the north face starting low and just left of a crumbly boulder.

LOST SOULS ROCK

Lost Souls Rock has a memorial cross inscribed at the base of the north face. Topo, p. 124; photos below and on page 126.

8 *Soul Daddy 12 feet V0–*
Climb big easy jugs up the east face.

9 *Lost Souls 16 feet V0 BL*

10 *Dead Souls 17 feet V0 ★ BL*

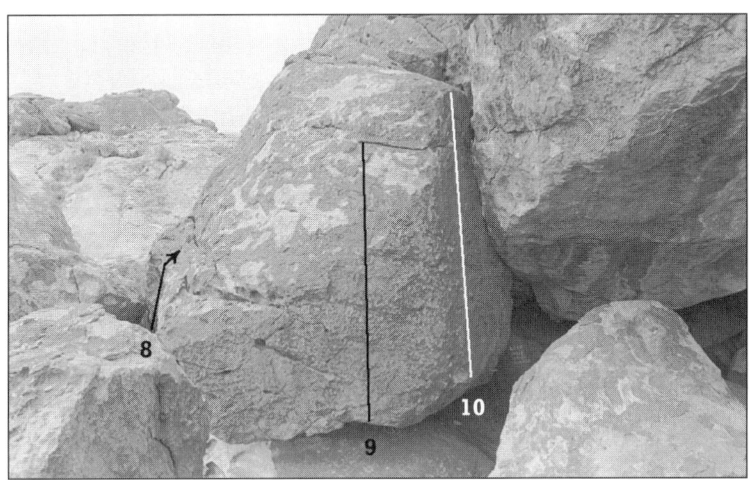

Lost Souls Rock

8 *Soul Daddy 12 feet V0–*
9 *Lost Souls 16 feet V0 BL*
10 *Dead Souls 17 feet V0 ★ BL*

SUPERGOOSE WALL

Topo, p. 124; photo, p. 125.

11 *Supergoose 8 feet V3 SD*
8 yards north of Lost Souls Rock is a long south facing streaked wall supporting the huge overhanging block on it's left and a smaller block (*Girls of Juarez*) on it's right. *Supergoose* (sit down start) underclings up the black streak 8 feet left of the contact with Girls of Juarez Boulder.

GIRLS OF JUAREZ WALL

Topo, p. 124; photo, p. 125.

12 *Girls Of Juarez 15 feet V4 BL*
Start at the right end of Supergoose Wall on a white stained jug/flake. Loose lips and gaping holes cross the 12-foot roof under the boulder. The topout is even worse.

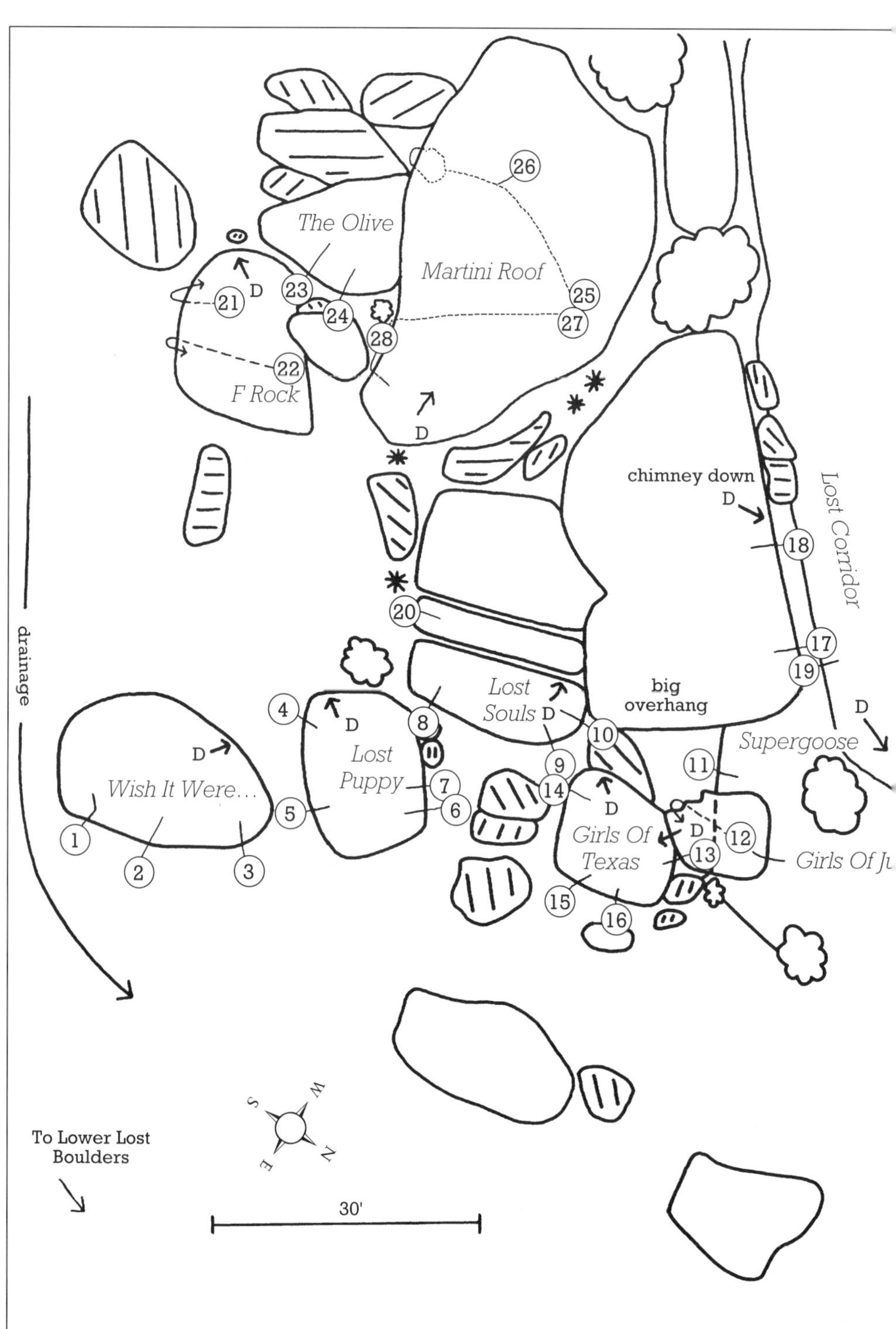

The Olive
Martini Roof
F Rock
Lost Corridor
chimney down
Lost Souls
big overhang
Supergoose
Lost Puppy
Wish It Were...
Girls Of Texas
Girls Of Ju
drainage
To Lower Lost Boulders
30'

Supergoose, Girls of Juarez Wall and Girls of Texas Wall

11 *Supergoose 8 feet V3 SD*
12 *Girls Of Juarez 15 feet V4 BL*
13 *Mexican Toprope 11 feet V2*

GIRLS OF TEXAS BOULDER

To the right of Supergoose Wall is the other boulder supporting *Girls Of Juarez*. This is the Girls Of Texas Boulder.

13 *Mexican Love Handle 11 feet V2*
On the left side of the west face are several big pockmarks in the ironrock. Pinch between two of these to get started. Exit through the gap under *Girls of Juarez.*

14 *Mastercool 13 feet V2 BL*
Hard to get to the undercling crack if you're short. Photo, p. 126.

15 *The Weather Wimp 16 feet V0+*
A 2 foot long by 3 inch wide right angling ramp/seam at 7 foot height is the starting hold. Photo, p. 126.

Upper Lost Boulders (topo at left)

1 *Gangrene Seam 15 feet V0*
2 *Not Again 17 feet V1*
3 *El Rauncho 19 feet V1*
4 *Cheapskate 11 feet V0+*
5 *The French Route 10 feet V0+*
6 *Fast Break 9 feet V1*
7 *El Marko 9 feet V2*
8 *Soul Daddy 12 feet V0–*
9 *Lost Souls 16 feet V0 BL*
10 *Dead Souls 17 feet V0 ★ BL*
11 *Supergoose 8 feet V3 SD*
12 *Girls Of Juarez 15 feet V4 BL*
13 *Mexican Love Handle 11 feet V2*
14 *Mastercool 13 feet V2 BL*
15 *The Weather Wimp 16 feet V0+*
16 *Girls of Texas 14 feet V5*
17 *Finders Keepers 20 feet V0*
18 *Get Lost 20 feet V0+ ★*
19 *Felchfest (aka Picking Straws) 15 feet V4*
20 *Significant Line 17 feet V1 ★*
21 *Fingerfucker 10 feet V4 SD*
22 *Fistfucker 22 feet V5 ★*
23 *Squeeze 11 feet V0-*
24 *Twist 11 feet V0-*
25 *Martini Roof (aka Left Martini) 34 feet V10 ★★★ SD*
26 *Schadenfraud 12 feet V5 ★ SD*
27 *Right Martini 45 feet V12 ★★★ SD*
28 *Big Iron On His Hip 25 feet V7 ★★*

Girls Of Texas Boulder

14 Mastercool 13 feet V2 BL
15 The Weather Wimp 16 feet V0+
16 Girls of Texas 14 feet V5

---

16 Girls of Texas 14 feet V5
Climb the middle of the east face starting low with both hands on the ample jug at 4-foot level. Thin moves follow. Topo, p. 124.

LOST CORRIDOR

On the level above and to the northwest of *Girls of Juarez, Supergoose, Dead Souls,* etc. is this east-west aligned corridor. Topo, p. 124.

17 Finders Keepers 20 feet V0
Climb the left side of the corridor's northwest-facing wall along a line starting 6 feet right of the bush at its left end. Loose top.

18 Get Lost 20 feet V0+ ★
Climb the same northwest facing wall 25 feet right of the bush. A black streak bounds the line on it's right.

19 Felchfest (aka Picking Straws) 15 feet V4
Climb the right side of the southeast facing wall of the corridor, 5 feet left of the bush.

20 Significant Line 17 feet V1 ★

THE F ROCK

Fistfucker Rock is a few yards to the south of the drainage and 20 yards west of Wish it Were Still Lost Boulder. From the drainage, a mean looking fistcrack can be seen exiting a cave. Topo, p. 124.

The F Rock

20 Significant Line 17 feet V1 ★
21 Fingerfucker 10 feet V4 SD
22 Fistfucker 22 feet V5 ★

21 ***Fingerfucker*** *10 feet V4 SD*
Start sitting down on a layaway hueco on the left side at the back of the cave.

22 ***Fistfucker*** *22 feet V5 ★*
Climbs the hand and fist crack under the boulder. Start at the north end. The crux is keeping your butt off the deck through the fist section. If it weren't for it's butt dragging nature, this would be a classic roof crack problem.

THE OLIVE

Topo, p. 124.

23 ***Squeeze*** *11 feet V0-*
Up the flake/trough. Loose.

24 ***Twist*** *11 feet V0-*
The loose flakes 5 feet right of *Squeeze.*

MARTINI ROOF

Great horizontal power jug climbing that always stays dry. Very popular since *Bucket Roof* was closed. Numerous link-ups abound and some mind-blowing ones await the next generation. Doubtless, it won't be long before someone reverses *Martini Roof* and finishes out *Martini Right.* Though the big-number link-ups get all the hype, shorter sections of these problems (minus the crux moves) give great climbing in the V5 to V7 range. Topo, p. 124.

25 ***Martini Roof (aka Left Martini)*** *34 feet V10 ★★★ SD*
The full version starts at the ample (2 hands plus) undercling hueco and crosses right to left across the back of the cave finishing by dismounting onto the 5 foot tall boulder at the left end. By avoiding the 11 feet at the righthand end, the problem is V6 going either right to left or left to right, or V7 going right to left then back right again.

26 ***Schadenfraud*** *12 feet V5 ★ SD*
Start in the obvious low hueco and climb up to the standard *Martini Roof* (right to left) finish.

27 ***Right Martini*** *45 feet V12 ★★★ SD*
Start the same as for *Martini Roof,* but quickly head out right via huecos and fingertip flakes finishing out the right-hand wall of the *Martini Roof* entrance. The final straight up moves are loose and scary – some parties chicken off onto the boulder at the right to finish.

Martini Roof
25 ***Martini Roof (aka Left Martini)*** *34 feet V10 ★★★ SD*
26 ***Schadenfraud*** *12 feet V5 ★ SD*
27 ***Right Martini*** *45 feet V12 ★★★ SD*

28 ***Big Iron On His Hip*** *25 feet V7 ★★*
The final 25 feet of *Right Martini* was a popular problem in itself before *Right Martini* was done. Start at the foot-wide hueco at the entrance to the cave. Traverse 10 feet right, then cruise straight up the scary, loose finish.

AREA 31

Map, p. 26

LITTLE ITTY BITTY ADOLESCENT TITTIES WALL

100 yards southwest of the East Parking Lot is a trail to the top of North Mountain. Three sets of chain handrails mark the trail, two short sets down low, and a much longer set along the top half of the trail. The Little Itty Bitty Adolescent Titties Wall is the north-facing brown waffle iron wall seen 20 feet south of the second (uphill) short set of chains. Overview photo, p. 118.

1 *Have A Seat Ted 10 feet V3*
A memorium to Ted Bundy. Dreadfully hard to pull up once you've sat down. On the lower wall left of Itty Bitty is this undercut wide open dihedral. Start with hands in the shallow hueco at the bottom of the left hand wall then crank up.

2 *Get Off Your Ass And Jam 25 feet V2*
Under the left side of Itty Bitty Wall is a long roof crack never more than 4 feet above the rock below until the dropoff under the lip. Jam this from 18 feet back.

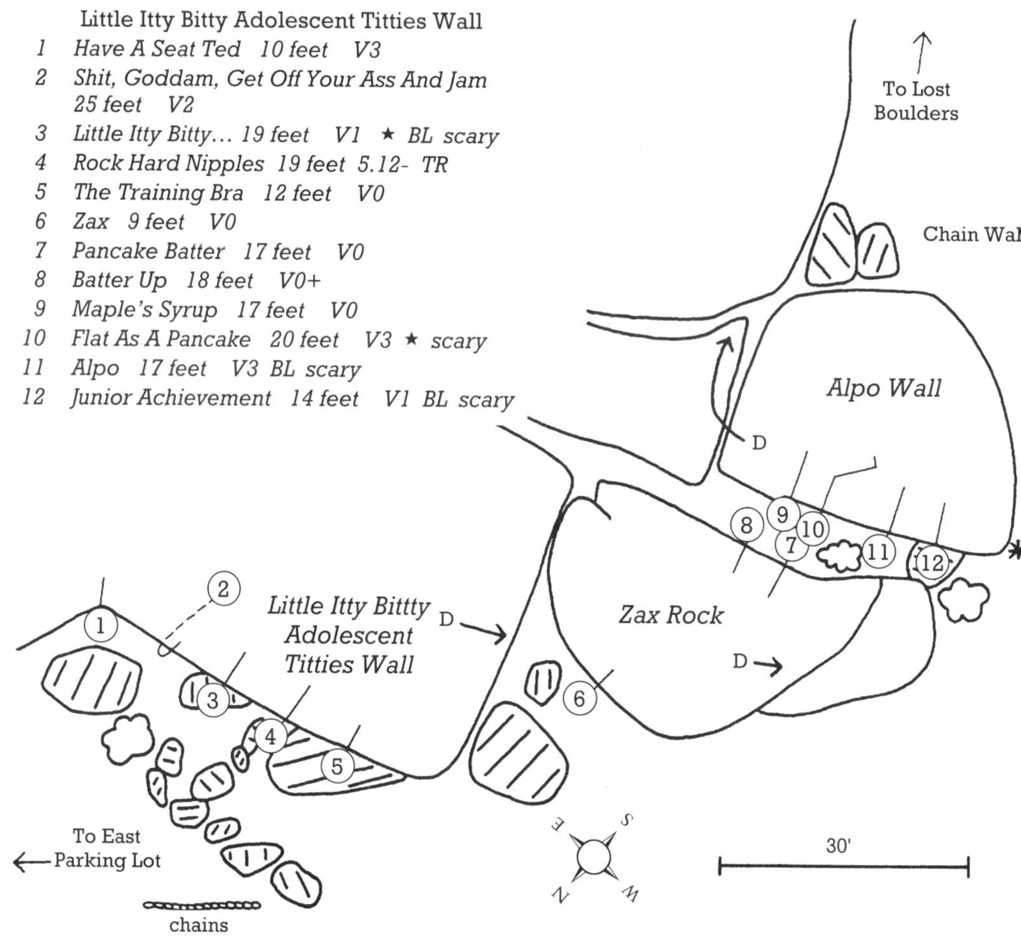

Little Itty Bitty... Wall

Top:

1 *Have A Seat Ted 10 feet V3*
2 *Shit, Goddam, Get Off Your Ass And Jam 25 feet V2*
3 *Little Itty Bitty Adolescent Titties 19 feet V1 ★ BL scary*
4 *Rock Hard Nipples 19 feet 5.12- TR*
5 *The Training Bra 12 feet V0*
6 *Zax 9 feet V0*

Bottom:

7 *Pancake Batter*
8 *Batter Up 18 feet V0+*
9 *Maple's Syrup 17 feet V0*
10 *Flat As A Pancake 20 feet V3 ★ scary*
11 *Alpo 17 feet V3 BL scary*
12 *Junior Achievement 14 feet V1 BL scary*

---

3 *Little Itty Bitty Adolescent Titties 19 feet V1 ★ BL scary*
4 *Rock Hard Nipples 19 feet 5.12- TR*
5 *The Training Bra 12 feet V0*

Zax Rock

Zax Rock, the next boulder around the corner right of Little Itty Bitty Adolescent Titties Wall has a bright green lichened 9 foot tall northeast face.

6 *Zax 9 feet V0*

7 *Pancake Batter 17 feet V0*
Climb the right angling flake on the left side of the south face. A catclaw is just to the left.

8 *Batter Up 18 feet V0+*
Start just left of a 4 foot high rock and 6 feet right of the catclaw. Climb the sweeping arched flakes above.

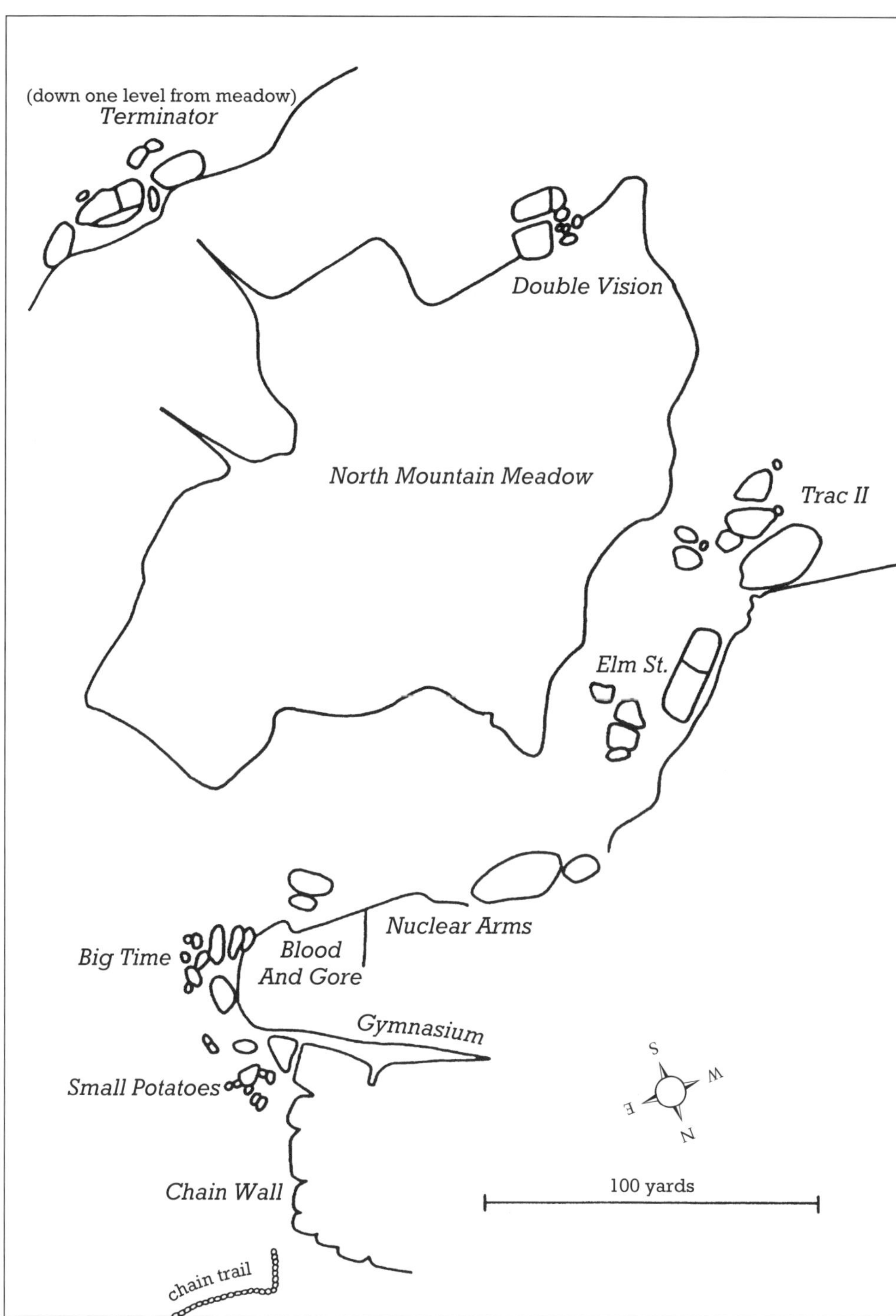

The Top of North Mountain

Alpo Wall

Alpo Wall is the next rock south. Topo, p. 128; photo, p. 129.

9 *Maple's Syrup 17 feet V0*

10 *Flat As A Pancake 20 feet V3 ★ scary*
Climb the glassy wall right of the *Maple's Syrup* corner. The corner is strictly off-route. Catclaw landing.

11 *Alpo 17 feet V3 BL scary*

12 *Junior Achievement 14 feet V1 BL scary*
Start 3 feet right of *Alpo,* standing on the bigger block to it's right.

THE TOP OF NORTH MOUNTAIN

The climbing areas on top of North Mountain are most easily found by walking up the chain trail west of the East Parking Lot. The third set of chains tops out just northeast of the Chain Wall and Small Potatoes area.

The Chain Wall

The Chain Wall is the southeast facing wall between the Small Potatoes and the top of the chains. Expect loose rock on all routes. Topo, p. 132.

1 *Bawl And Chain 20 feet V0+*

2 *Men In Chains 20 feet V0*

3 *Women In Chains 18 feet V0 ★*

4 *Chain Gang 18 feet V1 SD*
Start sitting down and jam out the A-frame to loose rock above.

Chain Wall

1 *Bawl And Chain 20 feet V0+*

2 *Men In Chains 20 feet V0*

3 *Women In Chains 18 feet V0 ★*

4 *Chain Gang 18 feet V1 SD*

13 *Frankenstem 20 feet V0 ★★★ BL*

THE SMALL POTATOES

From the top of the chains, it is 35 yards to the first of The Small Potatoes, The Baby Baker. The largest of the Small Potatoes, The Russet, is less than two feet away from the main cliff to its west. The topo is on page 132; route descriptions begin on page 133.

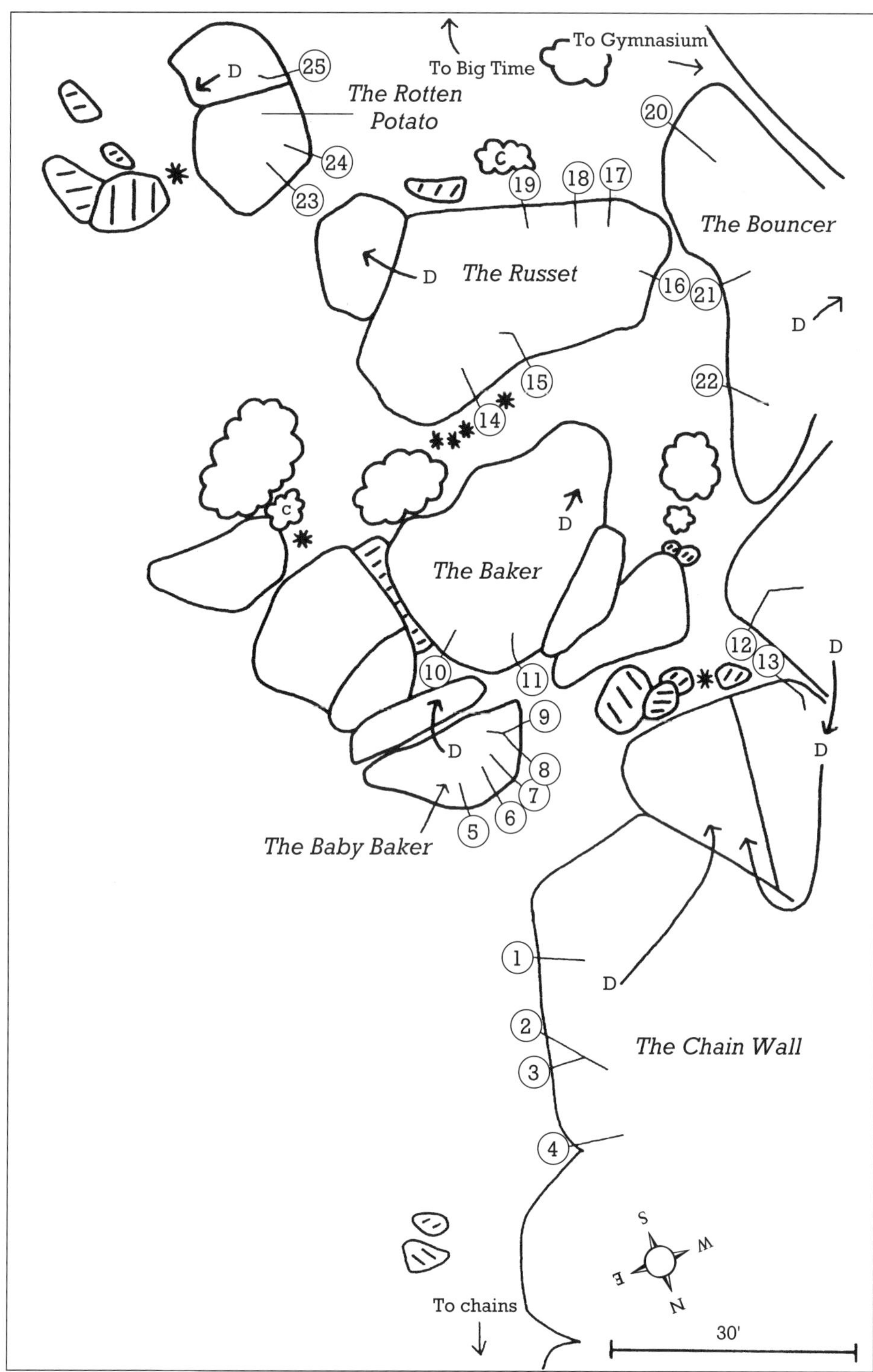

To Big Time
To Gymnasium
The Rotten Potato
D
25
24
23
C
19
18
17
20
The Russet
D
16
21
The Bouncer
D
15
14
22
C
D
The Baker
10
11
12
13
D
9
D
8
7
6
5
D
The Baby Baker
1
D
2
3
The Chain Wall
4
S
W
E
N
To chains
30'

Small Potatoes
The Baby Baker (left)
5 *The Honey Hole 11 feet V0*
6 *Bassin' 11 feet V0+ ★*
7 *Chive Sucker 12 feet V0*
8 *Baco Bit Left 14 feet V0*
9 *Baco...Right 14 feet V0 ★*
The Baker (right)
10 *Mr. Potatohead 14 feet V1 ★*
11 *Mrs. Potatohead 12 feet V1 ★*

The Baby Baker

The Baby Baker is the Small Potato closest to the chains. Five closely-spaced routes crowd it's ironrock north face.

5 *The Honey Hole 11 feet V0*
6 *Bassin' 11 feet V0+ ★*
7 *Chive Sucker 12 feet V0*
8 *Baco Bit Left 14 feet V0*
9 *Baco Bit Right 14 feet V0 ★*

The Baker

The Baker is the biggest of the many blocks immediately west of the Baby Baker. The "trail" ducks under the two blocks to it's north.

10 *Mr. Potatohead 14 feet V1 ★*
15 feet left of where the "trail" ducks between boulders is this route inside a corridor. A hueco 6 feet up is the first hand hold.

11 *Mrs. Potatohead 12 feet V1 ★*
6 feet right of *Mr. Potatohead's* hueco. Climb up to and over the sloped ledge 9 feet up. Start on a flake at the 5 foot level.

The Small Potatoes

1 *Bawl and Chain 20 feet V0+*
2 *Men in Chains 20 feet V0*
3 *Women in Chains 18 feet V0 ★*
4 *Chain Gang 18 feet V1 SD*
5 *The Honey Hole 11 feet V0*
6 *Bassin' 11 feet V0+ ★*
7 *Chive Sucker 12 feet V0*
8 *Baco Bit Left 14 feet V0*
9 *Baco Bit Right 14 feet V0 ★*
10 *Mr. Potatohead 14 feet V1 ★*
11 *Mrs. Potatohead 12 feet V1 ★*
12 *Beefy Reef 26 feet V3 ★ BL scary*
13 *Frankenstem 20 feet V0 ★★★ BL*
14 *Please Don't Eat The Dasileriums 15 feet V2 ★*
15 *The Peeler 14 feet V0*
16 *Mashed Potato 10 feet V0+*
17 *O'Grady's 12 feet V3*
18 *Suckah Inna Yucca 13 feet V0+*
19 *Cactus Casual 14 feet V1*
20 *Dip Chip Face 30 feet 5.9 TR*
21 *Monkey Man 29 feet 5.11 TR ★*
22 *Strong Arm 25 feet 5.11 TR*
23 *Spud Boy 9 feet V1*
24 *Eye Gouger 10 feet V0–*
25 *Man Of Leisure 9 feet V0–*

Main Cliff

North of the blocks the trail ducks through is a 20-foot hand to offwidth crack in a dihedral on the main cliff. This is *Frankenstem*. Topo, p. 132.

12 *Beefy Reef 26 feet V3 ★ BL scary*

13 *Frankenstem 20 feet V0 ★★★ BL*
Continuous; sometimes toproped. Photo, p. 131.

The Russet

The Russet is the biggest of the Small Potatoes. It lies 6 yards from the Gym's chimney entrance. Topo, p. 132.

14 *Please Don't Eat The Dasileriums 15 feet V2 ★*
Start between the 2 rightmost sotols along the northeast face. Climb up to the short right-facing flake above.

15 *The Peeler 14 feet V0*
Climb easy ground right of the rightmost sotol. A small right-facing corner lump is at the top.

16 *Mashed Potato 10 feet V0+*
The northwest face 4 feet left of the squeeze between The Russet and the main cliff.

17 *O'Grady's 12 feet V3*
Climb loose, flexing flakes on the far left side of the southwest face. Start 7 feet left of the big sotol. Bad landing.

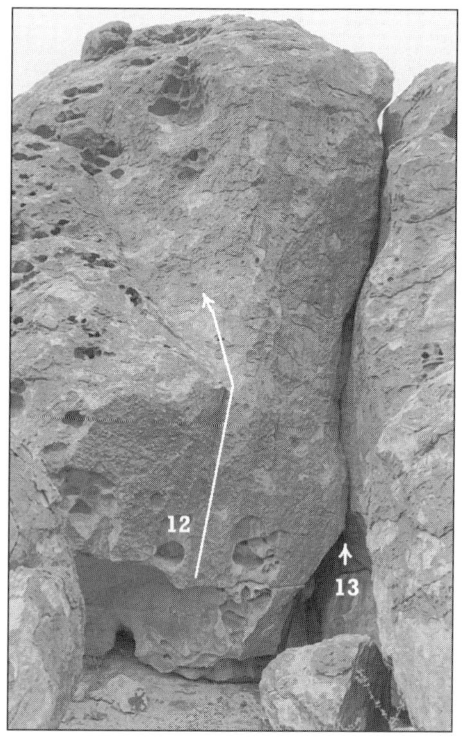

Small Potatoes Main Cliff

12 *Beefy Reef 26 feet V3 ★ BL scary*
13 *Frankenstem 20 feet V0 ★★★ BL*

The Russet

17 *O'Grady's 12 feet V3*
18 *Suckah Inna... 13 feet V0+*
19 *Cactus Casual 14 feet V1*
20 *Dip Chip Face 30 feet 5.9 TR*

18 Suckah Inna Yucca 13 feet V0+
Start 3 feet left of the sotol. Bad landing. Topo, p. 132.

19 Cactus Casual 14 feet V1
Start just right of the sotol in front of the prickly pear. Topo, p. 132.

The Bouncer

This 30-foot tall boulder forms the right side of the chimney entrance to the Gymnasium. It appears to part of the main cliff. To access the top, climb a short 5.8 face on the east side of the boulder. Topo, p. 132.

20 Dip Chip Face 30 feet 5.9 TR
Start 7 feet left of the squeeze between The Russet and The Bouncer. Climb loose flakes to the top.

21 Monkey Man 29 feet 5.11 TR ★
Start 6 feet right of the squeeze between The Russet and The Bouncer. Climb the overhanging concave face above.

22 Strong Arm 25 feet 5.11 TR
Climb the right angling crack 10 feet right of *Monkey Man.*

The Rotten Potato

This is the small cracked boulder southeast of the Russet. Topo, p. 132.

23 Spud Boy 9 feet V1
Sit down start at the black streak on the north face.

24 Eye Gouger 10 feet V0–
Easy huecos up the prow between the north and northwest faces.

25 Man Of Leisure 9 feet V0–
Casual jugs by the crack splitting the northwest face.

The Bouncer

21 Monkey Man 29 feet 5.11 TR ★
22 Strong Arm 25 feet 5.11 TR

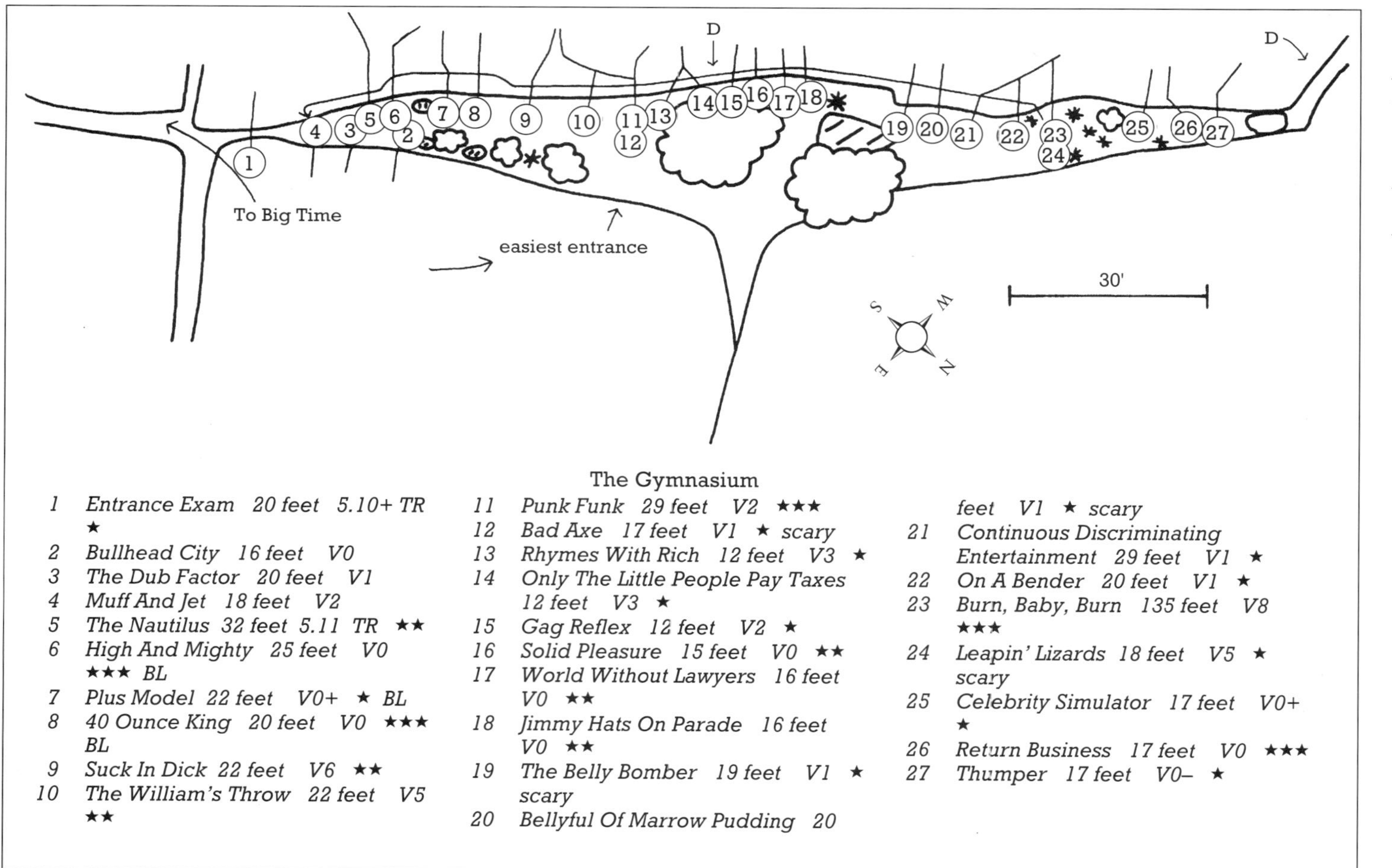
D
D
To Big Time
easiest entrance
30'
S
W
E
N
The Gymnasium
1 Entrance Exam 20 feet 5.10+ TR ★
2 Bullhead City 16 feet V0
3 The Dub Factor 20 feet V1
4 Muff And Jet 18 feet V2
5 The Nautilus 32 feet 5.11 TR ★★
6 High And Mighty 25 feet V0 ★★★ BL
7 Plus Model 22 feet V0+ ★ BL
8 40 Ounce King 20 feet V0 ★★★ BL
9 Suck In Dick 22 feet V6 ★★
10 The William's Throw 22 feet V5 ★★
11 Punk Funk 29 feet V2 ★★★
12 Bad Axe 17 feet V1 ★ scary
13 Rhymes With Rich 12 feet V3 ★
14 Only The Little People Pay Taxes 12 feet V3 ★
15 Gag Reflex 12 feet V2 ★
16 Solid Pleasure 15 feet V0 ★★
17 World Without Lawyers 16 feet V0 ★★
18 Jimmy Hats On Parade 16 feet V0 ★★
19 The Belly Bomber 19 feet V1 ★ scary
20 Bellyful Of Marrow Pudding 20 feet V1 ★ scary
21 Continuous Discriminating Entertainment 29 feet V1 ★
22 On A Bender 20 feet V1 ★
23 Burn, Baby, Burn 135 feet V8 ★★★
24 Leapin' Lizards 18 feet V5 ★ scary
25 Celebrity Simulator 17 feet V0+ ★
26 Return Business 17 feet V0 ★★★
27 Thumper 17 feet V0– ★

THE GYMNASIUM

The Gymnasium is one of the most classic bouldering walls at Hueco Tanks. It is also one of the coldest. To find it walk 70 yards southwest from the top of the chains. For 35 yards a 25-30 foot cliff line will be on your right split by several cracks. This is the Chain Wall. After 35 yards you will encounter lots of 10-15 foot high boulders, the Small Potatoes. Walk through these, under some, keeping the main rock bodies to your right. After squeaking past the last potato you should see a small tree, lots of cactus and a 40-foot hand to fist crack (*Entrance Crack*) splits the east face of the main rocks next to the entrance to a chimney. Scramble through this chimney. After 35 feet it opens up to form the Gymnasium. The last squeeze through the chimney can be avoided by staying high to the east and dropping in midway along the wall. Problem 1 on the topo is above this last chimney squeeze, before the Gymnasium proper is entered. Problems 2-4 are on the lower-angled southwest-facing wall. All of the other problems are on the classic overhung hueco wall. Midway along the overhanging wall is a prominent black water streak descending from a notch. Many of the following descriptions are based on distances from this streak. Descend down the tree next to this streak or off the northwest end of the wall. Photo, p. 118; map, p. 130.

Hairy Chingadera 45 feet 5.11+
Start on *Entrance Crack,* exit left and finish on the obvious overhanging, left-leaning crack at the top of the wall. Usually toproped. See photo, p. 140.

Entrance Crack 40 feet 5.10
This is the hand to fist crack on the east facing wall of the Gymnasium entrance chimney. Photo, pp. 118, 140.

1 *Entrance Exam 20 feet 5.10+ TR ★*
An overhanging east-facing hueco wall begins at the top of the ramp in the chimney, before it widens into The Gym proper. Start by leaning over the chimney to reach huge holds 7 feet left of a yellow smiley face. Pull up and climb huecos to the top. This route requires nerves of steel, or a toprope. Photo, p. 141.

The Gym Slab

2 *Bullhead City 16 feet V0 BL*
Climb big huecos, some sloping, up the left side of the wall.

3 *The Dub Factor 20 feet V1 BL*
Climb the center of the wall above a fresh broken patch at the 6 foot level.

4 *Muff And Jet 18 feet V2*
Climb the incipient seam line on the right side of the wall. The squeeze chimney starts 6 feet to your right.

The Gymnasium Wall Proper

Routes 5 to 9 are pictured on page 138.

5 *The Nautilus 32 feet 5.11 TR ★★*
Climb the wall 5 feet left of *High And Mighty,* finishing up a left-angling thin crack at the top.

6 *High And Mighty 25 feet V0 ★★★ BL*
Move right at the end for an easier top out. Don't fall.

7 *Plus Model 22 feet V0+ ★ BL*

8 *40 Ounce King 20 feet V0 ★★★ BL*
Start left, right, or directly to reach this line.

9 *Suck In Dick 22 feet V6 ★★*
A long undercling or grim liebacks on the scoop's left side are needed to succeed. As Dick said moments before a snapped hold sent him cratering, "All you gotta do is suck in."

Gymnasium Wall Proper

Far left side (top photo):

5 *The Nautilus 32 feet 5.11 TR* ★★
6 *High And Mighty 25 feet V0* ★★★ *BL*
7 *Plus Model 22 feet V0+* ★ *BL*
8 *40 Ounce King 20 feet V0* ★★★ *BL*

Left side (middle photo):

8 *40 Ounce King*
9 *Suck In Dick 22 feet V6* ★★
10 *The William's Throw 22 feet V5* ★★
11 *Punk Funk 29 feet V2* ★★★
12 *Bad Axe 17 feet V1* ★ *scary*
13 *Rhymes With Rich 12 feet V3* ★
23 *Burn, Baby, Burn 135 feet V8* ★★★

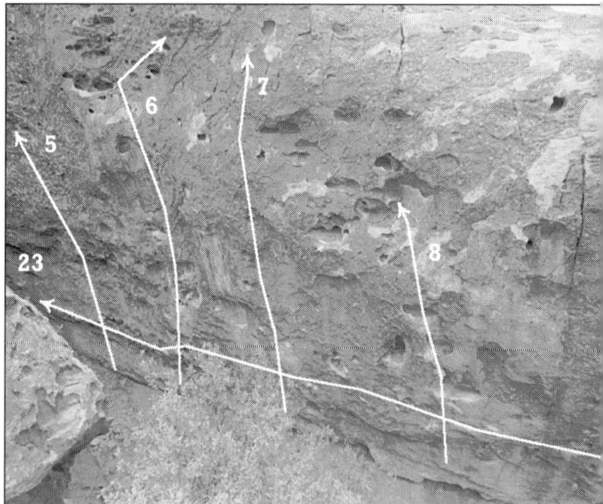

Gymnasium Wall Proper

Center (bottom photo)

13 *Rhymes With Rich 12 feet V3* ★
14 *Only The Little People Pay Taxes 12 feet V3* ★
15 *Gag Reflex 12 feet V2* ★
16 *Solid Pleasure 15 feet V0* ★★
17 *World Without Lawyers 16 feet V0* ★★
18 *Jimmy Hats On Parade 16 feet V0* ★★

The topo for problems 10-27 is on page 136.

10 *The William's Throw 22 feet V5* ★★

11 *Punk Funk 29 feet V2* ★★★

12 *Bad Axe 17 feet V1* ★ *scary*

13 *Rhymes With Rich 12 feet V3* ★

14 *Only The Little People Pay Taxes 12 feet V3* ★

15 *Gag Reflex 12 feet V2* ★

16 *Solid Pleasure 15 feet V0* ★★

The wall 10 feet right of the waterstreak. A small tree is just behind it.

17 *World Without Lawyers 16 feet V0* ★★

A delightful concept. The wall 13 feet right of the waterstreak.

18 *Jimmy Hats On Parade 16 feet V0* ★★

19 *The Belly Bomber 19 feet V1* ★ *scary*

20 *Bellyful Of Marrow Pudding 20 feet V1* ★ *scary*

21 *Continuous Discriminating Entertainment 29 feet V1* ★

22 *On A Bender 20 feet V1* ★

23 *Burn, Baby, Burn 135 feet V8* ★★★

Starting 2 feet right of the faded peace sign, traverse the wall from right to left, eliminating the slabby foot holds low down and the top of the waterstreak. It ends with both hands on a smile shaped jug 6 feet before the wall turns to a squeeze chimney at it's far left end. For those without long, strong arms it will probably end sooner. Pumper.

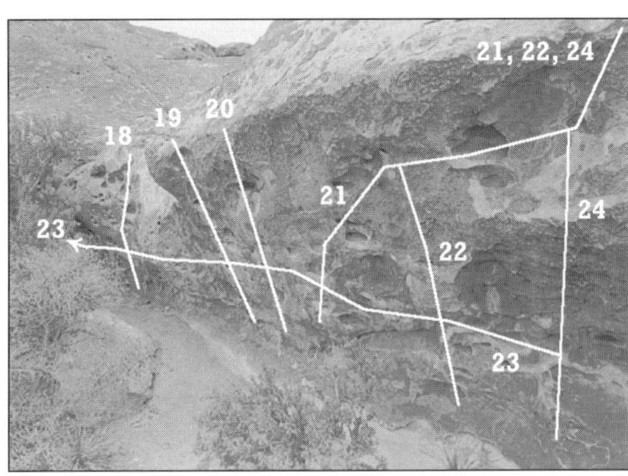

Gymnasium Wall Proper

Right side (above):

18 *Jimmy Hats On Parade*

19 *The Belly Bomber*

20 *Bellyful Of Marrow Pudding*

21 *Continuous Discriminating Entertainment*

22 *On A Bender*

23 *Burn, Baby, Burn*

24 *Leapin' Lizards*

Far right side (left photo):

23 *Burn, Baby, Burn*

24 *Leapin' Lizards*

25 *Celebrity Simulator*

26 *Return Business*

27 *Thumper 17 feet*

Big Time Boulder (left)

1 *See Spot Run 25 feet V6 ★★★*
21 *Free Delivery 22 feet V0+ scary*

24 *Leapin' Lizards 18 feet V5 ★ scary*
Some loose holds.
25 *Celebrity Simulator 17 feet V0+ ★*
26 *Return Business 17 feet V0 ★★★*
27 *Thumper 17 feet V0– ★*

AREA 34

Map, p. 26

THE BIG TIME

The Big Time is the cluster of 25-footers found between the Gymnasium and Nuclear Arms. Photo, p. 118; map, p. 130.

Big Time Boulder

This rock features a 25-foot north-facing arete with 3 prominent huecos on its left side. Of the Big Time boulders, it is the closest one to the Gymnasium's chimney entrance.

The Big Time (topo on right)

1 *See Spot Run 25 feet V6 ★★★*
2 *The Rack 16 feet V3 ★*
3 *Cracked Lips 8 feet V0–*
4 *XXX 25 feet 5.12 TR ★★*
5 *For Adults Only 25 feet V3 ★ scary*
6 *Sleaze 18 feet V0+ ★★*
7 *Movers And Shakers 25 feet V0+*
8 *Do Fries Go With That Shake? 25 feet V2 ★★*
9 *Little Big Time 20 feet V0+ ★*
10 *Wife On Ice 17 feet V1 ★*
11 *Aging Celtics 15 feet V1*
12 *Blubberhead 10 feet V1*
13 *Wild Turkey 14 feet + escape V8 ★*
14 *100 Proof Roof 22 feet V3 ★ scary*
15 *Fern Bar Possibilities 25 feet V1 scary*
16 *It's A Man's, Man's, Man's World 23 feet V2 scary*
17 *Dope Fiend 19 feet V3 scary*
18 *Waffling Big Time 21 feet V2 scary*
19 *Griddle Cake 22 feet V1 ★ BL*
20 *Tall Stack 22 feet V4 ★*
21 *Free Delivery 22 feet V0+ scary*

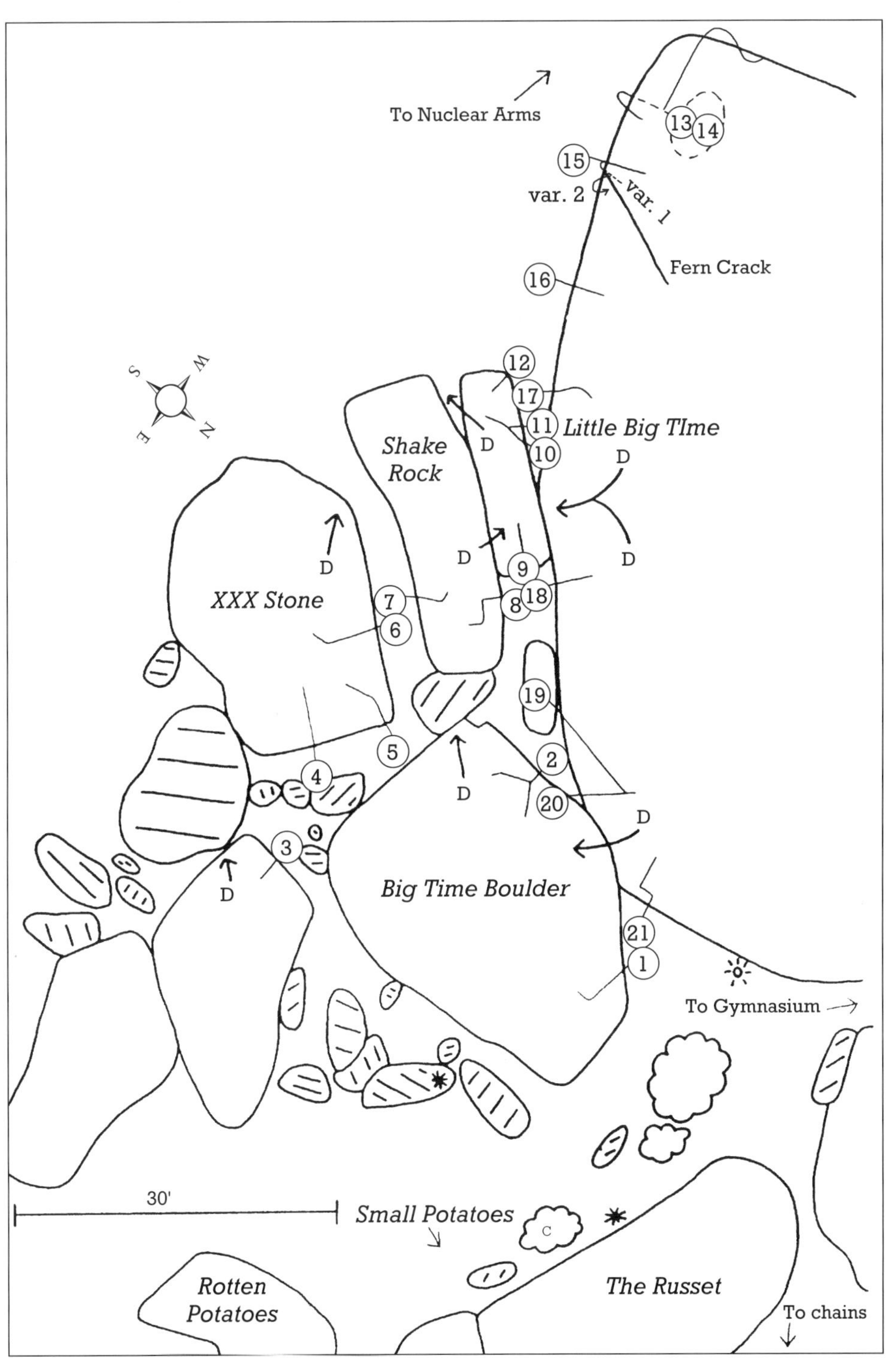

To Nuclear Arms
13
14
15
var. 2
var. 1
Fern Crack
16
S
W
E
N
12
17
11
Little Big TIme
10
Shake Rock
D
D
D
D
D
XXX Stone
9
D
7
8
18
6
19
5
2
4
D
20
D
3
D
Big Time Boulder
21
1
To Gymnasium
30'
Small Potatoes
C
Rotten Potatoes
The Russet
To chains

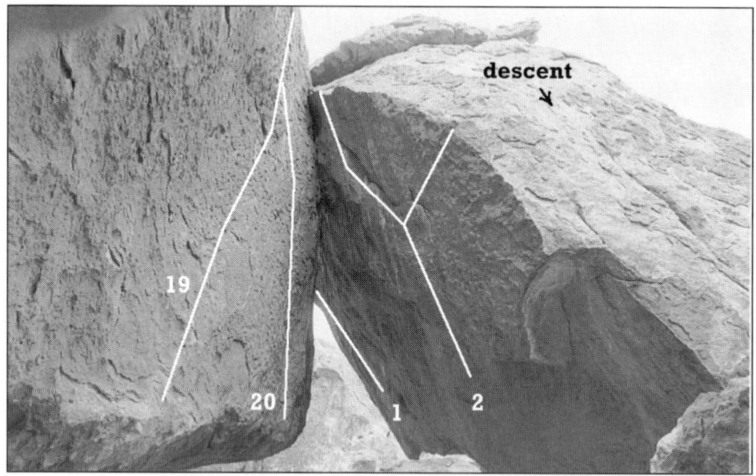

Big Time Boulder (right), Fern Crack Wall

1	*See Spot Run 25 feet V6 ★★★*	19	*Griddle Cake 22 feet V1 ★ BL*
2	*The Rack 16 feet V3 ★*	20	*Tall Stack 22 feet V4 ★*

XXX, Shake

4 *XXX 25 feet 5.12 TR ★★*
5 *For Adults Only 25 feet V3 ★ scary*
6 *Sleaze 18 feet V0+ ★★*
7 *Movers And Shakers 25 feet V0+*
8 *Do Fries Go With That Shake? 25 feet V2 ★★*
9 *Little Big Time 20 feet V0+ ★*
18 *Waffling Big Time 21 feet V2 scary*

1 *See Spot Run 25 feet V6 ★★★*
Angle left up the wall on the right side of the arete, topping out where a 3 foot vertical seam splits the lip 19 feet up. A desperate start followed by a mortifying top out. An even more desperate start begins around the corner to the left and climbs to a sloping hueco 10 feet up on the left edge of the arete, then moves right to finish up *See Spot Run.* The entire left side of the arete awaits a complete ascent--the section from the sloping hueco at 10 foot level to the top was topropped in the early '80s when a three foot cheater stone resided at the base. Photos above and on page 140.

2 *The Rack 16 feet V3 ★*
A long stretch gains a left angling crack. Either follow this crack left or top out straight up or to the right (both V3). Topo, p. 141.

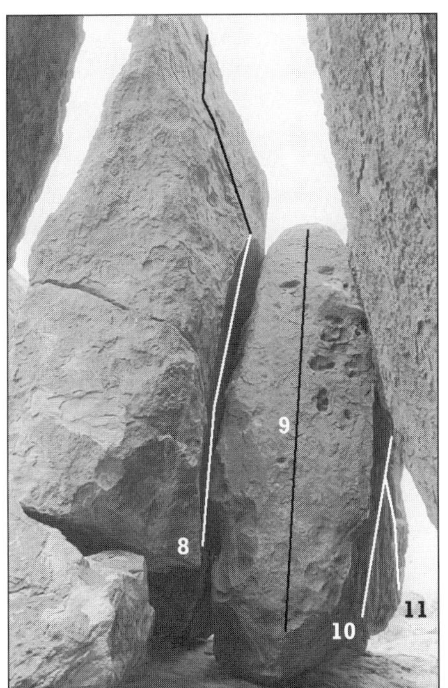

Shake Rock (left), Little Big Time Rock
8 *Do Fries... 25 feet V2 ★★*
9 *Little Big Time 20 feet V0+ ★*
10 *Wife On Ice 17 feet V1 ★*
11 *Aging Celtics 15 feet V1*

Little Big Time Rock
10 *Wife On Ice 17 feet V1 ★*
11 *Aging Celtics 15 feet V1*
12 *Blubberhead 10 feet V1*

XXX Stone

This is the 25-foot tall boulder south of Big Time Boulder. Topo, p. 141.

3 *Cracked Lips 8 feet V0–*
Eight feet east of XXX Stone is this scooped overhang with a fingercrack through it's lip. Start inside the scoop and climb out.

4 *XXX 25 feet 5.12 TR ★★*

5 *For Adults Only 25 feet V3 ★ scary*
The north arete climbed at first on it's left then on it's right.

6 *Sleaze 18 feet V0+ ★★*
Climb the center of the dark brown northwest face hitting the descent ramp at 18-foot level. Hard landing.

Shake Rock

This is the rock contacting Little Big Time's southeast face. Topo, p. 141.

7 *Movers And Shakers 25 feet V0+*

8 *Do Fries Go With That Shake? 25 feet V2 ★★*
Climb the undercut face on the rock 3 feet left of *Little Big Time.* Excellent holds take you to the crux traverse left at the 19-foot level. More scary moves to the top. Chickening out to *Little Big Time* is possible before the crux.

Fern Crack Wall
13 *Wild Turkey 14 feet + escape V8* ★
14 *100 Proof Roof 22 feet V3* ★ *scary*
15 *Fern Bar Possibilities 25 feet V1 scary*
16 *It's A Man's, Man's, Man's World 23 feet V2 scary*
17 *Dope Fiend 19 feet V3 scary*

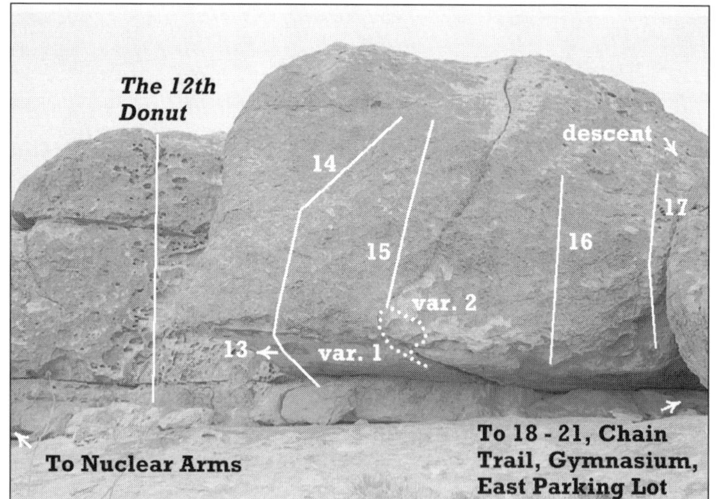

Little Big Time Rock

Little Big Time Rock leans against the main cliff at the west end of the corridor. Descend the chimney on the rock's west side. Topo, p. 141.

9 *Little Big Time 20 feet V0+* ★

10 *Wife On Ice 17 feet V1* ★

11 *Aging Celtics 15 feet V1*

12 *Blubberhead 10 feet V1*
Climb the right arete of the northwest face.

Fern Crack Wall

West of the Big Time's big boulders is a 36 foot wide by 12 foot deep roof that is part of the main cliff. A fern filled crack splits this roof and the face above. The first 4 problems listed are on this roof. The wall above the lip has lots of loose rock. Test your holds before yarding on them. Topo, p. 141.

13 *Wild Turkey 14 feet + escape V8* ★
Start on fingertip holds at the beginning of *100 Proof Roof,* but off-routing the *100 Proof Roof* starter boulder for the feet. Move left along very sloping lip holds until you can turn the lip via wide pinches on a blunt prow. Stand up on the lip then escape via easy moves to the huecoed ramp/dihedral to the left.

14 *100 Proof Roof 22 feet V3* ★ *scary*
Start with feet on a boulder under the left (west) end of the roof. Awesome moves to the lip, then looseness above

15 *Fern Bar Possibilities 25 feet V1 scary*
Pull the lip at the roof crack's end then climb loose holds above.
Variation 1: V5 Start halfway back under the roof on face holds next to the crack.
Variation 2: ***Barfly V7*** Starts with Variation 1 but turns the lip to the right of the crack, off-routing the crack.

16 *It's A Man's, Man's, Man's World 23 feet V2 scary*
Pull the lip 12 feet right of where the crack meets the lip. A bit more solid than it's mates.

17 *Dope Fiend 19 feet V3 scary*

18 *Waffling Big Time 21 feet V2 scary*

Cranking in the Gymnasium

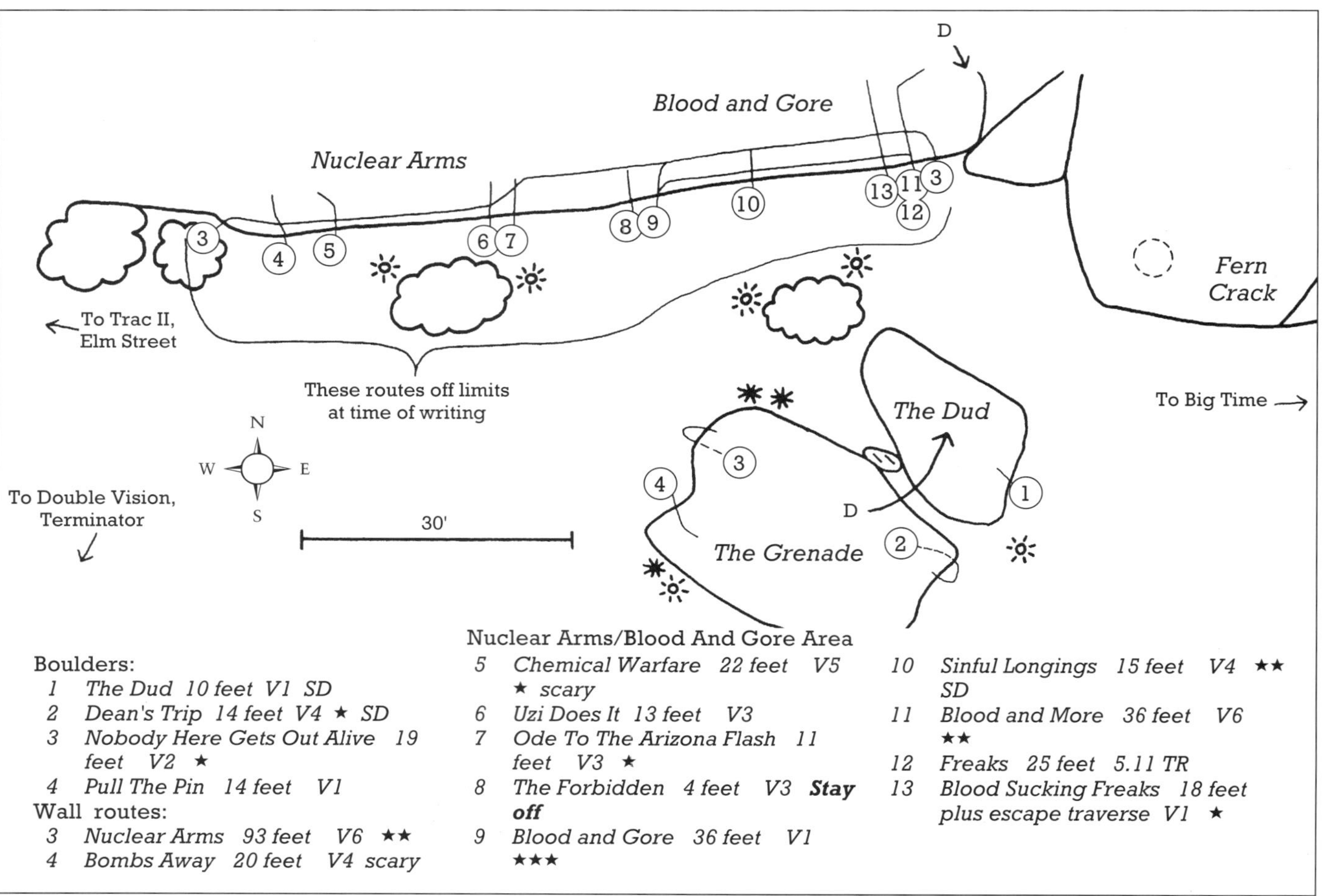

Boulders:
1 *The Dud 10 feet V1 SD*
2 *Dean's Trip 14 feet V4 ★ SD*
3 *Nobody Here Gets Out Alive 19 feet V2 ★*
4 *Pull The Pin 14 feet V1*

Wall routes:
3 *Nuclear Arms 93 feet V6 ★★*
4 *Bombs Away 20 feet V4 scary*

Nuclear Arms/Blood And Gore Area
5 *Chemical Warfare 22 feet V5 ★ scary*
6 *Uzi Does It 13 feet V3*
7 *Ode To The Arizona Flash 11 feet V3 ★*
8 *The Forbidden 4 feet V3* ***Stay off***
9 *Blood and Gore 36 feet V1 ★★★*
10 *Sinful Longings 15 feet V4 ★★ SD*
11 *Blood and More 36 feet V6 ★★*
12 *Freaks 25 feet 5.11 TR*
13 *Blood Sucking Freaks 18 feet plus escape traverse V1 ★*

Dud (right), Grenade
1 *The Dud 10 feet V1 SD*
2 *Dean's Trip 14 feet V4 ★ SD*

10 feet right of *Dope Fiend,* through the gap between it and *Little Big Time* is this undercut wall. Hard moves conquer the undercut, scary moves top it out. Stepping left to *Little Big Time* is an easy way to chicken out up high. Hard landing. Photo, p. 142.

19 *Griddle Cake 22 feet V1 ★ BL*
Start on the boulder on the corridor floor 10 feet right of *Waffling Big Time.* See photo, p. 142.

20 *Tall Stack 22 feet V4 ★*
Start 5 feet right of the boulder on the corridor floor. See photo, p. 142.

21 *Free Delivery 22 feet V0+ scary*
The Big Time Boulder is off-route.

NUCLEAR ARMS/BLOOD AND GORE AREA

This area used to see a lot of action when conditions were prohibitively cold or wet elsewhere in the park. Countless contrived variations have been done along the Blood And Gore side of the wall, some among the hardest in the park. To find it walk up the chain trail to its top, then along the main cliff faces, passing through the Small Potatoes and The Big Time. The Nuclear Arms/Blood And Gore Area is the next

The Grenade
3 *Nobody Here Gets Out Alive 19 feet V2 ★*
4 *Pull The Pin 14 feet V1*

Nuclear Arms/Blood And Gore Wall

3 *Nuclear Arms 93 feet V6 ★★*
4 *Bombs Away 20 feet V4 scary*
5 *Chemical Warfare 22 feet V5 ★*
6 *Uzi Does It 13 feet V3*
7 *Ode To...Flash 11 feet V3 ★*

---

wall left (west) of the Big Time's *Fern Crack Roof.* The wall is part of the main cliff and is currently closed to climbing. Map, p. 130.

The Dud

1 *The Dud 10 feet V1 SD*

The Grenade

This is the bigger of the two boulders immediately south of Blood and Gore.

2 *Dean's Trip 14 feet V4 ★ SD*

3 *Nobody Here Gets Out Alive 19 feet V2 ★*
Start as far back as you want.

4 *Pull The Pin 14 feet V1*
Climb the leaning scoop right of *Nobody Here Gets Out Alive.*

Nuclear Arms/Blood And Gore Wall

AT THE TIME OF THIS WRITING, ALL ROUTES ON THIS WALL ARE CLOSED TO CLIMBING. In the first edition of this guide, only the left side was closed. Because some climbers did not respect the ban, the right half was closed as well to punish climbers. If we ever want to climb on this wall again and if we want to see a reasonable and intelligent route closure policy that strives to protect the park's art and not to punish climbers, it is imperative that we police ourselves. If you see someone climbing on this wall, tell them to get off and explain why. There is great hope that sections of this wall and other areas in the park will reopen to climbing in the future, but only if we prove we are willing to cooperate with parks department. Topo, p. 146.

3 *Nuclear Arms 93 feet V6 ★★*
Traverse the entire wall under the roof (left to right). Right to left is 93 feet; V7 ★★.

4 *Bombs Away 20 feet V4 scary*
Start from the hand jam slot at the 5 foot level. Pull the upper roof on it's left end via huecos above it.

5 *Chemical Warfare 22 feet V5 ★ scary*
Start 3 feet right of *Bombs Away* at the same level.

6 *Uzi Does It 13 feet V3*

7 *Ode To The Arizona Flash 11 feet V3 ★*
The crux section of *Nuclear Arms* is a good problem in its own right.

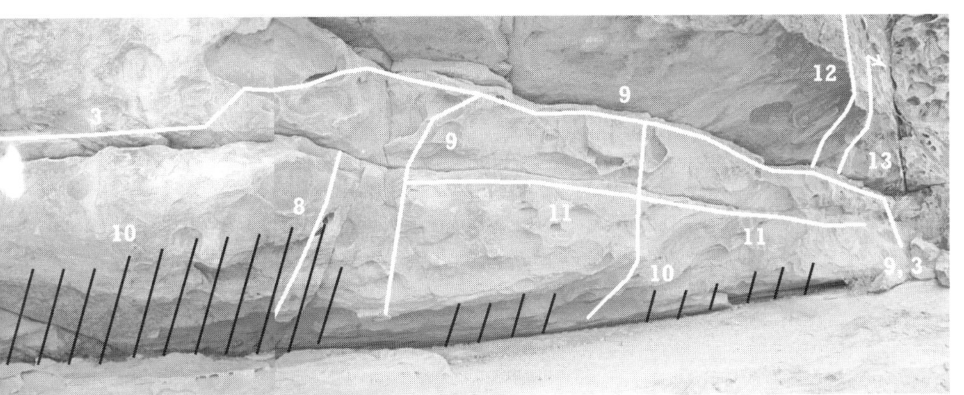

Nuclear Arms/Blood And Gore Wall

8	*The Forbidden*	11	*Blood and More*
9	*Blood and Gore*	12	*Freaks*
10	*Sinful Longings*	13	*Blood Sucking Freaks*

8 ***The Forbidden*** *4 feet V3 STAY OFF*
Just left of the seam is a beautiful red and yellow mask painting tucked in the back of the overhang about 2 feet above the ground. A crusty seam of a foothold is to its right. This was started in an undercling. Hard pulls followed eventually topping out 11 feet above ground level. PROTECT THE ROCK ART; DON'T DO THIS PROBLEM.

9 ***Blood and Gore*** *36 feet V1* ★★★
Traverse the right hand 36 feet of *Nuclear Arms*. Same grade in either direction.

10 ***Sinful Longings*** *15 feet V4* ★★ *SD*
14 feet right of the *Off Limits* seam is this good sit down problem.

11 ***Blood and More*** *36 feet V6* ★★
Traverse the wall from right to left off-routing all holds above the lower horizontal seam. Desperate individuals have added some unnecessary holds to this problem.

12 ***Freaks*** *25 feet 5.11 TR*
The roof 4 feet left of *Blood Sucking Freaks.* Loose at the lip.

13 ***Blood Sucking Freaks*** *18 feet plus escape traverse V1* ★
Start at the right end of the wall, where dirt meets slab. Climb up to the tooth in the horizontal crack beneath the roof, then climb the roof above. Traverse off right. Watch for loose holds over the lip.

The 12th Donut *35 feet 5.6* ★★
The straight up hueco line at the right end of Blood and Gore wall. Often soloed. See photo, p. 144. The large dihedral to the right of this, and the flake to its right, are easy climbs often toproped for first-timers.

TERMINATOR AREA

To find The Terminator Area, start at Double Vision Boulder (the obvious boulder with the quite overhung north face at the southwest corner of North Mountain Meadow).

Walk 75 yards due east along the south margin of the meadow. This should put you at the edge of the meadow where a grass and sotol filled 3-foot deep by 5-foot wide groove runs south across the slabs 25 yards to a bush at the horizon. Follow this groove to the bush.

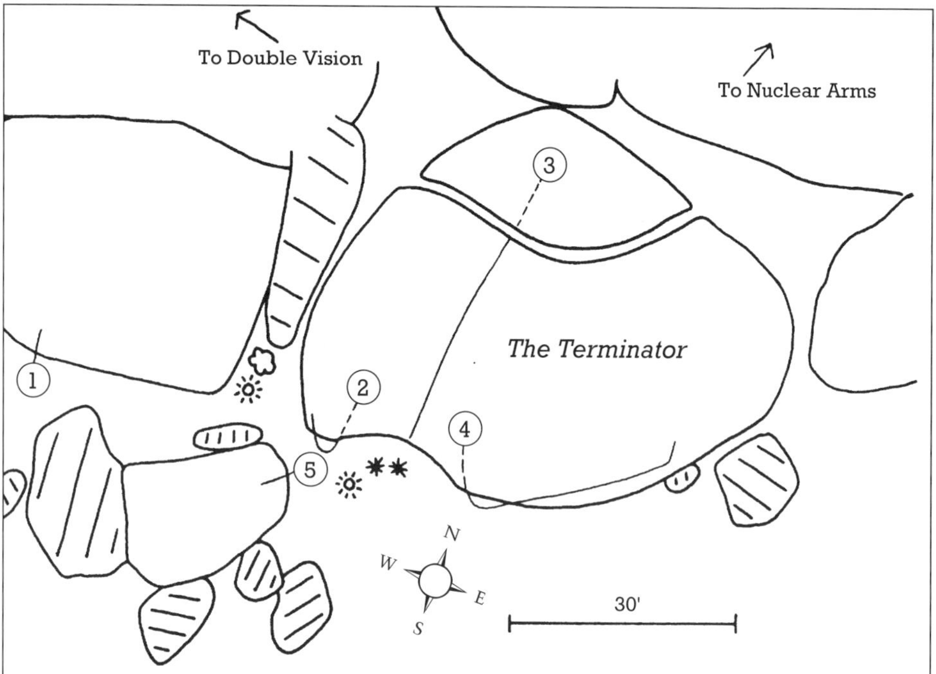

To Double Vision

To Nuclear Arms

The Terminator

30'

N W E S

Terminator Area

1 *Serious Attitude Problem 16 feet V4* ★
2 *Fuck You Asshole 18 feet V4* ★
3 *The Terminator 35 feet 5.12+ TR* ★★★
4 *The 40 Watt Range 30 feet V2* ★
5 *Dead Cat Face 12 feet V0 to V1*

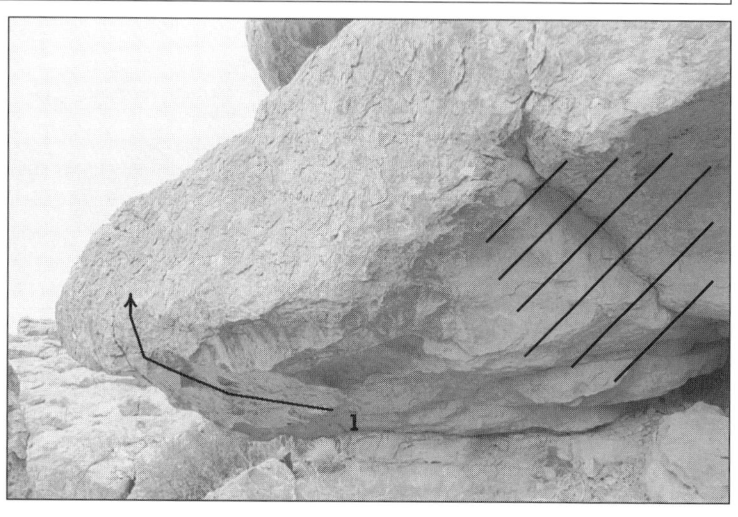

Terminator Area

1 *Serious Attitude Problem 16 feet V4* ★
Do not climb in hatched rock zone on right.

Terminator Approach

View from atop *The Grenade.* (near Nuclear Arms / Blood and Gore)

At the bush you should be able to see the flat area between North, East, and West Mountains. 12 yards to the southeast and slightly below you is the top of a boulder (though it may not look like a separate rock) split by a 12-inch wide curving crack running roughly east-west for 13 yards across the top of the rock.

This is the top of the Terminator rest chimney. Skirt this rock on its west side, dropping 15 feet down to the next level, hook a U-turn left around the rock and you should be looking at a 45-foot deep cave with an awe-inspiring crack running out the roof. This crack is *The Terminator,* a popular toprope challenge. Map, p. 130; topo, p. 150.

1 ***Serious Attitude Problem 16 feet V4 ★***

20 yards west of the *Terminator* is another overhang. A rotting seam splits this overhang on it's right. 12 feet left of this seam is a jug line out the 11 foot roof. Start in an undercling with feet at the back of the roof. Watch for loose holds over the lip. See photo on page 150.

Topo for problems 2-5 is on page 150.

2 ***Fuck You Asshole 18 feet V4 ★***

This climbs up to, then traverses left along, the finger seam on the left wall of the *Terminator* alcove.

3 ***The Terminator 35 feet 5.12+ TR ★★★***

Brutal, unforgiving, relentless - the one climb that deserves the name. Start at the back of the crack where it butts into the chimney. Starting halfway out the crack, off the low boulder, checks in at 5.12-. A spot is recommended until the climber is high enough up that a belayed fall will not cause one to swing into the sotol under the lip.

Terminator Start 10 feet V5 ★

The face start to *The Terminator* is a worthy challenge in it's own right. It has been added to The *Terminator* for an increased challenge (top roped, 5.13). Start on the fin at the back of the cave. Climb the roof to

Terminator Area

2 *Fuck You Asshole 18 feet V4 ★*
3 *The Terminator 35 feet 5.12+ TR ★★★*
4 *The 40 Watt Range 30 feet V2 ★*

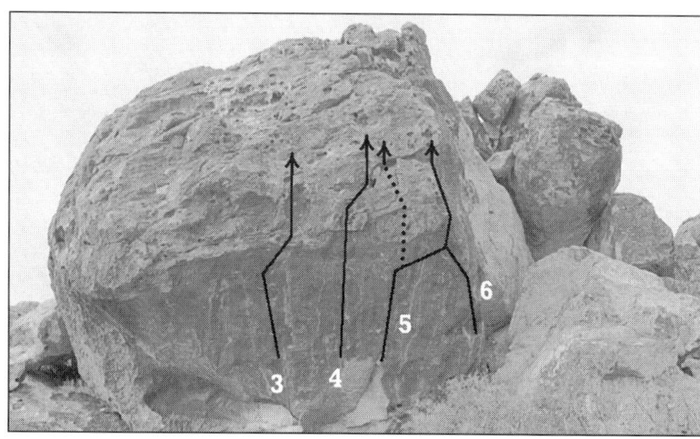

Double Vision Rock

3 *Double Vision (AKA 4 Eyes) (AKA Poke In The Eyes) 19 feet V7 ★★★*
4 *Optic Nerve 19 feet V2 ★ BL*
5 *Seka's Specialty 20 feet V2 ★★★*
6 *20-20 Hindsight 19 feet V2*

the upside down chimney rest. A large chunk of the *Terminator* crack can be safely tried unroped (a spot may be desired).

Terminator Chimney Drop 16 feet unrated

I once saw a young black boy fall out of the bottom of the *Terminator* rest chimney having obviously started from the top. To my knowledge, this feat remains unrepeated despite the large number of anorexics in the climbing community with the proper physique for this problem. Climbing up this chimney has yet to be done. It could be just the problem to hone up (or down) for *Astroman's* Harding Slot pitch.

4 *The 40 Watt Range 30 feet V2 ★*

Do the long hand traverse from left to right out the right side of the *Terminator* alcove. Start as far left as you can.

5 *Dead Cat Face 12 feet V0 to V1*

Hey Buddy, several variants have been done on the north face of this small boulder just behind the exit moves of *Fuck You Asshole.*

DOUBLE VISION ROCK AREA

The Double Vision Rock Area is the prominent boulder at the southwest end of North Mountain Meadow.

It features a very overhung north face (facing the meadow). Map, p. 130.

Slime Stone

1 *Partners In Slime 17 feet V3 BL*

The boulder directly behind (south) of Double Vision Rock has a slightly overhung offset finger seam in it's north face (in the gap between boulders).

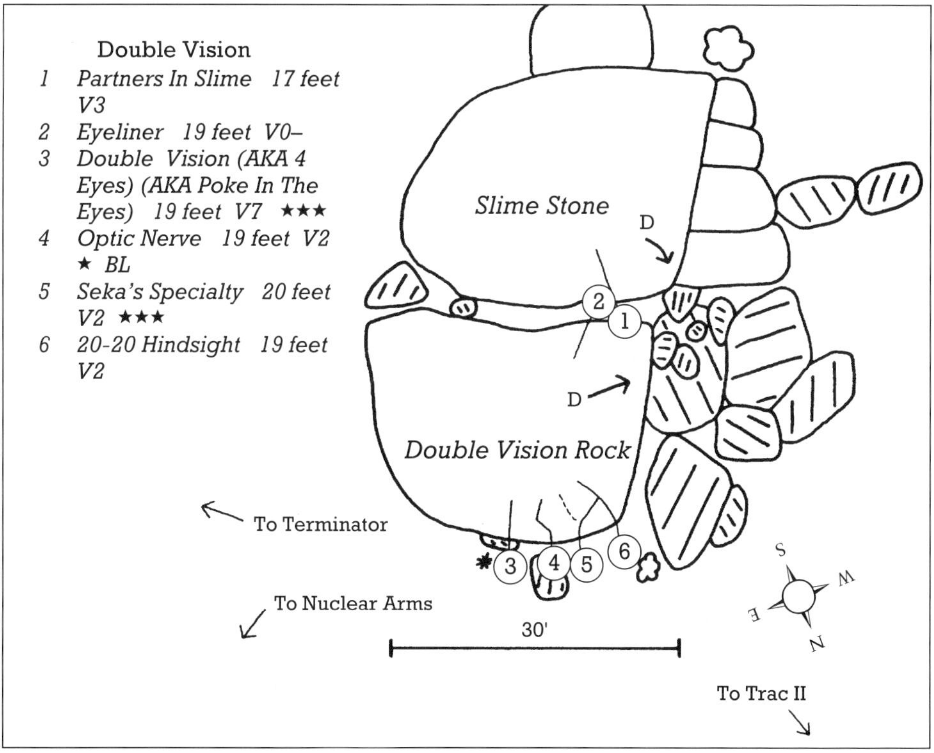

Double Vision

1 *Partners In Slime 17 feet V3*
2 *Eyeliner 19 feet V0–*
3 *Double Vision (AKA 4 Eyes) (AKA Poke In The Eyes) 19 feet V7 ★★★*
4 *Optic Nerve 19 feet V2 ★ BL*
5 *Seka's Specialty 20 feet V2 ★★★*
6 *20-20 Hindsight 19 feet V2*

Slime Stone
D
Double Vision Rock
To Terminator
To Nuclear Arms
30'
S
W
E
N
To Trac II

Double Vision Rock

2 *Eyeliner 19 feet V0– BL*
The easy companion crack across the gap from *Partners In Slime.*

3 *Double Vision (aka 4 Eyes) (aka Poke In The Eyes) 19 feet V7 ★★★*
Start off a rock at the base of the north face. Five holds have broken off, yet it still goes. Wild and intimidating. Photo on page 152.

4 *Optic Nerve 19 feet V2 ★ BL*
Start off the block fallen from the white corner. Crank ironrock wafers to the lip and a sketchy finish.

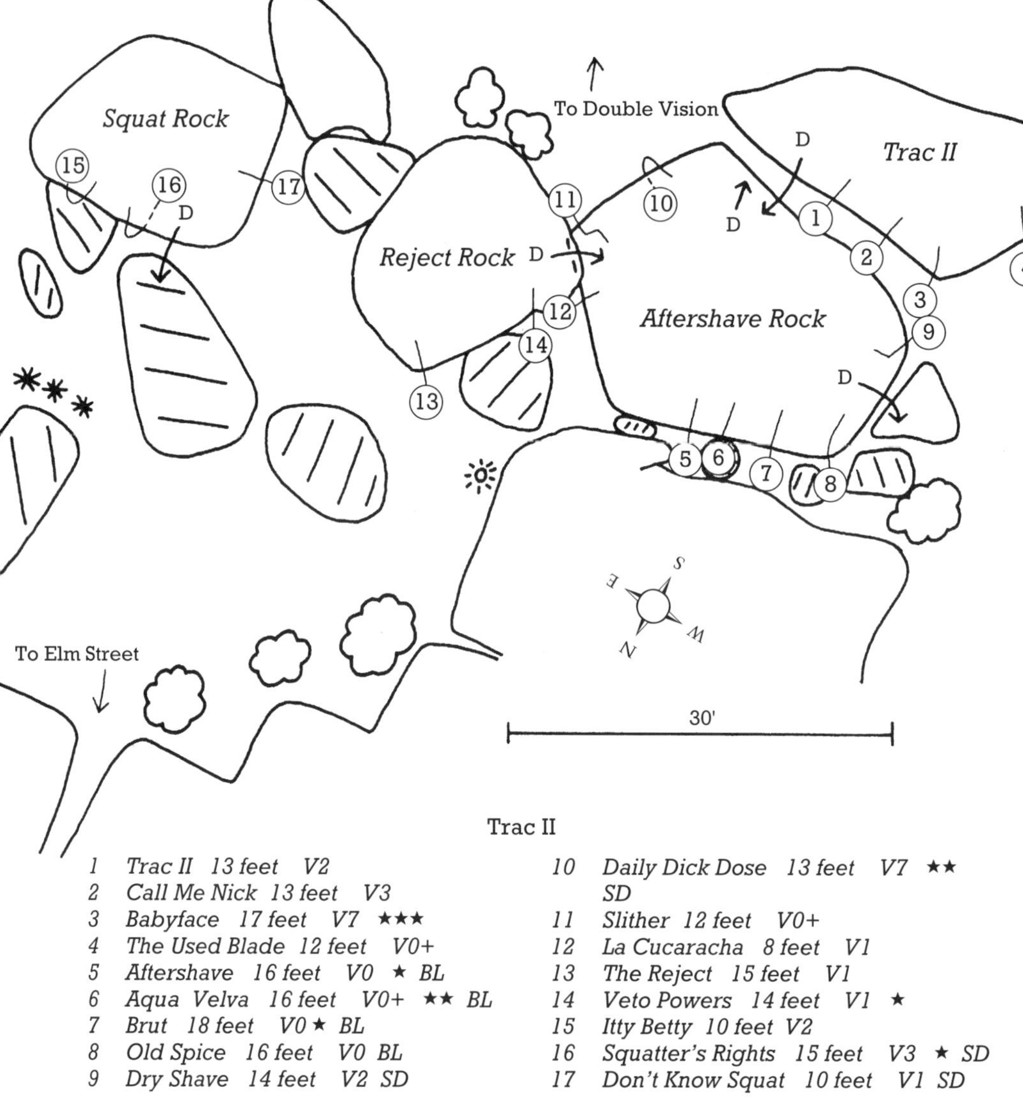

Trac II

1 *Trac II 13 feet V2*
2 *Call Me Nick 13 feet V3*
3 *Babyface 17 feet V7 ★★★*
4 *The Used Blade 12 feet V0+*
5 *Aftershave 16 feet V0 ★ BL*
6 *Aqua Velva 16 feet V0+ ★★ BL*
7 *Brut 18 feet V0 ★ BL*
8 *Old Spice 16 feet V0 BL*
9 *Dry Shave 14 feet V2 SD*
10 *Daily Dick Dose 13 feet V7 ★★ SD*
11 *Slither 12 feet V0+*
12 *La Cucaracha 8 feet V1*
13 *The Reject 15 feet V1*
14 *Veto Powers 14 feet V1 ★*
15 *Itty Betty 10 feet V2*
16 *Squatter's Rights 15 feet V3 ★ SD*
17 *Don't Know Squat 10 feet V1 SD*

Trac II Boulder
1 *Trac II 13 feet V2*
2 *Call Me Nick 13 feet V3*
3 *Babyface 17 feet V7 ★★★*
4 *The Used Blade 12 feet V0+*

5 *Seka's Specialty 20 feet V2 ★★★ scary*
Long cranks between jugs.
Variation: From the good incut (one long move up) continue straight over the roof. Photo on page 152.
6 *20-20 Hindsight 19 feet V2*

AREA 38 Map, p. 26

TRAC II ROCKS

Trac II Rocks, as well as Elm Street, lies on the rocky plateau overlooking the northwest end of North Mountain Meadow. The Trac II Boulder is 95 yards north-northwest across the meadow from Double Vision Rock. From Double Vision Rock, part of the large east facing roof on Aftershave Rock (the boulder just to the right of Trac II Boulder) can be seen. This roof is even more apparent when viewed from 20-40 yards northeast of Double Vision. Also visible, 30 yards right of Aftershave Rock, is a long boulder split by a wide crack. This is Elm Street. Map, p. 130.

Trac II Boulder

To descend hop across to Aftershave Rock and downclimb the slab on its south face.

1 *Trac II 13 feet V2*
The first blade pulls the skin tight while the second blade slices the flapper. Start off the big plate on the ground. Photo, p. 156.
2 *Call Me Nick 13 feet V3*

Aftershave Rock
5 *Aftershave 16 feet V0 ★ BL*
6 *Aqua Velva 16 feet V0+ ★★ BL*
7 *Brut 18 feet V0 ★ BL*
8 *Old Spice 16 feet V0 BL*

Trac II Boulder (left), Aftershave Rock
1 *Trac II 13 feet V2*
10 *Daily Dick Dose 13 feet V7 ★★ SD*
11 *Slither 12 feet V0+*

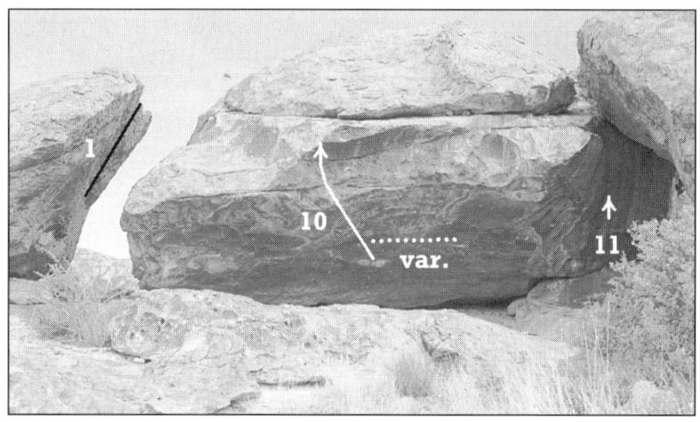

3 *Babyface 17 feet V7 ★★★*
A sit down start ups the grade to V8. Photo on page 155.
Variation 1: ***Flying Marcel 25 feet V10 ★★*** Start sitting down at a low flake/jug on the left end of the face. Traverse right and finish up *Babyface.*
Variation 2: ***Crybaby 16 feet V8 ★*** Climb the face left of *Babyface,* off-routing the arete on *Babyface.* Uses many of *Babyface's* left hand holds for the right hand. Super-sharp.

4 *The Used Blade 12 feet V0+*

Aftershave Rock

The Aftershave Wall is the north-facing wall on the Trac II descent rock. A classic ironrock face. Photo on page 155; topo, p. 154.

5 *Aftershave 16 feet V0 ★ BL*
Start on the ground at the left side of the wall. Straight up.

6 *Aqua Velva 16 feet V0+ ★★ BL*
Makes a man feel like a man. Start off the bad landing rock.

The topo for problems 7-12 is on page 154.

7 *Brut 18 feet V0 ★ BL*
Start low. Photo, p. 155.

8 *Old Spice 16 feet V0 BL*
Utilize a contrived start wedged between rocks. Photo, p. 155.

9 *Dry Shave 14 feet V2 SD*
A stupid sit down problem on Aftershave Rock, 9 feet north of *Babyface.* Climb the left side of the face right of the foot wide crack between boulders.

10 *Daily Dick Dose 13 feet V7 ★★ SD*
Start sitting down, with hands on holds left of "Alma".
Variation: ***Zuluflex 14 feet V6 ★*** Traverse into *Daily Dick Dose* from the right starting on a wide, but thin horizontal flake.

11 *Slither 12 feet V0+*
Start 12 feet right of *Daily Dick Dose.* Reject Rock is off-route.

12 *La Cucaracha 8 feet V1*
7 yards right of *Daily Dick Dose,* climb through the right hand gap between Aftershave Rock and Reject Rock.

Reject Rock

Reject Rock leans against the east side of Aftershave Rock. Topo, p. 154.

13 *The Reject 15 feet V1*
Climb the left side of the northwest face 3 feet right of the north arete. A tough, butt-

Squat Rock

15 Itty Betty 10 feet V2

16 Squatter's Rights 15 feet V3 ★ SD

dragging sit down start traversing in from the right (sometimes called P*umped Full Of Semen*) received only one or two ascents before it was retrochiseled.

14 Veto Powers 14 feet V1 ★
Start on a left-facing flake just under the lip of the northwest face. Over the lip is a left-facing corner. Carefully avoiding the boulder to your left, yard into the corner and layback to the top.

Squat Rock

This short rock is 5 yards northeast of Reject Rock. Topo, p. 154.

15 Itty Betty 10 feet V2
Start low at base of roof.

16 Squatter's Rights 15 feet V3 ★ SD
Start sitting down on a scooped grey ledge 3 feet off the ground.

17 Don't Know Squat 10 feet V1 SD
Start sitting down with hands in the horizontal crack at the lip of the west facing cave on the *Squatter's Rights* boulder. Up and left to a loose, flaky lip encounter.

Elm Street

1 Bowl Bound 25 feet V4 SD

2 Sleep Disorder 20 feet V2

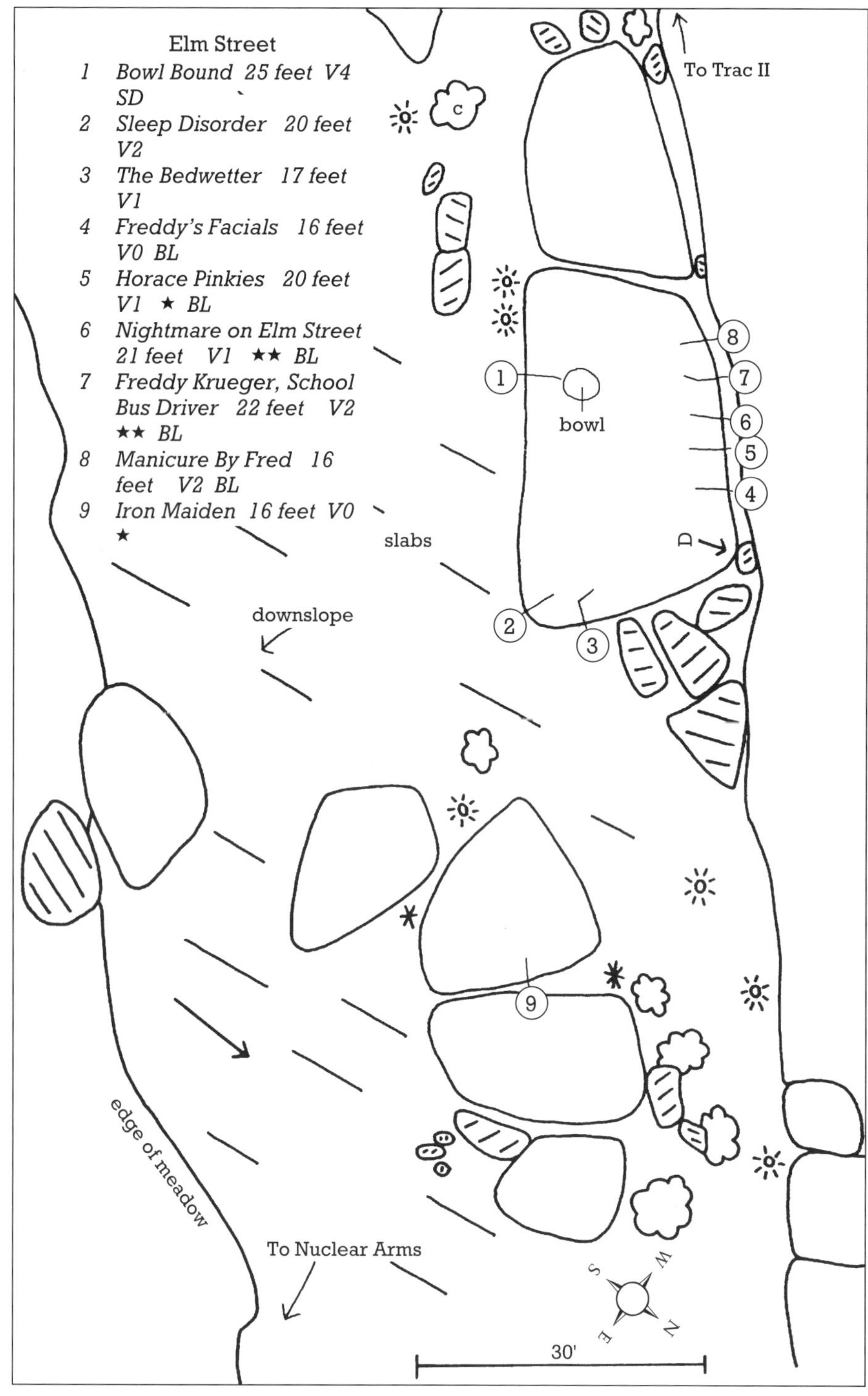
Elm Street
1 Bowl Bound 25 feet V4 SD
2 Sleep Disorder 20 feet V2
3 The Bedwetter 17 feet V1
4 Freddy's Facials 16 feet V0 BL
5 Horace Pinkies 20 feet V1 ★ BL
6 Nightmare on Elm Street 21 feet V1 ★★ BL
7 Freddy Krueger, School Bus Driver 22 feet V2 ★★ BL
8 Manicure By Fred 16 feet V2 BL
9 Iron Maiden 16 feet V0 ★
To Trac II
c
bowl
D
slabs
downslope
edge of meadow
To Nuclear Arms
W
S
N
E
30'

Elm Street

Left:

4 *Freddy's Facials 16 feet V0 BL*

5 *Horace Pinkies 20 feet V1 ★ BL*

6 *Nightmare on Elm Street 21 feet V1 ★★ BL*

7 *Freddy Krueger, School Bus Driver 22 feet V2 ★★ BL*

8 *Manicure By Fred 16 feet V2 BL*

Below:

2 *Sleep Disorder 20 feet V2*

3 *The Bedwetter 17 feet V1*

ELM STREET

Elm Street is a huge 75 foot long by 25 foot tall by 20 foot wide split boulder 36 yards northeast of Trac II Boulder on the same level. Map, p. 130; topo, p. 158.

1 ***Bowl Bound* 25 feet V4 SD**

2 ***Sleep Disorder* 20 feet V2**
At the far right end of the southeast face climb the left side of the prow from a sit down start.

3 ***The Bedwetter* 17 feet V1**
6 feet right of *Sleep Disorder,* on the northeast face, climb huecos and flakes up the wall left of the bush.

The northwest face rises menacingly out of a dark chimney that provides a bad landing, but convenient chickening out via a quick stem behind you. Five routes are on this face.

4 ***Freddy's Facials* 16 feet V0 BL**
This starts in the chimney, not at it's base.

5 ***Horace Pinkies* 20 feet V1 ★ BL**
Starting from the ground as far left as practical, climb straight up to big huecos at the very top.

6 ***Nightmare on Elm Street* 21 feet V1 ★★ BL**
Start on the ground. Ironrock at it's best. A small boulder under the wall, visible only from the base, marks the start.

7 ***Freddy Krueger, School Bus Driver* 22 feet V2 ★★ BL**
Start on the ground as far right as practical.

8 ***Manicure By Fred* 16 feet V2 BL**
Start in the chimney with hands on a tan streaked flake.

9 ***Iron Maiden* 16 feet V0 ★**
Climb great ironrock up the overhanging wall inside the tight chimney between the two large boulders east of Elm Street.

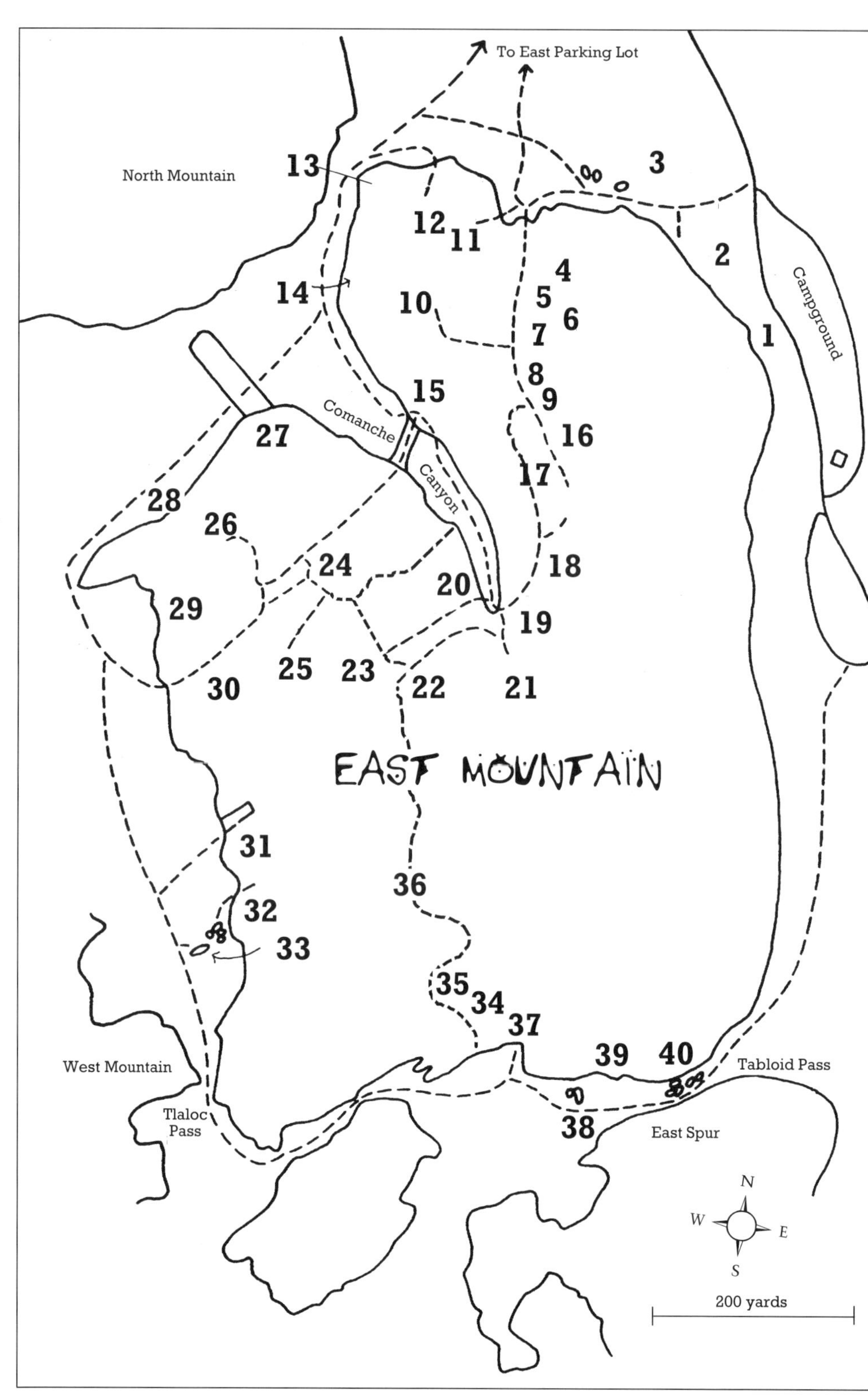
To East Parking Lot
North Mountain
Campground
Comanche
Canyon
EAST MOUNTAIN
West Mountain
Tlaloc Pass
Tabloid Pass
East Spur
N
W
E
S
200 yards
1
2
3
4
5
6
7
8
9
10
11
12
13
14
15
16
17
18
19
20
21
22
23
24
25
26
27
28
29
30
31
32
33
34
35
36
37
38
39
40

EAST MOUNTAIN

Descriptions go counterclockwise around East Mountain, starting at the campground. If you aren't registered for the campground, you may not park there. Most of the East Mountain areas are easily approached from the East parking lot. The Tabloid Boulders, Donkey Show Boulder, Mantle Illness Center and the south side of East Mountain are most quickly approached by walking on the trail south from the campground through the pass between East Mountain and East Spur (Tabloid Pass).

CAMPGROUND

There are several boulders in the campground, but the bouldering on them is marginal and besides the sites they're in are often occupied. Nevertheless, there is one good problem behind site #4 that doesn't infringe on campers' privacy.

Happy Camper 12 feet V4
★
10 yards west of site #4's picnic table is a low slab, 4 feet thick and flanked by bushes. Underneath this slab on it's west (uphill) side, invisible from site 4, is an 11 foot roof. Start on the lowest jug on the left. Crank out and right to the lip via jugs, a thin hold, and a wafer more deeply incut than one might wish.

The Star-eyed Man, somewhere on East Mountain.

EAST MOUNTAIN CLIMBING AREAS DIRECTORY

Oak Tree Wall
1 Bud The Chud

OAK TREE WALL

The Oak Tree Wall is located 40 yards west of campsite #1, and 30 yards southeast of the Amphitheater Rock (Amputator). It's hidden from view of the trail between site #1 and the Amphitheater by a 20 foot tall boulder called Chudstone. This 20 high boulder has a concrete slab at the base of it's north face. Behind Chudstone is the north facing Oak Tree Wall. It's two thin vertical face climbs are reminiscent of granite bouldering; good foot work is essential for success.

Chudstone

1 Bud The Chud 20 feet V0+ loose

Oak Tree Wall

2 Dueling Dicks 18 feet V3 ★

3 Escape From Planet Dread 18 feet V2 ★
Climb the wall 8 feet left of the right oak.

Oak Tree Wall
2 Dueling Dicks
3 Escape From Planet Dread

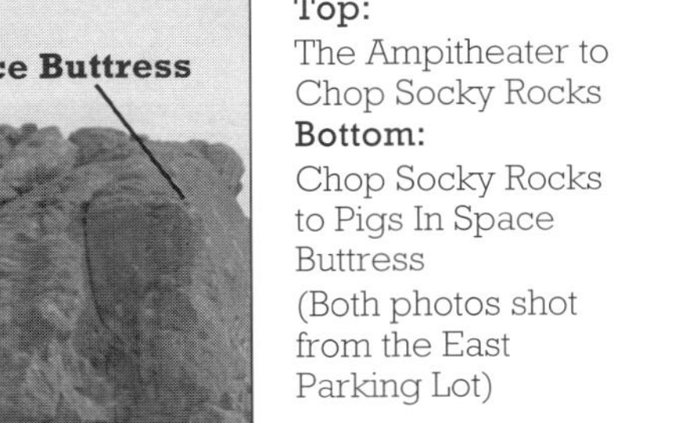

Top: The Ampitheater to Chop Socky Rocks
Bottom: Chop Socky Rocks to Pigs In Space Buttress
(Both photos shot from the East Parking Lot)

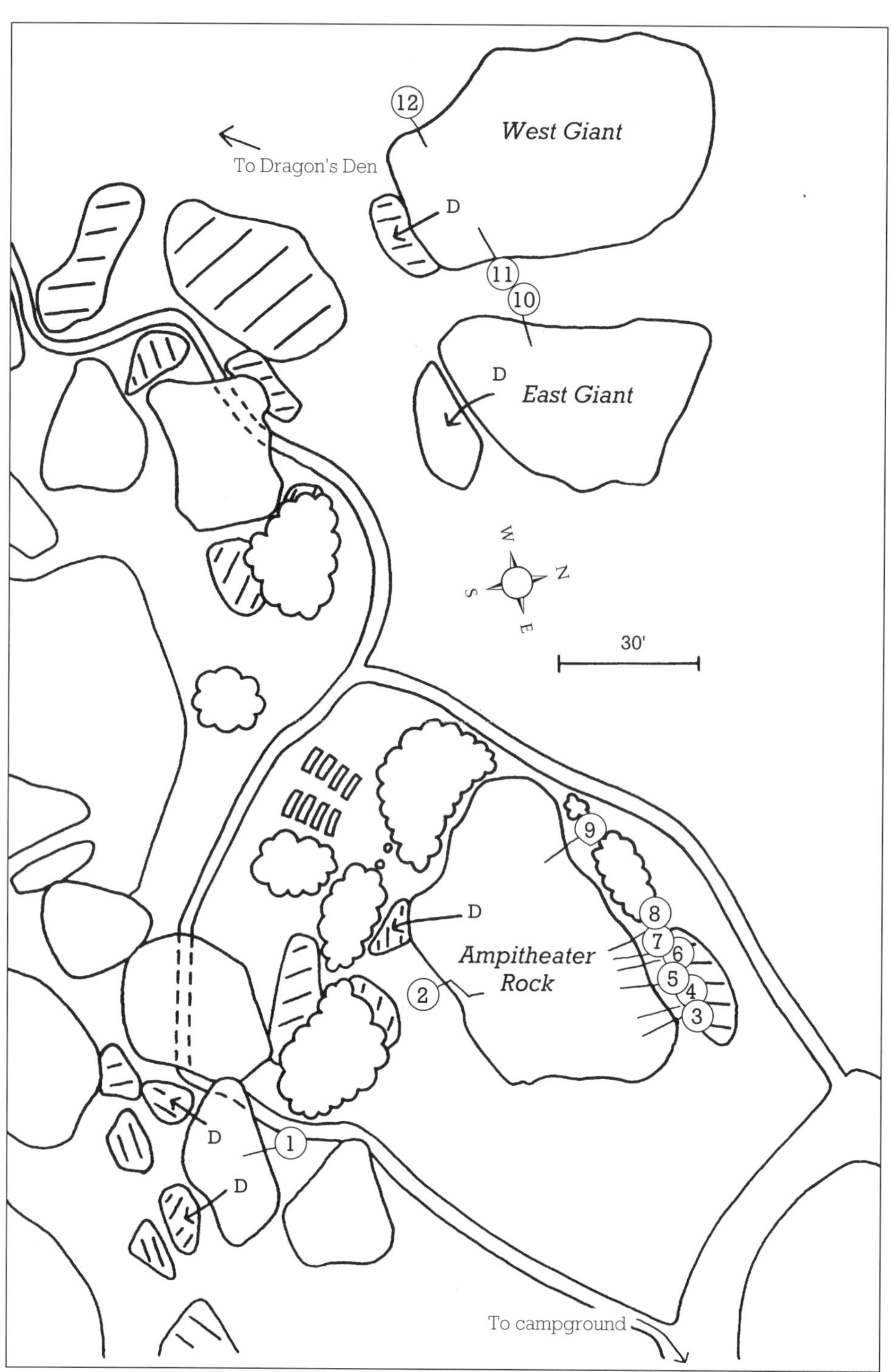

12
West Giant
To Dragon's Den
D
11
10
D
East Giant
W
N
S
E
30'
9
D
8
7
6
Ampitheater
Rock
5
4
3
2
D
1
D
To campground

Ampitheater Rock

2 Amputator 17 feet V3 ★

THE AMPHITHEATER

To get to the Amphitheater, start where the road enters the campground. Near the fork in the road, (Keep Right sign) is a rock lined path heading northwest. This path leads to the Amphitheater. Keep an eye out for the amphitheater sign on your left after 90 yards.

East Mountain

1 Opening Act 13 feet V4

25 yards along the trail west from the amphitheater sign the trail ducks between two rocks. The rock to the left (east) has a thin face problem in the middle of its north face. A six inch wide, first digit flake 6 feet up is the opening hold.

After ducking under the rocks the trail soon takes you to the Amphitheater and it's 8 split log benches. Two metal posts are standing where they once supported a slide screen. The humongous boulder behind and left of these posts is Amphitheater Rock. The small boulder behind the posts is the descent rock.

Amphitheater Rock

2 Amputator 17 feet V3 ★

Behind the metal posts, duck through the gap between rocks to access the cavernous south face of Amphitheater Rock. Climb blocky flakes up the overhang then karate chop the amputator jam out to the right to gain the final 4 foot right facing corner. Tape is recommended if you can't crank the crux statically.

The Ampitheater (topo at left)

1 Opening Act 13 feet V4
2 Amputator 17 feet V3 ★
3 Mr. Salty 17 feet V1
4 Maggots Are Falling Like Rain 18 feet V2 ★
5 Crack Deal 18 feet V0+ ★
6 Pusherman 18 feet V1 ★
7 Dirty Deeds 18 feet V1
8 Sex Packet 15 feet V0+ ★
9 Biochemically Compacted Sexual Affection 20 feet V0–
10 Mucho Loose-O 25 feet V0–
11 Pacific Sock Exchange 23 feet V0
12 Mouthful Of Vapo-Rub 9 feet V1

Ampitheater Rock

3	*Mr. Salty 17 feet V1*	6	*Pusherman 18 feet V1* ★
4	*Maggots Are Falling Like Rain*	7	*Dirty Deeds 18 feet V1*
5	*Crack Deal 18 feet V0+* ★	8	*Sex Packet 15 feet V0+* ★

3 *Mr. Salty 17 feet V1*

4 *Maggots Are Falling Like Rain 18 feet V2* ★

5 *Crack Deal 18 feet V0+* ★

6 *Pusherman 18 feet V1* ★

Climb the wall 3 feet right of the thin crack (the crack is off-route) via a midway mantle.

7 *Dirty Deeds 18 feet V1*

8 *Sex Packet 15 feet V0+* ★

Climb the wall above the scraggly bush 10 feet right of the thin crack. Some scrubbing would add an extra star to this.

9 *Biochemically Compacted Sexual Affection 20 feet V0–*

The right side of the north face. Start behind mesquite bushes at a head size hueco 5 feet up. Up and left along big flakes to the top.

The Giants

The Giants are the two enormous 25 foot tall boulders 30 and 50 yards northwest of the amphitheater. Topo, p. 164.

10 *Mucho Loose-O 25 feet V0–*

Walk up the west face of the East Giant.

11 *Pacific Sock Exchange 23 feet V0*

Climb the flaky east face of the West Giant.

12 *Mouthful Of Vapo-Rub 9 feet V1*

Mantle the lowest point on the lip of the west face's fire blackened cave.

Southwest and above the amphitheater is a lot of potential bouldering, mostly with bad landings. So far only a few problems have been done here. The adventurous reader is encouraged to explore this area without help from this guide. Descriptions resume at the Dragon's Den.

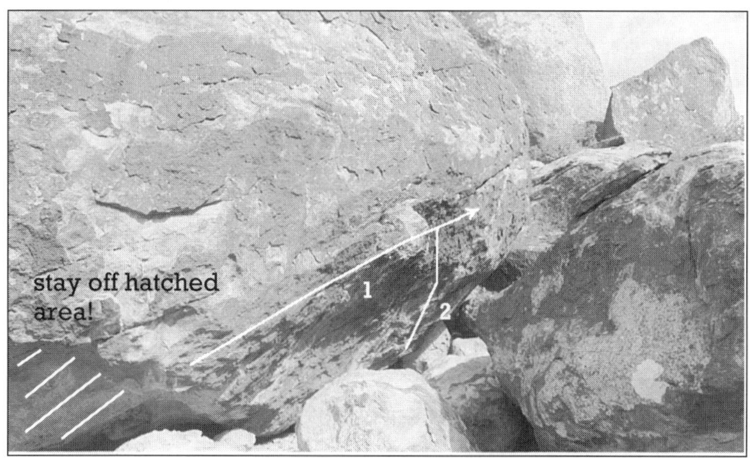

Camel's Back Boulder

1 *Camel's Back 25 feet V5* 2 *Tall People In A Blender 10 feet V5*

THE DRAGON'S DEN

The Dragon's Den boulders are located atop the major gully between the campground and the pass between East and North Mountains. This is the first gully west of the Amphitheater. Photo, p. 163.

Camel's Back Boulder

The Camel's Back Boulder is located at the bottom of the Dragon's Den approach gully on the left (east) side.

1 *Camel's Back 25 feet V5*
Beware of rock art to left of start.

2 *Tall People In A Blender 10 feet V5 SD*
Much harder if you're tall.

AREA 4
MAP, P. 160

DRAGON'S BOULDER AREA

From the East Parking Lot, the most striking feature of the Dragon's Den is a 50 foot tall boulder with a 30 foot tall, 6 foot thick flake leaning against it's east side. This is Dragon's Boulder and is on the east side of the approach gully. The base of this boulder is 50 feet above ground level.

1 *The Clawmarks 11 feet V0+*

2 *On Your Knees 14 feet V0+ ★ SD*

3 *Jugs 14 feet V0-*

4 *Rubberman 14 feet V3 ★*
On the same wall as Jugs, start under the big hanging block. Move up and left to big sloping horn then topout left of the hanging block.

5 *Dragon Lotion 50 feet 5.10 X*
Descend the outside of the leaning flake to the east.

Independent States

This is the first group of boulders east of Dragon's Boulder. Photos, pp. 168, 169.

1 *Half-pint 11 feet V2*

2 *Jerry's Not Home 14 feet V4 ★ SD*

3 *Instant Classic 14 feet V3 ★ SD*

Dragon's Boulder

1 *The Clawmark*
2 *On Your Knees*
3 *Jugs*
4 *Rubberman*
5 *Dragon Lotion*

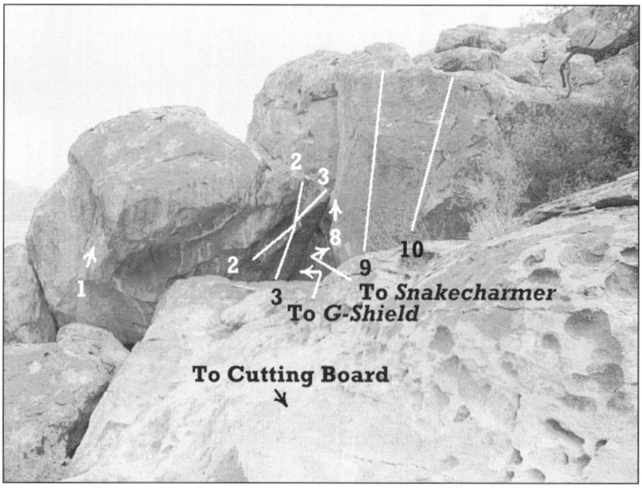

Independent States (viewed from near Cutting Board)

1 *Half-pint 11 feet V2*
2 *Jerry's Not Home 14 feet V4 ★ SD*
3 *Instant Classic 14 feet V3 ★ SD*
8 *Pistons Of Flesh*
9 *Crisis Of The Humanities*
10 *Johnny Butt*

The finishes to *Jerry's Not Home* and *Instant Classic* can be swapped without affecting the grade of either problem... or finish between the two finishes.

4 *Hat Trick 14 feet V4 ★ BL scary*

5 *The Snakecharmer 17 feet V7 ★★★ BL*
Start low, with hands on a 1-inch thick hueco lip 4 feet up. Up the brown rock 3 to 4 feet left of the arête. Freaky.

6 *The Anti-Hueco 16 feet V3*
The flake crack to the right is off route.

7 *Conservative Backlash 18 feet V1 ★*
Arête to the right is off route.

8 *Pistons Of Flesh 17 feet V0*
The arête.

9 *Crisis Of The Humanities 18 feet V0*

10 *Johnny Butt 16 feet V0-*

11 *Fear Of Frying 20 feet V0+ BL*

12 *The G-Shield 21 feet V1 ★ BL*

13 *The Hitman 22 feet V0+ ★ BL*

14 *Do You Feel Lucky? 22 feet V3 ★★★ BL scary*
Well do you, Punk? Start on incut flakes 6 feet up. Up and right to horizontal crack then up past "see-thru death flake" to the top. For Hueco Tanks experts only.

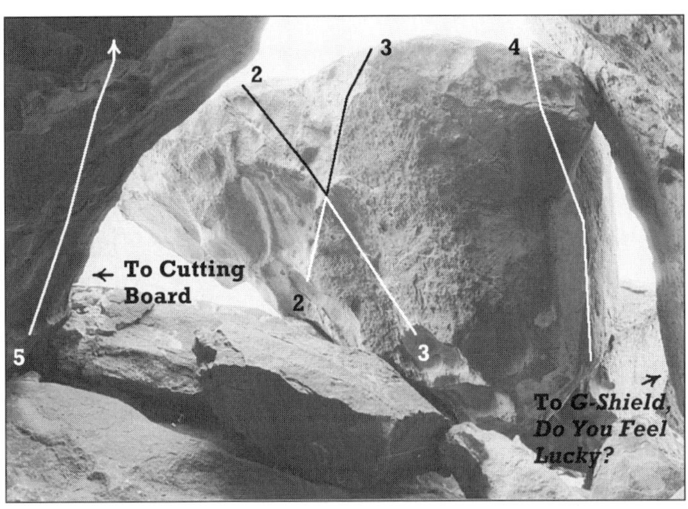

Independent States
Left:
2 *Jerry's Not Home 14 feet V4 ★ SD*
3 *Instant Classic 14 feet V3 ★ SD*
4 *Hat Trick 14 feet V4 ★ BL scary*
5 *Snakecharmer 17 feet V7 ★★★ BL*
Below:
5 *Snakecharmer*
6 *The Anti-Hueco 16 feet V3*
7 *Conservative Backlash 18 feet V1*

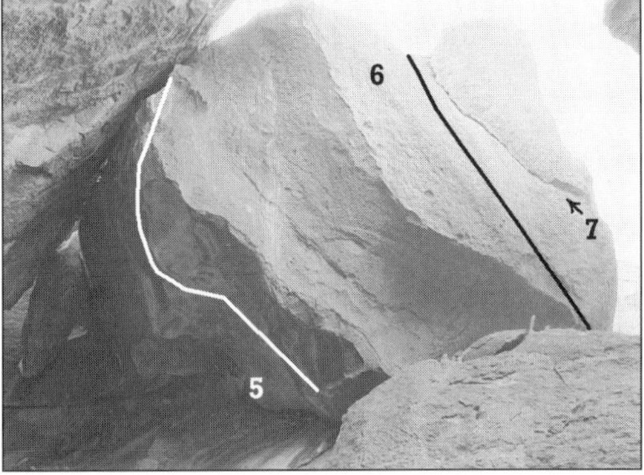

Independent States
Above:
11 *Fear Of Frying 20 feet V0+ BL*
12 *The G-Shield 21 feet V1 ★ BL*
13 *The Hitman 22 feet V0+ ★ BL*
Right:
14 *Do You Feel Lucky? 22 feet V3 ★★★ BL scary*

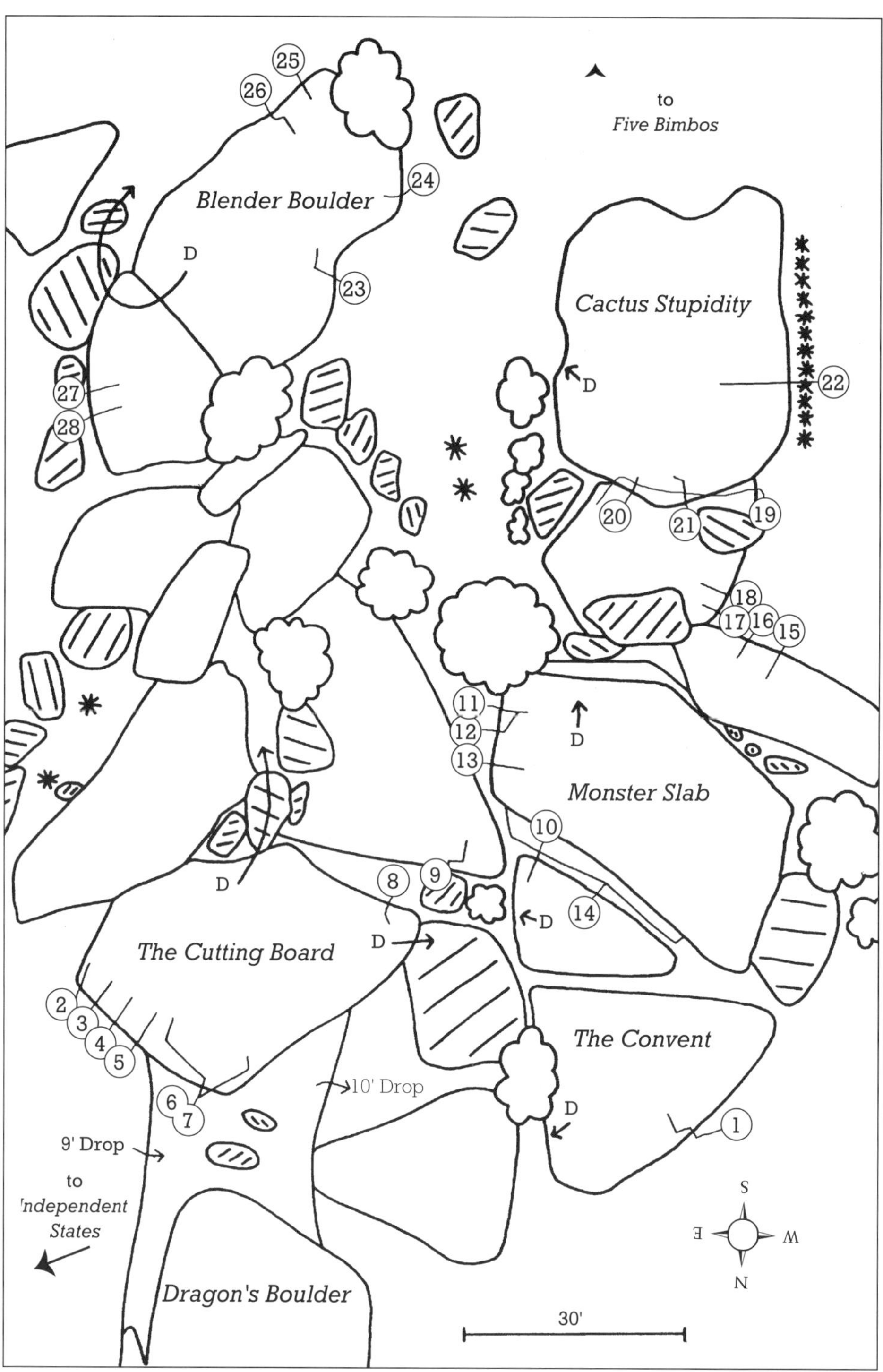

to
Five Bimbos
Blender Boulder
Cactus Stupidity
Monster Slab
The Cutting Board
The Convent
Dragon's Boulder
10' Drop
9' Drop
to
Independent
States
D
S
E
W
N
30'
1
2
3
4
5
6
7
8
9
10
11
12
13
14
15
16
17
18
19
20
21
22
23
24
25
26
27
28

The Convent
1 Nuns With The Runs

NORTH CENTRAL DRAGON'S DEN

The large boulder 8 yards south of Dragon's Boulder is The Cutting Board. An abundance of solid ironrock razors grace it's overhanging northeast face. The easiest approach line stays on the slabs in the gully until two junipers are reached near the top of the gully. 8 yards left (north) of the junipers is a boulder with a long flake running out a roof and an obvious trail running by the base. This boulder is the Convent. The best approach to the Cutting Board skirts the north end of The Convent. 25 yards south of the two junipers is Cactus Stupidity Rock, with a line of sotols and yuccas beneath its west face.

The Convent

1 *Nuns With The Runs 16 feet V1*
Nothing solid about this one. Hand traverse left out the flake, then say your prayers at the lip. Every bit as bad as its name.

North Central Dragon's Den (topo at left)

1 *Nuns With The Runs 16 feet V1*
2 *Sledge-O-Matic 10 feet V1 BL*
3 *Veg-O-Matic 11 feet V0+ ★*
4 *Butterknife 13 feet V2 ★*
5 *The Ginsu Wall 14 feet V4 ★★ BL scary*
6 *The Banzai Knife 24 feet V6 ★★★ BL*
7 *Folding Hunter 26 feet V4 BL scary*
8 *The Leftover 13 feet V0*
9 *Seedless 11 feet V1*
10 *The Backslabber 16 feet V0+*
11 *The Monster Mash 17 feet V3*
12 *The Monstrosity 18 feet V4*
13 *The Succubus 20 feet 5.12+ TR ★*
14 *The Monster Slab 20-25 feet V0 ★★*
15 *The Prankster 17 feet 5.12 TR*
16 *The Snap 16 feet 5.12+ TR*
17 *Mumblety-peg 15 feet 5.11+ TR*
18 *The Skinny 17 feet 5.13- TR*
19 *So Damn Insane 50 feet V5*
20 *Pushy, Pushy 8 feet V0*
21 *Obtuse As A Dog 13 feet V3*
22 *Cactus Stupidity 28 feet 5.12 TR ★*
23 *The Osterizer 15 feet V2 ★*
24 *Tri Hard 15 feet V4 ★*
25 *The Ostracizer 16 feet V2 SD*
26 *Hobbit In A Blender 15 feet V5 ★★★*
27 *Brutus 13 feet V5*
28 *The Ides Of March 16 feet V6 SD BL scary.*

The Cutting Board
2 *Sledge-O-Matic*
3 *Veg-O-Matic*
4 *The Butterknife*
5 *The Ginsu Wall*
6 *The Banzai Knife*
7 *Folding Hunter*

The Cutting Board

Map on page 170.

2 *Sledge-O-Matic 10 feet V1 BL*
Climb the left arête of the northeast face starting as low as you can.

3 *Veg-O-Matic 11 feet V0+* ★
Start where the arête meets the base.

4 *The Butterknife 13 feet V2* ★
Tall folks should start from the lower block for full value.

5 *The Ginsu Wall 14 feet V4* ★★ *BL scary*
A faint black streak descending from a flake on the summit marks the line. Sharp, scary, bad landing. A V10 sit down start, *Man Gum,* received but one ascent before several grades were chiseled out.

6 *The Banzai Knife 24 feet V6* ★★★ *BL*
What rating would you give to a problem that starts with 13 feet of severely overhung razors? Don't answer yet, because you also get 12 feet of pumping serrated flake traversing up and left. And there's still more, the crux is firing for the lip. All this for a bargain V6 rating and as a free bonus gift, we'll toss in a sloping mantle to top it off. Scary, but the elevated bad landing is thankfully only 12 feet below the lip. Start 2 feet left of the rounded prow.

7 *Folding Hunter 26 feet V4 BL scary*
Start as for *The Banzai Knife,* but cast off right to the big flake on the arête. Hand traverse this around the corner until it's easy to go up. This can also be started to the right, on the rounded prow.

8 *The Leftover 13 feet V0*
A south facing wall helps form the westernmost tip of the Cutting Board Boulder. Climb the south face 6 feet right of it's left end. This problem is at the lowest point of the Cutting Board Boulder, down a level from the northeast face problems.

9 *Seedless 11 feet V1*
10 feet south of the Cutting Board Boulder's westmost tip (its lowest point) is an undercut north facing ironrock wall. Climb the right side starting off a boulder to grab the watermelon size hueco.

Monster Slab

Monster Slab Boulder's south side lies 10 yards north of Cactus Stupidity Rock. Its north side is 10 yards southwest of the western tip of The Cutting Board Boulder. Monster Slab Boulder has a terrific 20-25 foot ironrock slab coming out of the chimney on it's north side.

Monster Slab

10	*The Backslabber*	12	*The Monstrosity*
11	*The Monster Mash*	13	*The Succubus*

10 *The Backslabber 16 feet V0+*
Actually on the boulder north of Monster Slab Boulder, starting in the same chimney as Monster Slab. Climb the right side of the south face starting at the 5 foot tall hueco.

11 *The Monster Mash 17 feet V3*

12 *The Monstrosity 18 feet V4*

13 *The Succubus 20 feet 5.12+ TR* ★

14 *The Monster Slab 20-25 feet V0* ★★
The north face can be climbed anywhere at the V0 grade, with the exception of the far left side which requires a V2 move to clear the initial overhang and gain the slab. Bad landing. Top ropes recommended for beginners.

The Little Demons

These four short toprope problems are on the west sides of the two short boulders between the Monster Slab and Cactus Stupidity Rock.

15 *The Prankster 17 feet 5.12 TR*

16 *The Snap 16 feet 5.12+ TR*
Lunge for a dubious looking hold.

17 *Mumblety-peg 15 feet 5.11+ TR*
The shortest toprope in the book, inspired by the sotol at the base. Climb the incut flakes just right of the notch between boulders.

18 *The Skinny 17 feet 5.13- TR*
Superthin problem just right of Mumblety-peg.

Cactus Stupidity Rock

This rock has a dozen sotols lining the base of its triangular (point down) west face. Named after the Euros who were assured by a famous U.S. hangdog that they'd be loved by all if they illegally bolted down the 28-foot west face top rope into a "sport" lead. Rather than provoking adulation, their actions led to a ban on all roped climbing in the park. What a bunch of geeks. Descend the groove down the middle of the east face by the juniper.

19 *So Damn Insane 50 feet V5*
Hand traverse the flake right into the A-frame tunnel then traverse the length of the tunnel until one pops out the east end. Will deserve a star once it gets cleaned off.

Monster Slab, Little Demons, Cactus Stupidity

15 The Prankster 17 feet 5.12 TR
16 The Snap 16 feet 5.12+ TR
19 So Damn Insane 50 feet V5
22 Cactus Stupidity 28 feet 5.12 TR ★

---

20 Pushy, Pushy 8 feet V0
Start on top of the large boulder supporting the north face, 7 feet right of dropping off the base boulder's left side, and 5 feet left of a Y-shaped seam. An 8 inch long seam angles into the lip at this point. Mantle the lip just right of the seam.

21 Obtuse As A Dog 13 feet V3
Start 6 feet right of the base of the Y-seam. An off-route boulder is one foot to your right. Strenuous pulls work up into the obtuse dihedral above.

22 Cactus Stupidity 28 feet 5.12 TR ★

Blender Boulder

23 The Osterizer 15 feet V2 ★

24 Tri Hard 15 feet V4 ★

25 The Ostracizer 16 feet V2 SD
Climb the hollow flake out the left side of the southeast overhang.

26 Hobbit In A Blender 15 feet V5 ★★★
Where they belong. Start low on two finger holds a foot apart and 5 feet above the dirt. Was V5 before someone chiseled the starting hold.

27 Brutus 13 feet V5
Start on flake 6 feet up.

28 The Ides Of March 16 feet V6 SD BL scary.
Beware. Incut starter hold is 4 feet up.

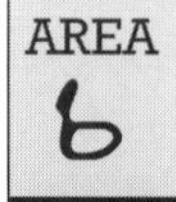

MAP, P. 160

DRAGON'S WALL

Dragon's Wall is the obvious 60-foot tall, west-facing wall east of the Dragon's Den. See photo on page 163.

1 Bob's Day Off 40 feet 5.11+
From the beginning of the left angling crack on the left side of Dragon's Wall, move up to a bolt then continue straight up. 4 bolts.

2 Short Dihedral 35 feet 5.9

Blender Boulder

23 *The Osterizer*

24 *Tri Hard*

Blender Boulder

25 *The Ostracizer*

26 *Hobbit In A Blender*

27 *Brutus*

28 *The Ides Of March*

Dragon's Wall and Dragon's Den

1 *Bob's Day Off* 40 feet 5.11+
2 *Short Dihedral* 35 feet 5.9
3 *Danger Bird* 55 feet 5.11+ ★
4 *Dangling Nerd* 60 feet 5.11– TR ★
5 *Ranger Turd* 60 feet 5.11+ TR
6 *The Skidmark* 60 feet 5.11+ TR
7 *Dragon's Breath* 60 feet 5.12 TR
8 *Tlaloc Straight Up* 60 feet 5.12
9 *Tlaloc* 60 feet 5.12– TR ★★
10 *A Dog's Life* 60 feet 5.12 TR ★
11 *Dog Legs And Feet* 55 feet 5.10+ ★★
12 *Save And Gain With Lobo* 55 feet 5.6
13 *Krispy Kritters* 55 feet 5.11 TR
14 *Dragon's Waltz* 55 feet 5.8
15 *Death And Texas* 55 feet 5.10

3 ***Danger Bird* 55 feet 5.11+ ★**
This takes a line 10 to 15 feet right of the black water streak on the northwest facing wall. Start directly at the overhanging base on unprotected 5.10 moves, or use the easier crack in the shallow left-facing dihedral to the left. Traverse right, then straight up past two horizontal cracks. 5 feet above the second horizontal is a bolt. Climb from the bolt to the left-facing overhanging dihedral. From the last bolt the route takes two variations over the bulge. The right-hand way is slightly easier than the left, but both are the crux of the climb.

4 ***Dangling Nerd* 60 feet 5.11– TR ★**
Climb up to *Danger Bird's* second horizontal crack, then traverse it right to a ledge on the edge of the buttress. Climb the brown streak up the buttress above. There is a single bolt at the base of the streak, used to back off on a failed lead attempt.

5 ***Ranger Turd* 60 feet 5.11+ TR**
Do the same start as *Dangling Nerd* to gain the ledge. Move right 10 feet from *Dangling Nerd* then climb the plates above. Finish up the brown streak 13 feet right of *Dangling Nerd.*

6 ***The Skidmark* 60 feet 5.11+ TR**
This follows a brown streak 10 feet right of the guano stained wide crack splitting Dragon's Wall. Start at a rotten roof crack or on big flakes 8 feet right of the roof crack. Either way, reach the horizontal crack above. Traverse this left to a vertical corner crack, or go straight up the face to the big ledge above. From the ledge follow the brown streak up.

7 ***Dragon's Breath* 60 feet 5.12 TR**
Use any route to gain the big ledge 25 feet up. Climb the left side of the concave wall above. Follow the right border of the grey streak. This will be much harder after a few key holds snap.

8 ***Tlaloc Straight Up* 60 feet 5.12 ★★**
Start as for *Tlaloc,* doing the same crux section 25 feet up, then instead of following the buttress to the right, climb left of it, up the right side of the concave face. The top section, though not the crux, is harder than the the top of *Tlaloc.*

9 ***Tlaloc* 60 feet 5.12– TR ★★**
15 yards left of *Save And Gain With Lobo,* climb a bulge 13 feet up, then instead of stepping left along the easy ramp, follow the left angling seam above the bulge. Finish up the bulging buttress on the right side of the concave wall above. A huge hanging flake 25 feet up runs between *Tlaloc* and *Dog Legs And Feet*

10 ***A Dog's Life* 60 feet 5.12 TR ★**
Climb the overhanging right-facing lieback flakes directly beneath the *Dog Legs And Feet Flakes.* Join *Dog Legs And Feet* 25 feet up. The nut placements are there, but this has yet to be led.

11 ***Dog Legs And Feet* 55 feet 5.10+ ★★**
Climb a light grey right-facing flake system to a thin right-leaning crack. Start on the easy ramp to the right.

***Huehung* 55 feet 5.9+ TR**
Toprope the wall between *Dog Legs And Feet* and *Save And Gain With Lobo.*

12 ***Save And Gain With Lobo* 55 feet 5.6**
Climb the wide flared corner crack. This is the left hand of three crack climbs (2 offwidths, 1 chimney) at the south end of Dragon's Wall.

13 ***Krispy Kritters* 55 feet 5.11 TR**
The prow halfway between *Save And Gain With Lobo* and *Dragon's Waltz.*

14 ***Dragon's Waltz* 55 feet 5.8**
Dragon's Waltz is the middle of the three cracks at Dragon's Wall's south end.

15 ***Death And Texas* 55 feet 5.10**
Climb the curving hand crack which turns into an overhanging chimney 10 feet right of *Dragon's Waltz.* A large jammed block is in the bottom of the chimney flare.

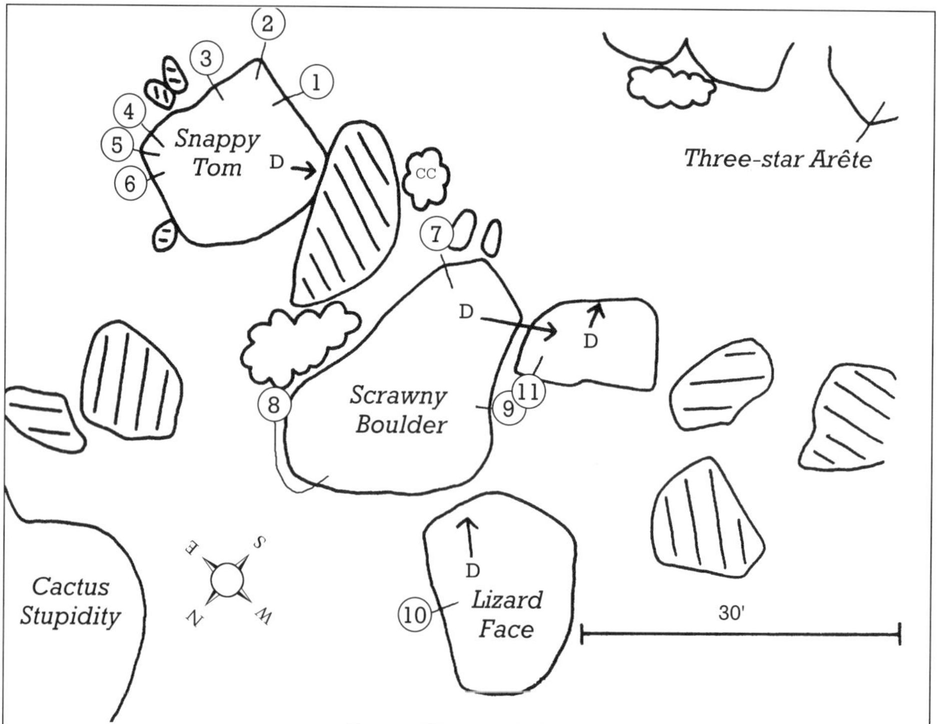

Central Dragon's Den

1 *Spice 14 feet V0+*
2 *The Juicer 14 feet V2*
3 *Satta 13 feet V1*
4 *Snappy Tom 13 feet V4*
5 *Potty Breath 13 feet V0+*
6 *All The Rage 13 feet V0– ★★*
7 *Tug-A-Dug 14 feet V2 ★*
8 *The Siphon 17 feet V3 ★*
9 *Scrawny Hardon 17 feet V0+*
10 *Lizard Face 11 feet V0 ★*
11 *Brawny Hardon 13 feet V3*

Snappy Tom
2 *The Juicer*
3 *Satta*
4 *Snappy Tom*
5 *Potty Breath*
6 *All The Rage*

CENTRAL DRAGON'S DEN

Snappy Tom Rock

Snappy Tom Rock is the 14 foot tall boulder halfway between the Blender Boulder and the Five Bimbos. See topo, p. 178.

1 *Spice 14 feet V0+*
Climb the center of the south face.

2 *The Juicer 14 feet V2*

3 *Satta 13 feet V1*

4 *Snappy Tom 13 feet V4*

5 *Potty Breath 13 feet V0+*

6 *All The Rage 13 feet V0–* ★★

Scrawny Boulder

7 *Tug-A-Dug 14 feet V2* ★
Climb the east face's left side, 9 feet left of the juniper trunk, 3 feet right of a small boulder. A sit down start beginning 5 feet to the right is V4.

8 *The Siphon 17 feet V3* ★
Drains you. Start 2 feet right of the juniper and traverse the low, sloping lip to the right.

9 *Scrawny Hardon 17 feet V0+*
Climb the west face via a series of 1 to 2 inch wide, foot long, right-facing corners. *Brawny Hardon* is on the boulder 6 feet to the right.

Lizard Face

10 *Lizard Face 11 feet V0* ★
The north face above "V."

Brawny Boulder

11 *Brawny Hardon 13 feet V3*
Sharp holds lead up the northwest face's left side, four feet right of the face's left edge.

THE FIVE BIMBOS

These are the five big boulders lined up roughly northeast to southwest. The left (northeast) two have a large juniper guarding their north sides. The southernmost boulder has an oak in front of its northwest face. Topo, p. 180.

Alicia

1 *Press On With Scott And Dick 18 feet V0+*
Climb the left side of the north arête. The descent is 6 feet to the left.

2 *Barbara's Knolls 18 feet V2*
Climb the right side of the north arête. The crack to the right is off route.

3 *Scarlett Unleashed 17 feet V0* ★
The shallow crack in the right-facing dihedral.

4 *Bimbo Akimbo 20 feet V2*
5 feet right of the shallow crack, thrash through branches to enter the scoop above.

Barbie

5 *The Little Spermaid 20 feet V0*

Cindy

6 *B-Movie Bimbos 17 feet V1*
Climb the left side of the east face (6 feet south of where *Barbie* contacts *Cindy*). A catclaw is 6 feet behind the start.

7 *The Porker 12 feet V1* ★
Starts 4 feet left of *I Own It* at a face size hueco on the left side of a blunt arête.

8 *I Own It 15 feet V3* ★
Climb the north facing overhang 6 feet left of the *3 Star Arête*. Sit down start is V5.

9 *3 Star Arête 20 feet V2* ★★★
With a sit-down start this is V4.

10 *Texas Happy Hour 22 feet 5.13– TR* ★

11 *Red 22 feet V5*

12 *The Urge To Purge 15 feet V0*
Low start opposite *Sorority Babes...*

Danielle

13 *DG Crack 12 feet V2*
Traverse left out the southeast end of the crack between *Danielle* and *Ellie May*. It keeps getting wider.

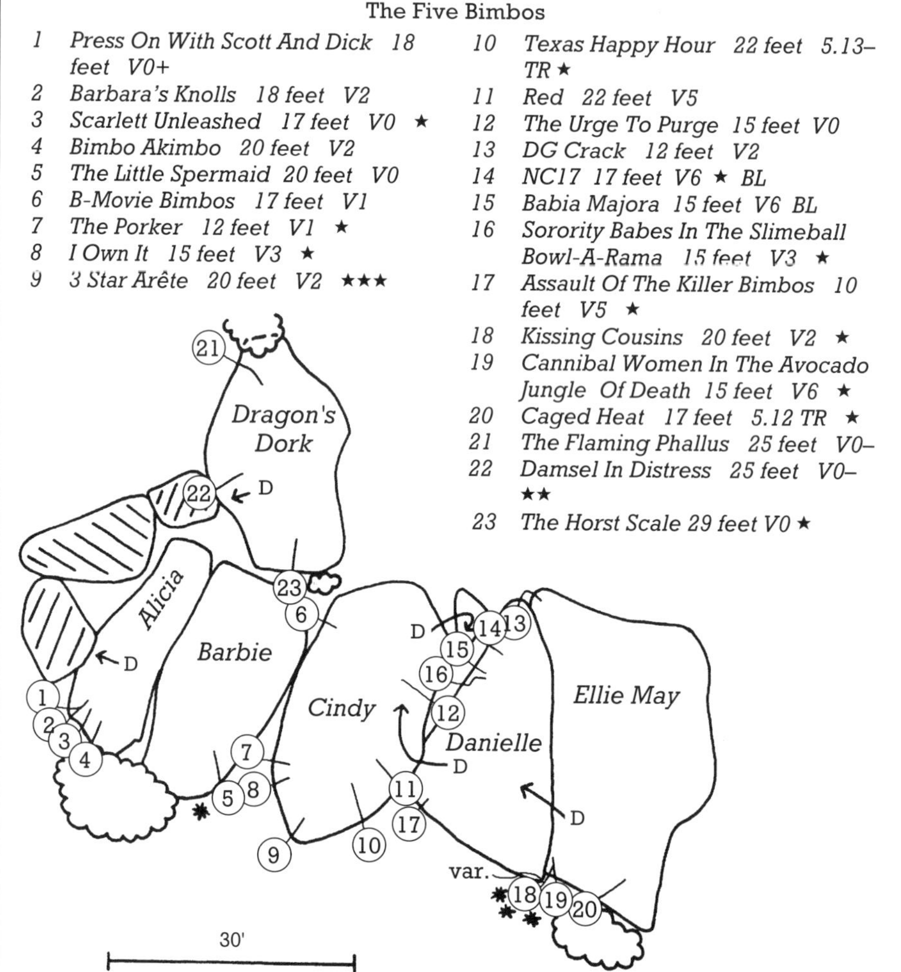

Danielle

View from the southeast.

13 *DG Crack 12 feet V2*

14 *NC17 17 feet V6 ★ BL*

15 *Babia Majora 15 feet V6 BL*

16 *Sorority Babes In The Slimeball Bowl-A-Rama 15 feet V3 ★*

The Five Bimbos

View from the northwest.

5 *The Little Spermaid 20 feet V0*

8 *I Own It 15 feet V3 ★*

9 *3 Star Arête 20 feet V2 ★★★*

10 *Texas Happy Hour 22 feet 5.13– TR ★*

11 *Red 22 feet V5*

17 *Assault Of The Killer Bimbos 10 feet V5 ★*

18 *Kissing Cousins 20 feet V2 ★*

19 *Cannibal Women In The Avocado Jungle Of Death 15 feet V6 ★*

20 *Caged Heat 17 feet 5.12 TR ★*

14 *NC17 17 feet V6 ★ BL*
Start on a perfect hand-sized scoop 7 feet up.

15 *Babia Majora 15 feet V6 BL*
The wall 2 feet left of the cream-colored streak.

16 *Sorority Babes In The Slimeball Bowl-A-Rama 15 feet V3 ★*
Start 6 feet left of Danielle's contact with Cindy. A left angling crack at the top turns into a low angle left-facing dihedral over the lip. The lip moves aren't as simple as they look.

17 *Assault Of The Killer Bimbos 10 feet V5 ★*
Climb the left side of Danielle's northwest face, starting low on the incut fingertip flake 4 feet up. The blunt arête one foot left is off route. The tiny 3 fingertip knob one foot right of a broken patch 7 feet up the arête is on (although even this has been off-routed before, turning the problem into a desperate dynamic). Go right at the lip for a grim bonus mantle.

Ellie May

18 *Kissing Cousins 20 feet V2 ★*
Climb the 2-6 inch wide crack between Danielle and Ellie May. A wild top out.
Variation: No Rebate.

19 *Cannibal Women In The Avocado Jungle Of Death 15 feet V6 ★*
Climb sharp slopers straight up entering *Kissing Cousins'* crack 3 feet from the top.

20 *Caged Heat 17 feet 5.12 TR ★*
Start 2 feet right of *Cannibal Women...*, then angle up and right past the tree to a flexing flake at the lip.

The Dragon's Dork

The Dragon's Dork is the 25 foot tall spire behind (southeast) of Alicia and Barbie.

Five Bimbos, Hardman Rock areas

1 *Press On With Scott And Dick 18 feet VO+*
2 *Barbara's Knolls 18 feet V2*
3 *Scarlett Unleashed 17 feet VO ★*
4 *Bimbo Akimbo 20 feet V2*
21 *The Flaming Phallus 25 feet V0–*
22 *Damsel In Distress 25 feet V0– ★★*
23 *The Horst Scale 29 feet V0 ★*
26 *Bladerunner 11 feet V0+*
27 *Eager Beaver 11 feet V0–*
28 *Cute Dimples 14 feet V0–*
29 *I've Got The Handle 10 feet V0+*

21 *The Flaming Phallus 25 feet V0–*
The right side of the east face.

22 *Damsel In Distress 25 feet V0–* ★★
Straight up the center of the north face, using a right-facing flake near the top. This is also the easiest route to descend.

23 *The Horst Scale 29 feet V0* ★
The center of the west face.

HARDMAN ROCK AREA

Hardman Rock is the rock immediately southeast of the Dragon's Dork. An oak tree grows between the two rocks. Access this well hidden boulder either by scrambling around the south side of the Dragon's Dork or drop in from the north along the east side of The Blade. Topo on page 184; photos, p.185.

The Blade

24 *The Blade 14 feet V0+*
Climb the middle of the east face of the blade of rock perched above and north of Hardman Rock. The south edge of this blade comes within 3 feet of *Lip Service's* lip. Loose.

25 *The International Herb 9 feet V1* ★
Mantle the northeast arête.

26 *Bladerunner 11 feet V0+*
Climb the arête on the left edge of the west face.

27 *Eager Beaver 11 feet V0–*

28 *Cute Dimples 14 feet V0–*

29 *I've Got The Handle 10 feet V0+*
You got the blade. Start with your hands 5 feet up.

Hardman Rock

30 *Dragonfly (aka Dogmatics) 21 feet V5* ★★★
The left hand finish is a bit harder, but has a much safer landing. A hard sit down start has been added.

31 *Dry Dock 15 feet V7* ★★★
Either hug the bottom of the keel and fire up and right to a hueco, or do a huge swing from the ground to get started. This problem and *Lip Service* formerly had a horrific landing that added greatly to the thrills at the lip until a couple of pansy asses smashed off the pointed end of the boulder below.

Hardman Rock
30 *Dragonfly (aka Dogmatics)*

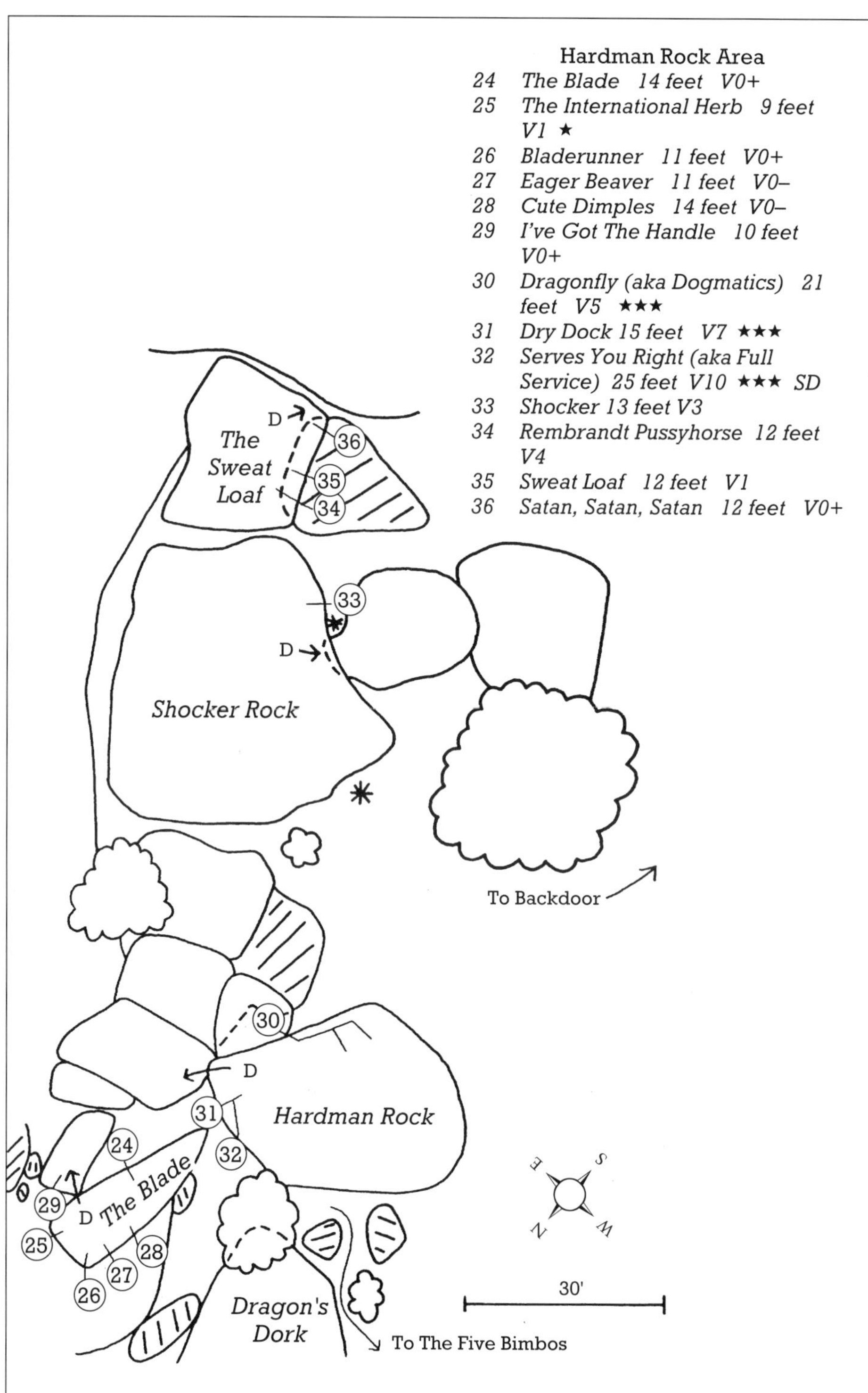
Hardman Rock Area
24 The Blade 14 feet V0+
25 The International Herb 9 feet V1 ★
26 Bladerunner 11 feet V0+
27 Eager Beaver 11 feet V0–
28 Cute Dimples 14 feet V0–
29 I've Got The Handle 10 feet V0+
30 Dragonfly (aka Dogmatics) 21 feet V5 ★★★
31 Dry Dock 15 feet V7 ★★★
32 Serves You Right (aka Full Service) 25 feet V10 ★★★ SD
33 Shocker 13 feet V3
34 Rembrandt Pussyhorse 12 feet V4
35 Sweat Loaf 12 feet V1
36 Satan, Satan, Satan 12 feet V0+
The Sweat Loaf
Shocker Rock
Hardman Rock
The Blade
Dragon's Dork
To Backdoor
To The Five Bimbos
30'
D
S
E
N
W

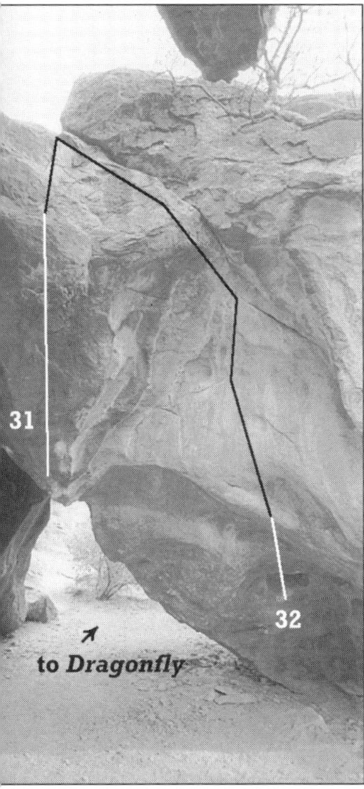

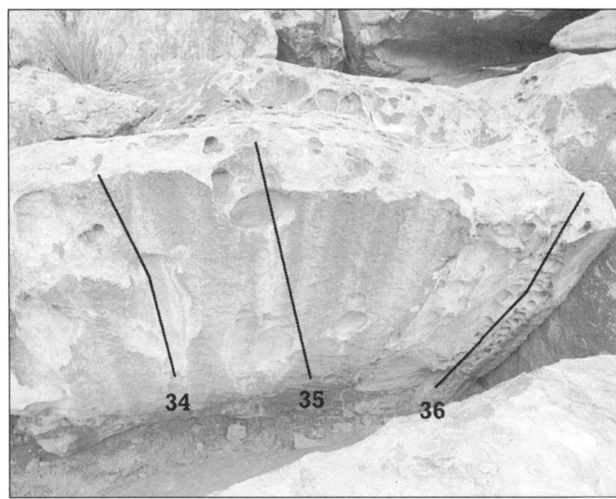

Hardman Rock (left)

31 *Dry Dock 15 feet V7 ★★★*
32 *Serves You Right (aka Full Service) 25 feet V10 ★★★ SD*

The Sweat Loaf (above)

34 *Rembrandt Pussyhorse 12 feet V4*
35 *Sweat Loaf 12 feet V1*
36 *Satan, Satan, Satan 12 feet V0+*

32 *Serves You Right (aka Full Service) 25 feet V10 ★★★ SD*
The stand-up start from the low boulder is *Lip Service* (17 feet V4 ★).

Shocker Rock

33 *Shocker 13 feet V3*
Start on a rock next to a sotol to grab the initial flakes. Move up and right to the lip mantle.

The Sweat Loaf

34 *Rembrandt Pussyhorse 12 feet V4 SD*
35 *Sweat Loaf 12 feet V1 SD*
36 *Satan, Satan, Satan 12 feet V0+ SD*

WARM UP ROOF AREA

The Warm Up Roof lies atop the rocky slabs on the other side of the gully (west) from the Dragon's Den (see the Dragon's Den photo). Its 140 foot long roof band faces west, away from the Dragon's Den. Situated between the Warm Up Roof and the Dragon's Den, and visible from much of the Dragon's Den, is the low, east- facing Kid's Stuff Wall. Topo on next page.

Kid's Stuff Wall

This popular warm up wall catches a lot of sun.

1 *Tiger Beat 11 feet V1 SD*
2 *Juvenile Offender 11 feet V0 SD*

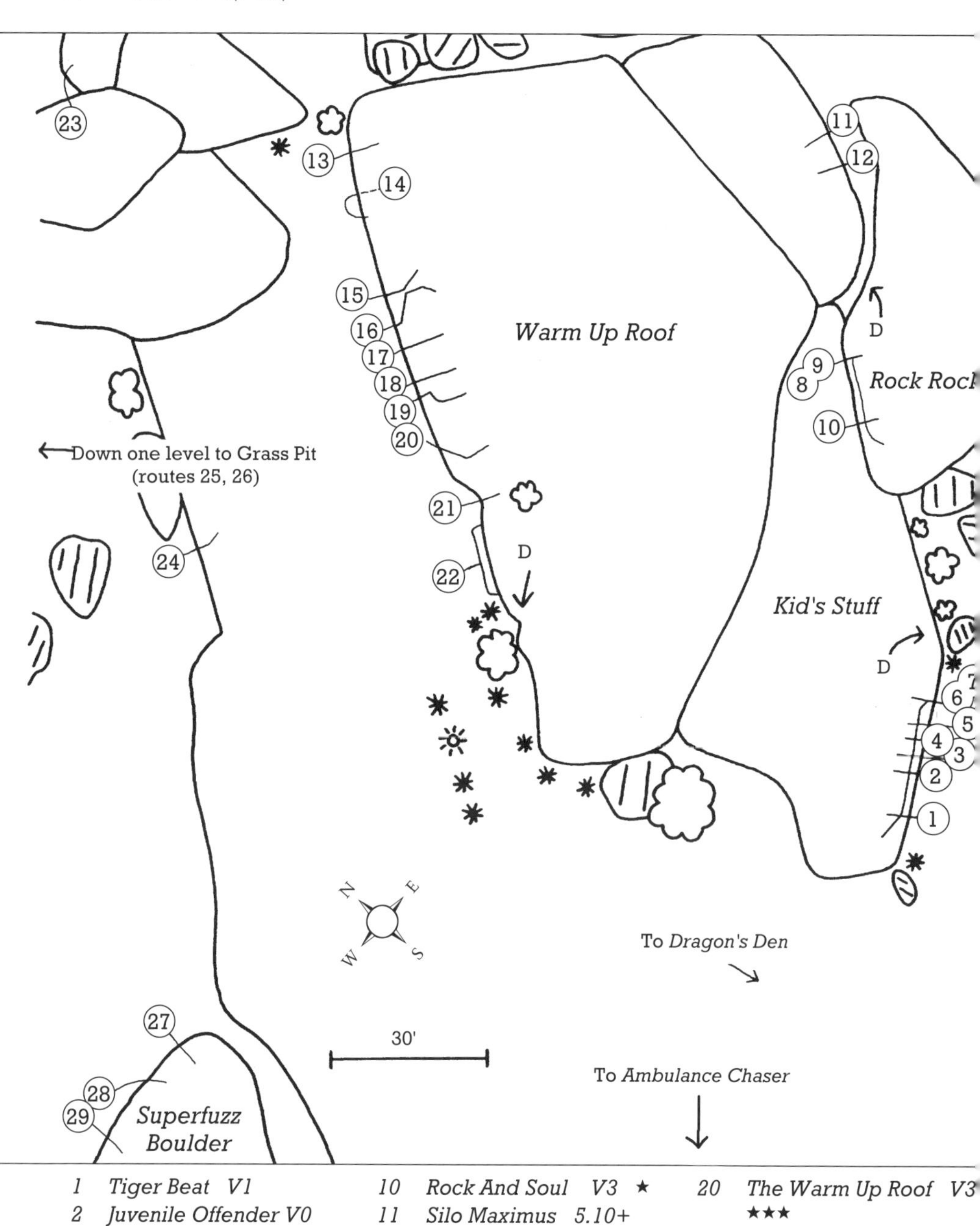

1 *Tiger Beat* V1
2 *Juvenile Offender* V0
3 *Jiffy Lube* V0+
4 *Greasy Kid Stuff* V4 ★
5 *Young Guns* V4
6 *Babyfat* V6
7 *Adolescent Behavior* V6
8 *Rock And Roll* V1 ★
9 *Rock And Roll Is Dead* V3 ★
10 *Rock And Soul* V3 ★
11 *Silo Maximus* 5.10+
12 *Dragon's Claw* 5.10
13 *Left Out* V2
14 *Thorny Toad* V5
15 *Slamdunk* V3
16 *The Guillotine* V2
17 *The Execution* V3 ★
18 *Crispy Critters* V3
19 *Automatic Choke* V1 ★
20 *The Warm Up Roof* V3 ★★★
21 *Warm Up Seam* V1 ★
22 *Hug-A-Jug Wall* V0
24 *The Burnout* V1
27 *Least Of Your Problems* V0 ★
28 *Superfuzz Bigmuff* V0-
29 *It's Not Pretty Being Easy* V0-

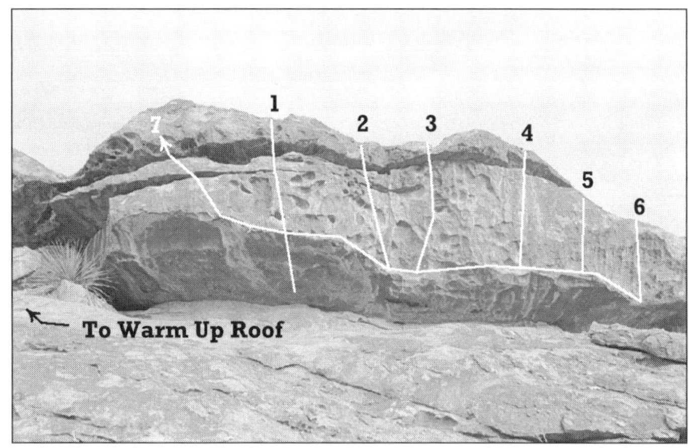

Kid's Stuff Wall (top)
1 *Tiger Beat 11 feet V1 SD*
2 *Juvenile Offender 11 feet V0 SD*
3 *Jiffy Lube 11 feet V0+ SD*
4 *Greasy Kid Stuff 11 feet V4 ★ SD*
5 *Young Guns 11 feet V4 SD*
6 *Babyfat 8 feet V6 SD*
7 *Adolescent Behavior 27 feet V6 ★*

Rock Rock (bottom)
8 *Rock And Roll*
9 *Rock And Roll Is Dead*
10 *Rock And Soul*

3 *Jiffy Lube 11 feet V0+ SD*
4 *Greasy Kid Stuff 11 feet V4 ★ SD*
5 *Young Guns 11 feet V4 SD*
6 *Babyfat 8 feet V6 SD*
7 *Adolescent Behavior 27 feet V6 ★*

Rock Rock

Rock Rock is 23 yards north of Kid's Stuff Wall. From Kid's Stuff Wall one can see a large roof on Rock Rock's south side. The 2 routes are on the west face.

8 *Rock And Roll 11 feet V1 ★ SD*
Sit down start off a rocking block between 2 big blocks.
9 *Rock And Roll Is Dead 20 feet V3 ★*
10 *Rock And Soul 11 feet V3 ★ SD*

Claw Wall

This is the 40 foot tall east-facing wall at the top of the Dragon's Den approach gully. Rock Rock obscures the left half from view.

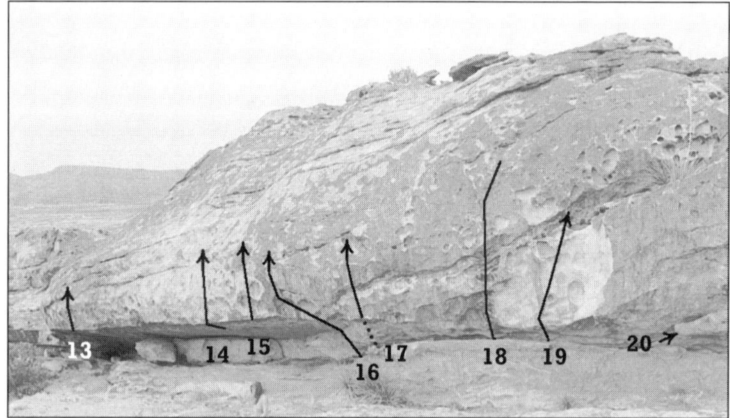

Warm Up Roof

Left side (top):

13 *Left Out*
14 *Thorny Toad*
15 *Slamdunk*
16 *The Guillotine*
17 *The Execution*
18 *Crispy Critters*
19 *Automatic Choke*
20 *The Warm Up Roof*

Right side (bottom):

20 *The Warm Up Roof 25 feet V3* ★★★
21 *Warm Up Seam 12 feet V1* ★
22 *Hug-A-Jug Wall 10-14 feet V0*

11 *Silo Maximus 38 feet 5.10+*
Climb the steep wall 15 feet left of Dragon's Claw. A 5 foot long left-angling seam is halfway up.

12 *Dragon's Claw 45 feet 5.10*
This route is normally toproped.

Warm Up Roof

13 *Left Out 14 feet V2*
Start with hands at lip.

14 *Thorny Toad 15 feet V5*
Start in hueco 4 feet back from lip.

15 *Slamdunk 15 feet V3*
If you're tall enough to reach the first holds you belong in the NBA. 3 feet left of the tip of the Guillotine flake are some well spaced jugs. To get to them one must leap to grab small holds at the lip (the crux), then ladder up the jugs until you can get your feet on the rock. Finish straight up. Spud Webb doesn't use cheater stones.

16 *The Guillotine 17 feet V2*
Start on the horizontal crack behind the sotols, crank out to the flake, pray it doesn't break, then pull the chossy lip.

17 *The Execution 14 feet V3 ★*
Start at a first digit flake on the lip, or add a grade and start from the back of the roof.

18 *Crispy Critters 17 feet V3*
Start on the horizontal crack. Climb straight up the wall using a crispy sharp flake as the first hold after the starter crack.

19 *Automatic Choke 18 feet V1 ★*
Start on the horizontal crack.

20 *The Warm Up Roof 25 feet V3 ★★★*
Start on the horizontal crack at the back. More like the Warm Out roof. For and added pump, this has been started at the far left end of the horizontal crack (left of *Thorny Toad*).

21 *Warm Up Seam 12 feet V1 ★*

22 *Hug-A-Jug Wall 10-14 feet V0*
Any of several hueco hauls along the 30 foot stretch of rock right of Warm Up Seam.

23 *Contest Problem 11 feet V0 ★★ SD*
Beginner power climbing. Traverse right to left to the lip.

Photo of routes 24 to 29 is on page 170.

24 *The Burnout 18 feet V1*
40 feet west of the Warm Up Roof and down one level is a severely overhung wall with potential for several 5.16 topropes. Between the catclaw to it's right and a boulder to it's left is this west facing line of big huecos hardly worth mentioning.

The Grass Pit

Fifty yards northwest and two levels below Warm Up Roof is this very grassy pit/bowl with two routes ascending its 20 foot tall west-facing wall. Beware of friable holds.

25 *Weed With Roots In Hell 20 feet V2*

26 *Lodemabola 20 feet V2 ★*

Superfuzz Boulder

This is the big boulder 35 yards southwest of Warm Up Roof. A good place to warm up for Warm Up Roof.

27 *Least Of Your Problems 12 feet V0 ★*
Begin on jugs at the lip of the undercut roof.

28 *Superfuzz Bigmuff 14 feet V0-*
Start near right end of roof.

29 *It's Not Pretty Being Easy 15 feet V0-*

Contest Problem
(Looking from the north) The Warm Up Roof is behind these boulders.
23 *Contest Problem*

Grass Pit and Superfuzz Boulder

View from the northwest.

23 *Contest Problem 11 feet V0 ★★ SD*
24 *The Burnout 18 feet V1*
25 *Weed With Roots In Hell 20 feet V2*
26 *Lodemabola 20 feet V2 ★*
27 *Least Of Your Problems 12 feet V0 ★*
28 *Superfuzz Bigmuff 14 feet V0-*
29 *It's Not Pretty Being Easy 15 feet V0-*

Ambulance Chaser Rock

The top of this rock is on the same level as Warm Up Roof and Kid's Stuff Wall, but located 60 yards southwest of the south end of Kid's Stuff Wall. It is hard to find because the problems are in a narrow corridor that isn't apparent until you are nearly standing on top of it. If you walk any further southwest, you will be forced to drop over cliffs leading down toward Comanche Canyon Dam.

1 *Satan's Little Helper 29 feet V0+ BL scary*

2 *Ambulance Chaser 28 feet V0 ★★ BL*
Start on the northwest facing slab around the corner to the right. Go up 10 feet to a left-diagonaling crack. Traverse 12 feet left on this crack then turn the roof at the finger crack.

3 *Holey Shit 25 feet V0*
Climbs the loose huecos up the southwest facing wall at the entrance to the *Ambulance Chaser* chimney.

Ambulance Chaser Rock

1 *Satan's Little Helper*
2 *Ambulance Chaser*
3 *Holey Shit*

AREA 11 MAP, P. 160

CHOP SOCKY ROCKS (AKA NORTH DRAGON'S DEN)

Chop Socky Rocks lie below Dragon's Den gully on the northwest side of the entrance. Two 25 foot high walls, one facing north, one east, form a giant corner easily seen when approaching the Dragon's Den from the north.

1 *Spam In A Cabin 10 feet V1 STAY OFF*
Sit down start at the left end of southeast facing wall. The hueco line 2 feet right of corner bounding the wall. There is rock art on this marginal problem - DON'T DO IT.

2 *Kickboxer 13 feet V2*
20 feet left of the off width roof is this sit down problem 11 feet right of Spam In A Cabin. Start by jamming the horizontal crack beneath the roof. Turn the lip on ironrock flakes. Move left to the hueco line at the top.

3 *Enter The Dragon (AKA Dragon's Buckets) 15 feet V0 ★ BL*
The eastern most projection of Chop Socky Rocks sports an overhanging off width emerging from an art-filled cave. Francrico Arsapea painted his name in big black letters here, complete with a backwards "N". DO NOT CLIMB IN THIS CAVE. 12 feet right of the off width is a black water streak next to a hueco line. Climb the huecos.

4 *French Fry Head Intellectual 16 feet V2*
15 feet right of Enter The Dragon is another black water streak on a north facing wall. The lower half of the streak is partially obscured by a right-facing flake. Climb the flake and the wall straight above it. Loose top. Intimidating.

Chop Socky Main Wall

5 *Giant Cheater 22 feet 5.12 TR ★★*
Start on a low boulder 15 feet left of *BL Striker.* This has also been started from the ground left of the low boulder (5.13-).

6 *B. L. Striker 25 feet V2 ★★★*
B. L. for bad landing. This also has been finished straight up (top rope, 5.11).

7 *Check It Out 24 feet 5.13 TR ★★★ BL*
More climbers will check this out than will ever check it off. The left angling crack in the right (east-facing) wall of the big corner.

Chop Socky Main Wall and Joe Bob Boulder

5 *Giant Cheater*
6 *B. L. Striker*
7 *Check It Out*

Chop Socky Rocks

3 *Enter The Dragon (aka Dragon's Buckets)* 15 *feet* V0 ★
BL
4 *French Fry Head Intellectual* 16 *feet* V2
5 *Giant Cheater* 22 *feet* 5.12 *TR* ★★
6 *B. L. Striker* 25 *feet* V2 ★★★
8 *V.B.L.* 20 *feet* V0+ ★

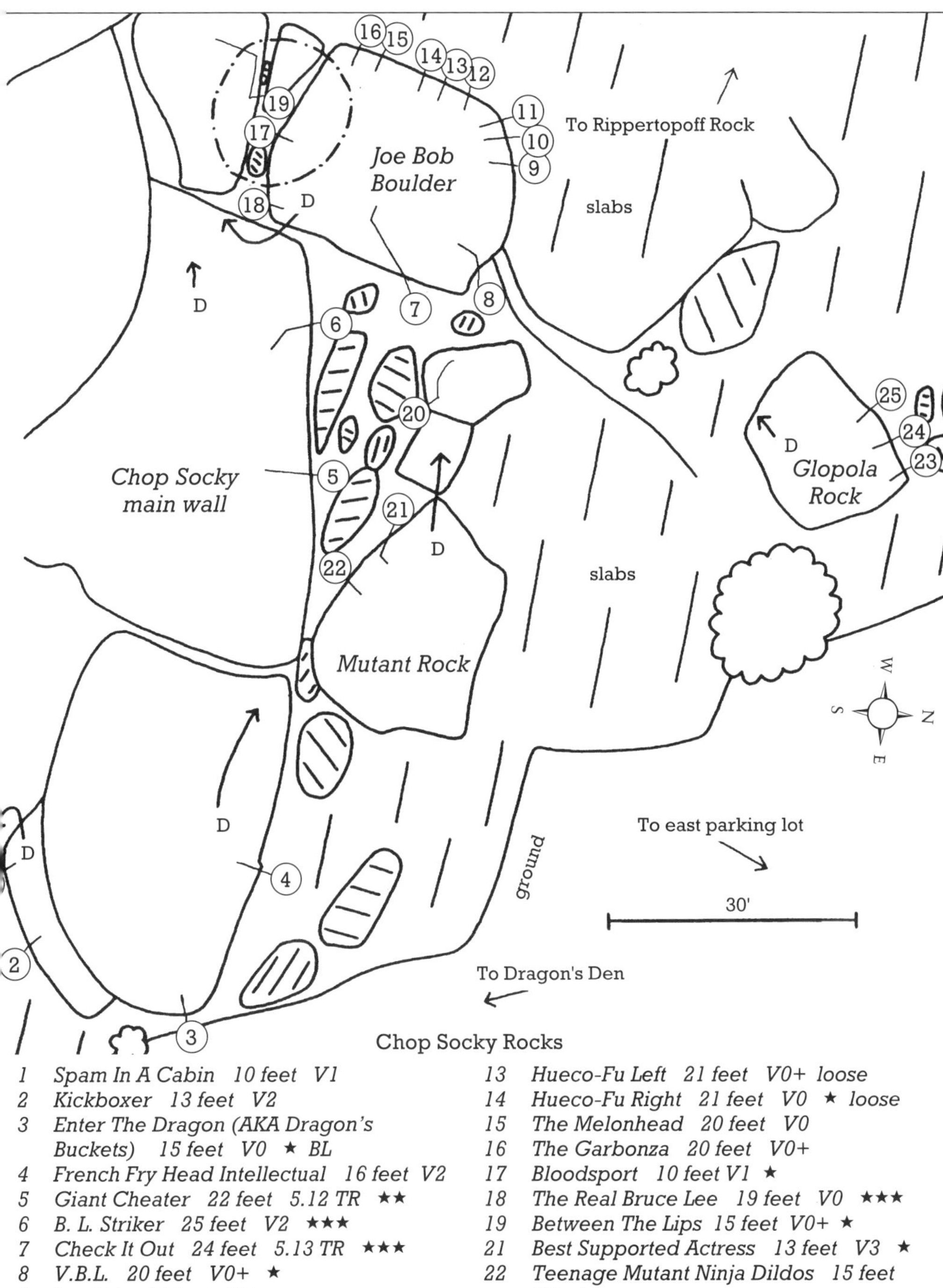

Chop Socky Rocks

1 *Spam In A Cabin 10 feet V1*
2 *Kickboxer 13 feet V2*
3 *Enter The Dragon (AKA Dragon's Buckets) 15 feet V0 ★ BL*
4 *French Fry Head Intellectual 16 feet V2*
5 *Giant Cheater 22 feet 5.12 TR ★★*
6 *B. L. Striker 25 feet V2 ★★★*
7 *Check It Out 24 feet 5.13 TR ★★★*
8 *V.B.L. 20 feet V0+ ★*
9 *Joe Bob 19 feet V0–*
10 *Chop Socky 20 feet V0–*
11 *Nekkid Breasts 20 feet V0+*
12 *Non-gratuitous Violence 21 feet V1 ★*
13 *Hueco-Fu Left 21 feet V0+ loose*
14 *Hueco-Fu Right 21 feet V0 ★ loose*
15 *The Melonhead 20 feet V0*
16 *The Garbonza 20 feet V0+*
17 *Bloodsport 10 feet V1 ★*
18 *The Real Bruce Lee 19 feet V0 ★★★*
19 *Between The Lips 15 feet V0+ ★*
21 *Best Supported Actress 13 feet V3 ★*
22 *Teenage Mutant Ninja Dildos 15 feet V2 ★★*
23 *Stunt Breasts 17 feet V3*
24 *Monkey-Fu 17 feet V1 ★*
25 *Jason The Mongolard 13 feet V0*

Chop Socky Rocks
6 *B. L. Striker 25 feet V2* ★★★
8 *V.B.L.*
9 *Joe Bob*
10 *Chop Socky*
11 *Nekkid Breasts*
Glopola Rock
23 *Stunt Breasts 17 feet V3*
24 *Monkey-Fu 17 feet V1* ★
25 *Jason The Mongolard 13 feet V0*

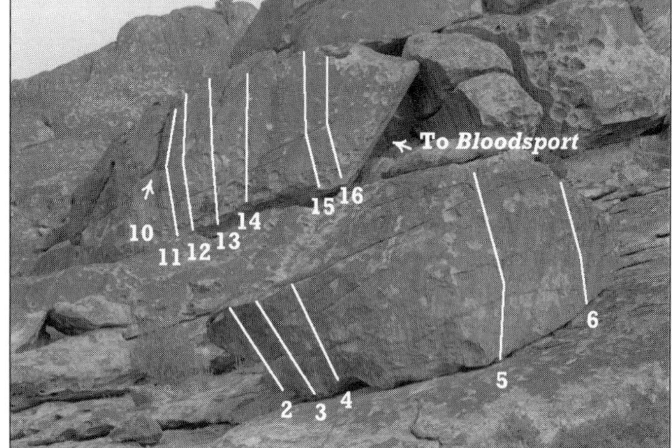

Joe Bob Boulder
10 *Chop Socky 20 feet V0–*
11 *Nekkid Breasts 20 feet V0+*
13 *Hueco-Fu Left 21 feet V0+ loose*
14 *Hueco-Fu Right 21 feet V0* ★ *loose*
15 *The Melonhead 20 feet V0*
16 *The Garbonza 20 feet V0+*

Rippertopoff Rock
2 *Striptease 11 feet V1*
3 *Rip Her Top Off 12 feet V1*
4 *Rip His Top Off 13 feet V1* ★
5 *Ripaway Jersey 16 feet V1*
6 *Karnivore 9 feet V0*

---

8 *V.B.L. 20 feet V0+* ★ *BL*
We ain't talking socks. The V is for very. Start on the outside corner between the east and north faces. Move up and right via some long reaches. Towards the top one risks a fall into the chimney below.

9 *Joe Bob 19 feet V0–*

10 *Chop Socky 20 feet V0–*

11 *Nekkid Breasts 20 feet V0+*
Parallel *Chop Socky* 4 feet to it's right, finishing up the blunt prow.

12 *Non-gratuitous Violence 21 feet V1* ★
Start 7 feet right of *Chop Socky* at a flaky football size hueco 7 feet up. Straight up exhilarating jugs.

13 *Hueco-Fu Left 21 feet V0+ loose*
The northwest face has a 5 foot wide line of big huecos ascending the face near its left side. Climb the left side of this hueco line.

14 *Hueco-Fu Right 21 feet V0 ★ loose*
The right side of the 5 foot wide line of huecos.

15 *The Melonhead 20 feet V0*
Start in the crumbly hueco 2 feet right of "JW".

16 *The Garbonza 20 feet V0+*
Start with a cantaloupe-sized hueco 6 feet up.

17 *Bloodsport 10 feet V1 ★ BL*
Starts inside the cave, on the south face 3 feet left of a crumbling boulder and 2 feet right of a white streak. Sink fingers behind the juicy incut, then lunge 5 feet for the incut at the lip. A half-assed attempt could be costly.

18 *The Real Bruce Lee 19 feet V0 ★★★ BL*
Also inside the cave, but on the right side of the south face. Ironrock doesn't get any better. Start off a boulder to reach holds 2 feet right of a 4 inch wide black streak. Short climbers might have trouble reaching the first good holds. Climb the blunt arête until it disappears, then move right to top out.

19 *Between The Lips 15 feet V0+ ★*
Unique. Climb up to the roof then hand traverse right until you can grab "the tonsils" and squeeze through the gullet under the capstone.

20 *Meine Kleine Buzzbomb 11 feet V4 SD*

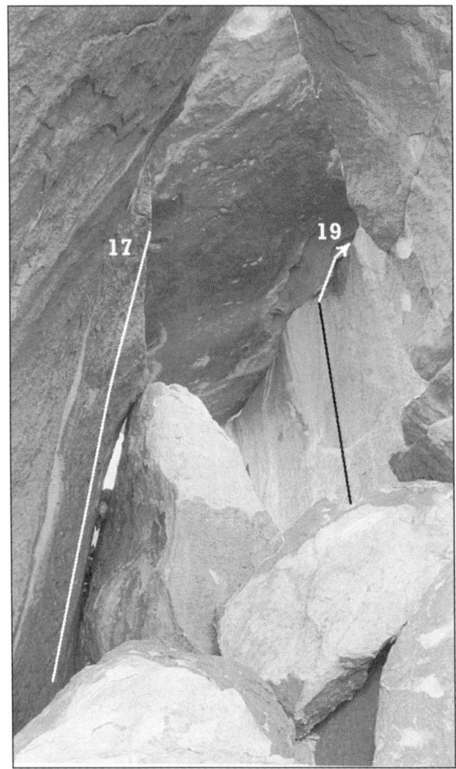

Joe Bob Boulder, south face left
17 *Bloodsport*
19 *Between The Lips*

Joe Bob Boulder, south face right
18 *The Real Bruce Lee*

Mutant Rock
21 *Best Supported Actress 13 feet V3* ★
22 *Teenage Mutant Ninja Dildos 15 feet V2* ★★

Mutant Rock

21 *Best Supported Actress 13 feet V3* ★
Start sitting down between blocks littering the base of the southwest face. Move right out the horizontal crack lines until you can crank to a notch at the lip.

22 *Teenage Mutant Ninja Dildos 15 feet V2* ★★
Start sitting down 11 feet right of *Best Supported Actress.* You'll be sitting on a projection off a small block. A brown, black, and grey scoop will be at your face. Climb positive holds out and right to the lip.

Glopola Rock

This, the northernmost of the Chop Socky Rocks, is only 10 feet up the slab from ground level. Photo, page 194.

23 *Stunt Breasts 17 feet V3*

24 *Monkey-Fu 17 feet V1* ★

25 *Jason The Mongolard 13 feet V0*
Start where the northwest face touches the rock below it.

RIPPERTOPOFF ROCK

Rippertopoff Rock is a lone boulder elevated 20 feet above ground level on the slabs 30 yards northwest of Chop Socky Rocks. Brownish pink paint has been used to cover graffiti on it's north and west faces. Beware of loose holds when topping out.

Photo, page 194.

1 *The Rip-Off 11 feet V2* ★
Climb the roof on the rounded corner left (east) of the north face. Start with hands at the back of the roof, not on the big flake halfway out.

2 *Striptease 11 feet V1*
A vertical seam 2 to 5 feet off the base marks the start of this route on the left side of the north face.

3 *Rip Her Top Off 12 feet V1*
5 feet right of Striptease. Straight up to a 9-inch diameter hueco a foot below the lip.

4 *Rip His Top Off 13 feet V1* ★
Start at the white paint splotch 5 feet up.

5 *Ripaway Jersey 16 feet V1*
This faces due west. A patch of orange lichen is under the base 4 feet left of the start. The top half is loose.

6 *Karnivore 9 feet V0*
The loose right side of the west face, 4 feet right of the pink paint.

AREA 13 MAP, P. 160

PORN AGAIN

Porn Again is well hidden. From the spot where East Mountain and North Mountain come closest to each other, approach via a thin incised gully to the right of a low rock inscribed "Jo Wharton." This boulder is 5 feet from the trail. Porn Again is on the backside (east side) of the boulder behind the Jo Wharton boulder. When approaching along the right side of the Porn Again Boulder, be careful not to reach out and touch the Indian horse paintings on the south face.

1 *Porn Again 12 feet V7* ★
Start low and climb the overhanging huecoed trough on the right side of the east face. The right arête is off route. Mantel big knobs on the right side of the lip to top out. Two V0 slab lines are around the corner to the right on the north face.

AREA 14 MAP, P. 160

THE BUCKET ROOF

To get to the Bucket Roof walk southwest from the east parking lot through the gap between East and West Mountains. 60 yards southwest of the gap is a small grove of trees with a bench and a garbage can. The overhanging rocks (east) of the bench have Indian paintings on them. On the same cliff band 60 yards south (to the right) of the main gallery of paintings is the Bucket Roof. You will have to ascend some easy slabs to get to the problems.

Boney's Meat Market 11 feet V0–
40 yards south of the main gallery of paintings, at the base of the approach slab to the Bucket Roof, is this small boulder with a vertical east face. Climb the left side of the east face. A 3 foot vertical crack marks the top.

The Koppelateher 12 feet V0+
The face 6 feet right of *Boney's Meat Market.*

ALL ROUTES ON THE BUCKET ROOF ARE CURRENTLY CLOSED TO CLIMBING.
There are Indian paintings at the very back of the cave. None of the established climbing routes come close enough to the paintings to ever damage them, nevertheless, we are not allowed to climb here. If you agree that these route closures are illogical and unjust, make your feelings known to the rangers, the superintendent, and the Texas Parks and Wildlife Department in Austin. Without a concious lobbying effort, areas like the Bucket Roof and Kiva Cave will remain closed.

The following descriptions are given in the hopes that these routes will be opened in the future. Until that time, refrain from climbing on this wall. If this wall ever is reopened, do not climb further back in the cave behind the established *Bucket Roof* and *Steep Hill* lines.

The Bucket Roof consists of four different sections that can be mixed and matched to provide several different levels of desperation. If you don't have the artillery to blast V4 and up problems, this is the place to gun up. It's also a great place to practice no-hands roof rests. The four sections are as follows.

***Intro Pump* 22 feet V4 (a-b on photo)**
The lower 1-3 feet of rock below the horizontal seam at the base is off route. The Intro Pump ends at a horizontal hand to fist jam slot, the first hold for the following two problems.

***The Devil In Chris Jones* 29 feet V8 ★★★ (b-d-e)**
Start in the horizontal jam slot at the end of *Intro Pump*. Climb out the first 2 monster huecos of *Bucket Roof*, then head southwest in a beeline for the lip moves of *Bucket Roof*. One big hueco and two finger flakes is all it takes to reach the big flexing flake at the beginning of *Bucket Roof's* lip crux sequence. Finish up this sequence to the glue dripping holds at the lip, then traverse the lip 5 feet right to where you stem back onto the rocks behind you to get off.

***The Bucket Roof* 35 feet V6 ★★★ (b-c-d-e)**
Start at the horizontal jam slot at the end of *Intro Pump*. Crank out for the first basketball sized hueco in the roof, then move down and right with the help of two equally huge huecos. Next, move across 8 feet of fin moves until the Helmet hueco

The Bucket Roof

1 *Lady Di-hedral 30 feet 5.12 TR* ★
Intro Pump 22 feet V4 (a-b on photo)
The Devil In Chris Jones 29 feet V8 ★★★ *(b-d-e)*
The Bucket Roof 35 feet V6 ★★★ *(b-c-d-e)*
The "Steep" Hill Finish 17 feet V7 ★★★ *(c-f-e)*
Dynamic Tension 57 feet V7 ★★★ *(a-b-c-f-e)*
Judgement Day 58 feet V8 ★★★ *(a-b-d-e)*
Jones Crusher 51 feet V9 ★★★
Bad Judgement 65 feet V9 ★★★ *(a-b-d-c-f-e)*

---

can be grabbed. (A human head fits almost perfectly inside the Helmet. It's possible to hang no hands, no feet from this headlock. Nobody has broken their neck doing this, yet.) From the Helmet grasp one more gaping hueco, then power out west to the 18 inch long, 3 inch thick flexing flake. Fingery moves to gain the lip follow. The lip holds have been reinforced with glue which can be seen dripping along their sides. Traverse these holds right until you can step off to the boulders behind.

The "Steep" Hill Finish 17 feet V7 ★★★ *(c-f-e)*

Start at the Helmet hueco. Instead of moving west for the lip like *Bucket Roof*, move south into the 5 foot diameter inverted bowl. Wild moves follow to get set up for the crux undercling to the lip. Move left at the lip and step off a la *Bucket Roof*.

The following desperate variations have been done:

Dynamic Tension 57 feet V7 ★★★ *(a-b-c-f-e)*
Judgement Day 58 feet V8 ★★★ *(a-b-d-e)*
Jones Crusher 51 feet V9 ★★★
Bad Judgement 65 feet V9 ★★★ *(a-b-d-c-f-e)*

Comanche Canyon (from atop the dam)

COMANCHE CANYON (AKA MESCALERO CANYON)

AREA 15 MAP, P. 160

Comanche Canyon is the major canyon on the north side of East Mountain. To get there start at the East Parking Lot. Walk south through the gap where East and North Mountains come closest to each other then continue walking along the base of East Mountain until you run into a 20 foot tall stone dam. Comanche Canyon is the drainage blocked by this dam. The name is a misnomer, Comanches didn't live at Hueco Tanks. The rangers call this drainage Mescalero Canyon.

The following areas are most easily approached from this canyon: on the northeast side of the canyon (from north to south) – the Mines of Moria, the Backdoor Boulder, the Homeboy Boulder, and the Dark Heart; at the back of the canyon (south end) – Water Dog Wall, Tanks For The Mammaries, and Obscured By Clouds; southwest of the end of the canyon – Maiden Gully and The Waffle Iron; on the west side of the canyon – Bulbicide Wall, The Aircraft Carrier, Top Of Doldrums Gully, and The Veranda.Water Dog Wall is the only area at ground level in the canyon. The top of Doldrums Gully and The Veranda can also be approached from the west side of East Mountain up Doldrums Gully.

***Damn Comanches* 25 feet 5.11 TR**

15 yards above the northeast end of Comanche Canyon Dam. *Damn Comanches* is the 15 foot roof graced with a left-angling flake from base to lip. At the start, there is a long reach and at the finish, a desperate lip move.

MINES OF MORIA

AREA 16 MAP, P. 160

The Mines of Moria routes are well hidden in the corridors between the Dragon's Den and the Dark Heart. The Backdoor Boulder is located on the level 20 feet below Crunchy Toad Boulder. Access the routes by: 1) Walking south from Hardman Rock (in the Dragon's Den) and scrambling through the dark corridors formed by huge boulders to your right (west) and the main wall to your left (east). 2) Getting atop the west-facing walls in the Dark Heart (Mazola Marginal, Dark Angel crack), then entering the maze of huge boulders to the northeast. Duck through the passageways (deeper and darker than approach 1) trending northeast until against the main wall (huge undercut roofs beneath it). Follow dark corridors north along this wall to the routes. 3) Find the Backdoor Boulder then solo hazardous, loose rock up the 20 foot wall to it's east to get on the next level up. You should end up in the gap between Crunchy Toad Boulder and another huge boulder south of it (Repeated Audacity). A distinctive 30

Approach #1 to the Mines of Moria: From 20 yards southeast of Hardman Rock.

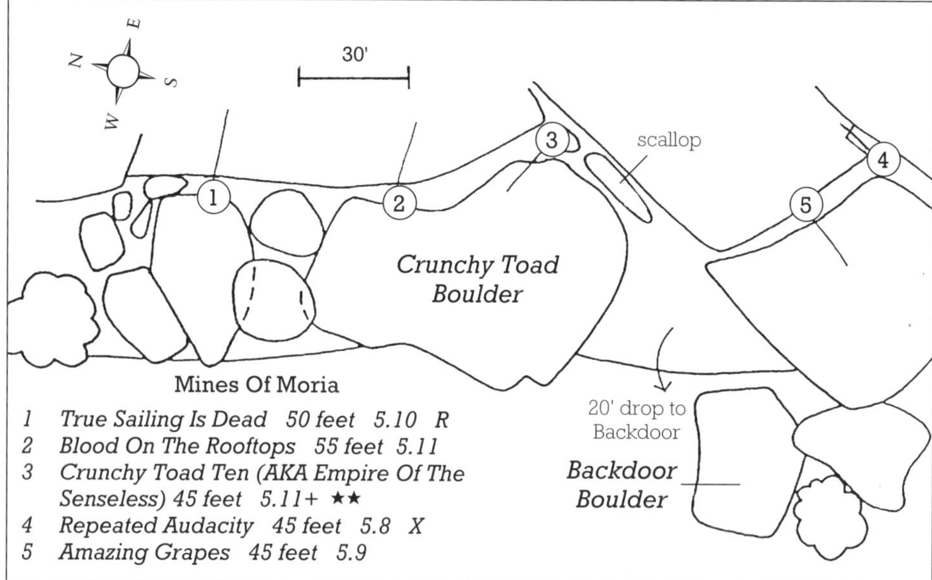

foot tall scallop shaped flake is wedged in the corridor on the southeast side of Crunchy Toad Boulder. Or 4) Get off-route on the slabs above and east of the Mines, peer over the cliff edge, lose your footing and fall to the base of the routes.

Routes in the Mines Of Moria are described from north to south.

1 ***True Sailing Is Dead 50 feet 5.10 R***
This route is the zig-zagging crack, in a black water streak, on the west-facing wall near the north entrance to the Mines of Moria. Climb the crack to small huecos.

2 ***Blood On The Rooftops 55 feet 5.11***
Climb a steep thin wall, with a bolt and a pin, 27 feet to the right of *True Sailing Is Dead.* The first bolt is 25 feet up.

3 ***Crunchy Toad Ten (AKA Empire Of The Senseless) 45 feet 5.11+ ★★***
This is on the east face of a huge boulder seperate from the main cliff. Follow a line of four bolts up the sweeping scoop to a two bolt anchor. *Blood On The Rooftops* is 50 feet to the north on the opposite wall.

4 ***Repeated Audacity 45 feet 5.8 X***
On the huge boulder immediately south of Crunchy Toad Boulder, climb the northeast-facing wall starting 20 feet north of *Amazing Grapes.*

5 ***Amazing Grapes 45 feet 5.9***
From the base of the large scallop-shaped flake next to Crunchy Toad Boulder, walk 20 yards south into the curved chimney to a dihedral on the left (east) side. Begin in a 1 to 2 foot wide crack which leads to a thin crack in the dihedral above.

BACKDOOR/HOMEBOY

The Homeboy and Backdoor boulders lie 30 yards and 60 yards north of The Dark Heart, respectively. They are on the same level as the Dark Heart. The Mines of Moria are one level above them to the east. Approach the Homeboy and Backdoor from the northern exit of the Dark Heart (by the Swirl Wall), or work your way up the slabs from the bottom of Comanche Canyon. Walking north from the Backdoor on the same level will eventually place you in the Dragon's Den. Overview photo on page 200; photo, p.204.

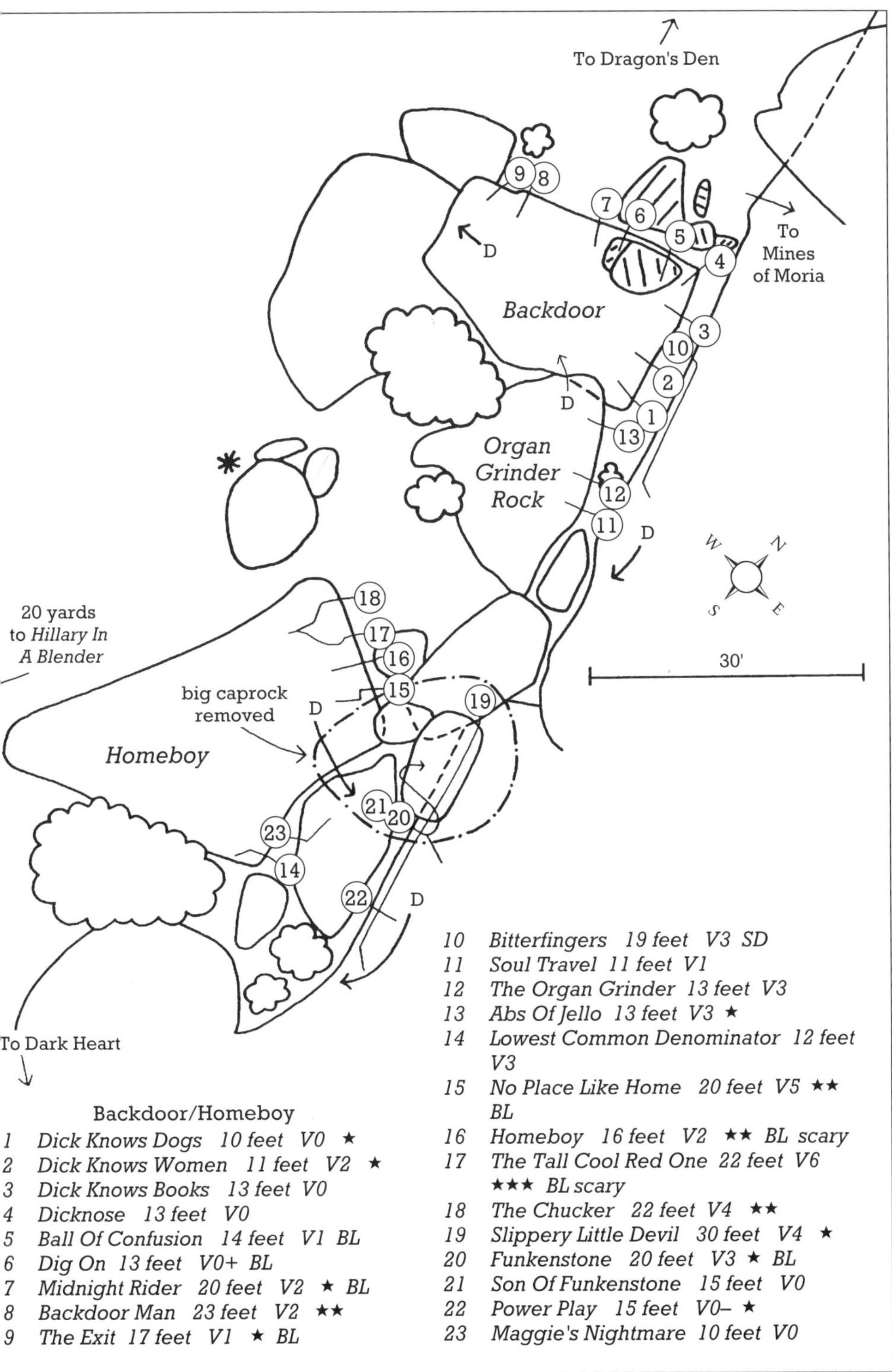

Backdoor/Homeboy

1 *Dick Knows Dogs 10 feet V0 ★*
2 *Dick Knows Women 11 feet V2 ★*
3 *Dick Knows Books 13 feet V0*
4 *Dicknose 13 feet V0*
5 *Ball Of Confusion 14 feet V1 BL*
6 *Dig On 13 feet V0+ BL*
7 *Midnight Rider 20 feet V2 ★ BL*
8 *Backdoor Man 23 feet V2 ★★*
9 *The Exit 17 feet V1 ★ BL*
10 *Bitterfingers 19 feet V3 SD*
11 *Soul Travel 11 feet V1*
12 *The Organ Grinder 13 feet V3*
13 *Abs Of Jello 13 feet V3 ★*
14 *Lowest Common Denominator 12 feet V3*
15 *No Place Like Home 20 feet V5 ★★ BL*
16 *Homeboy 16 feet V2 ★★ BL scary*
17 *The Tall Cool Red One 22 feet V6 ★★★ BL scary*
18 *The Chucker 22 feet V4 ★★*
19 *Slippery Little Devil 30 feet V4 ★*
20 *Funkenstone 20 feet V3 ★ BL*
21 *Son Of Funkenstone 15 feet V0*
22 *Power Play 15 feet V0– ★*
23 *Maggie's Nightmare 10 feet V0*

Backdoor Boulder

4 *Dicknose 13 feet V0*
5 *Ball Of Confusion 14 feet V1 BL*
6 *Dig On 13 feet V0+ BL*
7 *Midnight Rider 20 feet V2 ★ BL*
8 *Backdoor Man 23 feet V2 ★★ scary*
9 *The Exit 17 feet V1 ★ BL*

Organ Grinder Rock
(Looking from the northeast)

11 *Soul Travel 11 feet V1*
12 *The Organ Grinder 13 feet V3*
13 *Abs Of Jello 13 feet V3 ★*

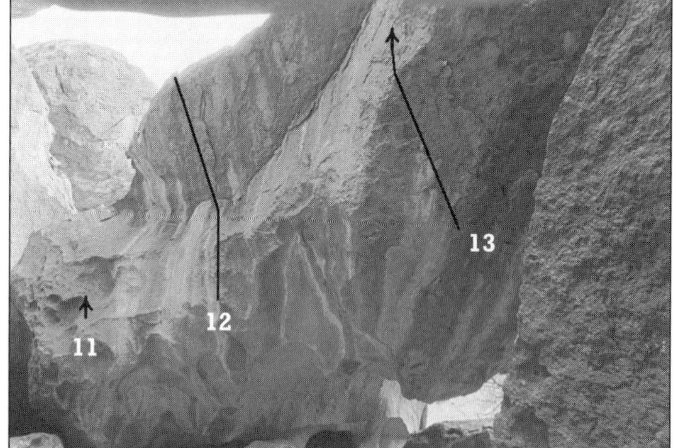

The Homeboy

15 *No Place Like Home 20 feet V5 ★★ BL*
16 *Homeboy 16 feet V2 ★★ BL scary*
17 *The Tall Cool Red One 22 feet V6 ★★★ BL scary*
18 *The Chucker 22 feet V4 ★★ scary*

Backdoor Boulder

1 *Dick Knows Dogs 10 feet V0 ★*
The blunt prow 4 feet right of the left end of Backdoor Boulder's east face.

2 *Dick Knows Women 11 feet V2 ★*
Thin moves up the center of the east face. Starts opposite Bitterfingers start.

3 *Dick Knows Books 13 feet V0*
Start a foot left of the 2 foot high rock at the base.

4 *Dicknose 13 feet V0*
Start on the rock at the base.

5 *Ball Of Confusion 14 feet V1 BL*
Start on the rock at the base. Photo, page 204.

6 *Dig On 13 feet V0+ BL*
Start off the taller boulder. Straight up over the loose top or hand traverse right.

7 *Midnight Rider 20 feet V2 ★ BL*
Start on the ground between *Dig On*'s starter block and The Backdoor Boulder.

8 *Backdoor Man 23 feet V2 ★★ scary*

9 *The Exit 17 feet V1 ★ BL*
Start from a foot high rock next to a bush.

10 *Butterfingers 19 feet V3 SD*
Traverse the wall 5 feet east of the Backdoor Boulder from left to right. Starts sitting down on a 6 foot wide block lying under the overhang. Finish up just left of a scrawny tree.

11 *Soul Travel 11 feet V1*
Harder than it looks mantel.

12 *The Organ Grinder 13 feet V3*

13 *Abs Of Jello 13 feet V3 ★*

The Homeboy

14 *Lowest Common Denominator 12 feet V3*
Sit down start with feet on a detached flake at the base. Climb the far left side of the east (not the northeast) face of the Homeboy, exiting left to the arête at the 12 foot level.

15 *No Place Like Home 20 feet V5 ★★ BL*
Start on the ground between many stones. A 1½ inch thick undercling flake is at the 5 foot level. Freaky. Add a sit down start and the problem is V6 ★★★.

16 *Homeboy 16 feet V2 ★★ BL scary*
Climb the center of the northeast face starting from the sloping boulder behind it.

17 *The Tall Cool Red One 22 feet V6 ★★★ BL scary*
The best highball problem in the park.

18 *The Chucker 22 feet V4 ★★ scary*
Loose top, but more solid if you move left.

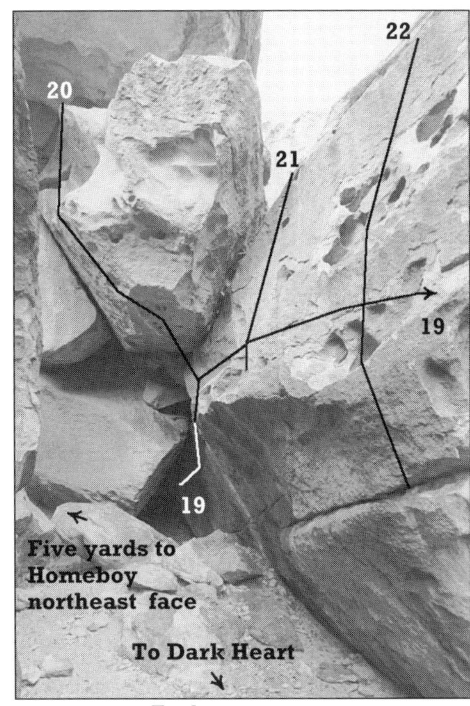

Funkenstone, etc.

19 *Slippery Little... 30 feet V4 ★*

20 *Funkenstone 20 feet V3 ★ BL*

21 *Son Of Funkenstone 15 feet V0*

22 *Power Play 15 feet V0– ★*

The following routes are on the west-facing wall 4-10 yards east of the Homeboy's southeast and east face. A 12 foot high by 20 foot long boulder lies between the Homeboy and this wall. See photo, page 205.

19 ***Slippery Little Devil* 30 feet V4 ★**
Start back in the A-frame cave at the left end of the wall. 4 to 5 feet off the ground is a long sloping edge. Traverse it from left to right. After 18 feet it turns to jugs. Step off at the tree.

20 ***Funkenstone* 20 feet V3 ★ BL**
Start where slopers turn to jugs on *Slippery Little Devil.* Get stood up on the slope, then undercling out the bottom side of the boulder suspended above. After a hard move from the lower to upper lip either stand up on the first lip and step off backwards (preferable) or finish with a junky traverse to he right. Combined with *Slippery Little Devil* this is *Funkenstone vs. The World* (33 feet, V4, ★★)

21 ***Son Of Funkenstone* 15 feet V0**

22 ***Power Play* 15 feet V0– ★**

23 ***Maggie's Nightmare* 10 feet V0**
A jug haul up and left with no feet.

***Hillary In A Blender* 15 feet V5 ★**
This is on a boulder 20 yards south of the south tip of Homeboy Boulder. Climb the south face starting with hands in the horizontal crack at the back of the five-foot roof. Photo, p. 200.

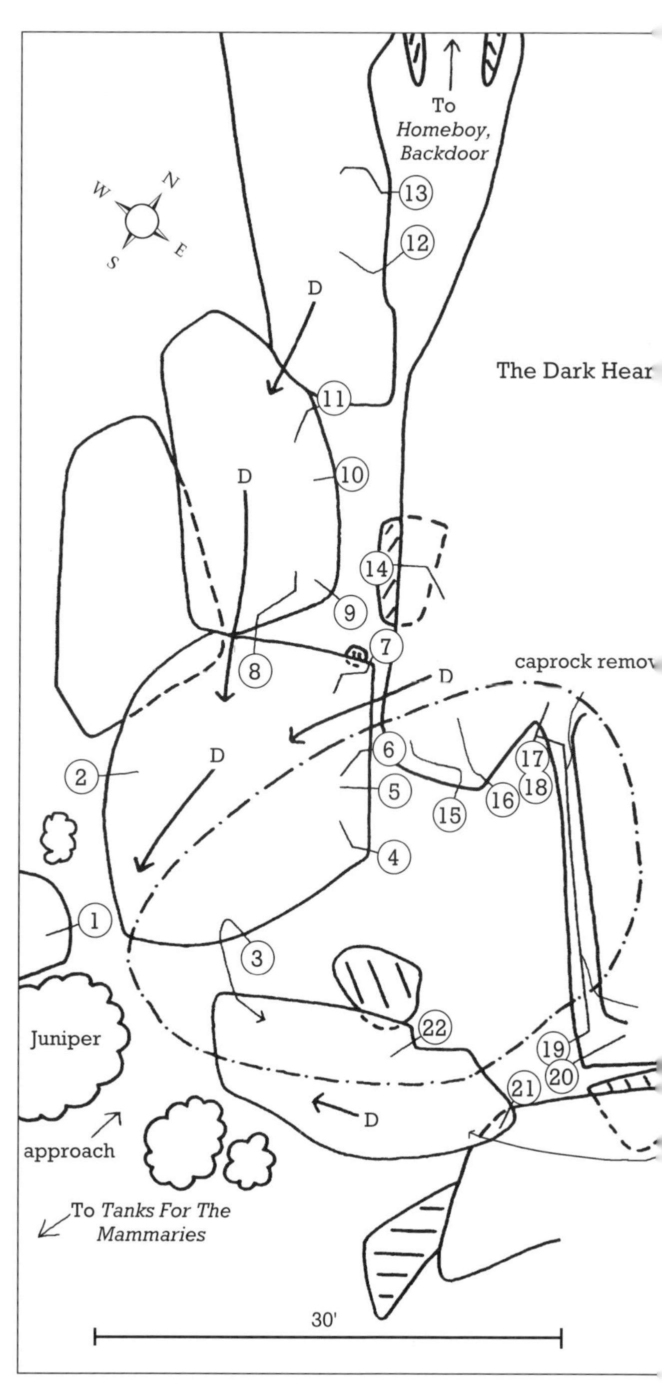

AREA 18

MAP, P. 160

THE DARK HEART

The Dark Heart is at the extreme southeast end of Comanche Canyon, 30 yards uphill (northeast) of Water Dog Wall. A huge juniper guards the entrance. An even bigger boulder caps the Dark Heart Boulder complex. To approach the Dark Heart walk to the south end of Comanche Canyon, past Water Dog Wall on your right, to where Tanks for the Mammaries blocks the end of the canyon. Head up slabs between boulders northeast of Tanks for the Mammaries to reach the juniper and northeast of it the Dark Heart Boulders. Overview photo on page 200.

1 *Infield Single 10 feet V0*
The short east face 5 feet north of the big juniper's trunk.

2 *Generation Excrement 9 feet V3 SD*
The current "worst line in the park" starts 6 feet left of the bush and climbs past several broken flakes.

3 *Dark Heart Roof 18 feet V0+ ★★*
Climb the line between the brown and tan rock to the roof formed by the huge caprock above. Reach behind you to holds under the roof. Undercling out then swing your feet across to the nearby rock to the southeast.

4 *Red Fox 12 feet V2*

5 *William's Lectric Shave 11 feet V4*
The thin sharp face 5 feet right of the prow. Start off a small immobile rock at the base.

6 *Rocket Boosters 11 feet V2*
Start immediately right of the immobile cheat stone of *William's Lectric Shave.*

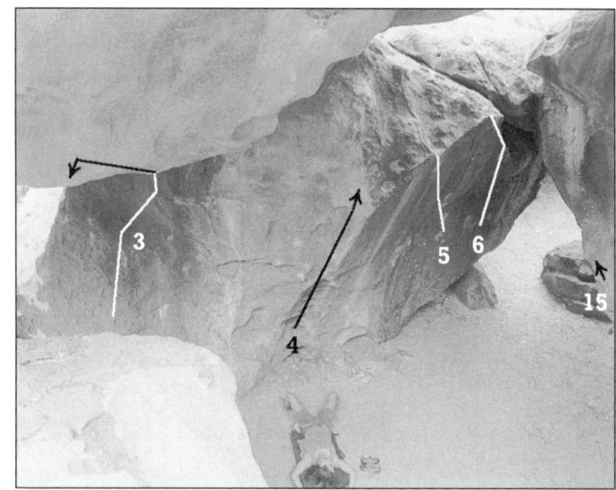

The Dark Heart

3 *Dark Heart Roof 18 feet V0+ ★★*
4 *Red Fox 12 feet V2*
5 *William's Lectric Shave 11 feet V4*
6 *Rocket Boosters 11 feet V2*
15 *The Ventral Fin 15 feet V1 ★*

The Dark Heart (topo at left)

1 *Infield Single 10 feet V0*
2 *Generation Excrement 9 feet V3 SD*
3 *Dark Heart Roof 18 feet V0+ ★★*
4 *Red Fox 12 feet V2*
5 *William's Lectric Shave 11 feet V4*
6 *Rocket Boosters 11 feet V2*
7 *Darth Vader 13 feet V1*
8 *Something Different 15 feet was V8 ★★★*
9 *The Bear 13 feet V4 ★*
10 *Politics Or Pontiacs 12 feet V4 ★*
11 *Spaceship Romex 12 feet V0+*
12 *Jiffy Pop 20 feet V4 ★*
13 *Swirl Wall 18 feet V3*
14 *Mazola Marginal 16 feet V1 BL*
15 *The Ventral Fin 15 feet V1 ★*
16 *Cowboyectomy 17 feet V3 ★ scary*
17 *Dark Angel 19 feet V0 ★★*
18 *Heartbreak Traverse (left to right) 30 feet V0+*
19 *Heartbreak Traverse (right to left) 30 feet V3 ★ scary*
20 *Moonwalk 21 feet V0 ★*
21 *Botch-A-Notch 16 feet V1*
22 *The Pipeloader 14 feet V2*

The Dark Heart
8 *Something Different*
9 *The Bear*
10 *Politics Or Pontiacs*
11 *Spaceship Romex*

7 *Darth Vader 13 feet V1*
Climb the arête between the north and east faces. Traverse a crack right to top out. The base boulder is off route.

8 *Something Different 15 feet V8 ★★★*
Everyone calls this something different. Start off the good incut flakes 5 feet off the ground. Easier barefoot or in slippers. Even easier sinceone retrochiseled it. A V9 variant (*Same Difference*) moves left at the start to a big sloper, then back right to join the regular route.

9 *The Bear 13 feet V4 ★*

10 *Politics Or Pontiacs 12 feet V4 ★*
Thin holds up center of the east face.

11 *Spaceship Romex 12 feet V0+*

12 *Jiffy Pop 20 feet V4 ★*
Via the fingertip seam.

13 *Swirl Wall 18 feet V3*
Start anywhere 6-10 feet left of the detached flake under the right end of the wall. Tops out at the right side of the swirling rock. Freaky moves, some friable holds.

14 *Mazola Marginal 16 feet V1 BL*
A swinging lunge off the 3 high boulder nails a solid hueco, one of the few solid holds on the route. Move right at the top.

15 *The Ventral Fin 15 feet V1 ★*
See photo, page 207.

16 *Cowboyectomy 17 feet V3 ★ scary*
Holds on *The Ventral Fin* are off route for the hands.

17 *Dark Angel 19 feet V0 ★★*

18 *Heartbreak Traverse (left to right, high) 30 feet V0+*
Finish at roof level around the right corner of the sizable caprock.

The Dark Heart
7 *Darth Vader*
12 *Jiffy Pop*
13 *Swirl Wall*

19 *Heartbreak Traverse (right to left, low) 30 feet V3 ★ scary*
Start up *Moonwalk*, but move to the left of the huecos once your feet are 6 feet up. Continue straight left around the arête to a 2 foot long shelf angling down and left. Crank or throw from the shelf for the 5 foot long angling ledge to your left. Hand traverse this to it's left end then up to the roof and top out left.

20 *Moonwalk 21 feet V0 ★*

21 *Botch-A-Notch 16 feet V1*
Start in the inverted notch between boulders. Finish in the notch above. Use both rocks. Lousy. A better variant doesn't use the left wall. Start in the inverted notch and head out right onto the face and up the wall avoiding the left arête above the notch (V5 BL scary).

22 *The Pipeloader 14 feet V2*
The 3 foot tall boulder at your right is off route.

Dark Heart

4 *Red Fox 12 feet V2*
5 *William's Lectric Shave 11 feet V4*

15 *The Ventral Fin*
16 *Cowboyectomy*
17 *Dark Angel*
18 *Heartbreak Traverse L to R*
19 *Heartbreak Traverse R to L*

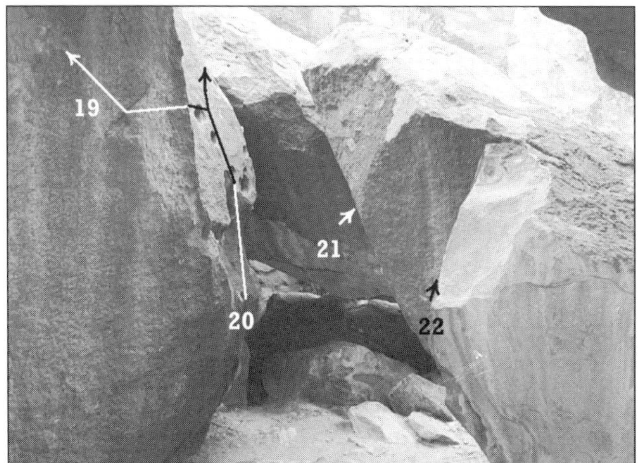

The Dark Heart

19 *Heartbreak Traverse R to L*
20 *Moonwalk*
21 *Botch-A-Notch*
22 *The Pipeloader*

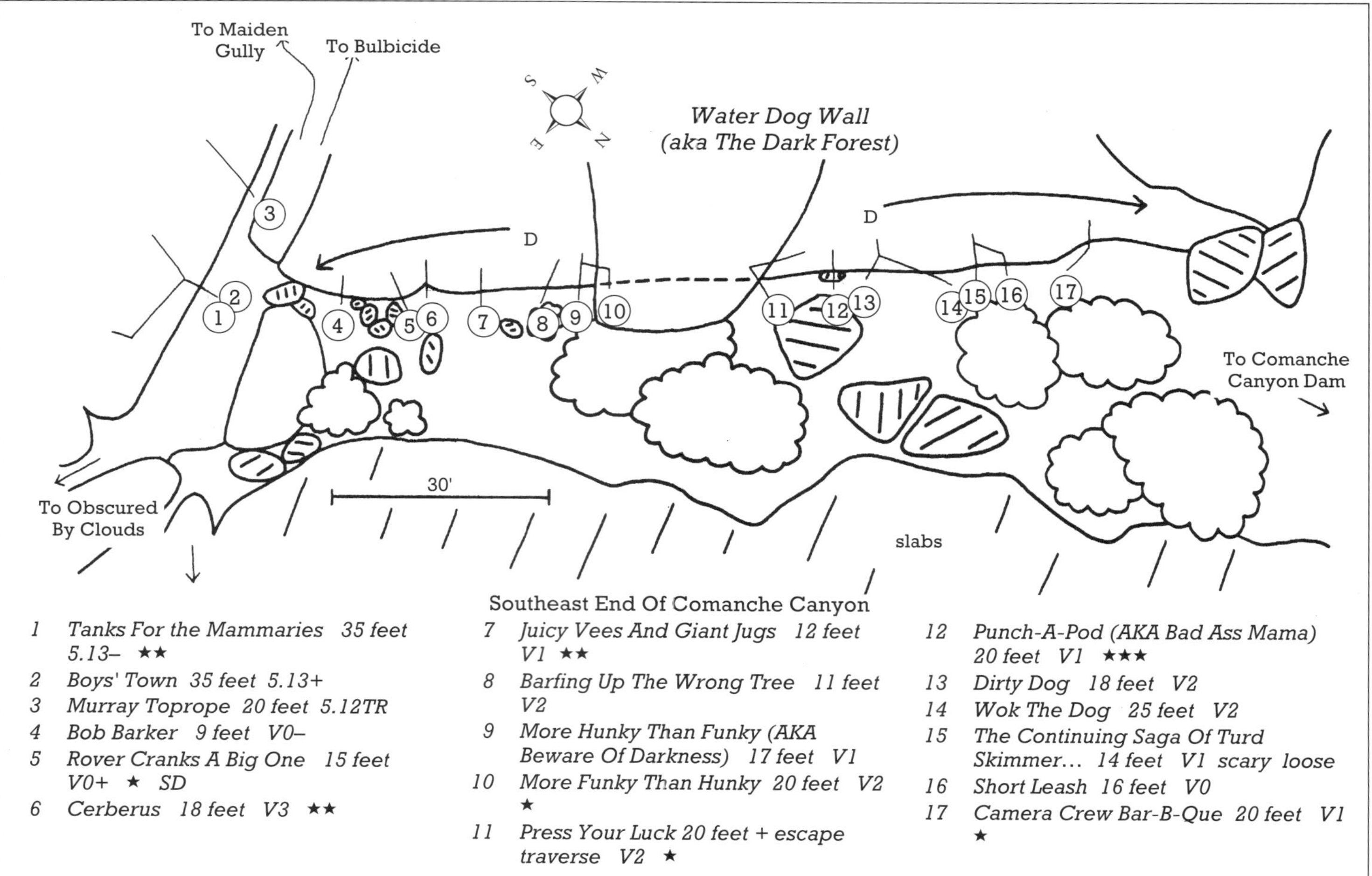
To Maiden Gully
To Bulbicide
S
W
E
N
Water Dog Wall
(aka The Dark Forest)
D
D
To Comanche Canyon Dam
To Obscured By Clouds
30'
slabs
1
2
3
4
5
6
7
8
9
10
11
12
13
14
15
16
17
Southeast End Of Comanche Canyon
1 Tanks For the Mammaries 35 feet 5.13– ★★
2 Boys' Town 35 feet 5.13+
3 Murray Toprope 20 feet 5.12TR
4 Bob Barker 9 feet V0–
5 Rover Cranks A Big One 15 feet V0+ ★ SD
6 Cerberus 18 feet V3 ★★
7 Juicy Vees And Giant Jugs 12 feet V1 ★★
8 Barfing Up The Wrong Tree 11 feet V2
9 More Hunky Than Funky (AKA Beware Of Darkness) 17 feet V1
10 More Funky Than Hunky 20 feet V2 ★
11 Press Your Luck 20 feet + escape traverse V2 ★
12 Punch-A-Pod (AKA Bad Ass Mama) 20 feet V1 ★★★
13 Dirty Dog 18 feet V2
14 Wok The Dog 25 feet V2
15 The Continuing Saga Of Turd Skimmer… 14 feet V1 scary loose
16 Short Leash 16 feet V0
17 Camera Crew Bar-B-Que 20 feet V1 ★

Southeast Comanche Cyn.
1 *Tanks For the Mammaries*
2 *Boys' Town*
3 *Murray Toprope*

AREA 19
MAP, P. 160

SOUTHEAST END OF COMANCHE CANYON

1 *Tanks For the Mammaries 35 feet 5.13– ★★*
This is the severely overhanging hueco wall at the south end of Comanche Canyon. Formerly a proud toprope, it has since been reduced to a silly two bolt lead. Climb up and left to the twin DD-cup huecos, then crank a thin move or a huge dyno to grasp the summit jugs.

2 *Boys' Town 35 feet 5.13+*
Where the whores hang. A gluey mess rumored to have been chiseled prior to the first ascent. At least one key hold has broken since. Bring big gear for the huecos between the bolts.

3 *Murray Toprope 20 feet 5.12 TR*

AREA 20
MAP, P. 160

WATER DOG WALL (AKA THE DARK FOREST)

This 12-foot long, northeast facing wall contains many excellent problems that aren't as dirty as they first appear. The moves are reminiscent of climbing in the Shawangunks. Most of these problems sport bad landings. The wall is located at the south end of Comanche Canyon. At the left end of Water Dog Wall, the canyon ends abruptly at the very overhung Tanks For The Mammaries Wall. Midway along the Water Dog Wall the bill of a big caprock juts over the wall. To descend from routes left of the bill, walk off the left (southeast) end of the wall. Routes right of the bill descend to the northwest. Overview photo on page 200.

4 *Bob Barker 9 feet V0–*
At the left end of the wall is a slanting crack through a roof 4 feet off the ground. Climb the big huecos above the crack.

5 *Rover Cranks A Big One 15 feet V0+ ★ SD*

6 *Cerberus 18 feet V3 ★★*

7 *Juicy Vees And Giant Jugs 12 feet V1 ★★*

8 *Barfing Up The Wrong Tree 11 feet V2*
Start 6 feet left of roof crack. A long stretch or a mid-roof undercling gains the lip and a thrash through branches to top out.

Water Dog Wall

Top:

5 *Rover Cranks A Big One 15 feet V0+ ★ SD*

6 *Cerberus 18 feet V3 ★★*

7 *Juicy Vees And Giant Jugs 12 feet V1 ★★*

8 *Barfing Up The Wrong Tree 11 feet V2*

Bottom:

8 *Barfing Up The Wrong Tree 11 feet V2*

9 *More Hunky Than Funky (AKA Beware Of Darkness) 17 feet V1*

10 *More Funky Than Hunky 20 feet V2 ★*

9 *More Hunky Than Funky (AKA Beware Of Darkness) 17 feet V1*

10 *More Funky Than Hunky 20 feet V2 ★*

11 *Press Your Luck 20 feet + escape traverse V2 ★*

12 *Punch-A-Pod (AKA Bad Ass Mama) 20 feet V1 ★★★*
Start on the ground or on a 3 foot high boulder. Excellent, scary, crux at the top.

13 *Dirty Dog 18 feet V2*

14 *Wok The Dog 25 feet V2*

15 *The Continuing Turd Saga 14 feet V1 scary loose*

16 *Short Leash 16 feet V0*
Climb the wall right of the black streak. Top out at the top of streak.

17 *Camera Crew Bar-B-Que 20 feet V1 ★*

Water Dog Wall

Above:

11 *Press Your Luck 20 feet + escape traverse V2* ★

12 *Punch-A-Pod (AKA Bad Ass Mama) 20 feet V1* ★★★

13 *Dirty Dog 18 feet V2*

14 *Wok The Dog 25 feet V2*

15 *The Continuing Turd Saga 14 feet V1 scary loose*

Left:

15 *The Continuing Saga 14 feet V1 scary loose*

16 *Short Leash 16 feet V0*

17 *Camera Crew Bar-B-Que 20 feet V1* ★

If one walks directly from the middle of Water Dog Wall up the slabs to the Dark Heart (not going via Tanks For The Mammaries Wall) one will pass by a large boulder perched on the slab at about the halfway point. ***Sam's Problem (V8)*** climbs the side of this boulder facing the Dark Heart

1 Obscured By Clouds

OBSCURED BY CLOUDS

AREA 21 MAP, P. 160

20 yards south of the top of Tanks For The Mammaries Wall (the wall marking the south end of Comanche Canyon) is the Obscured By Clouds overhang. To get to Obscured By Clouds scramble up the chimney systems behind (south of) Tanks For The Mammaries. The entrance to these chimneys is marked "Clate and Donna Cave." Overview photo on page 228.

1 *Obscured By Clouds (left finish: 22 feet V2 ★) (right finish: 15 feet V2 ★★)*

MAIDEN GULLY (AKA OBSCURED GULLY)

AREA 22 MAP, P. 160

Maiden Gully is the boulder choked gully west of Obscured By Clouds. The chimney system behind (south of) Tanks For The Mammaries runs underneath this gully for hundreds of yards. Starting at Obscured By Clouds and boulder hopping along the top of the gully is the simplest approach, but involves much scrambling. Less scrambling is involved if one walks up the slabs above Water Dog Wall (start on it's left side) until the Tanks For The Mammaries Wall becomes short enough to step over. After crossing over this wall, drop south into the gully and join the second half of the boulder hopping approach above. The boulders are clustered near a

Maiden Gully (topo at right)

1 *The Maiden 30 feet 5.9+ ★★★*
2 *Maidenform 29 feet 5.12– TR ★★*
3 *Maidenhead 25 feet 5.11 TR*
4 *The White Stuff 15 feet V1*
5 *Cowabunghole 12 feet V6 ★ SD*
6 *Free The Gerbils 13 feet V0*
7 *Snakelady 9 feet V1 SD*
8 *Trivial Pursuit 9 feet V0 SD*
9 *Lifestyles Of The Steep And Heinous 22 feet + 9 foot downclimb off V8 ★★*
10 *General Fisher's Half-Inch Journey Of Delight 9 feet V0+ SD*
11 *Death Flake 2000 10 feet V0 BL+*
12 *Beer, Pizza, And A Three Foot Toothless Girl 28 feet V6 ★★*
13 *Lucky, The Wonder Poodle 10 feet V2 ★*
14 *Fucking Lucky 12 feet V4 ★*
15 *Lucky Strike 15 feet V1*
16 *Dreamy 15 feet V2 ★ SD*
17 *Creamy 20 feet V3 ★★*
18 *Captain Fertility 19 feet V0 scary*
19 *Gutbuster Plus 19 feet V5 ★ SD BL*
20 *Head Trip 24 feet V4 BL scary*
21 *If You're Not Now, You Never Will Be 17 feet V1 ★★ BL*
22 *Surf And Slam 24 feet V0 ★★★ BL*
23 *Skidip 20 feet V1 ★*
24 *Slimer 14 feet V1*
25 *The Hidden 13 feet V3 ★*
26 *Soylent Green 17 feet V2 BL scary*
27 *That Loving Feeling 12 feet V2 loose*
28 *Three Years Dead And She Still Burnt Me 15 feet V6 ★ SD*
29 *Here's The Scoop 12 feet V3 SD*
30 *Otimojoginkbrute 8 feet V0 SD*

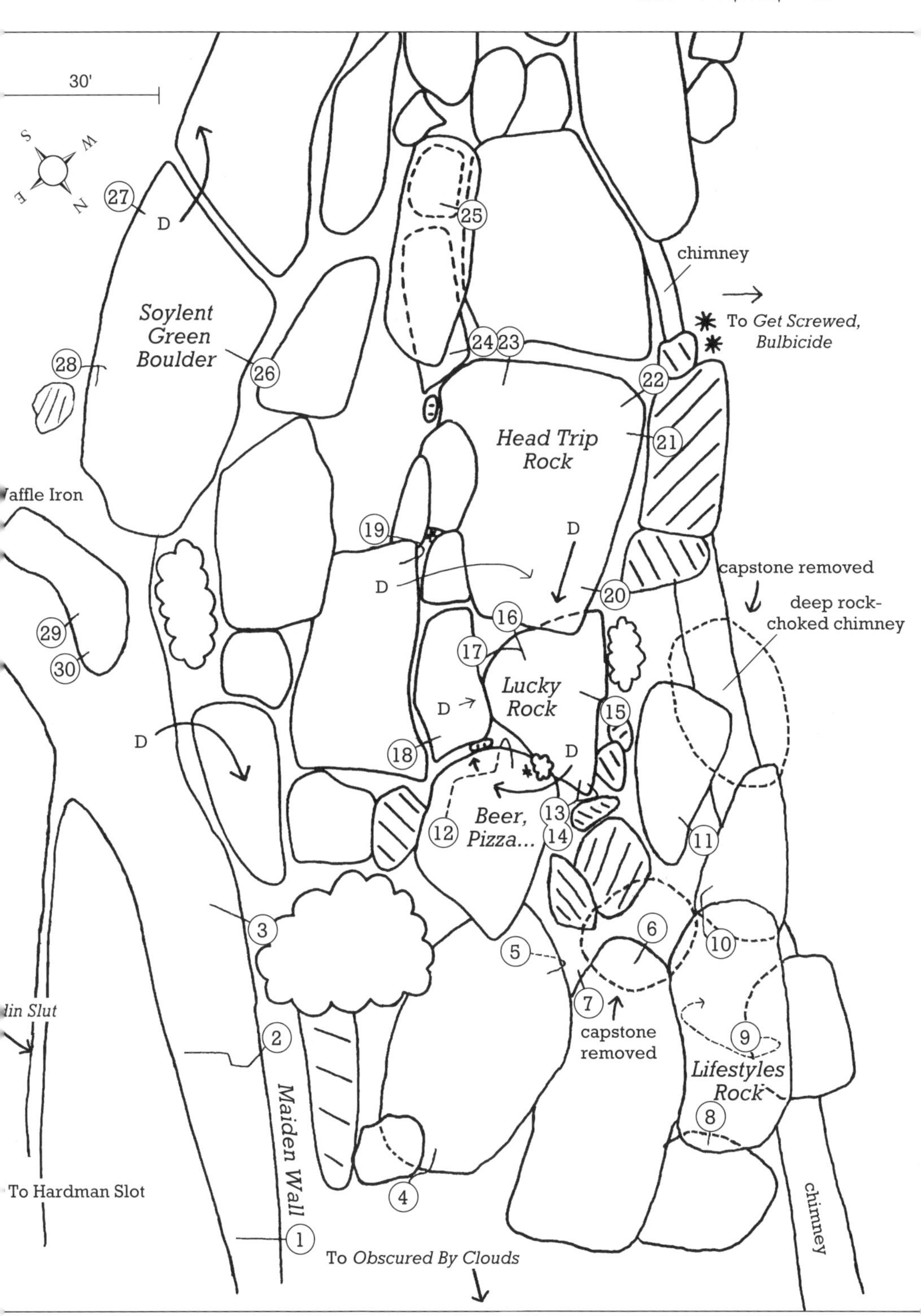
30'
S
W
E
N
27
D
25
chimney
To Get Screwed, Bulbicide
Soylent Green Boulder
24 23
28
26
22
Head Trip Rock
21
affle Iron
19
D
D
capstone removed
20
deep rock-choked chimney
16
29
17
30
Lucky Rock
D
15
D
18
D
Beer, Pizza...
13
12
14
11
3
6
5
10
7
lin Slut
capstone removed
9
2
Maiden Wall
Lifestyles Rock
8
To Hardman Slot
4
chimney
1
To Obscured By Clouds

Maiden Gully (from 20 yards southwest of *Tanks For The Mammaries*)

1 *The Maiden 30 feet 5.9+* ★★★

2 *Maidenform 29 feet 5.12– TR* ★★

large oak. The Maiden Wall (which contains several 30 foot toprope problems) is south and east of this oak.

The most fun approach, and the least practical with a pack, is to enter the chimney system behind *Tanks For The Mammaries*, then rather than ascending to *Obscured...*, walk west along the floor of the chimney for 100 yards (dark, cold and inhabited by bats) until you are forced to chimney up at its far west end. This chimney tops out at Maiden Gully boulders.

The Maiden Wall

1 *The Maiden 30 feet 5.9+ ★★★*
This is the line of big huecos on the left side of Maiden Wall. Start 50 feet left of the big oak tree and 10 feet right of a juniper. Pull over the 3 foot roof on large huecos and cruise to the top. Photo on page 228.

2 *Maidenform 29 feet 5.12– TR ★★*
25 feet left of the oak, start at a right-facing arch. Move left out of the arch to huecos, then finish up the small left-facing dihedral above.

3 *Maidenhead 25 feet 5.11 TR*
Start at the oak. Move left to huecos 15 feet up, then angle up and right along flakes to the top.

Above and behind (southeast) the Maiden Wall are two narrow slots with developed bouldering, The Hardin Slut and The Hardman Slot.

Maiden Gully Boulders

4 *The White Stuff 15 feet V1*

Maiden Gully Boulders

Left:

4 *The White Stuff 15 feet V1*

Below:

5 *Cowabunghole 12 feet V6 ★ SD*

6 *Free The Gerbils 13 feet V0*

9 *Lifestyles Of The Steep And Heinous 22 feet + 9 foot downclimb off V8 ★★*

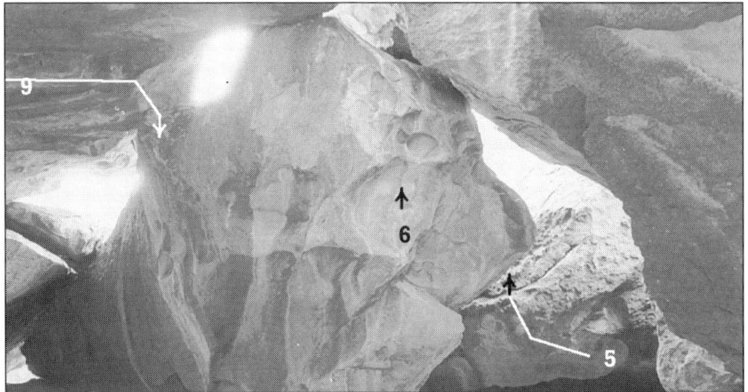

Maiden Gully Boulders

8 *Trivial Pursuit 9 feet V0 SD*
9 *Lifestyles Of The Steep And Heinous 22 feet + 9 foot downclimb off V8 ★★*

5 *Cowabunghole 12 feet V6 ★ SD*
Sit down on slab with 3 foot long "ripple" at your back. Bearhug a 2-foot wide brown protrusion and move left via a thin hueco lip, big hueco, and cool moves to the lip.

6 *Free The Gerbils 13 feet V0*
Everything goes to squirm out the gap to the sunshine.

7 *Snakelady 9 feet V1 SD*
Start where the diagonal crack meets the horizontal crack 4 feet up. Up right, then left to a sloped topout.

8 *Trivial Pursuit 9 feet V0 SD*

9 *Lifestyles Of The Steep And Heinous 22 feet + 9 foot downclimb off V8 ★★*
Up the 8 foot slab, out the 14 foot honeycombed roof, then dismount onto the boulder to the south and downclimb.

10 *General Fisher's Half-Inch Journey Of Delight 9 feet V0+ SD*
On the 8-foot tall boulder supporting the west end of Lifestyles Rock, start at an 8-inch diameter hueco 3 feet up. Traverse good ironrock holds up and left and out the gap.

11 *Death Flake 2000 10 feet V0 BL+*
A closed casket funeral if the flake blows.

12 *Beer, Pizza, And A Three Foot Toothless Girl 28 feet V6 ★★*
The climb that has it all. 12 feet of hand jams under a roof, followed by

Maiden Gully Boulders

11 *Death Flake 2000*
13 *Lucky, The Wonder Poodle*
14 *Fucking Lucky*
15 *Lucky Strike*

12 feet of funky jug swinging under the same roof, followed by 4 feet of overhanging 1st digit flake pulling to top it off. Find the big boulder immediately northwest and partially covering the northwest end of White Stuff Rock. The oak leaves are only 6 feet southeast of *Beer, Pizza, And A Three Foot Toothless Girl* Rock. There is also a small sub sandwich-size guano stain atop this boulder, as well as a sotol and a small bush growing between it and the top of the boulder to it's west, Lucky Rock. The route starts far underneath the boulder (enter easily from under the lip at the west end). Sit down as far back along the roof crack as you can. Jam the crack until it butts into another boulder. This other boulder is off-route. Move left here across jugs heading for the exit gap to the west. Finish up sharp flakes to the top. The quintesential Hueco Tanks climb.

On the east face of Lucky Rock, 16 feet right of *Beer, Pizza, And A Three Foot Toothless Girl's* exit (*Beer, Pizza, And A Three Foot Toothless Girl* is not on this rock) are the next two problems.

13 Lucky, The Wonder Poodle 10 feet V2 ★

Start sitting down at the bomber jug flake 3 feet up. Yard straight out to the sloping lip with a tricky move to get over.

14 Fucking Lucky 12 feet V4 ★

The same starting hold as *Lucky, The Wonder Poodle,* but go right instead, around the very overhung blunt arête. Climb the face right of the arête to the top. Avoiding the boulder behind with your behind is the crux.

15 Lucky Strike 15 feet V1

Climb the left-facing dihedral in the north face. It's easiest to start on the face right of the dihedral.

Immediately west of *Beer, Pizza, And A Three Foot Toothless Girl's* exit is a triangular shaped room between 3 boulders. The next 2 problems climb the south facing wall in this room.

16 Dreamy 15 feet V2 ★ SD

Start sitting down at the south face's far left side. Up and right out good horizontal edges.

17 Creamy 20 feet V3 ★★

Let *Creamy* cream you. Traverse the finger crack from right to left then up big holds to the top. Start far right on the face, on 9 inch long cream stained fingertip flake 6 inches below the right end of the crack.

Maiden Gully Boulders

12 *Beer, Pizza, And A Three Foot Toothless Girl*
13 *Lucky, The Wonder Poodle*
14 *Fucking Lucky*

Maiden Gully Boulders

16 Dreamy 15 feet V2 ★ SD
17 Creamy 20 feet V3 ★★

18 Captain Fertility 19 feet V0 scary
Off route arête on right until last move.

19 Gutbuster Plus 19 feet V5 ★ SD
An delightful treat for the roof crack connoisseur. Start with both hands on the flake at the back of the crack.

Head Trip Rock

This is the next boulder west of Lucky Rock.

20 Head Trip 24 feet V4 BL scary
Halfway up is a key hold the size of a pack of King Size cigarettes attached by a surface area no bigger than a pack of matches. The next few holds are friable as well.

21 If You're Not Now, You Never Will Be 17 feet V1 ★★ BL

22 Surf And Slam 24 feet V0 ★★★ BL

23 Skidip 20 feet V1 ★
Climb the west facing wall inside the chimney starting 10 feet left of it's right end. A left-facing 4 fingertip flake 7 feet up is the first handhold.

24 Slimer 14 feet V1
Climb the discontinuous north facing arête at the junction of the 2 chimneys.

Maiden Gully Boulders

18 Captain Fertility 19 feet V0 scary

Head Trip Rock, Etc.
Above:

20 *Head Trip 24 feet V4 BL scary*

21 *If You're Not Now, You Never Will Be 17 feet V1 ★★ BL*

22 *Surf And Slam 24 feet V0 ★★★ BL*

23 *Skidip 20 feet V1 ★*

Left (Soylent Green Boulder from the north):

26 *Soylent Green*

Soylent Green Boulder from the south

27 *That Loving Feeling 12 feet V2 loose*

28 *Three Years Dead And She Still Burnt Me 15 feet V6 ★ SD*

29 *Here's The Scoop 12 feet V3 SD*

30 *Otimojoginkbrute 8 feet V0 SD*

The Wild Wild West, Doldrums

25 *The Hidden 13 feet V3 ★*
From the south end of the north-south chimney on Head Trip Rock's west side, *(Skidip* and *Slimer* are in this chimney) turn west along the perpendicular chimney system. 20 feet back in the dark is this overhung northeast-facing arête. Climb the right side hopefully finding all the holds in the darkness. Spooky.

26 *Soylent Green 17 feet V2 BL scary*
This is one level up and to the south from the other Maiden Gully routes. It's not really in the gully at all. Find the 2 big boulders separated by a 25 foot deep 3 to 5 foot wide north-south trending chimney. These are 30 yards south of Head Trip Rock. Climb the north face of the eastern one of this pair, staying on the right margin of the green lichen streak. A test in footwork trust.

27 *That Loving Feeling 12 feet V2 loose*
Start at face level flakes. A chiseled sit down attempt has deservedly failed.

28 *Three Years Dead And She Still Burnt Me 15 feet V6 ★ SD*
Start in undercling/lieback 3 feet up. Straight up top out is loose. You can easily traverse off right at the lip.

Seventy yards southwest of *Three Years Dead* is an interesting 24 foot right-angling crack through a horizontally slashed overhang (V3).

29 *Here's The Scoop 12 feet V3 SD*
Start in low roof scoop 15 feet left of the northeast end of the boulder. Out left of the first scoop, then straight over the top via a turkey-sized undercling hueco.

30 *Otimojoginkbrute 8 feet V0 SD*
Up and left to a left-facing fingercrack/flake at the lip.

Waffle Iron

The Waffle Iron is located atop the mountain 80 yards south from the top of the Maiden. This unusual wall is a knobby, dark-brown north face shaped like a blimp.

Save The Cows 25 feet 5.10+ TR
Start standing on the handcrack in the block below. There is a single ¼-inch stud on top. Better to bring an extra rope and some big hexes to fix an anchor on the backside of the boulder.

More Cows Than Last Year 23 feet 5.10
Several other lines have doubtless been toproped on this face, but not reported.

Waffle Iron
Save The Cows (left) and More Cows Than Last Year

BULBICIDE

You can climb up this ironrock nipple wall virtually anywhere at V1. Turning the lip is usually the crux. The easiest approach is directly up the slabs atop Water Dog Wall (gain the slabs from the left of the wall). You won't be able to see the Bulbicide Wall until you're almost to it. It's just one level below the top of the mountain. Approaching from the Maiden Gully Boulders is also possible (The Bulbicide Wall is 45 yards northwest of Head Trip Rock), although this approach involves some third class slab moves on loose rock. *Get Screwed* is at the top of these slabs. As with the first approach, the Bulbicide wall cannot be seen until you're at it. Overview photo, p.228.

1 *Get Screwed 18 feet V4 ★*
Start on a big white jug 6 feet up and 8 feet southwest of the roof crack. More moves could be tacked on. Loose over lip.

2 *Bulbicide Traverse 65 feet V5 ★*
Traverse the wall in either direction. Lots of ironrock nipple pinching. Tough on the skin, pumper, bad landings in places.

3 *Tough Titties 16 feet V1 BL*
Climb the wall 8 feet left of the black streak. The boulder behind you is cracked at this point.

4 *Big Black 16 feet V1*

5 *Mr. Brown 16 feet V1 BL*

6 *Young And Tender 16 feet V1 BL*

7 *Adolph's 15 feet V2 BL*

8 *Searing Flesh 12 feet V1*

9 *Savage With A Cinder 10 feet V0*

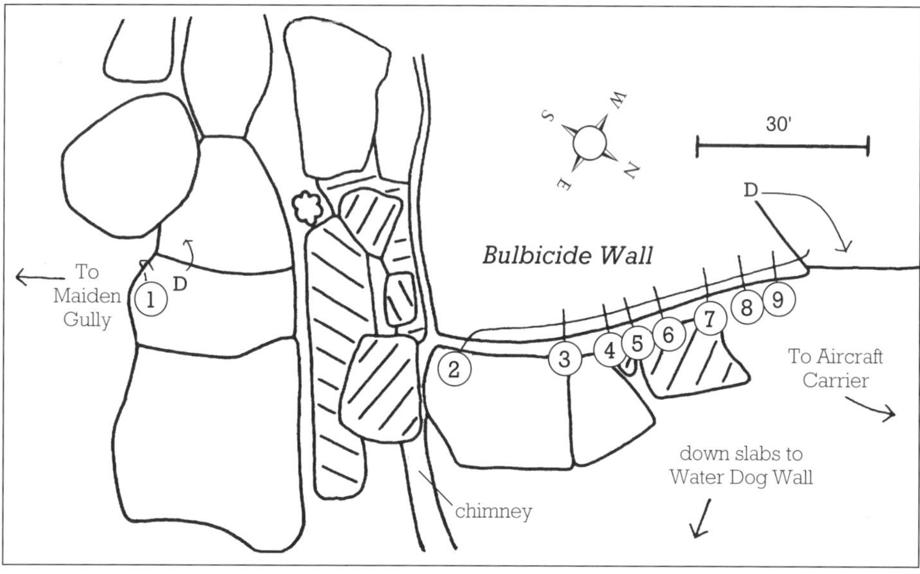

Bulbicide Area

1 *Get Screwed 18 feet V4* ★

Bulbicide Wall

2 *Bulbicide Traverse 65 feet V5* ★
3 *Tough Titties 16 feet V1 BL*
4 *Big Black 16 feet V1*
5 *Mr. Brown 16 feet V1 BL*
6 *Young And Tender 16 feet V1 BL*
7 *Adolph's 15 feet V2 BL*
8 *Searing Flesh 12 feet V1*
9 *Savage With A Cinder 10 feet V0*

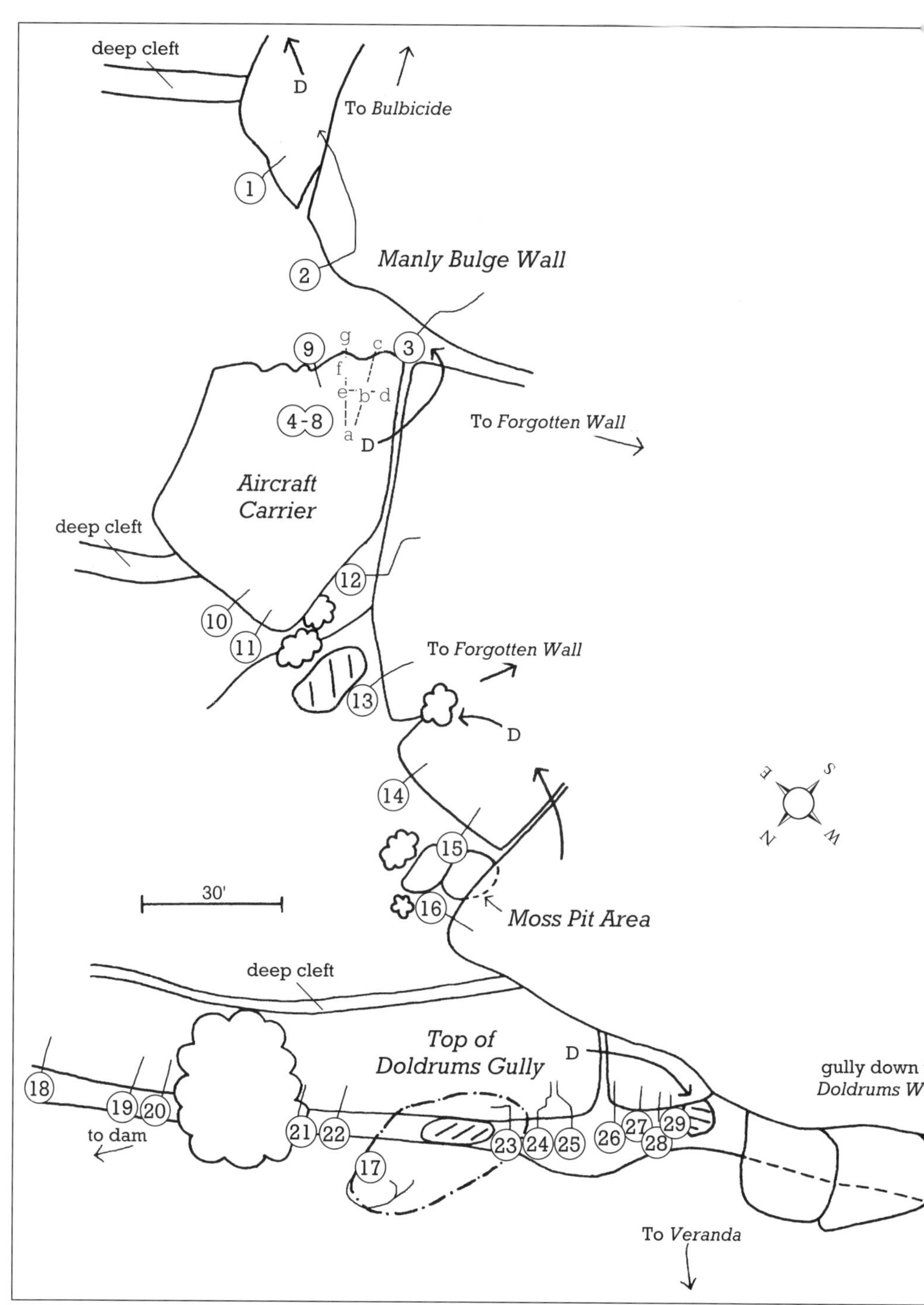
deep cleft
D
To Bulbicide
1
2
Manly Bulge Wall
9
g
c
3
f
e
b
d
4-8
a
D
To Forgotten Wall
Aircraft
Carrier
deep cleft
12
10
11
To Forgotten Wall
13
D
14
15
16
Moss Pit Area
30'
deep cleft
Top of
Doldrums Gully
D
18
19
20
to dam
21
22
17
23
24
25
26
27
28
29
To Veranda
E
S
N
W

AREA 24

MAP, P. 160

AIRCRAFT CARRIER TO TOP OF DOLDRUMS GULLY

Doldrums Gully runs northeast-southwest across the northwest chunk of East Mountain.

The northeast end is the first major fracture system emptying into the west side of Comanche Canyon upstream from the dam. At this point near ground level, the fracture system forms a large north-facing overhang with a collection of pornographic Indian paintings under it.

The southwest end of Doldrums Gully features the Doldrums, a northwest-facing wall above the gully with, so far, three lead climbs. The approach to the top of the gully is about the same from either end.

From the northeast end its easiest to start on the top of the Comanche Canyon Dam and follow the slabs up to the southwest. Do not cross any deep chimney or fracture systems on the way up.

When you reach the top of the mountain you should be between two major fracture systems, both straddled by enormous chockstones. Doldrums gully is the fracture system to the south. The large chockstone is above one of the problems.

To approach from the southwest, just walk up the gully beneath the Doldrums. Progress is easier on the slabs than in the bottom of the gully, but at the top you should drop back down into the gully itself where you'll have to duck under several big chockstones on the way to the problems.

On the level to the southeast and above the Top of Doldrums Gully climbs are problems 1-16.

The Aircraft Carrier can be approached directly up the slabs from Comanche Canyon starting 100 yards downstream of the northwest end of Water Dog Wall.

Midnight Express and *Winged Victory* are located near the 10 foot diameter moss pit 20 yards southeast of the topouts of the Doldrums Gully routes.

See the approach photo (shot near the Backdoor Boulder) on page 228.

Aircraft Carrier to Top Of Doldrums Gully

1 *The Locksmith 11 feet V3*
2 *Manly Bulge 28 feet V8 ★★★ BL scary*
3 *TK 1000 23 feet V0+ scary*
4 *The Elements of Style 25 feet V5 ★★★ BL scary (a-b-c)*
5 *The Dry Heaves 20 feet V7 ★★★ BL (b-d)*
6 *Superchunk 30 feet V8 ★★★ BL scary (d-b-c)*
7 *Snakebelly 28 feet V7 ★★★ (e-f-g)*
8 *The Fin 15 feet V3 ★ (f-g)*
9 *Fish Lips 11 feet V3*
10 *Chicken Of The Sea 15 feet V3 ★★ BL scary*
11 *Sorry Charlie 13 feet V1*
12 *Fashion Land 18 feet V2 ★*
13 *Bearded Clam Chomper 16 feet V3*
14 *Rabbi Roof 13 feet V2*
15 *Midnight Express 13 feet V2 ★ BL scary*
16 *Winged Victory 14 feet V5 ★★*

Top of Doldrums Gully

17 *Wanking Dreams (aka Love, Vomit, And Jellybeans) 35 feet V3 ★★ BL*
18 *Drawing Blanks 12 feet V1*
19 *The Two-toothed Terror 12 feet V3*
20 *Tarzan 13 feet V2*
21 *Jane 14 feet V0+*
22 *Unconditional Love 17 feet V0*
23 *Hit With The Ugly Stick 22 feet V3 ★*
24 *Tom And Jor And Bert And Stef 23 feet V2 ★ scary*
25 *Anything But Dull 21 feet V1 ★*
26 *Ter it Up 13 feet V3 SD*
27 *On a Ter 10 feet V2*
28 *Jumping Jive 12 feet V2*
29 *Tet Offensive 12 feet V3*

Aircraft Carrier approach (view from near Backdoor Boulder)

Manly Bulge Wall (view from atop the Aircraft Carrier)

1 *The Locksmith 11 feet V3*
2 *Manly Bulge 28 feet V8 ★★★ BL scary*
3 *TK 1000 23 feet V0+ scary*

Manly Bulge Wall

This wall faces the southern aspect of the Aircraft Carrier.

1 *The Locksmith 11 feet V3*

2 *Manly Bulge 28 feet V8 ★★★ BL scary*
Start 2 feet right of a 5-foot diameter hueco in the slab at the base. Up 18 feet to the right end of the horizontal crack then traverse the crack left and off.

3 *TK 1000 23 feet V0+ scary*

The wall between *TK 1000* and *Manly Bulge* has been traversed in sections. The link up from right to left and finishing up *Manly Bulge* is a last great problem in waiting.

The Aircraft Carrier

Despite the long approach this boulder has become quite popular in recent years. Except for the final lip moves, the south overhang routes always stay dry. Like the Bucket Roof, the Aircraft Carrier has many link-ups and has potential for many more. The routes are listed by their coordinates on page 230.

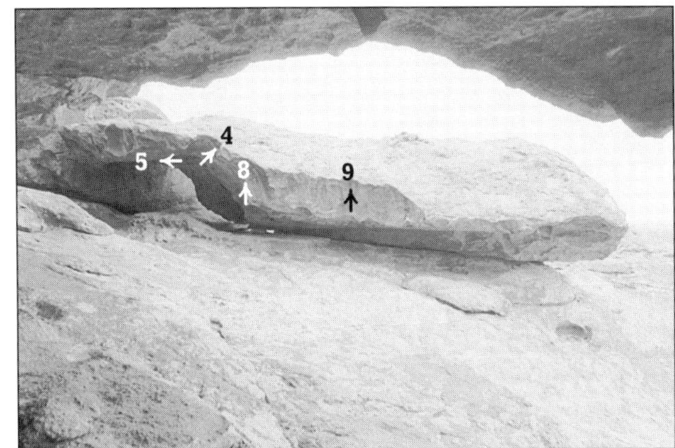

Aircraft Carrier

4 *The Elements of Style 25 feet V5 ★★★ BL scary*
5 *The Dry Heaves 20 feet V7 ★★★ BL*
8 *The Fin 15 feet V3 ★*
9 *Fish Lips 11 feet V3*

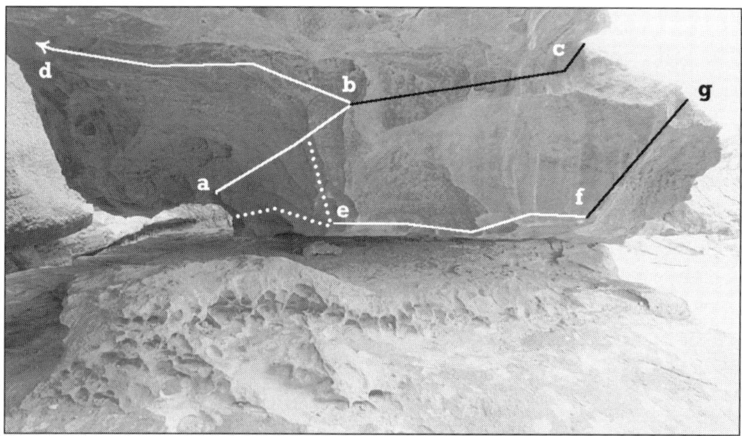

Aircraft Carrier
(The big south overhang)

4 *The Elements of Style 25 feet V5 ★★★ BL scary*
Do a-b-c; the e-b-c sit down variant is the same difficulty.

5 *The Dry Heaves 20 feet V7 ★★★ BL*
Do b-d then squeeze up the short chimney to summit or downclimb the wall to the west.

6 *Superchunk 30 feet V8 ★★★ BL scary*
Climb up wall to west then reverse **Dry Heaves** and finish out *The Elements Of Style. d-b-c.*

7 *Snakebelly 28 feet V7 ★★★*
Do e-f-g. The a-e low arch traverse start begs to be added on.

8 *The Fin 15 feet V3 ★*
Do f-g. For a real pump, be the first to do the a-e-f-g-c-b-d-b-a loop.

9 *Fish Lips 11 feet V3*

10 *Chicken Of The Sea 15 feet V3 ★★ BL scary*

11 *Sorry Charlie 13 feet V1*
Reachy start.

12 *Fashion Land 18 feet V2 ★*
From the gravelly drainage below the east face of the main cliff, mantle the white scoop at the lip of the roof 6 feet up. Continue up and left along the narrow ramp above. The west side of The Aircraft Carrier is right behind you.

13 *Bearded Clam Chomper 16 feet V3*
Start back in the hollow. Undercling to sharp flakes.

Aircraft Carrier

10 *Chicken Of The Sea 15 feet V3 ★★ BL scary*

11 *Sorry Charlie 13 feet V1*

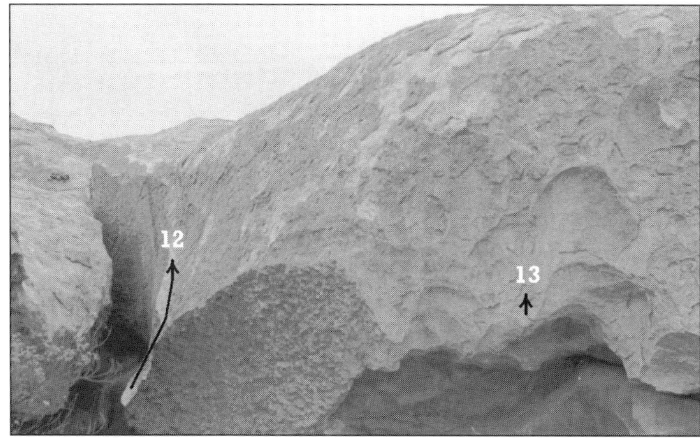

The wall immediately west of the Aircraft Carrier

12 *Fashion Land 18 feet V2 ★*

13 *Bearded Clam Chomper 16 feet V3*

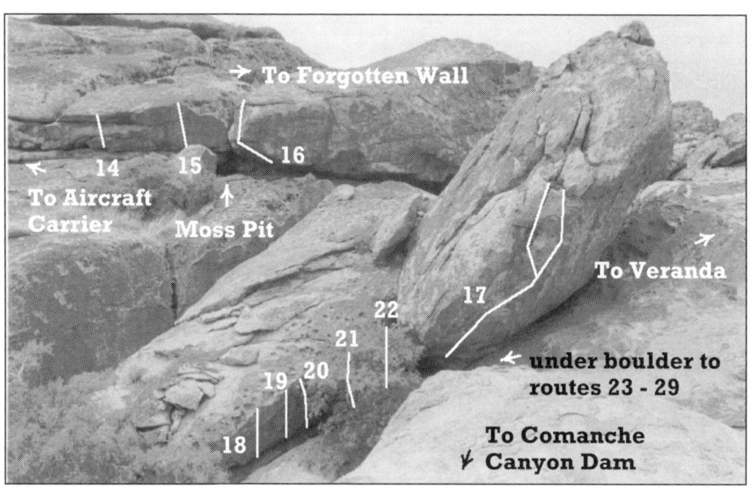

Moss Pit and Top Of Doldrums Gully

14 *Rabbi Roof 13 feet V2*

15 *Midnight Express 13 feet V2 ★ BL scary*

16 *Winged Victory 14 feet V5 ★★*

17 *Wanking Dreams 35 feet V3 ★★ BL*

18 *Drawing Blanks 12 feet V1*

19 *The Two-toothed Terror 12 feet V3*

20 *Tarzan 13 feet V2*

21 *Jane 14 feet V0+*

22 *Unconditional Love 17 feet V0*

Moss Pit Area

14 *Rabbi Roof 13 feet V2*

Watch your tip at the lip. 18 feet left of the Moss Pit, 10 feet left of the sotol jam the horizontal crack under the middle of the roof. Grab a hueco 3 feet out the roof, then grovel over the lip. Less fun than getting it caught in your zipper.

15 *Midnight Express 13 feet V2 ★ BL scary*

Start between the Moss Pit to your right and the sotol to your left. The boulder behind you had a nasty thumb, "the coatpeg," on it at this point.

16 *Winged Victory 14 feet V5 ★★*
Start 4 feet north of the Moss Pit at two holds under the roof 6 feet up. Note the paucity of footholds. Monkey out to the lip, then pull a thin move to get stood up. Great acrobatic moves.

Top of Doldrums Gully

17 *Wanking Dreams (aka Love, Vomit, And Jellybeans) 35 feet V3 ★★ BL*
Start low, where a fall will deposit you much lower. Of the two finishes the right is better. Most folks downclimb the last few moves to get off.

18 *Drawing Blanks 12 feet V1*
Start 6 feet from left end of lower block.

19 *The Two-toothed Terror 12 feet V3*
Start on lower block lip, then up to a very incut flake and small ironrock nub to the lip.

20 *Tarzan 13 feet V2*
Up huecos and out left branches.

21 *Jane 14 feet V0+*
Up huecos directly in front of tree then out right through branches.

22 *Unconditional Love 17 feet V0*
Start on a seperate small block 3 feet right of the lowerblock routes 18-21 start on.

23 *Hit With The Ugly Stick 22 feet V3 ★*
A fall from the crux would probably clip the boulders at the base. Undercling the roof left then downclimb to get off.

24 *Tom And Jor And Bert And Stef 23 feet V2 ★ scary*

25 *Anything But Dull 21 feet V1 ★*

26 *Ter it Up 13 feet V3 SD*
Climb seam left of "Ter" from a sit down start. The arête on the left is off-route. Branch thrashing at top.

27 *On a Ter 10 feet V2*
Grab huecos at the lip and thrash over.

28 *Jumping Jive 12 feet V2*
Start right of the boulder. Jump to the hueco, then up.

29 *Tet Offensive 12 feet V3*
A tall person's start.

Top Of Doldrums Gully

23 *Hit With The Ugly Stick 22 feet V3 ★*
24 *Tom And Jor... 23 feet V2 ★ scary*
25 *Anything But Dull 21 feet V1 ★*

Top Of Doldrums Gully

26 Ter it Up
27 On a Ter
28 Jumping Jive
29 Tet Offensive

Forgotten Wall

1 Amnesia
2 Rip Van Winkle
3 Leggo My Egg Hole
4 Forgotten Falls Left
5 Forgotten Falls Right

FORGOTTEN WALL

The wall is located 75 yards southwest of The Aircraft Carrier (see topo on page 226.). The descent chimney for the Aircraft Carrier is along the same fracture system as the Forgotten Wall.

1 Amnesia 12 feet V0+
2 Rip Van Winkle 15 feet V0
3 Leggo My Egg Hole 15 feet V0
4 Forgotten Falls Left 14 feet V1
5 Forgotten Falls Right 14 feet V2

Lower half of Forgotten Wall and Lower Forgotten Wall

6 *Plate In My Head*

Lower Forgotten Wall

7	*Reinert High*	10	*Hypno High*
8	*Monkey High*	11	*Premium Miniature*
9	*Baboon High*	12	*Windy City*

6 *Plate In My Head 17 feet V1 scary*
Big time looseness. At the far right end of Forgotten Wall is this nightmare climbing up to hollow, but seemingly interlocked plates.

Lower Forgotten Wall

Walk left to descend off the south end. Hard starts from low in the chimney have been added to some of these.

7 *Reinert High 18 feet V0+*
Start down and left between boulders.

8 *Monkey High 18 feet V0+*
Low start in chimney for maximum jug haul action.

9 *Baboon High 11 feet V1 ★ SD*

10 *Hypno High 11 feet V2 SD*

11 *Premium Miniature 11 feet V3 ★ SD*

12 *Windy City 10 feet V1 SD*

The Veranda

1 *Gap Tooth Grin*
2 *Jump Or Dump*
3 *The Bubba Vote*
4 *Playing With Matches*
11 feet V3 ★ SD

The Veranda (The Overlook)

5 *Flaking Waste 15 feet V0+*
6 *In Like Flint 16 feet V0*
7 *Stone Age 18 feet V0– ★*
8 *The Microlith 20 feet V0+*

THE VERANDA AREA (AKA THE OVERLOOK)

The Veranda Area is located atop East Mountain above The Great Wall (which contains the lead climbs Stardust and Tarts Of Horsham). Many of the Veranda area climbs are on the two monstrous boulders that dominate the northwest summit of East Mountain. See photo on page 241.

From the north and west these boulders look like a brobdignadian hamburger patty cut in half. Approach by walking and scrambling northwest from the top of Doldrums Gully. Another gully crossing is necessary (easiest to the west of the big chockstone wedged above the second gully).

1 *Gap Tooth Grin 10 feet V1 BL*
Start on the white rock topping the 6 foot deep chimney.

2 *Jump Or Dump 13 feet V2 ★ BL*
Start teetering over the right side of the chimney on 2 good horizontal incuts. Go for the fearsome lunge to the top.

3 *The Bubba Vote 13 feet V2 ★*
Start at the left edge of a scraggly bush, 4 feet right of Jump or Dump.

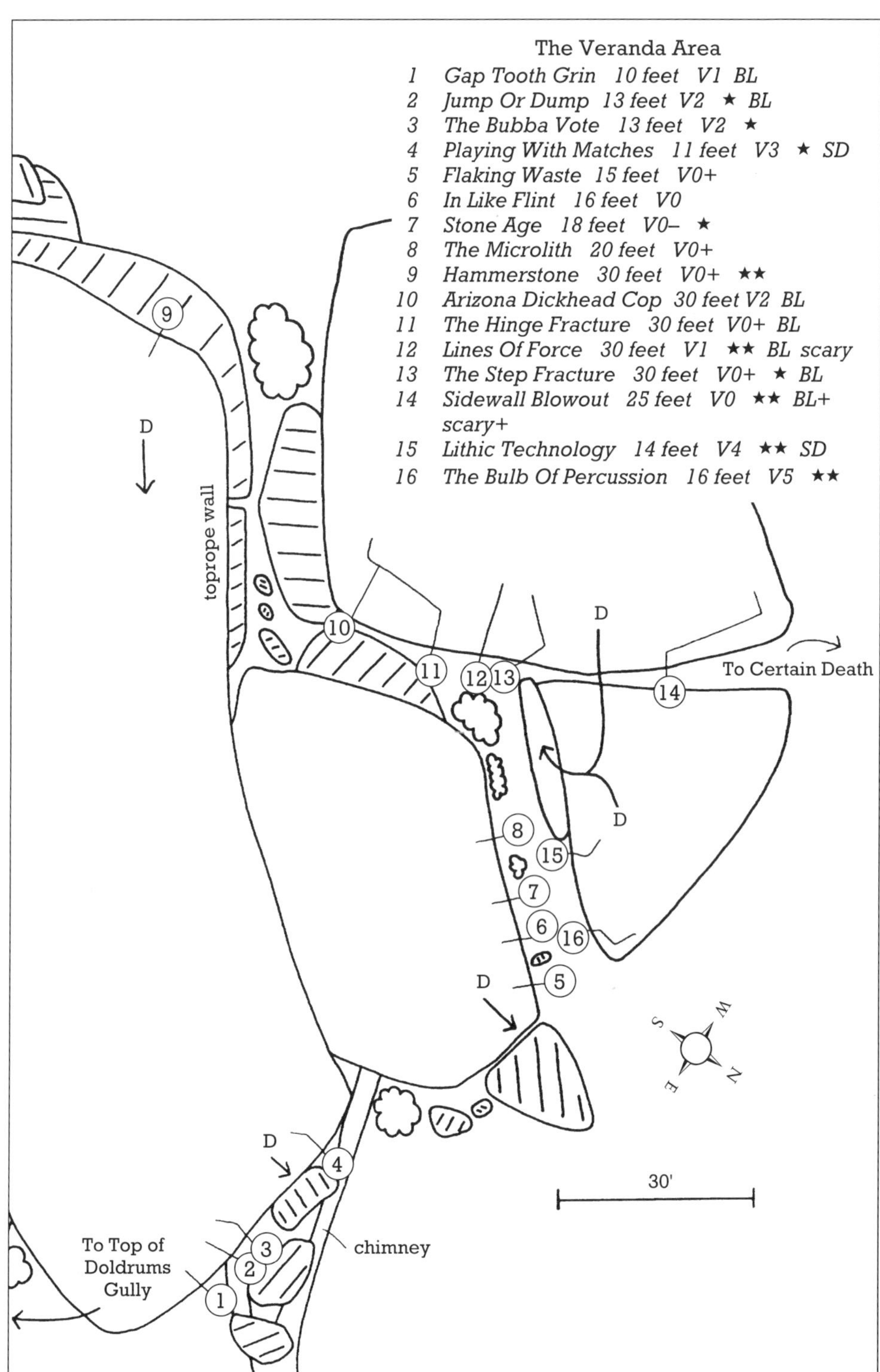
The Veranda Area
1 Gap Tooth Grin 10 feet V1 BL
2 Jump Or Dump 13 feet V2 ★ BL
3 The Bubba Vote 13 feet V2 ★
4 Playing With Matches 11 feet V3 ★ SD
5 Flaking Waste 15 feet V0+
6 In Like Flint 16 feet V0
7 Stone Age 18 feet V0– ★
8 The Microlith 20 feet V0+
9 Hammerstone 30 feet V0+ ★★
10 Arizona Dickhead Cop 30 feet V2 BL
11 The Hinge Fracture 30 feet V0+ BL
12 Lines Of Force 30 feet V1 ★★ BL scary
13 The Step Fracture 30 feet V0+ ★ BL
14 Sidewall Blowout 25 feet V0 ★★ BL+ scary+
15 Lithic Technology 14 feet V4 ★★ SD
16 The Bulb Of Percussion 16 feet V5 ★★
toprope wall
To Certain Death
chimney
To Top of Doldrums Gully
30'
D

The Veranda
Left:
9 *Hammerstone 30 feet V0+ ★★*
Below:
10 *Arizona Dickhead Cop 30 feet V2 BL*
11 *The Hinge Fracture 30 feet V0+ BL*
12 *Lines Of Force 30 feet V1 ★★ BL scary*
13 *The Step Fracture 30 feet V0+ ★ BL*

4 *Playing With Matches 11 feet V3 ★ SD*
5 *Flaking Waste 15 feet V0+*
6 *In Like Flint 16 feet V0*
7 *Stone Age 18 feet V0– ★*
8 *The Microlith 20 feet V0+*
9 *Hammerstone 30 feet V0+ ★★*
Climb classic big huecos up the west facing overhang. An oak tree is in the gully 10 feet northwest (left) of the start. The 30-foot wall extending left of *Hammerstone* has several 5.10– topropes.
10 *Arizona Dickhead Cop 30 feet V2 BL*
11 *The Hinge Fracture 30 feet V0+ BL*
12 *Lines Of Force 30 feet V1 ★★ BL scary*
The crux is at the top. Scary.
13 *The Step Fracture 30 feet V0+ ★ BL*
14 *Sidewall Blowout 25 feet V0 ★★ BL+ scary+*
A fall at the end would send the climber to the morgue. From the start of *The Step Fracture*, crawl under the gap to the right (the passage to the Veranda and it's scenic

The Veranda
12 *Lines Of Force 30 feet V1 ★★ BL scary*
15 *Lithic Technology 14 feet*
16 *The Bulb Of Percussion*

views) to enter the chimney between the two huge rocks. Stem up onto the left (east-facing) wall (the same wall as 10-12) then traverse right over the death drop to gain the lip. Be sure to test your holds.

15 *Lithic Technology 14 feet V4 ★★ SD*
To start, grab the bottom of the dimpled scoop, 2 feet off the ground. One of the lowest sit down starts in Hueco Tanks.

16 *The Bulb Of Percussion 16 feet V5 ★★*
Avoid the loose flakes just above the fin.

PIGS IN SPACE BUTTRESS

Pigs In Space Buttress is the 150 foot buttress on the northwest side of the entrance to Comanche Canyon. Comanche Canyon Dam is 140 yards left (southeast) of Pigs In Space Buttress. To descend, walk north down the sloped rock then turn left towards a ledge with a tree to the east. Climb down the hueco covered wall east of the tree to the base of Plastic Fantastic. **NOTE: BEWARE OF THE BEES THAT RESIDE BETWEEN *PORK SHUTTLE* AND *PIGS IN SPACE*, 10 FEET RIGHT OF THE GREAT WHITE HUECO. THEY HAVE ATTACKED MANY CLIMBERS.** See photo on page 241.

1 *Fryebaby 30 feet 5.13- TR*
Toprope the right side of the north-facing wall south and slightly above *Plastic Fantastic*. The approach used to set up anchors on top of *Plastic Fantastic* passes under this wall.

2 *Rejection Slip 40 feet 5.12 TR*

3 *Plastic Fantastic 40 feet 5.11 TR ★★★*
Toprope ever steepening rock 5 to 10 feet left of the black streak. Follow the huecos to a small notch in the lip of the overhang. Access the anchors by scrambling around the corner to the left (5.6).
Variation: Plastic Surgery 40 feet 5.11+ TR ★★ Finish up the right-facing flake/crack halfway between the Plastic Fantastic notch to the left and the black streak notch to the right.

4 *Death Dihedral 120 feet 5.8 ★*
Start in a chimney with a chockstone at head level, and climb to a large hueco-alcove 35 feet up. From here, climb left then back right to the dihedral at the bushy tree 70 feet above the base. Continue up the dihedral to the top.

5 *Pork Shuttle 140 feet 5.10 ★★ BEWARE OF BEES*
Climb the first part of *Death Dihedral* to the alcove 35 feet up. Continue up the right-hand wall of the corner on huecos to a short, right-slanting crack below *The Great White Hueco. The Great White Hueco* is 6 feet right of *Death Dihedral's* tree and can provide a unique rest. Traverse left to a hueco with a bolt inside, then climb straight up and right, following good huecos to a bolt and the steep face above.

Pigs To Pork 140 feet 5.10+ ★★★ BEWARE OF BEES
Start on *Pigs In Space* and go directly up and left to *The Great White Hueco,* bypassing the belay ledge. Finish up **Pork Shuffle.** This route is done in one long pitch and requires many slings to reduce rope drag.

6 *Pigs In Space 140 feet 5.10 ★★ BEWARE OF BEES*
Begin in the chimney with a chockstone at head level (base of *Death Dihedral*). Step up right from the chockstone to the base of the overhanging rock. Follow good huecos and 2 bolts in a brown water streak to a stance left of a ledge. Step right to the ledge and belay. The second pitch climbs straight up to easier ground.

7 *Pig Riders 150 feet 5.10 ★*
Start on a ramp (20 feet right of *Death Dihedral's* base) which leads to a bulge 30 feet up. Climb the bulge on its right side (1 bolt) and continue on steep rock past 2 pins to a headwall with a bolt at its base. Traverse left under the headwall, to a prow and climb straight up.

Variation: Party Pigs 150 feet 5.10 R Instead of traversing left under the headwall on Pig Riders, climb straight over the headwall on the right side. Continue on steep, hard to protect rock to the top.

8 *Pigs On A Rope 35 feet 5.10-5.11 TR*
Toprope the rotting, overhanging cracks at the start of *Kings' Highway*. This could be led with gear in manky rock.

9 *Kings Highway 150 feet 5.9 ★*
This route follows the obvious crack line on the north face of the *Pigs In Space* Buttress. Climb moderate rock 25 feet to the right of the cracks. After climbing a bulge atop a right-facing corner, traverse left to the crack system. Ascend the cracks, then step right and climb easier rock to the top.

Pigs In Space Buttress

1	*Fryebaby*	4	*Death Dihedral*	7	*Pig Riders*
2	*Rejection Slip*	5	*Pork Shuttle*		
3	*Plastic Fantastic*	6	*Pigs In Space*		

The Great Wall

7 *Pig Riders 150 feet 5.10 ★*
8 *Pigs On A Rope 35 feet 5.10-5.11 TR*
9 *Kings Highway 150 feet 5.9 ★*
10 *Star Dust 70 feet 5.12 ★★★*
11 *Tarts of Horsham 75 feet 5.12+ ★★*
12 *Wasp Warrior 130 feet 5.11 ★*

AREA 28

MAP, P. 160

THE GREAT WALL

This is the large, overhanging wall which dominates the northwest side of East Mountain. See photo on page 241.

10 *Star Dust 70 feet 5.12 ★★★*
This line is 30 feet right of a right-facing corner with a honeycomb halfway up. Scramble up to the large ledge with the tree. Rope up and follow the protection. A wired nut placement is useful and often fixed. 4 bolts, 2 bolt anchor.

11 *Tarts of Horsham 75 feet 5.12+ ★★*
Start at the right end of the ledge, 60 feet right of the honeycomb corner. Angle right past two bolts. At the third bolt go straight up to the top. This used to be easier and more popular.

12 *Wasp Warrior 130 feet 5.11 ★*
60 feet to the right of *Tarts of Horsham* is an energetic problem made all the more exciting by the numerous wasp nests in this area. There are two ways to mount the ledge at the start of this climb: start with a direct bolt protected boulder problem-type move, or traverse in from the right where the ledge is closest to the ground level. The line then departs from the highest point of the ledge. Ascend straight toward and over the small overhanging bulge halfway up (4 more bolts). Continue to the top of the wall for the belay. Medium sized nuts are useful.

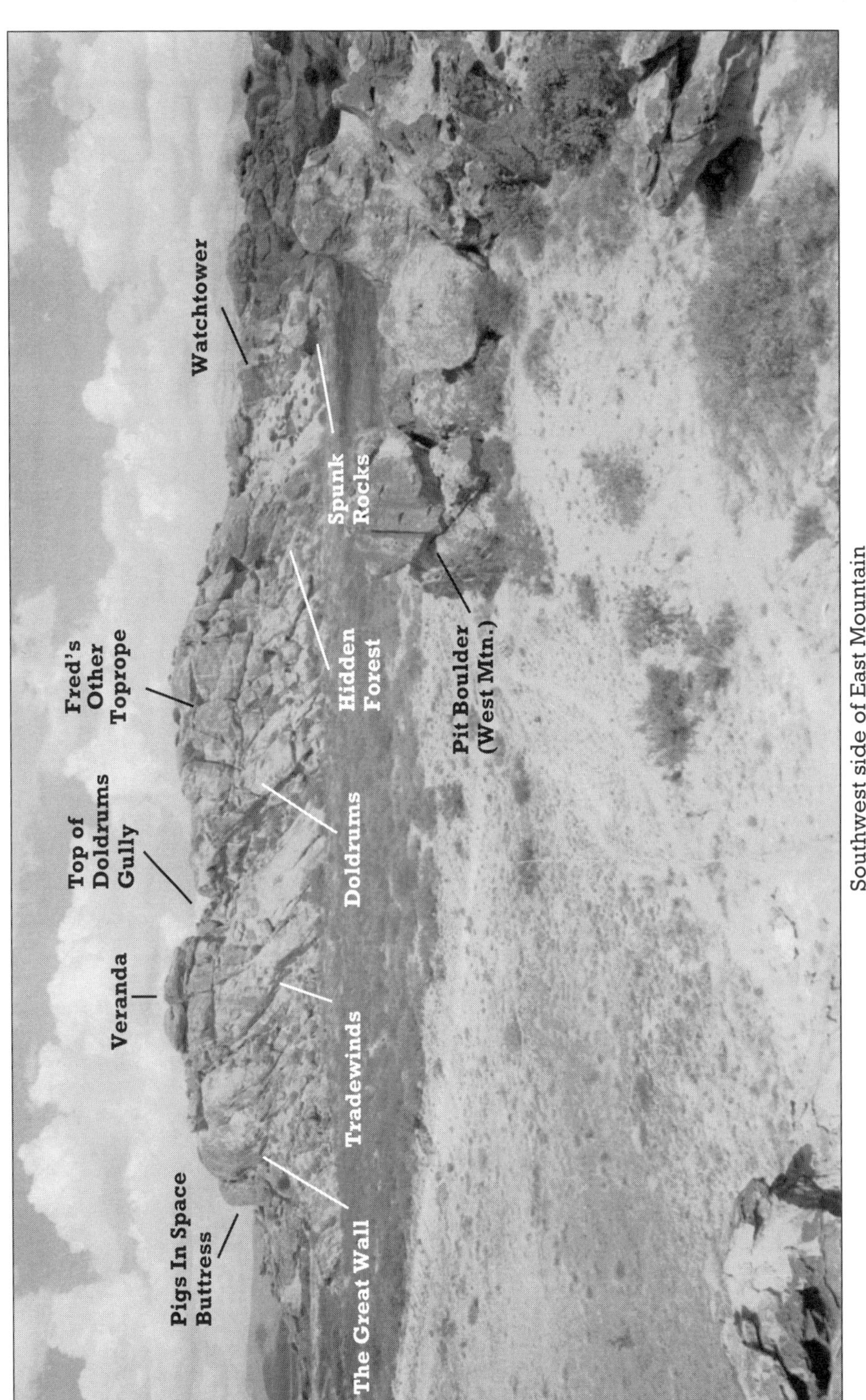

Southwest side of East Mountain

SOUTHWEST SIDE OF EAST MOUNTAIN

This area is embodies four parallel, east to west trending "canyons": The Trade Winds, The Doldrums, The Hidden Forest, and The Watchtower. The routes in the canyons are on the northwest faces. The four canyons that make up this general area can be seen from the north end of the Main Dam and on the photo on page 241.

TRADE WINDS

The Trade Winds is the northwestmost canyon on the southwest side of East Mountain.

This area is characterized by a short overhanging ironrock wall 70 yards uphill from the canyon's base.

1 *Upwind 50 feet 5.11 TR*
20 feet uphill from Downwind.

2 *Downwind 60 feet 5.11*
Climb the rightmost ironrock staying left of the green lichen. A bolt is 10 feet up.

THE DOLDRUMS

This canyon features the biggest wall on the southwest side of East Mountain. Three routes start 100 yards up the canyon on a big ledge which is accessed from the right.

The ledge is 20 feet off the ground and features a viscious looking jamcrack overhanging its right end.

Tradewinds (left)

1 *Upwind 50 feet 5.11 TR*

2 *Downwind 60 feet 5.11*

At the base of Doldrums Gully (below)

The Trickster 12 feet V2 ★★ SD

The Doldrums
1 *The Wild, Wild, West 120 feet 5.12– ★*
2 *Central Latitudes 70 feet 5.11+ ★★★*
3 *Horse Latitudes 50 feet 5.11 ★★★*

The Trickster 12 feet V2 ★★ SD
This problem is found on a boulder at ground level at the western base of the Doldrums gully. Please leave it as you found it.

1 *The Wild, Wild, West 120 feet 5.12– ★*
A convenient belay ledge is located 5 feet from the top. This long, one-pitch route requires many slings to prevent rope drag.

2 *Central Latitudes 70 feet 5.11+ ★★★*
Step left from the large sloping ledge to the left-facing dihedral as for *Wild, Wild, West.* Climb up and right on spectacular grey overhanging rock past three bolts. When the angle eases move right to the tree above *Horse Latitudes* or continue (5.11) on clean gear straight up to the top.

3 *Horse Latitudes 50 feet 5.11 ★★★*
The obvious overhanging hand crack on the right side of the ledge. Tape is recommended.

HIDDEN FOREST

This canyon is easily identified by its steep, brown northwest face and the huge roof block which caps the back of the canyon. The Hidden Forest is between The Doldrums and The Watch Tower. At the entrance to the Hidden Forest is *Captain Reality,* an obvious crack leaning severely to the left. Most people climb the routes from *Invisible Sun* to *Lizard King* only to the horizontal break 60 feet up where anchors can be set. To descend from the horizontal break traverse left to a 5.5 downclimb at the left end of the wall, below the big roof block.See photo on page 241.

1 *Fred's Other Toprope 65 feet 5.11 ★*
To get to this climb scramble up the Hidden Forest wall approach until above the 3rd class boulders, then traverse left on a wide sloping ledge to the base. To set up anchors, 3rd class up the gully left of the route.

2 *F.H.I.T.A. 80 feet 5.12– TR*
This climbs the left side of the south facing wall in Hidden Forest canyon. Start low.

3 *Invisible Sun 55 feet 5.10+ ★*
Climb over the small roof on the left side of the wall above the 5 foot long horizontal Friend slot. This is 15 feet left of *Waiting For The Sun.*

4 *Waiting For The Sun 55 feet 5.11 ★★*
This route climbs a steep hueco line 18 feet left of *Gecko Master.* 1 pin, 1 bolt.

Hidden Forest

1 *Fred's Other Toprope 65 feet 5.11* ★

2 *F.H.I.T.A. 80 feet 5.12– TR*

5 *Gecko Master 60 feet 5.11* ★★
This amazing route follows the orange water streak up the center of the wall past one pin and one bolt.

6 *Lizard King 65 feet 5.11* ★★
Climb the first 40 feet of *Gecko Master* to the pin. Traverse right on the horizontal crack 2 feet below the pin for 10 feet, then climb straight up huecos past one bolt to the horizontal break. The first ascent started at *Waiting For The Sun* and traversed the horizontal from there.

7 *Now It's Dark 100 feet 5.12–*
This is the white streak 25 feet right of *Lizard King*. Start from the first big chockstone uphill (left) from *My Captain*.

8 *My Captain 60 feet 5.11* ★
This is a direct start to *Captain Reality* which was previously lead without the ring bolt.

9 *Captain Reality 90 feet 5.10* ★
At the entrance to the Hidden Forest is an obvious severely left-leaning crack. Traverse the crack for 50 feet to a bulge, then climb straight up a steep line of flakes past two bolts to a two bolt belay on a ledge 60 feet up.

10 *Reality Check 50 feet 5.10 X*
The black water streak right of *Captain Reality*.

THE WATCHTOWER

The Watchtower is two canyons south of The Hidden Forest and directly east of Spunk Rock. It is characterized by a conspicuous white point of rock at the entrance to the canyon. See overview photo on page 241.

The routes ascend the steep northwest face above the shallow canyon. See photo on page 246.

1 *Watchtower 50 feet 5.11*
At the base of the wall, start on the face to the right of a small dihedral, and climb up on small holds 10 feet right of the black streak above the dihedral.

2 *Crankbugs 50 feet 5.11 TR*
Toprope the center of The Watchtower wall, 20 feet right of the black streak. A basketball-size hueco is ⅔rds of the way up.

3 *Stress Fracture 50 feet 5.11*
Toprope the face 10 feet right of *Crankbugs*. A small bush is at the summit.

Hidden Forest

3 *Horses Latitudes 50 feet 5.11* ★★★
4 *Waiting For The Sun 55 feet 5.11* ★★
5 *Gecko Master 60 feet 5.11* ★★
6 *Lizard King 65 feet 5.11* ★★
7 *Now It's Dark 100 feet 5.12–*
8 *My Captain 60 feet 5.11* ★
9 *Captain Reality 90 feet 5.10* ★
10 *Reality Check 50 feet 5.10 X*

The Watchtower

1 *Watchtower 50 feet 5.11*
2 *Crankbugs 50 feet 5.11 TR*
3 *Stress Fracture 50 feet 5.11*

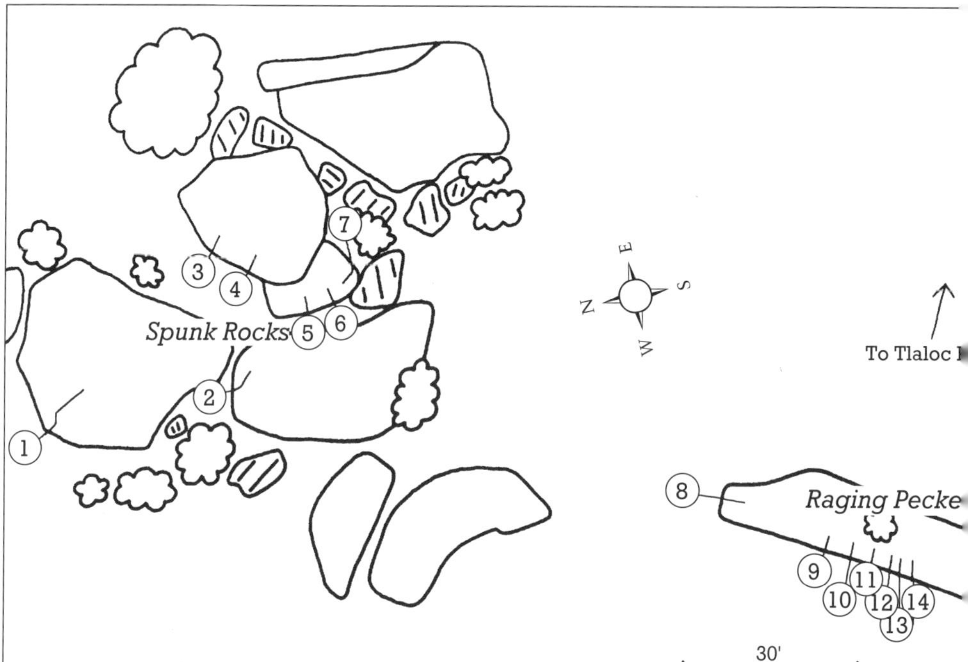

Spunk Rocks
Raging Pecke
To Tlaloc
30'
N E S W
1 2 3 4 5 6 7 8 9 10 11 12 13 14

Raging Pecker Area

1 *Wild Cat 35 feet 5.12* ★
2 *Spunk 17 feet V2* ★
3 *All That Jizz 15 feet V0–* ★
4 *The Cornhologram 16 feet V0*
5 *Kinjite 12 feet V0+*
6 *Mr. Happy 13 feet V3*
7 *Spunky's Playhouse 13 feet V2* ★
8 *Three Pulls And... 12 feet V1*
9 *Weenie Route 10 feet V0–*
10 *Dickweed 11 feet V0+*
11 *Peckercracker 12 feet V1* ★
12 *Peckerwood 13 feet V3*
13 *Pinker Would 11 feet V1*
14 *Dr. Pecker 10 feet V0––*

RAGING PECKER AREA

AREA 33 MAP, P. 160

The Raging Pecker is found 95 yards north of the pass between East and West Mountain (Tlaloc Pass).

It's a 50 foot long phallic-shaped boulder pointing towards the Spunk Rocks 60 yards to the northeast.

Spunk Rocks

1 *Wild Cat 35 feet 5.12* ★
On the west side of the largest boulder, toprope the impressive left arête pulling onto the face on the left when possible then following that face to the top.

2 *Spunk 17 feet V2* ★
Climb ironrock flakes up and left to a 3-4 inch wide sloping ramp, the key to the summit. Start 6 feet left of the tree.

3 *All That Jizz 15 feet V0–* ★
The easy blunt arête above the bushes.

4 *The Cornhologram 16 feet V0*
The face 8 feet right of All That Jizz.

5 *Kinjite 12 feet V0+*
The thin left side of the west face. A right-facing flake 6-8 feet up is 3 feet left of the line and is off-route.

6 *Mr. Happy 13 feet V3*
The undercut face 6 feet right of *Kinjite.*

7 *Spunky's Playhouse 13 feet V2* ★
Sit down start at the right end of horizontal crack on the south face. Traverse the crack 8 feet left then do a long crank to the lip. Mantle over.

Raging Pecker

8 *Three Pulls And It's All Over 12 feet V1*

9 *Weenie Route 10 feet V0–*

10 *Dickweed 11 feet V0+*

11 *Peckercracker 12 feet V1* ★

12 *Peckerwood 13 feet V3*

13 *Pinker Would 11 feet V1*

Mechan's Cracked

Raging Pecker

8 *Three Pulls And It's All Over 12 feet V1*
A no-foot flake haul up the tip of the rock.

9 *Weenie Route 10 feet V0–*
12 left of *Peckercracker.*

10 *Dickweed 11 feet V0+*
6 feet left of Peckercracker.

11 *Peckercracker 12 feet V1 ★*
The finger crack that splits the Raging Pecker. Start low for an added challenge.

12 *Peckerwood 13 feet V3*
The face 3 feet right of *Peckercracker.*

13 *Pinker Would 11 feet V1*
The face 6 feet right of *Peckercracker* using holds on both sides of the fresh patch. The crack to their right is off-route.

14 *Dr. Pecker 10 feet V0––*
The easy intermittent thin crack.

Mechan's Cracked 40 feet 5.11+ ★
60 yards south of Watchtower canyon is this right-leaning, overhanging crack in a diminishing right-facing dihedral. Move left out of the crack at the top.

THE SOUTH SIDE OF EAST MOUNTAIN

This area, extending between the Maiden Gully/Waffle Iron and the Mantel Illness Center has seen much development since the last guide. The most popular boulders are at The Meddle Shop, Home Of The Stars, and Moonshine Roof. Approaches can be convoluted, zigzagging back forth through low draws between outcrops. Stay on the rocks as much as possible to minimize erosion of the fragile soil.

THE MEDDLE SHOP

This area is elevated 20 feet above ground level and is best distinguished by the big A-frame entrance chimney that leads into the majority of problems. Topo on page 250.

The South Side of East Mountain (west half)

View from atop *Keelhauler* (East Spur).

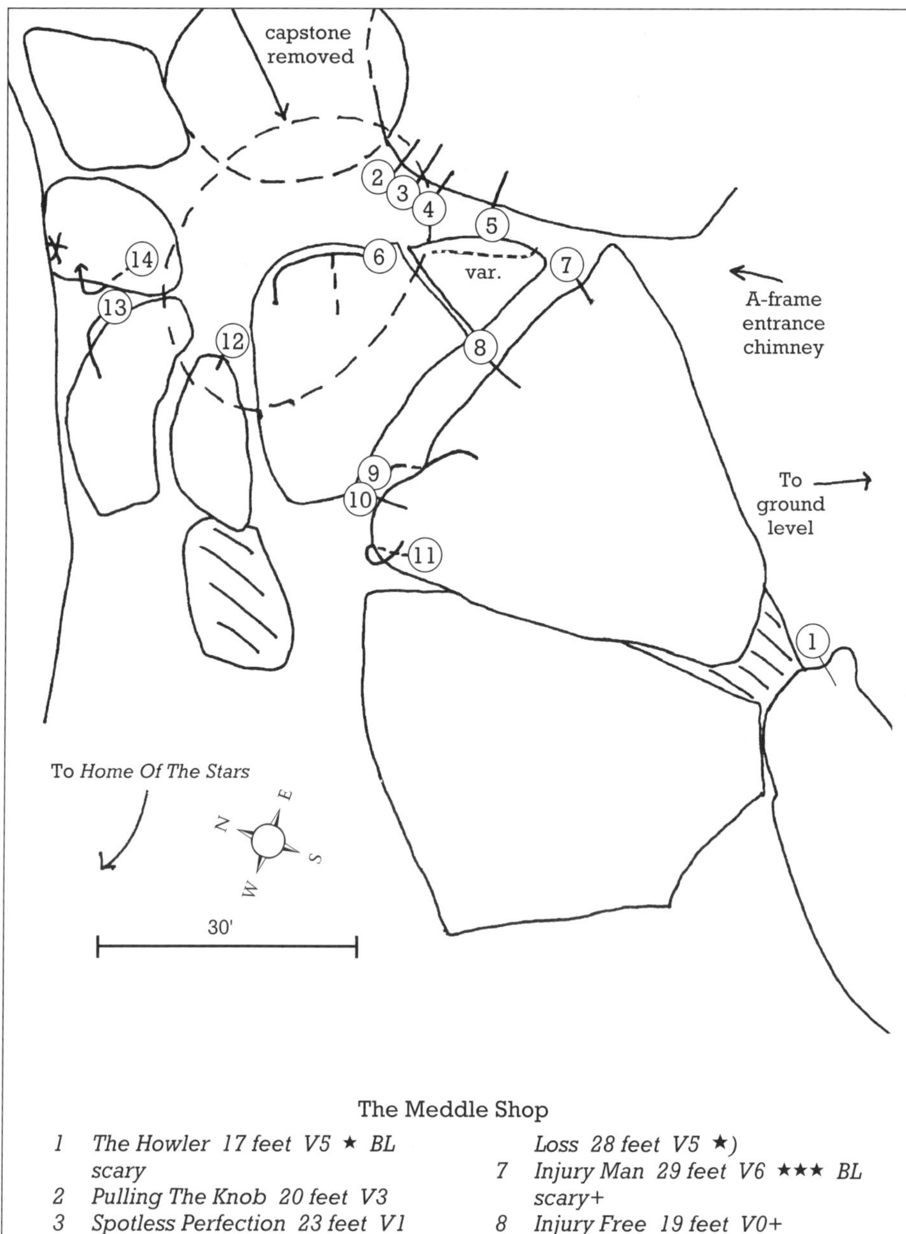

The Meddle Shop

1 *The Howler 17 feet V5 ★ BL scary*
2 *Pulling The Knob 20 feet V3*
3 *Spotless Perfection 23 feet V1*
4 *Bouting The Best 25 feet V3 SD ★*
5 *Screwface 20 feet V1 BL scary*
6 *Short Term Memory Loss 16 feet V3 ★*
Variation 1: 12 feet, V2.
Variation 2: (Long Term Memory Loss 28 feet V5 ★)
7 *Injury Man 29 feet V6 ★★★ BL scary+*
8 *Injury Free 19 feet V0+*
9 *Liquid Meddle 24 feet V2*
10 *Freak Boy 12 feet V0+ SD*
11 *Funk's Arête 20 feet V8 ★★★ SD BL*
12 *Meddle Mania 11 feet V2*
13 *Scrap Meddle 13 feet V1 SD*
14 *Funk Moe 12 feet V6*

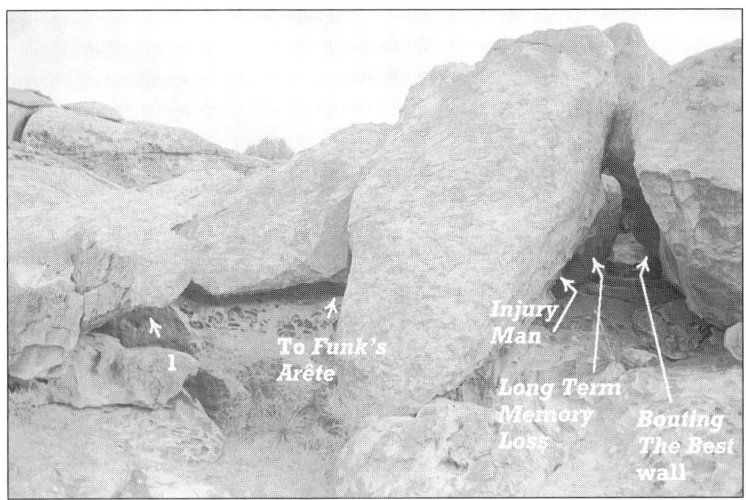

Meddle Shop

1 *The Howler*

Meddle Shop

4 *Bouting The Best 25 feet V3 SD ★*

5 *Screwface 20 feet V1 BL scary*

1 *The Howler 17 feet V5 ★ BL scary*
Start in the undercling crank and crank out the northeast-facing scoop above.

2 *Pulling The Knob 20 feet V3*
Start at an 18-inch wide white scar a foot over the lip. Up to a small knob and finish up the slab above. Easy once your feet are over the lip.

3 *Spotless Perfection 23 feet V1*
Reachy start 4 feet right of Pull The Knob.

4 *Bouting The Best 25 feet V3 SD ★*
Start in a fingerlock, then immediately move out left and climb the blunt prow.

5 *Screwface 20 feet V1 BL scary*
Start in a small, left-facing corner.

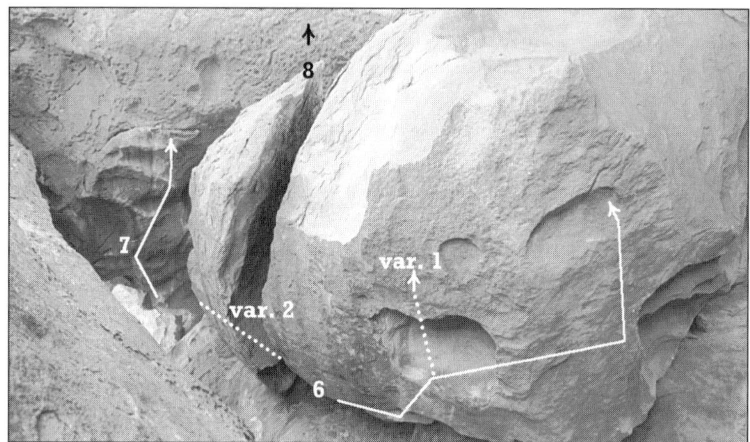

Meddle Shop

6 *Short Term Memory Loss*
7 *Injury Man*
8 *Injury Free*

Meddle Shop

7 *Injury Man*
8 *Injury Free*
9 *Liquid Meddle*
10 *Freak Boy*
11 *Funk's Arête*

---

6 *Short Term Memory Loss 16 feet V3 ★*
Start inside the roof/scoop. Both sides of the scoop are on route. Traverse right to the prow and finish up it, off-routing the easy ground right of the prow.
Variation 1: 12 feet, V2.
Variation 2: (Long Term Memory Loss 28 feet V5 ★) traverses the left hand boulder before dropping into the roof/scoop and finishing with *Short Term Memory Loss.*

7 *Injury Man 29 feet V6 ★★★ BL scary+*
Start next to a sotol, on a pointy dark brown flake 4 feet above the slab. Climb the blunt prow.

8 *Injury Free 19 feet V0+*
Start with your feet down in the chimney and with a 6-inch-wide crack at your back. Straight up.

Meddle Shop
12 *Meddle Mania*
13 *Scrap Meddle*
14 *Funk Moe*

9 *Liquid Meddle 24 feet V2*
Start on the ground and worm your way up the left-angling trough.

10 *Freak Boy 12 feet V0+ SD*
Start sitting down on the big boulder and climb big holds up the left side of the prow above Liquid Meddle's trough.

11 *Funk's Arête 20 feet V8 ★★★ SD BL*
Start at the base of the arête with your hand in a hueco 4 feet up the right side of the arête.

12 *Meddle Mania 11 feet V2*
Sloped, crumbly topout.

13 *Scrap Meddle 13 feet V1 SD*
Traverse the diagonaling crack on the north-facing wall of the alcove. Start at the left end.

14 *Funk Moe 12 feet V6*
Sharp, and now missing a hold. On the southwest-facing wall of the alcove start with feet on the cracked slab 3 feet under the roof. Grab the "udder," traverse left, and finish up serrated flakes. This has also been started without using the slab for the feet.

HOME OF THE STARS

Some folks consider this to be part of the Meddle Shop. Other folks call this the Meddle Shop, not knowing the location or the existence of the original Meddle Shop. See photo on page 249.

This magnificent chunk of overhanging stone is the western tip of the rounded south-facing wall bounding the north side of the Meddle Shop. During the two minute approach from the Meddle Shop, the overhang is hidden from view until you round the corner and are right at it.

1 *Full Dreamers aka Dreams You Right 31 feet V9 ★★★*
Start at the base of the roof on a horizontal crack. Climb out and left then along the crease in the back of the dihedral, finishing up the handcrack/layback. Started from the fingertip slot at the start of the seam (minus the first 7 feet) this is the original Dreamers.

2 *Meddle Detector 35 feet V6 ★★★*
Same start as *Full Dreamers...* but keep going straight out the roof 5 feet right of the corner. Traverse to the crack where it opens up.

Home Of The Stars

1 *Full Dreamers aka Dreams You Right 31 feet V9 ★★★*
2 *Meddle Detector 35 feet V6 ★★★*
3 *Try Now, Spray Later 22 feet V7 ★★ BL scary+ loose*

Home Of The Stars Area (20 yards east of *Meddle Detector*)

1 *I Saw Mommy Frenching Santa Claus*
2 *Ho Ho Ho 17 feet*

---

3 *Try Now, Spray Later 22 feet V7 ★★ BL scary+ loose*
Depending on one's skill level, this is either a true test of Hueco Tanks expertise or a suicide mission. Parallel *Meddle Detector* to its right for 7 feet (*Meddle Detector* holds are off route), then shoot out right over the bad landing, past twin fragile lipped huecos to a loose topout.

The following two routes are on the northwest-facing wall even with the top of *Meddle Detector* and 20 yards to its east.

1 *I Saw Mommy Frenching Santa Claus 16 feet V0 ★ BL*
2 *Ho Ho Ho 17 feet V0 ★★ BL+ scary*

Moonshine Roof Area
1 *The Sound Of Power*

Moonshine Roof
2 *Moonshine Roof Left 28 feet V6*
3 *Moonshine Roof Center 16 feet + topout slab V4* ★★★
4 *Moonshine Roof Right 16 feet + topout slab V5* ★★★
5 *Shitfaced 10 feet V3 SD*

MOONSHINE ROOF AREA

The long approach to this area is rewarded with the best V4 roof in the park. The Moonshine Roof is 150 yards uphill from The Home Of The Stars as the crow flies and is hard to find. Pass the first low rock ridge 30 yards northwest of the Meddle Detector on its right, then hook back left to skirt a cluster of large boulders on its left (Sound of Power is on the westernmost of these rocks). Moonshine Roof is the deep, south-facing roof pointing toward you from the next cluster of boulders uphill to the northwest. A thick, bushy tree stands guard at the left edge of the lip. Everything on this side of the mountain looks pretty similar and there are no prominent landmarks, so check the photos to help navigate. See photo on page 249

1 ***The Sound Of Power 11 feet V4*** ★

This roof attracts a lot of attention from Moonshine Roof, from which it is easily seen downhill and to the left (east). Only the last 11 feet of the flake have been climbed, but doubtless the first 8 feet will be tacked on soon making this a desperate 3-star classic.

The Moonshine Roof

All three Moonshine Roof lines start at the same two finger tip huecos at the back of the roof and climb out to the twin 6-foot long parallel fin-rails midway out the roof. Some ameoba-brained potlicker gouged out a new foothold at the start, but thankfully the first move is easier without this dastardly cheater hold. Photo, p. 255.

2 *Moonshine Roof Left 28 feet V6*
From the twin fins hang a left, skirting the tree on its north side to top out on loose holds.

3 *Moonshine Roof Center 16 feet + topout slab V4 ★★★*

4 *Moonshine Roof Right 16 feet + topout slab V5 ★★★*

5 *Shitfaced 10 feet V3 SD*
Sharp holds, loose top.

A number of problems in the V0 to V2 range have been done on the boulders immediately surrounding Moonshine Roof, particularly around its backside.

6 *Don't Call Me Picard 13 feet V4 straight up or V6 ★ left finish*
This sharp hold problem is in the Moonshine boulder cluster on the uphill (north) side. The straight up version follows a fingercrack at the top. The left finish moves left before any fingerjamming. Both problems start low.

7 *Go With The Finish 55 feet V3 ★★ SD*
This problem is found in the long, but narrow tree-choked notch 75 yards southwest of Moonshine Roof. It's a level down and on the opposite side of the drainage from Moonshine Roof. Start sitting down next to a sotol at the right end of a long horizontal crack. Hand traverse 40 feet to the left end of the crack then crank up the easy, but intimidating wall above. Easier and not such a crunchfest if you're short.

8 *Another Lonely Felchboy 13 feet V0+*
Start at a 3-inch diameter hueco 6 feet up.

The short cliffbands uphill and downhill from *Go With...* have a number of mediocre established problems.

Moonshine Roof Area

View looking southeast from 50 yards south of *Three Years Dead.*

6 *Don't Call Me Picard 13 feet V4 straight up or V6 ★ left finish*

Moonshine Roof Area

7 *Go With The Finish 55 feet V3 ★★ SD*

8 *Another Lonely Felchboy 13 feet V0+*

The South Side of East Mountain (east half)

View from atop *Keelhauler* (East Spur).

MANTEL ILLNESS CENTER

There are no topos for the routes at The Mantel Illness Center.

To get there start at the Donkey Show Boulder (next page) and walk west along the base of East Mountain for 70 yards (this is most easily done on a wide trail that stays 20-30 yards out from the side of the Mountain). If you took the wide trail, you should now be able to see a 50 foot tall, south facing overhanging wall to your northeast. It has a distinct buttress at it's west end. A narrow trail heads northeast through the grass towards this wall. 15 yards along this narrow trail, on it's right side, is a 4 foot tall tree stump. Follow the trail past the tree stump and two 20 foot tall oaks. The trail deposits you in a room between boulders. This room is just northwest around the corner from the 50 foot wall (which has been toproped on it's left side).

An undercut sloping mantelshelf graces the 10 foot tall boulder in the northwest corner of this room. This is ***Mantel Illness (10 feet, V1-4***, ★). Selective off-routing of holds, and shifting positions along the lip can change the difficulty dramatically. The pure lip mantel without using holds above is the V4 variant.

At the entrance to the room (south end near the forked oak trunk) is a desperate 10 foot roof crack. This is ***Crackpot (15 feet, V8***, ★). Start with both hands at the base of the roof and swing out the horrifically technical flared tips and thin hand jams to locker jams at the lip. This can also be finished in shorter fashion (if you possess an adequate reach) by moving to the lip right of the crack after 2 jams. This inferior finish removes the quality star.

THE DONKEY SHOW BOULDER

The Donkey Show Boulder is located at ground level along the south flank of East Mountain 110 yards west of the Tabloid boulders (the pass between East Mountain and East Spur). The southwest face of the Donkey Show Boulder, with it's concentration of hard bouldering and UV rays, is a popular hang on cold winter days. To descend, hop over to the boulder to the southwest.

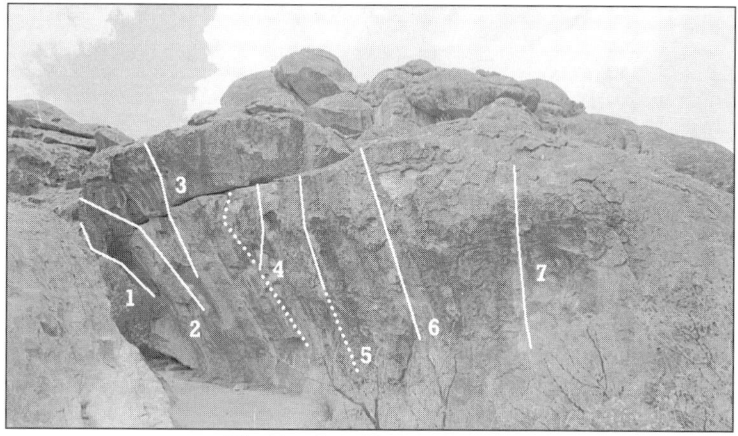

The Donkey Show Boudler

1. *Nuns And Donkeys 15 feet V6* ★
2. *Left Donkey Show 16 feet V5* ★★★
3. *Buttcracker (aka Right Donkey Show) 16 feet V5* ★★★ *BL*
4. *El Burro 13 feet V3* ★★
5. *Beast Of Burden 13 feet V4* ★
6. *Steel Toed Gourd Kickers 13 feet V3*
7. *Two Moves For Sister Sarah 12 feet V3*

1 *Nuns And Donkeys 15 feet V6* ★
Start in an undercling 4 feet right of the left end of the southwest face. Climb straight up the sharp flakes above. Starting on holds above the undercling knocks off a V grade.

2 *Left Donkey Show 16 feet V5* ★★★
Start on a blunt horn, 6 feet up the left side of the 3 foot wide black stain. Work into a fingertip undercling at the top of the stain. Head left to the horizontal jam slot then up and slightly left to the top.

3 *Buttcracker (aka Right Donkey Show) 16 feet V5* ★★★ *BL*
Climb straight up the 3 foot wide tan streak with the white boarders. A Hueco Tanks mega-classic and standard for V5.

4 *El Burro 13 feet V3* ★★
Harder than it looks. A sit down start adds length to this, but not difficulty.

5 *Beast Of Burden 13 feet V4* ★
Done with a sit down start, this problem becomes harder, but not a full grade.

6 *Steel Toed Gourd Kickers 13 feet V3*

7 *Two Moves For Sister Sarah 12 feet V3*

8 *Honky On A Donkey 11 feet V0* ★
The northeast prow of the descent rock, the tallest line on that rock.

AREA 39

MAP, P. 160

BEEHIVE BOULDERS

The two easiest approaches into this group of boulders pass very close to an active beehive. BEWARE OF BEES. Once at the problems, one is distant enough from the bees that they shouldn't be a problem. At least not until the killer bees make their way up the Rio Grande to El Paso. The Uncut Yogi/Humidifier approach involves some crawling through bushes. One can go directly from the *Humidifier* to *Modern Maturity*, *Three Seam Wall*, etc. and stay clear of the beehive by scrambling through the cool ground level passageway beneath the northwest end of *Three Seam Wall* and climbing out the boulder-choked east end of this tunnel.

The Beehive Boulders is a very three dimensional group of boulders to navigate through and problems exist on several levels. *Uncut Yogi*, *Strange Brew*, and the *Humidifier* are all at ground level. *Three Seam Wall*, *Sneaker Blast*, and *Discombobulator* all start on a level as high or higher than the tops of the aforementioned problems. *Modern Maturity* and *French Kiss From Grandma* start off of dirt, but at a level somewhat in between the two groups already mentioned. It's confusing, but the photos should help. See photo on page 257.

Ground Level Problems

1 *An Inch Of Fred 14 feet V0-* ★
The easy, narrow prow facing Uncut Yogi.

2 *Uncut Yogi 11 feet V6* ★
Start on the guano-stained two-hand shelf 4 feet up.

Beehive Boulders (Ground Level)
2 *Uncut Yogi*

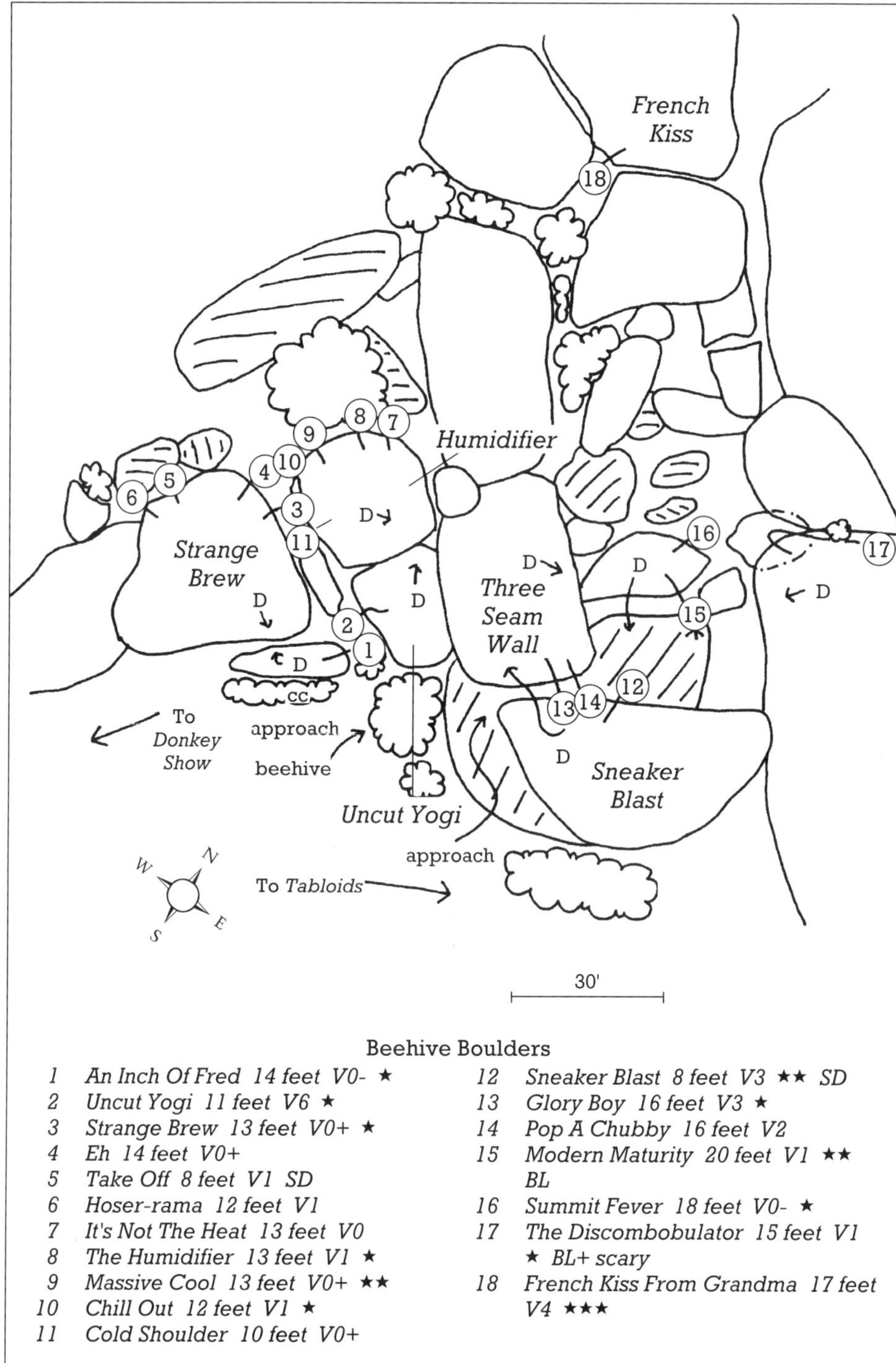
French Kiss
18
Humidifier
9
8
7
4
10
3
11
5
6
D
Strange Brew
D
2
1
D
cc
Three Seam Wall
D
D
16
17
D
15
D
12
13
14
D
Sneaker Blast
To Donkey Show
approach beehive
Uncut Yogi
approach
To Tabloids
W
N
S
E
30'
Beehive Boulders
1 An Inch Of Fred 14 feet V0- ★
2 Uncut Yogi 11 feet V6 ★
3 Strange Brew 13 feet V0+ ★
4 Eh 14 feet V0+
5 Take Off 8 feet V1 SD
6 Hoser-rama 12 feet V1
7 It's Not The Heat 13 feet V0
8 The Humidifier 13 feet V1 ★
9 Massive Cool 13 feet V0+ ★★
10 Chill Out 12 feet V1 ★
11 Cold Shoulder 10 feet V0+
12 Sneaker Blast 8 feet V3 ★★ SD
13 Glory Boy 16 feet V3 ★
14 Pop A Chubby 16 feet V2
15 Modern Maturity 20 feet V1 ★★ BL
16 Summit Fever 18 feet V0- ★
17 The Discombobulator 15 feet V1 ★ BL+ scary
18 French Kiss From Grandma 17 feet V4 ★★★

Strange Brew Boulder
3 *Strange Brew 13 feet V0+* ★
4 *Eh 14 feet V0+*

Strange Brew Boulder

3 *Strange Brew 13 feet V0+* ★

4 *Eh 14 feet V0+*
Top out through branches.

5 *Take Off 8 feet V1 SD*
Start on hueco 3.5 feet above the right hand block at the base. Climb the wall right of the seam.

6 *Hoser-rama 12 feet V1*
Start standing in dirt right of right hand block at base. Angle up and left to the right end of the horizontal crack then up and over.

The Humidifier

7 *It's Not The Heat 13 feet V0*

8 *The Humidifier 13 feet V1* ★

9 *Massive Cool 13 feet V0+* ★★

10 *Chill Out 12 feet V1* ★
Reachy start.

11 *Cold Shoulder 10 feet V0+*
Up big flakes 3 to 4 feet left of the gap between boulders. Could benefit from a sit down start.

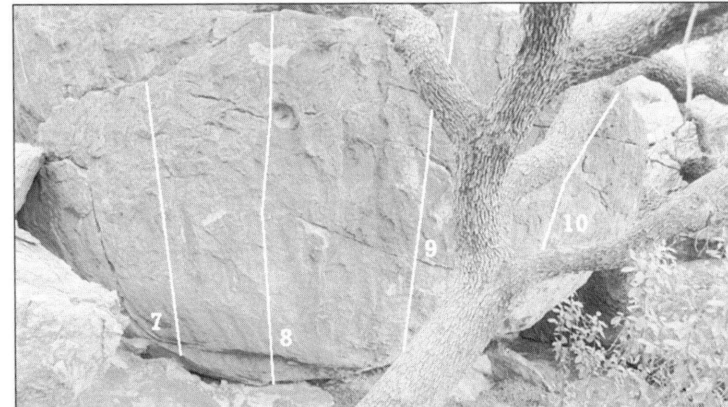

The Humidifier
7 *It's Not The Heat 13 feet V0*
8 *The Humidifier 13 feet V1* ★
9 *Massive Cool 13 feet V0+* ★★
10 *Chill Out 12 feet V1* ★

Beehive Boulders area

12 *Sneaker Blast 8 feet V3 ★★ SD*
13 *Glory Boy 16 feet V3 ★*
14 *Pop A Chubby 16 feet V2*
15 *Modern Maturity 20 feet V1 ★★ BL*

Upper level problems

12 *Sneaker Blast 8 feet V3 ★★ SD*
A fine one move problem, originally done in sneakers. Start on the low two-hand finger flake.

Three Seam Wall

Three Seam Wall is distinguished by its parallel, left-arcing seams.

13 *Glory Boy 16 feet V3 ★*
Start 3 feet left of the main seam. Climb up to the seam where it arcs left and go straight over.

14 *Pop A Chubby 16 feet V2*
Start 1 foot right of the arcing seam. Climb straight up to the higher arcing seam then over. The arête to the right is off route.

Mid level problems

The following two problems are on the same boulder and top out at nearly the same level from which the upper level problems start.

15 *Modern Maturity 20 feet V1 ★★ BL*
Climbs an awesome line through the gap between boulders. See the topout in photo on page 999; follow the line straight down to the dirt.

16 *Summit Fever 18 feet V0- ★*
The nice ironrock slab around the corner right from Modern Maturity.

Other problems

17 *The Discombobulator 15 feet V1 ★ BL+ scary*
The A-frame roof crack in the main wall northeast of *Modern Maturity*. Start on the boulder at the back of the crack and hand jam out over the deep gap between boulders. A psycho level problem.

18 *French Kiss From Grandma 17 feet V4* ★★★
This is easiest to approach from above. Once found, the base can be reached via the chimneys on either side. This can be climbed straight up, or for more moves, start on the boulder to the right, climb across the chimney, then go up.

Beehive Boulders
18 *French Kiss From Grandma*

TABLOIDS

The Tabloids sit atop the low pass between East Mountain and East Spur (Tabloid Pass). From the trail you can touch the southeast side of the Star Boulder. Topo on page 264.

Weekly World Boulder

Photos of this boulder are on page 265

1 *World's Hottest Gossip 14 feet V1* ★
Start in a depression in the slab below the boulder's northwest face.

2 *Hide Pounds Fast 11 feet V0*
Start with hands low at the finger width ribs on the left side of the scoop 5 feet up.

3 *Mom Sells Kidney To Buy Furniture 11 feet V0* ★★
Layaway the horn on the right side of *Hide Pounds Fast's* scoop to gain the sloping scooped ledge up and to the right.

Weekly World Boulder
1 *World's Hottest Gossip 14 feet V1* ★
2 *Hide Pounds Fast 11 feet V0*
3 *Mom Sells Kidney To Buy Furniture 11 feet V0* ★★

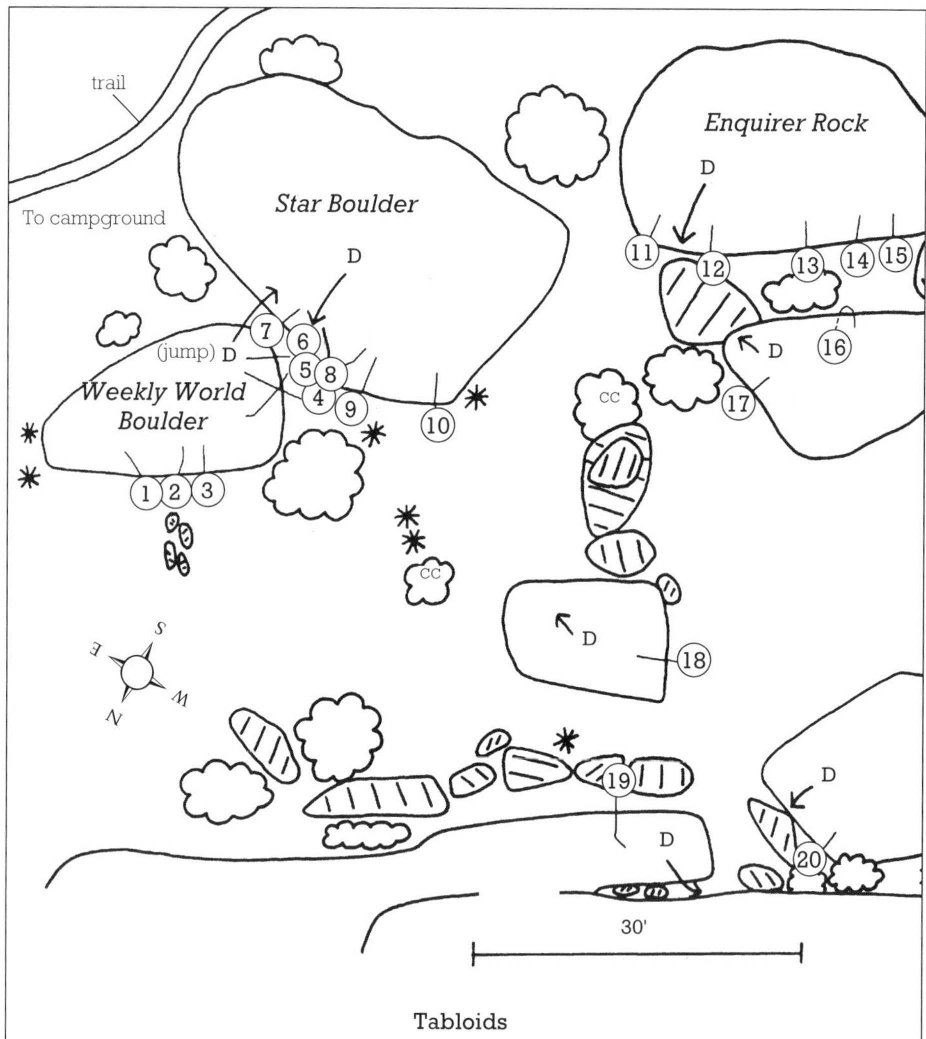

Tabloids

1 *World's Hottest…* 14 feet V1 ★
2 *Hide Pounds Fast* 11 feet V0
3 *Mom Sells Kidney To Buy Furniture* 11 feet V0 ★★
4 *Bigfoot Is A Woman* 13 feet V3
5 *Kidnapped By Monkeys* 14 feet V3 ★
6 *The Astonishing Flying Guru* 14 feet V4
7 *The Baffling Chair Of Death* 9 feet V0+ ★ SD
8 *Incredible Pix* 16 feet V1 ★★
9 *Sex After Death* 19 feet V9 ★★★
10 *Legless Little Hero* 10 feet V5
11 *Pygmy Shocker* 8 feet V0+
12 *Dwarf Toss Tragedy* 9 feet V2 SD
13 *Miracle Baby* 10 feet V3 ★ SD BL
14 *Amazing Little Halfboy* 9 feet V5 ★ SD BL
15 *Human Shot Putt* 8 feet V1 ★★ SD BL
16 *Castro's Bizarre Wormburger* 9 feet V4
17 *Midge* 8 feet V1 SD BL
18 *Elvis Had Gay Affair* 11 feet V0–
19 *Baby Born With Wooden Leg* 15 feet V2 BL
20 *Baboon Boy* 14 feet V3 ★

Weekly World, Star boulders
4 *Bigfoot Is A Woman 13 feet V3*
5 *Kidnapped By Monkeys 14 feet V3 ★*
6 *The Astonishing Flying Guru 14 feet V4*
7 *The Baffling Chair Of Death 9 feet V0+ ★ SD*

4 *Bigfoot Is A Woman 13 feet V3*
Start in the diagonal crack on the west face. Leave the crack and move up and right via switching layaways to a desperate, loose lip encounter. Contrived.

5 *Kidnapped By Monkeys 14 feet V3 ★*
Start low, at the bottom of the diagonal crack. Climb the crack, crossing *Bigfoot Is A Woman,* then throw for the summit. Yet another grim top out.

6 *The Astonishing Flying Guru 14 feet V4*
Start just right of the diagonal crack. Probably harder since a lip hold broke off.

The Star Boulder

7 *The Baffling Chair Of Death 9 feet V0+ ★ SD*
Start sitting down 6 feet left of the crack that runs along the descent ramp.

8 *Incredible Pix 16 feet V1 ★★*
Start on the 9 inch by 24 inch ledge just right of the descent ramp crack at the 6-foot level. Climb beautiful ironrock incuts up the prow above.

9 *Sex After Death 19 feet was V9 ★★★*
Top scientists prove what top perverts knew all along. Start sitting down 4 feet right of *Incredible Pix* with fingers in a good 3 finger pocket 4 feet up. This pocket had been enlarged by some ego-bloated tosser who found that this hold didn't fit his ability. The ledge on *Incredible Pix* is off-route, but the one digit tooth 2 feet to it's right is on. Easier with chiseled holds and small fingers. It's even been climbed in stocking feet.

10 *Legless Little Hero 10 feet V5*
Starting on the rock at the base, crank or jump to the downward jam crack. Either go right along the crack or straight over.

Star Boulder
8 *Incredible Pix*
9 *Sex After Death*
10 *Legless Little Hero*

Enquirer Rock

11	*Pygmy Shocker*	14	*Amazing Little Halfboy*
12	*Dwarf Toss Tragedy*	15	*Human Shot Putt*
13	*Miracle Baby*	17	*Midge 8 feet V1 SD BL*

Enquirer Rock

11 *Pygmy Shocker 8 feet V0+*
Start with hands 5 feet up on the base of a 2 foot wide by 3 foot tall oblong scoop.

12 *Dwarf Toss Tragedy 9 feet V2 SD*
Start with hands on fins in a cream colored hueco 3 feet up. For years the face right of this attracted attention. Climbers wondered who would be the man or woman hard enough to pull off the hideous razor edge move (also a key hold for a traverse of this rock). We'll never know – some raisin-balled retrograde filed away the business end of the crux hold and with it any glory an ascent could have provided.

13 *Miracle Baby 10 feet V3 ★ SD BL*

14 *Amazing Little Halfboy 9 feet V5 ★ SD BL*

15 *Human Shot Putt 8 feet V1 ★★ SD BL*

Miscellaneous Rocks

16 *Castro's Bizarre Wormburger 9 feet V4*
A tough lock-off problem coming out the roof facing Enquirer Rock.

17 *Midge 8 feet V1 SD BL*
Start with hands on a 1 inch wide by 10 inch long smile.

18 *Elvis Had Gay Affair 11 feet V0–*
Barely a route. Climb the left side of the west face starting at the short bush.

19 *Baby Born With Wooden Leg 15 feet V2 BL*
The southeast face starting at the gap between the two boulders closest to it's base. Some loose holds at the top.

20 *Baboon Boy 14 feet V3 ★*
Well hidden behind an 8 foot tall flake and an even bigger bush. Battle through the branches up the north arête.

The Meddle Detector, Home of the Stars

North end of East Spur

EAST SPUR

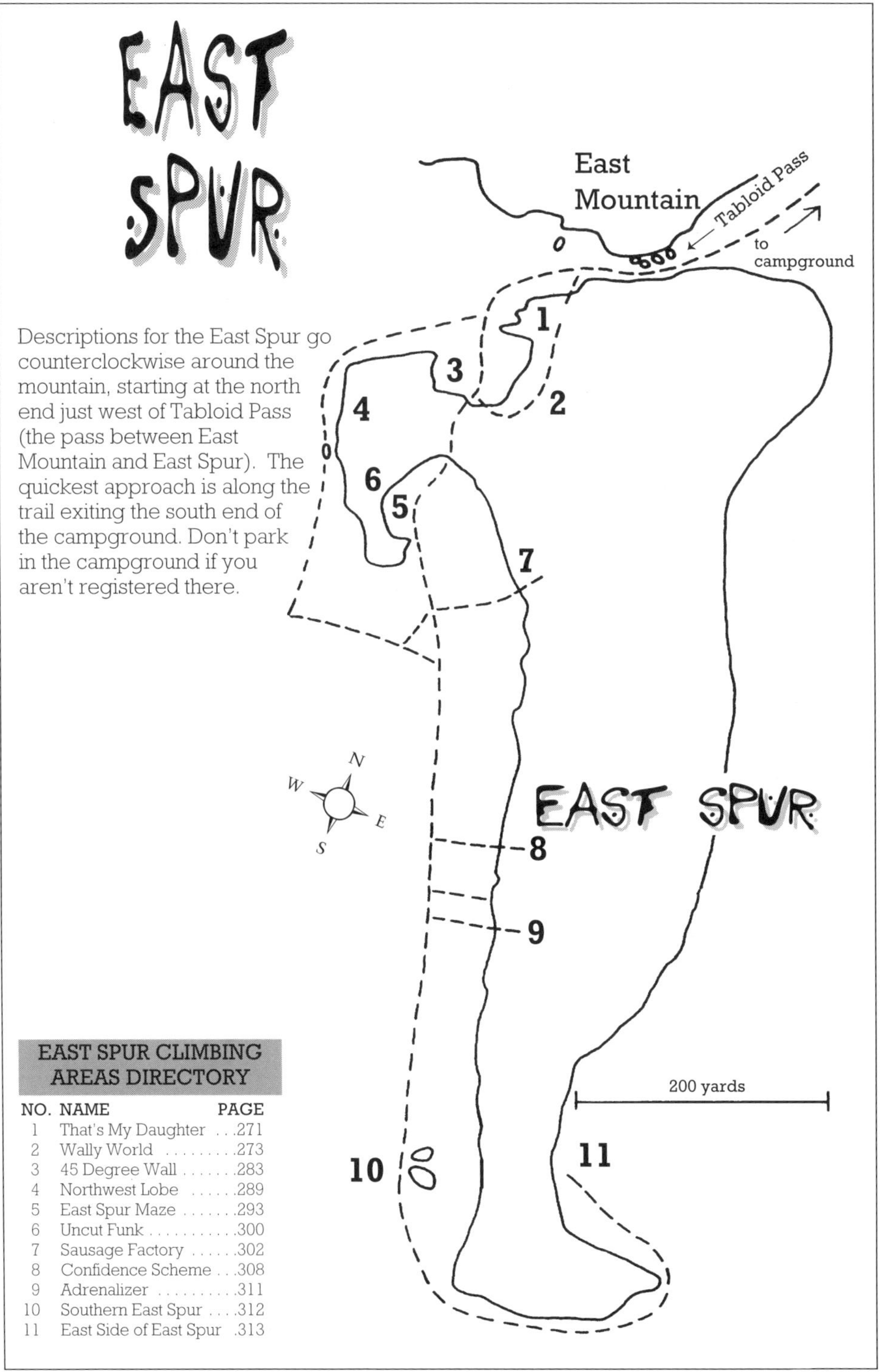

Descriptions for the East Spur go counterclockwise around the mountain, starting at the north end just west of Tabloid Pass (the pass between East Mountain and East Spur). The quickest approach is along the trail exiting the south end of the campground. Don't park in the campground if you aren't registered there.

EAST SPUR CLIMBING AREAS DIRECTORY

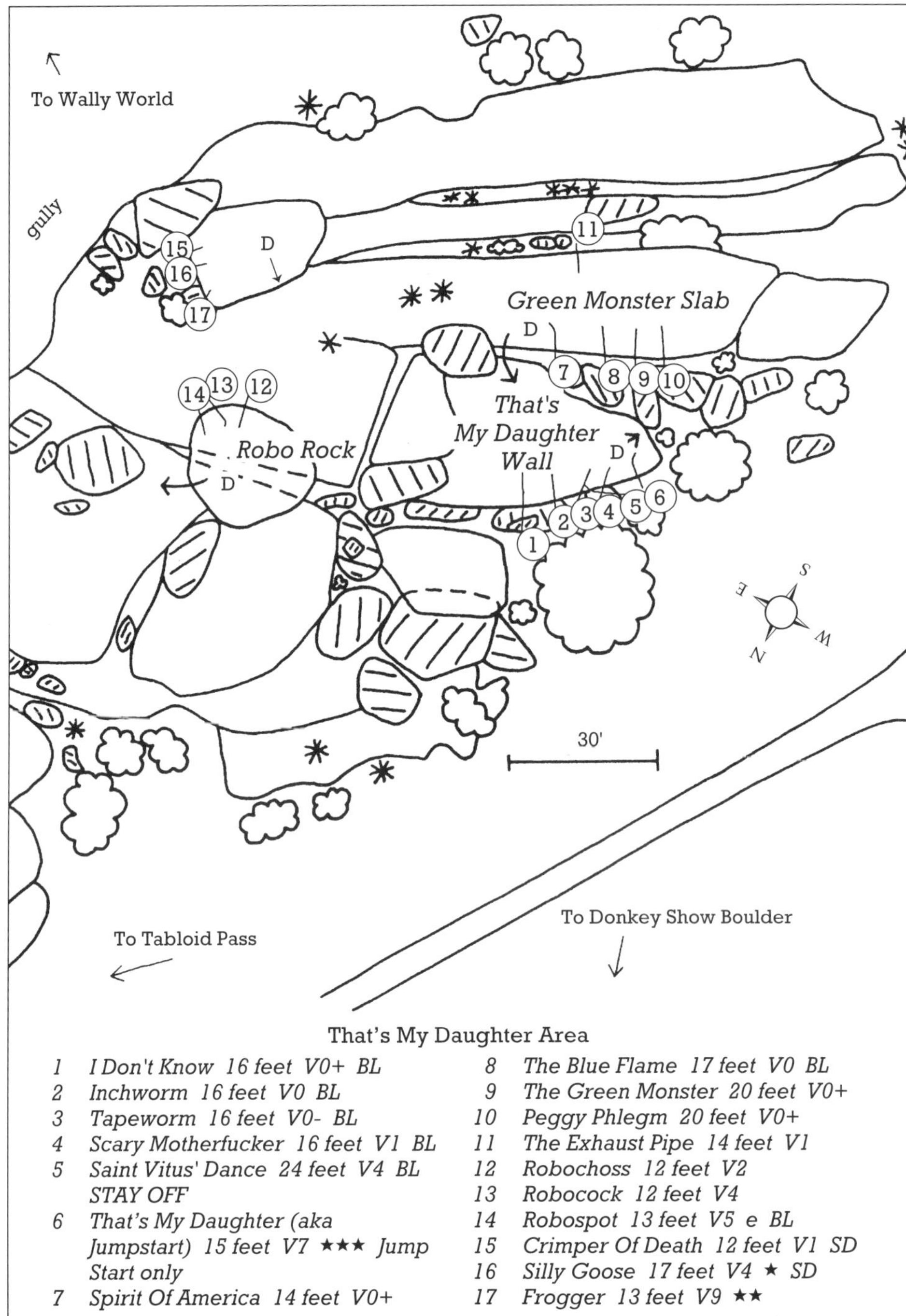
To Wally World
gully
D
Green Monster Slab
Robo Rock
That's My Daughter Wall
D
D
D
S
E
W
N
30'
To Donkey Show Boulder
To Tabloid Pass
That's My Daughter Area
1 I Don't Know 16 feet V0+ BL
2 Inchworm 16 feet V0 BL
3 Tapeworm 16 feet V0- BL
4 Scary Motherfucker 16 feet V1 BL
5 Saint Vitus' Dance 24 feet V4 BL STAY OFF
6 That's My Daughter (aka Jumpstart) 15 feet V7 ★★★ Jump Start only
7 Spirit Of America 14 feet V0+
8 The Blue Flame 17 feet V0 BL
9 The Green Monster 20 feet V0+
10 Peggy Phlegm 20 feet V0+
11 The Exhaust Pipe 14 feet V1
12 Robochoss 12 feet V2
13 Robocock 12 feet V4
14 Robospot 13 feet V5 e BL
15 Crimper Of Death 12 feet V1 SD
16 Silly Goose 17 feet V4 ★ SD
17 Frogger 13 feet V9 ★★

THAT'S MY DAUGHTER AREA

This area is at the north end of the East Spur, 100-150 yards west of the pass between East Spur and East Mountain. That's My Daughter is the one problem on this topo that starts in the dirt at ground level. The other problems start atop blocks or other levels. *That's My Daughter* is on the severely undercut northwest face 55 yards south of the Donkey Show Boulder. A big oak obscures the undercut part of this face, but from the Donkey Show Boulder the top with two angling thin cracks and the overhung right end can be seen through the vegetation. Approach the right side of this wall to get to routes 1-3.

1 *I Don't Know 16 feet V0+ BL*

2 *Inchworm 16 feet V0 BL*

3 *Tapeworm 16 feet V0- BL*

4 *Scary Motherfucker 16 feet V1 BL*

5 *Saint Vitus' Dance 24 feet V4 BL STAY OFF*

This starts 12 feet left of Jumpstart and traverses holds left along the lip to finish up *Tapeworm* or *Scary Motherfucker.* A number of Indian paintings are immediately underneath this problem and the odds of touching them with one's feet are too high to risk. Why this route is open while the Kiva Cave and Bucket Roof are closed is a mystery. Please refrain from doing this route.

6 *That's My Daughter (aka Jumpstart) 15 feet V7 ★★★ Jump Start only*

8 feet from the right end of the wall is this classic. Jump to the first holds (a running start might be necessary), then slap your way to the top. Please respect the Indian art work below this problem DON'T ATTEMPT A STATIC OR SITDOWN START. Only do the jump start. This way your feet will stay safely clear of the artwork.

That's My Daughter...

Above, and left:

1 *I Don't Know 16 feet V0+ BL*

2 *Inchworm 16 feet V0 BL*

3 *Tapeworm 16 feet V0- BL*

4 *Scary Motherfucker 16 feet V1 BL*

5 *Saint Vitus' Dance 24 feet V4 BL STAY OFF*

6 *That's My Daughter (aka Jumpstart) 15 feet V7 ★★★ Jump Start only*

Avoid hatched rock art zone underneath That's My Daughter..

Green Monster Wall

7 *Spirit Of America 14 feet V0+*
8 *The Blue Flame 17 feet V0 BL*
9 *The Green Monster 20 feet V0+*
10 *Peggy Phlegm 20 feet V0+*

Green Monster Wall

Green Monster Wall is the ironrock wall behind (south of) *That's My Daughter.* The bottom half is covered with green lichen. Photo, p. 268.

7 *Spirit Of America 14 feet V0+*

8 *The Blue Flame 17 feet V0 BL*

9 *The Green Monster 20 feet V0+*

10 *Peggy Phlegm 20 feet V0+*

The backside of the Green Monster Wall has the following worthless route.

11 *The Exhaust Pipe 14 feet V1*
Start at the upper end of the chimney under the Southeast face, just left of a scraggly bush. Grab a hardball size hueco and do a long crank to the lip.

Roborock

Roborock bridges the east end of the fissure system that formed That's My Daughter Wall. The next 3 problems are on it's sweeping southeast side. Photo, p. 268.

12 *Robochoss 12 feet V2*

13 *Robocock 12 feet V4*
This and *Robospot* start on the same first hold, a horizontal fingerslot 5 feet up.

14 *Robospot 13 feet V5 ★ BL*
Starting from the slot on *Robocock,* dig in to the left facing flake above and mo to the lip. Sharp.

Roborock

12 *Robochoss 12 feet V2*
13 *Robocock 12 feet V4*
14 *Robospot 13 feet V5 ★ BL*

Frogger Rock
15 *Crimper Of Death 12 feet V1 SD*
16 *Silly Goose 17 feet V4 ★ SD*
17 *Frogger 13 feet V9 ★★*

Frogger Rock

15 *Crimper Of Death 12 feet V1 SD*
16 *Silly Goose 17 feet V4 ★ SD*
17 *Frogger 13 fcct V9 ★★*
Start with hands low.

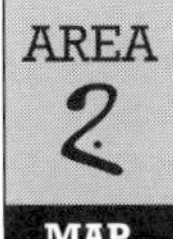

WALLY WORLD

Wally World is used to refer to the boulders above the 45 Degree Wall, 50-100 yards to the east. It's broken into 2 sections in this book – the Stableboy Rock area to the north and east of 45 Degree Wall, and the Gunks Area to the southeast of 45 Degree Wall.

Stableboy Rock Area

Stableboy Rock lies a few yards away from the main cliff which overhangs Stableboy Rock's east face. It can be found by walking southwest along the base of the main cliff starting at Tabloid Pass. After 115 yards (from the Star Boulder in Tabloid Pass, do not drop elevation from the pass) you should see Indian paintings under the overhang to your left (east) and a juniper in front of you. Problems 12 and 13 are on the main wall next to a forked oak just past this juniper. Stableboy Rock is the enormous boulder 20 yards south of the juniper. A tunnel squeezes along the base of it's east face. Purina Rock is one level below Stableboy Rock Problems 1 through 5 are found on boulders downhill from Purina Rock. Topo, page 275.

Headcracker 70 feet 5.12 ★
40 yards north of Stableboy rock on the main cliff is this obvious crack splitting an 11 foot roof (14 feet above the ground) and the bulges above. The listed approach for Stableboy Rock passes beneath this roof.

Longshot Rock

This is the tall, prominent boulder at the lower end of the southeast side of the gully between That's My Daughter Area and Wally World. Longshot Rock is at ground level.

1 *Longshot 18 feet V3 ★★★*
Start 4 feet right of a bush. The right end of a hollow flake is above the undercut start. Grab a good undercling 5 feet up and stretch for the left angling edge above. Positive edges keep appearing – always at arm's length. Committing, scary, bad landing.
2 *The Control Tower 29 feet V3 ★★ Scary+ loose*

Longshot Rock, Tropicana

1 *Longshot 18 feet V3* ★★★

2 *The Control Tower 29 feet V3* ★★ *Scary+ loose*

3 *Hot Oil And Silicon 12 feet V1*

4 *Feed The Kitty 10 feet V1*

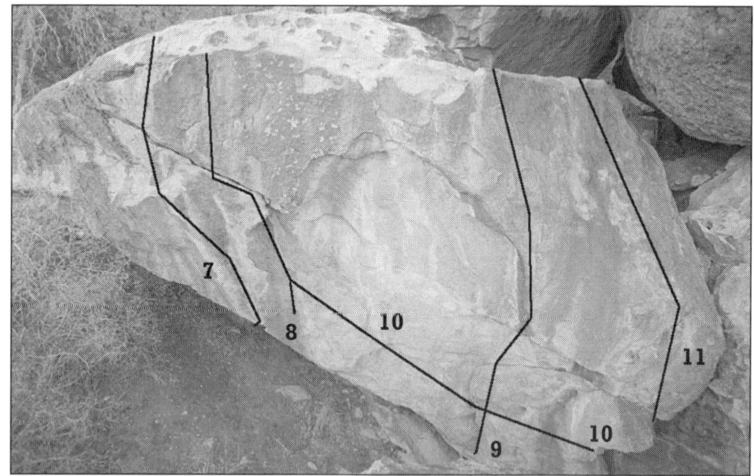

Purina Wall (below)

7 *That Hi-Pro Glow 17 feet V6* ★★

8 *Puppy Chow 15 feet V0* ★

9 *Chow Chow Chow 20 feet V4* ★★ *BL scary*

10 *Gravy Train Tryout 25 feet V5* ★

11 *You Bring Out The Mess In Me 21 feet V1* ★ *BL*

The Tropicana

3 *Hot Oil And Silicon 12 feet V1*

Climb the center of the northwest face using a sloping 4 finger hueco 8 feet up.

4 *Feed The Kitty 10 feet V1 SD*

Sit down start on the south face. From the well incut flake crank 4 feet up the overhang to an 18 inch long hollow fingertip flake over the lip.

Purina Wall

There is an active beehive in the trunk above and to the north of this wall.

5 *Seagram's VO 11 feet V0*

The short convex overhang southwest of Purina Wall.

6 *Instant Expert 9 feet V5 SD*

Around the corner left of *Hi-Pro Glow* is this problem now buried under a fallen tree.

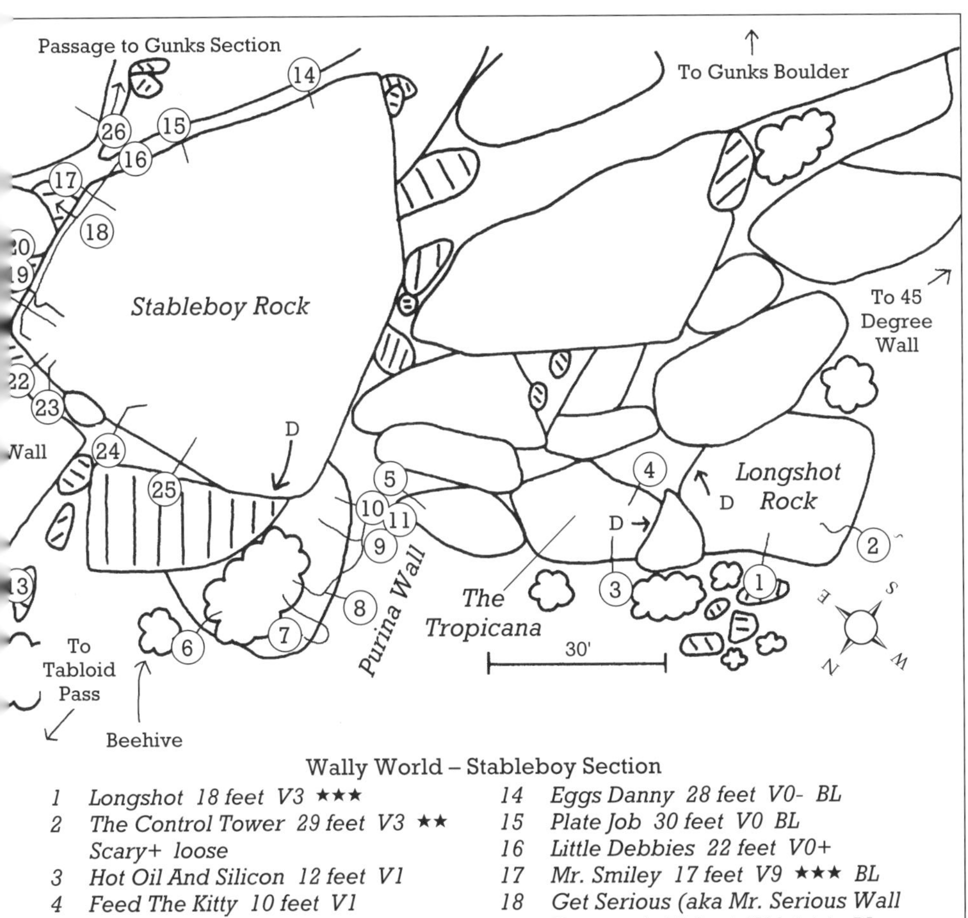

Wally World – Stableboy Section

1 *Longshot 18 feet V3* ★★★

2 *The Control Tower 29 feet V3* ★★ *Scary+ loose*

3 *Hot Oil And Silicon 12 feet V1*

4 *Feed The Kitty 10 feet V1*

5 *Seagram's VO 11 feet V0*

6 *Instant Expert 9 feet V5 SD*

7 *That Hi-Pro Glow 17 feet V6* ★★

8 *Puppy Chow 15 feet V0* ★

9 *Chow Chow Chow 20 feet V4* ★★ *BL scary*

10 *Gravy Train Tryout 25 feet V5* ★

11 *You Bring Out The Mess In Me 21 feet V1* ★ *BL*

12 *The N.A.M.B.L.A. Hoedown 12 feet V0 SD*

13 *Man-Boy 12 feet V0+ SD*

14 *Eggs Danny 28 feet V0- BL*

15 *Plate Job 30 feet V0 BL*

16 *Little Debbies 22 feet V0+*

17 *Mr. Smiley 17 feet V9* ★★★ *BL*

18 *Get Serious (aka Mr. Serious Wall Traverse) 55 feet V11* ★★★ *BL*

19 *Mr. Serious 14 feet V8* ★★★

20 *Dead Legends 13 feet V5* ★★

21 *A Good Day For Swiss Crisp Mix 16 feet V10* ★★★ *low SD*

22 *Eazy Duz It 13 feet V1 BL*

23 *Horse Tranquilizer 19 feet V1 BL*

24 *Stableboys 19 feet V2 BL scary*

25 *Tips From The Stableboy 18 feet V1 BL*

26 *Devastating Mic Control 20 feet V5* ★★ *BL scary+*

7 *That Hi-Pro Glow 17 feet V6* ★★

Start under the roof at a guano-stained sloper 4 feet above the ground. Climb out the right side of the roof to a big incut flake 2.5 feet over the lip. Head left to finish. The foot-wide dihedral to the right is off route.

8 *Puppy Chow 15 feet V0* ★

The right-facing dihedral.

Main Wall

12 The N.A.M.B.L.A. Hoedown 12 feet V0 SD
13 Man-Boy 12 feet V0+ SD

9 *Chow Chow Chow 20 feet V4 ★★ BL scary*

10 *Gravy Train Tryout 25 feet V5 ★*
Start at the right end of the wall then traverse left and finish up *Puppy Chow.*

11 *You Bring Out The Mess In Me 21 feet V1 ★ BL*
Weird slabby finish.

Main Wall

12 *The N.A.M.B.L.A. Hoedown 12 feet V0 SD*
Descend the tree.

13 *Man-Boy 12 feet V0+ SD*
Descend the tree.

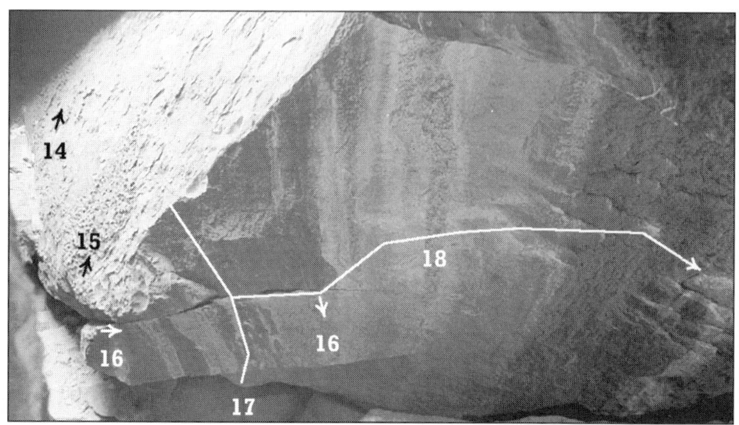

Stableboy Rock

14 Eggs Danny 28 feet V0- BL
15 Plate Job 30 feet V0 BL
16 Little Debbies 22 feet V0+
17 Mr. Smiley 17 feet V9 ★★★ BL
18 Get Serious (aka Mr. Serious Wall Traverse) 55 feet V11 ★★★ BL

Stableboy Rock

14 *Eggs Danny 28 feet V0- BL*

15 *Plate Job 30 feet V0 BL*

16 *Little Debbies 22 feet V0+*
Hand traverse the flake at the left end of the east face. Start at the left end of the flake. At the right end, step off to the boulder behind.

17 *Mr. Smiley 17 feet V9 ★★★ BL*
Start on the horizontal crack under the roof. This problem only lasted a month or two before the holds were doctored by some pansy-assed wannabe. Easier now. The face to the left has also been chiseled. Way to fuck up a great boulder.

18 *Get Serious (aka Mr. Serious Wall Traverse) 55 feet V11 ★★★ BL*
This climbed *Mr. Smiley* up to the *Little Debbies* crack, traversed the wall right to Mr. Serious, then finished up that. An outrageous achievement which will unfortunately go unrepeated because of the flea brain who applied the grade reducer to *Mr Smiley*. An undoctored, but easier, version could be done starting with *Little Debbies.*

19 *Mr. Serious 14 feet V8 ★★★*
Do a-b-c. The small holds right of the cream colored streak are on-route.
Variation: (10 feet V4) Start standing up and climb the cream-colored streak.

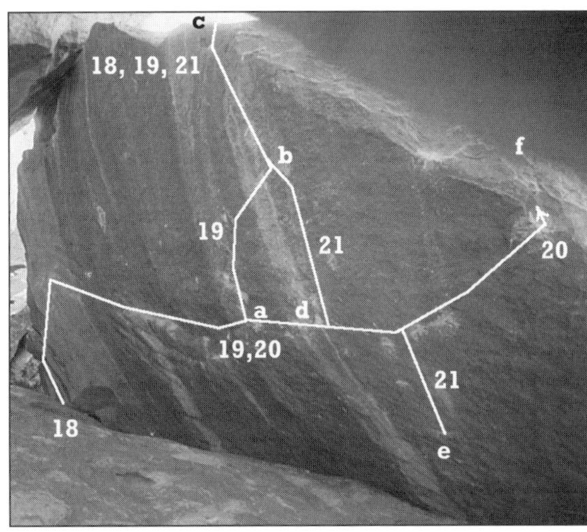

Stableboy Rock

Left:

18 *Get Serious (aka Mr. Serious Wall Traverse) 55 feet V11 ★★★ BL*

19 *Mr. Serious 14 feet V8 ★★★*

20 *Dead Legends 13 feet V5 ★★*

21 *A Good Day For Swiss Crisp Mix 16 feet V10 ★★★ low SD*

Below:

22 *Eazy Duz It 13 feet V1 BL*

23 *Horse Tranquilizer 19 feet V1 BL*

24 *Stableboys 19 feet V2 BL scary*

25 *Tips From The Stableboy 18 feet V1 BL*

20 *Dead Legends 13 feet V5 ★★*
Do a-d-f.

21 *A Good Day For Swiss Crisp Mix 16 feet V10 ★★★ low SD*
Do e-d-b-c. Once again, after the first ascent, some pigeon molester doctored a hold on the upper (d-b) stretch of this, but fortunately it's easier to do the route without the chipped hold.

Dead Serious 18 feet V10 ★★★ SD
Do e-d-a-b-c.

Serious Legends 25 feet V9 ★★
Do f-d-a-b-c. Start with foot hooked at Dead Legends' lip.

22 *Eazy Duz It 13 feet V1 BL*
Start standing atop a crumbly shelf 5 feet up. Pull up the smooth left side of the north facing wall above.

23 *Horse Tranquilizer 19 feet V1 BL*

24 *Stableboys 19 feet V2 BL scary*

25 *Tips From The Stableboy 18 feet V1 BL*

26 *Devastating Mic Control 20 feet V5 ★★ BL scary+*
So far the enormous "Death Flake" at the top has not pulled off even though it's been pulled on. It's possible to gingerly climb to the left of it.

Stableboy Rock
15 *Plate Job 30 feet V0 BL*
26 *Devastating Mic Control 20 feet V5 ★★ BL scary+*

Wally World — Gunks Section

The Gunks section of Wally World is located 50 yards east of the 45 Degree Wall, atop slabs 40 to 50 feet above ground level. Topo, page 280. Overview photo, p. 268.

Gunks Boulder

The moves on the northeast face of this boulder have Gunks written all over them. Countless variants can be done up these horizontal overlaps. 3 suggested lines are given.

1 *Fight Or Flight 16 feet V4 ★★★*
The first hold is a left-facing flake with a cornish game hen size hueco behind it. It's 7 feet up on the right side of a whitish stained patch. V6 ★★★ with the sit-down start.

2 *Straight Outta Conway 16 feet V5 ★ BL scary loose*
Start on the same first hold as *Fight Or Flight.*

3 *Full Monty 11 feet V11 ★★*
Start on the same first hold as *Layback And Like It.* Climb up the south face.

4 *Layback And Like It 29 feet V2 ★*
Crouch under the left side of the face, almost around the corner, to start on the left end of the sloping block next to the sotol. Either prostrate yourself across this sloping block to the right, or reach out the roof to a traverse flake. Traverse the wall right until the horizontal line takes you around the lip's right end.

5 *The Vulgarian 13 feet V1 ★★*
Start low for added challenge.

Gunks Boulder

1 *Fight Or Flight 16 feet V4 ★★★*
2 *Straight Outta Conway 16 feet V5 ★ BL scary loose*
7 *Y Chihuahua 13 feet V5 ★*

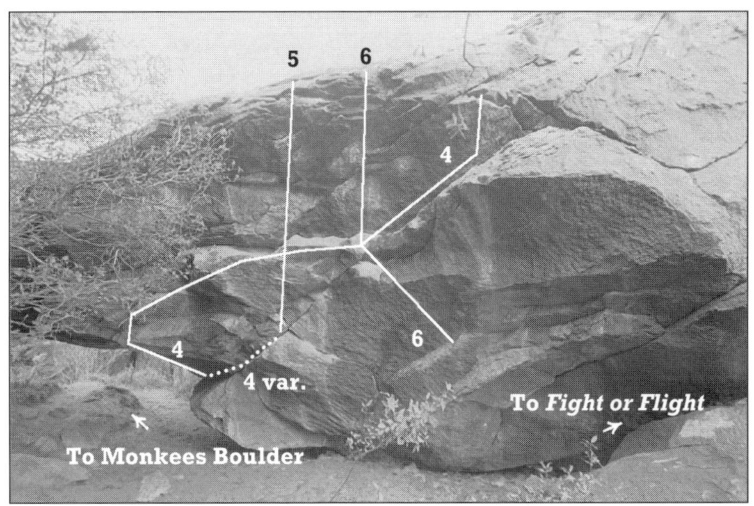

Gunks Boulder

4 *Layback And Like It 29 feet V2 ★*
5 *The Vulgarian 13 feet V1 ★★*
6 *Walrus In A Blender 13 feet V5 ★★ BL*

---

6 *Walrus In A Blender 13 feet V5 ★★ BL*
Either move left to top out as for The Vulgarian, or do a tougher top out straight up.

7 *Y Chihuahua 13 feet V5 ★*
Start low, with a fingerlock right next to where the rocks touch.

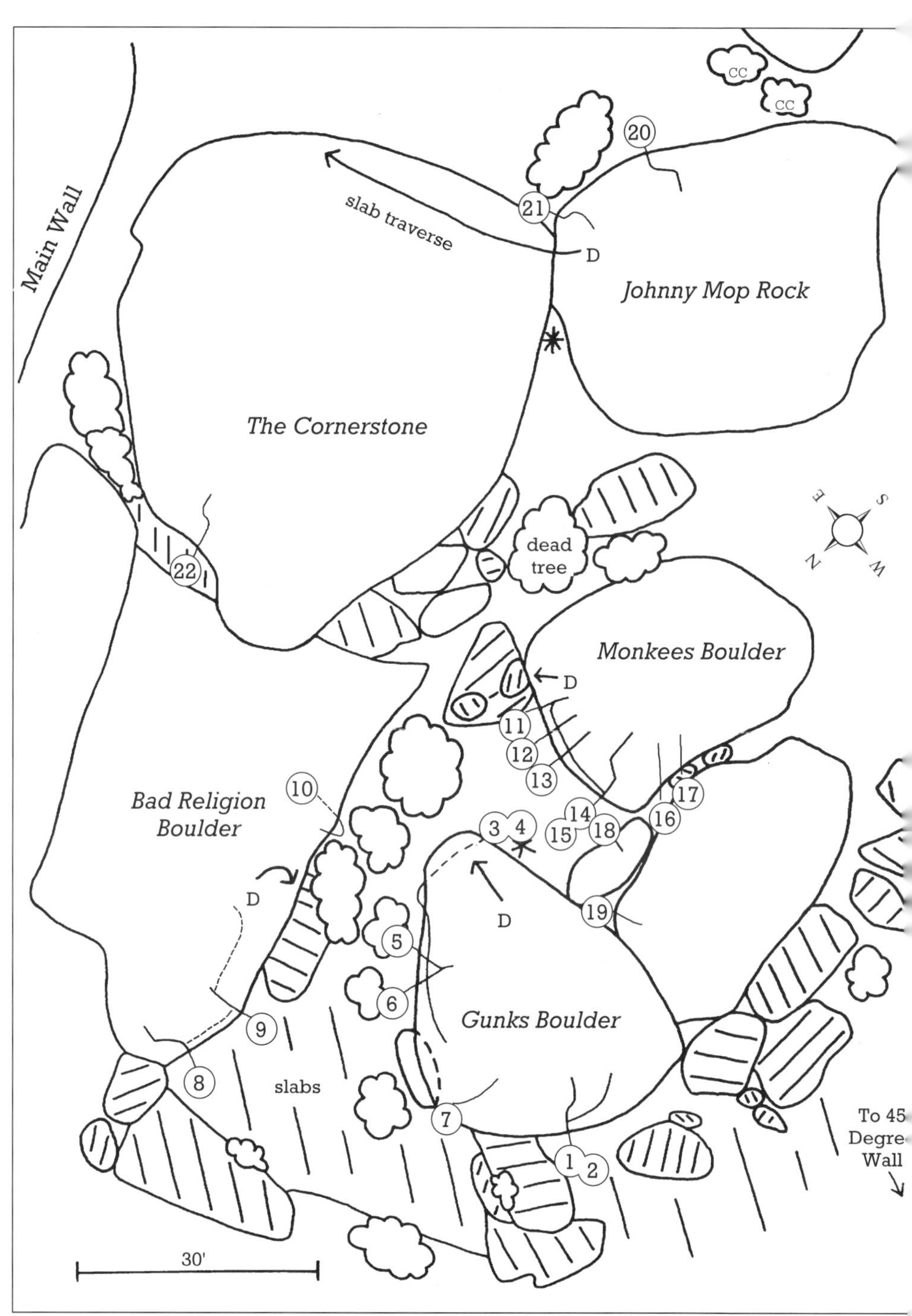
CC
CC
20
21
slab traverse
D
Main Wall
Johnny Mop Rock
The Cornerstone
dead tree
22
Monkees Boulder
D
11
12
13
10
Bad Religion Boulder
14
17
16
3 4
15 18
D
D
19
5
6
Gunks Boulder
9
8
slabs
7
1 2
To 45 Degre Wall
30'
E S N W

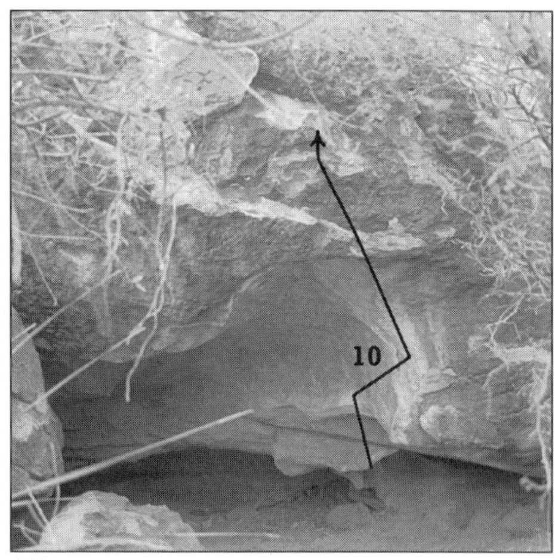

Above:
10 The Hunger Artist (aka Alf In A Blender) 15 feet V6 ★ SD

Left (Bad Religion Wall):
8 All The Idiots 15 feet V3
9 New Religion 16 feet V7 ★★★

Bad Religion Wall

8 *All The Idiots 15 feet V3*
Begin on huecos 4 feet up and 5 feet right of the face's left end. Use the prow on the left to top out.
Variation: (21 feet V5) Start at beginning of *New Religion*, then traverse left into All The Idiots.

9 *New Religion 16 feet V7 ★★★*
Start on a right facing flake 4½ feet up.
Variation: Brand New Religion V8. Does the crux of *New Religion*, then traverses right along and just beneath the lip. Bad landing for a move or two.

10 *The Hunger Artist (aka Alf In A Blender) 15 feet V6 ★ SD*

Wally World – Gunks Section (topo at left)

1 *Fight Or Flight 16 feet V4 ★★★*
2 *Straight Outta Conway 16 feet V5 ★ BL scary loose*
3 *Full Monty. 11 feet V11 ★★*
4 *Layback And Like It 29 feet V2 ★*
5 *The Vulgarian 13 feet V1 ★★*
6 *Walrus In A Blender 13 feet V5 ★★ BL*
7 *Y Chihuahua 13 feet V5 ★*
8 *All The Idiots 15 feet V3*
9 *New Religion 16 feet V7 ★★★*
10 *The Hunger Artist (aka Alf In A Blender) 15 feet V6 ★ SD*
11 *Last Train To Clarksville 16 feet V1 ★ BL*
12 *The Banana Splits 18 feet V4*
13 *The Monkees Get Canceled 12 feet V0+*
14 *Mickey 14 feet V0+*
15 *Hey, Hey, Hey We're The Monkees 27 feet V5 ★★*
16 *Ape Shit 13 feet V0*
17 *Monkey Business 16 feet V0*
18 *Ultrashit 10 feet V0+*
19 *UTEP Two Step 9 feet V0 ★*
20 *Johnny Mop 15 feet V2 ★★ BL*
21 *The Plunger 19 feet V4 ★*
22 *Dahmervision 21 feet V2 ★ BL+*

Monkees Boulder

11 *Last Train To Clarksville 16 feet V1 ★ BL*
12 *The Banana Splits 18 feet V4*
13 *The Monkees Get Canceled 12 feet V0+*
14 *Mickey 14 feet V0+*
15 *Hey, Hey, Hey We're The Monkees 27 feet V5 ★★*
16 *Ape Shit 13 feet V0*
17 *Monkey Business 16 feet V0*

The Monkees Boulder

The Monkees Boulder is 6 yards southeast of the Gunks Boulder. Problems 8 to 12 are on the north face.

11 *Last Train To Clarksville 16 feet V1 ★ BL*

12 *The Banana Splits 18 feet V4*

13 *The Monkees Get Canceled 12 feet V0+*

14 *Mickey 14 feet V0+*
Start on the right end of the 2-3 inch wide horizontal ledge 4½ feet up. Climb the wall up and left without using the ledge to the right (7 feet up).

15 *Hey, Hey, Hey We're The Monkees 27 feet V5 ★★*
Start as for Mickey, then traverse the horizontal line left and finish up *Last Train to Clarksville.*

16 *Ape Shit 13 feet V0*
Start off the sloped shelf. Up flakes between huecos to the right and the arete on the left.

17 *Monkey Business 16 feet V0*
Up past six shallow huecos.

18 *Ultrashit 10 feet V0+*
On the rock right of *Hey, Hey, We're The Monkees'* start. The name says it all.

19 *UTEP Two Step 9 feet V0 ★*

Johnny Mop Rock
Left:
View from east side of Monkees Boulder.
Below:
21 The Plunger 19 feet V4 ★

Johnny Mop Rock

West of the Monkees Boulder is a dead tree with a 30-35 foot overhang behind (east of) it. The right (south) end of this overhanging wall contacts another large rock to it's southwest, Johnny Mop Rock.

20 Johnny Mop 15 feet V2 ★★ BL
Climbs great rock on the east face. A toilet bowl size hueco is 3 feet below the lip. Start down and right of the toilet bowl at a 4 finger hueco 6 feet up. Lunge to a slope, then move left to the bowl. Dig your tips under the rim on the right side and move to the top. This would get a third star if the descent weren't so bad. To descend climb over onto the boulder to the north then traverse right across it's loose south face until you can downclimb.

21 The Plunger 19 feet V4 ★

The Cornerstone

22 Dahmervision 21 feet V2 ★ BL+
Blow it and it will eat you up. Start on a slab in the chimney between Bad Religion Boulder and The Cornerstone. A four-foot-tall triangular block is atop the slab immediately left of the line. Climb out of the chimney, up the headwall and over the top.

The prominent dihedral on this boulder's east side may have been done (probably on TR).

THE 45 DEGREE WALL

The 45 Degree Wall is at the back (south end) of a cul-de-sac in the north end of East Spur. It is at ground level and will be found 100 yards south of That's My Daughter. The best way to find it is to start at Tabloid Pass (the pass between East Mountain and East Spur) and walk 75 yards west, dropping about 30 feet elevation from the pass, until you reach a 5 foot wide trail. Follow this wide trail another 75 yards past That's My Daughter to where the trail forks. Take the left fork, heading south into the cul-de-sac. The trail initially points towards the 45 degree wall 80 yards to the south. A big juniper is on the wall's left.

The Keelhauler
Seppuku Roof
Fluff Wall
45 Degree Wall

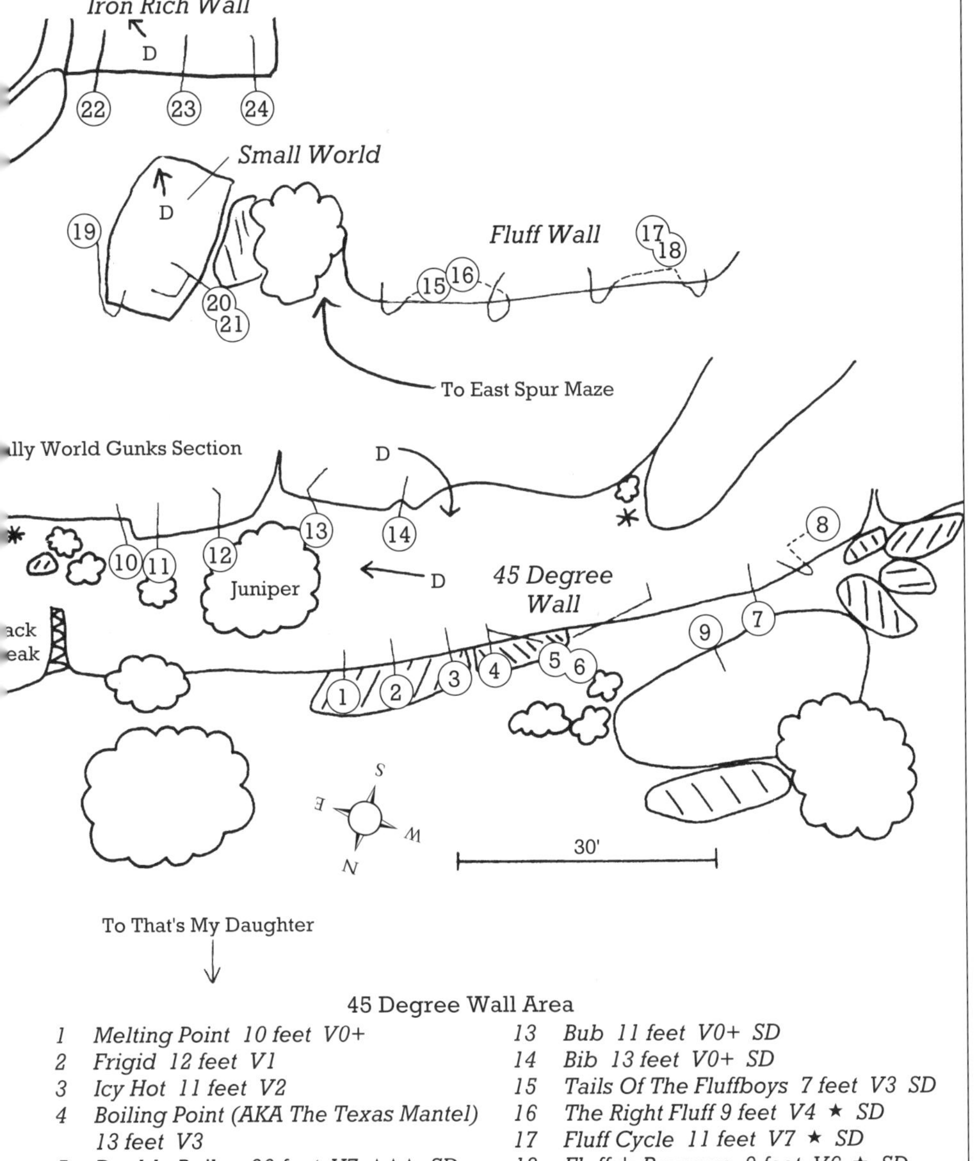

45 Degree Wall Area

1 *Melting Point 10 feet V0+*
2 *Frigid 12 feet V1*
3 *Icy Hot 11 feet V2*
4 *Boiling Point (AKA The Texas Mantel) 13 feet V3*
5 *Double Boiler 20 feet V7 ★★★ SD*
6 *The 45 Degree Wall 24 feet V5 ★★★★ SD*
7 *Absolute Zero 14 feet V3 BL scary*
8 *The Deep Freeze 24 feet V1 ★ SD*
9 *Bob Dog Press 6 feet D2 ★*
10 *True Grot 10 feet V0*
11 *Knee Deep 11 feet V3 ★ BL*
12 *The Happy Hooker 12 feet V4 ★ BL*
13 *Bub 11 feet V0+ SD*
14 *Bib 13 feet V0+ SD*
15 *Tails Of The Fluffboys 7 feet V3 SD*
16 *The Right Fluff 9 feet V4 ★ SD*
17 *Fluff Cycle 11 feet V7 ★ SD*
18 *Fluffy's Revenge 9 feet V6 ★ SD*
19 *It's A Small World After All 10 feet V2 SD*
20 *Jaded 9 feet V2 SD*
21 *Talking Short 8 feet V1 SD*
22 *Iron Rich 15 feet V0 ★*
23 *The Coolidge Effect 16 feet V2*
24 *It's A Tall World After All 17 feet V1*

45 Degree Wall

1 *Melting Point 10 feet V0+*
2 *Frigid 12 feet V1*
3 *Icy Hot 11 feet V2 BL*
4 *Boiling Point (AKA The Texas Mantel) 13 feet V3*
5 *Double Boiler 20 feet V7 ★★★ SD*
6 *The 45 Degree Wall 24 feet V5 ★★★★ SD*
7 *Absolute Zero 14 feet V3 BL scary*
8 *The Deep Freeze 24 feet V1 ★ SD*

Don't climb in hatched rock art zone

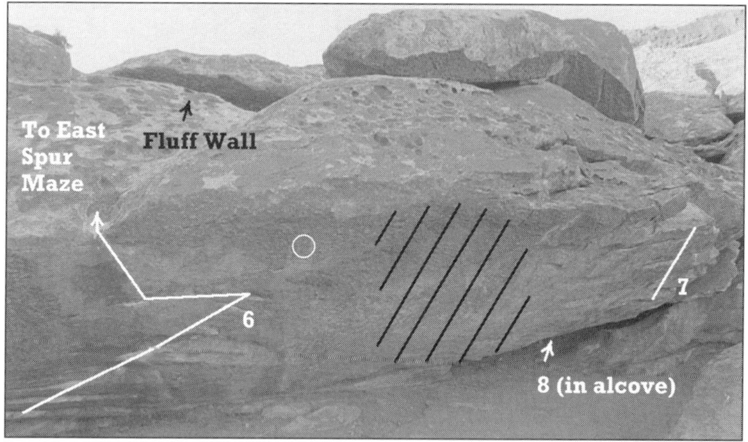

Seppuku Roof (aka Female Alligator Wrestlers In Bondage) 13 feet V3 SD
Climbs the roof crack out the very low cave. The summit is only chest high.

1 *Melting Point 10 feet V0+*
Start 27 feet left of the start of 45 degree Wall, just left of a rocky lump on the slab below. 2 vertical seams mark the line. Crank from the flake to a point at the lip and waddle over.

2 *Frigid 12 feet V1*
Turn the lip 10 feet left of *Boiling Point*. Start between the rocky lumps on the slab.

3 *Icy Hot 11 feet V2 BL*
Mantel the lip 5 feet left of *Boiling Point*.

4 *Boiling Point (AKA The Texas Mantel) 13 feet V3*
Start 10 feet left of the start of 45 Degree Wall, at a flexing flake 7 feet above an 18 inch deep grinding hole. Please leave the hole empty and uncovered.

5 *Double Boiler 20 feet V7 ★★★ SD*
Was slated to be upgraded to V8 then a talent-free, nth-degree loser gouged one of the finger flakes to make it a bit bigger.

6 *The 45 Degree Wall 24 feet V5 ★★★★ SD*
My editor doesn't like quality ratings to exceed 3 stars, but as this is probably the finest boulder problem in the world, I couldn't help myself. Bad landing if you fall off the lip moves. On the crux move to the lip, most falls miss the grinding holes by a safe margin. The name was given for its steepness, but applies just as well to the average

winter temperature (in degrees F) at the wall. One of the coldest spots in the park. The grinding holes have been repeatedly filled up with dirt (and sometimes tapewads, butts, etc.) to smooth out the landing. Park officials do not considered this an acceptable use of the resource. Please leave these holes empty, as well as the one under *Double Boiler* and all others in the park.

The ugly gouged-out hold (see circle on 45 Degree Wall photo, page 286) and associated beat marks 4 feet to the right of 45 Degree Wall are courtesy of Alf Randall and Dylan Estcourt. The tempting undercling to the right should not be climbed because it would endanger the artwork beneath it. Further attempts to climb this could get the entire wall closed. Please stay off the section of wall between 45 Degree Wall and Absolute Zero.

7 *Absolute Zero 14 feet V3 BL scary*
At the right end of the wall, 11 yards from 45 Degree Wall's start, is a thin walled football width hueco 8 feet up. Undercling this, hoping it doesn't snap, and keep chugging to the lip.

8 *The Deep Freeze 24 feet V1 ★ SD*
The 45 degree Wall is actually a 3 foot thick zig zag flake at it's right end. Start sitting down and hand traverse out to the lip.

9 *Bob Dog Press 6 feet D2 ★*
The boulder just north of the 45 Degree Wall is often used as a vantage point for taking pictures of the 45 Degree Wall. Bob the dog has cranked the sloping mantle on its southeast face. This went years without a canine repeat, but has since been done several times. Despite an extreme height and reach disadvantage, this was flashed by Pepe the pit bull; most impressive.

Above the 45 Degree Wall

Immediately above the left end of the 45 Degree Wall is a short wall divided into left and right halves by a wide crack.

10 *True Grot 10 feet V0*
The left angling undercling/lieback flake. Grotty.

11 *Knee Deep 11 feet V3 ★ BL*
Only use holds to the right of *True Grot.*

12 *The Happy Hooker 12 feet V4 ★ BL*

Above the 45 Degree Wall

10 *True Grot 10 feet V0*
11 *Knee Deep 11 feet V3 ★ BL*
12 *The Happy Hooker 12 feet V4 ★ BL*

A crack divides this wall into halves. The right half (Bib and Bub) is well suited to concocting variations. The two easiest lines are given

13 *Bub 11 feet V0+ SD*
The hueco line 6 feet right of the divider crack.

14 *Bib 13 feet V0+ SD*
The hueco line at the right end of the wall, 9 feet left of the descent, 15 feet right of the divider crack. A 5 foot reach to the lip notch is required (the lip right of the notch is off-route).

Fluff Wall

15 *Tails Of The Fluffboys 7 feet V3 SD*

16 *The Right Fluff 9 feet V4 ★ SD*

17 *Fluff Cycle 11 feet V7 ★ SD*
V5 for short folks.

18 *Fluffy's Revenge 9 feet V6 ★ SD*

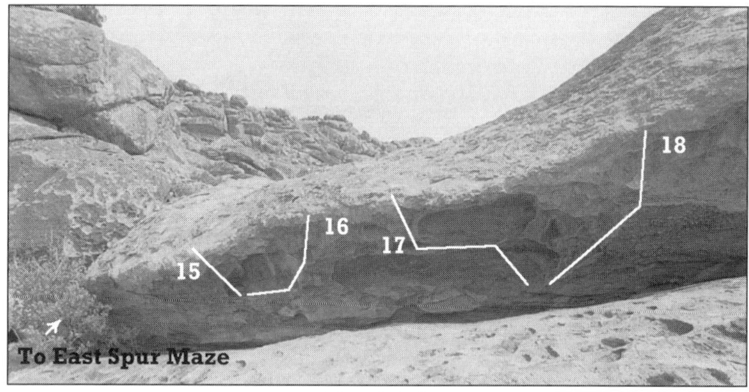

Fluff Wall

15 *Tails Of The Fluffboys*
16 *The Right Fluff*
17 *Fluff Cycle*
18 *Fluffy's Revenge*

Iron Rich Wall, left, and Small World

19 *It's A Small World After All*
22 *Iron Rich*
23 *The Coolidge Effect*
24 *It's A Tall World After All*

Small World

This diminutive boulder lies 5 yards east of Fluff Wall.

19 *It's A Small World After All 10 feet V2 SD*

The awe-inspiring west face has two sit down problems starting from the same holds.

20 *Jaded 9 feet V2 SD*
Move left and up.

21 *Talking Short 8 feet V1 SD*
Straight up.

Iron Rich Wall

This wall is 6 feet south of Small World.

22 *Iron Rich 15 feet V0 ★*

23 *The Coolidge Effect 16 feet V2*

24 *It's A Tall World After All 17 feet V1*
Reachy start.

To the southeast of 45 Degree Wall is a dense maze of boulders which have seen mild development. Most of the problems done so far are in the V1 to V5 range and sport bad landings. Check it out if you're looking for an easily-accessible area to explore in without the led-by-the-hand approach.

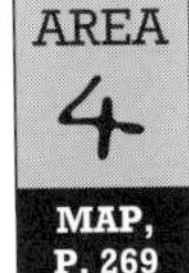

NORTHWEST LOBE OF EAST SPUR

1 *Pirelli 12 feet V5 ★ BL scary*
A lip encounter more reminiscent of granite bouldering.

2 *The Blow Out 24 feet V4 ★ BL*
The roof crack with the lovely flared exit notch. Start at the far back end of the crack. A contest problem one year which many super(sic)experts, noticing the cameras were rolling, felt the need to strip their shirts off for. It was ugly.

3 *The Handcuff Trick 30 feet 5.7 ★★*
A beautiful handcrack up the face inside the chimney immediately east of *Paddled Severely During Sorority Initiation.*

Nortwest Lobe of East Spur

1 *Pirelli 12 feet V5 ★ BL scary*

2 *The Blow Out 24 feet V4 ★ BL*

Northwest Lobe of East Spur

4 *Paddled Severely During Sorority Initiation 26 feet 5.11+* ★
This route is located on a free standing boulder at the westernmost projection of the north end of the East Spur. If one walks along the base of the East Spur counterclockwise from the 45 Degree wall to the East Spur Maze (as opposed to crossing the pass above 45 Degree Wall), they will pass this boulder at the halfway point. Three bolts; at presstime, the second bolt was hangerless.

5 *The Keelhauler 45 feet 5.11+ TR* ★
Start on the ramp right of the prow, shinny up the prow, then move back to the right side for the final moves.

A no-foot ascent of the 45° Wall

East Spur Maze

View south from the pass above the 45 Degree Wall.

EAST SPUR MAZE

South of The 45 Degree Wall is another cul-de-sac in the rocks, this one opening to the south. The East Spur Maze is the group of boulders on the southwest side of this cul-de-sac. Sheltered from the wind, it is one of the warmest areas in the park. Walking over the pass atop the 45 Degree Wall is the quickest approach. Topo, page 294.

Big Dick Jim 15 feet V3 ★

This route is found between the pass above 45 Degree Wall and the East Spur Maze. See photo, p. 292. Start at the bottom of the gap between boulders. Sharp.

Godzillatron Boulder

This 25 foot tall boulder is the furthest boulder south of this size in the East Spur Maze.

1 *Thumpasaurus 25 feet V0+ scary*
Climb the east face topping out in the notch on the left end of the summit. The crux is near the top.

2 *Jingus Bells 23 feet V5* ★★★
A 13 foot boulder lies next to the north face, providing a sloping landing for falls off the last move crux. The last move is an intimidating jump for the flat spot on the lip. With a good spot the landing from the last move isn't bad. Falls before this move could prove disastrous.

3 *Slayride 20 feet V2* ★ *BL*

4 *Funkicidal Vibrations 17 feet V2 BL scary loose*
Start right of the *Jingus Bells* landing block, climbing the wall that overhangs the block's right (west) end. Loose.

5 *The Godzillatron Cush 14 feet V3* ★
Start with a jump to a 2 hand jug 8½ feet up.

Godzillatron Boulder

1 *Thumpasaurus 25 feet V0+ scary*
2 *Jingus Bells 23 feet V5* ★★★
3 *Slayride 20 feet V2* ★ *BL*
4 *Funkicidal Vibrations 17 feet V2 BL scary loose*
5 *The Godzillatron Cush 14 feet V3* ★

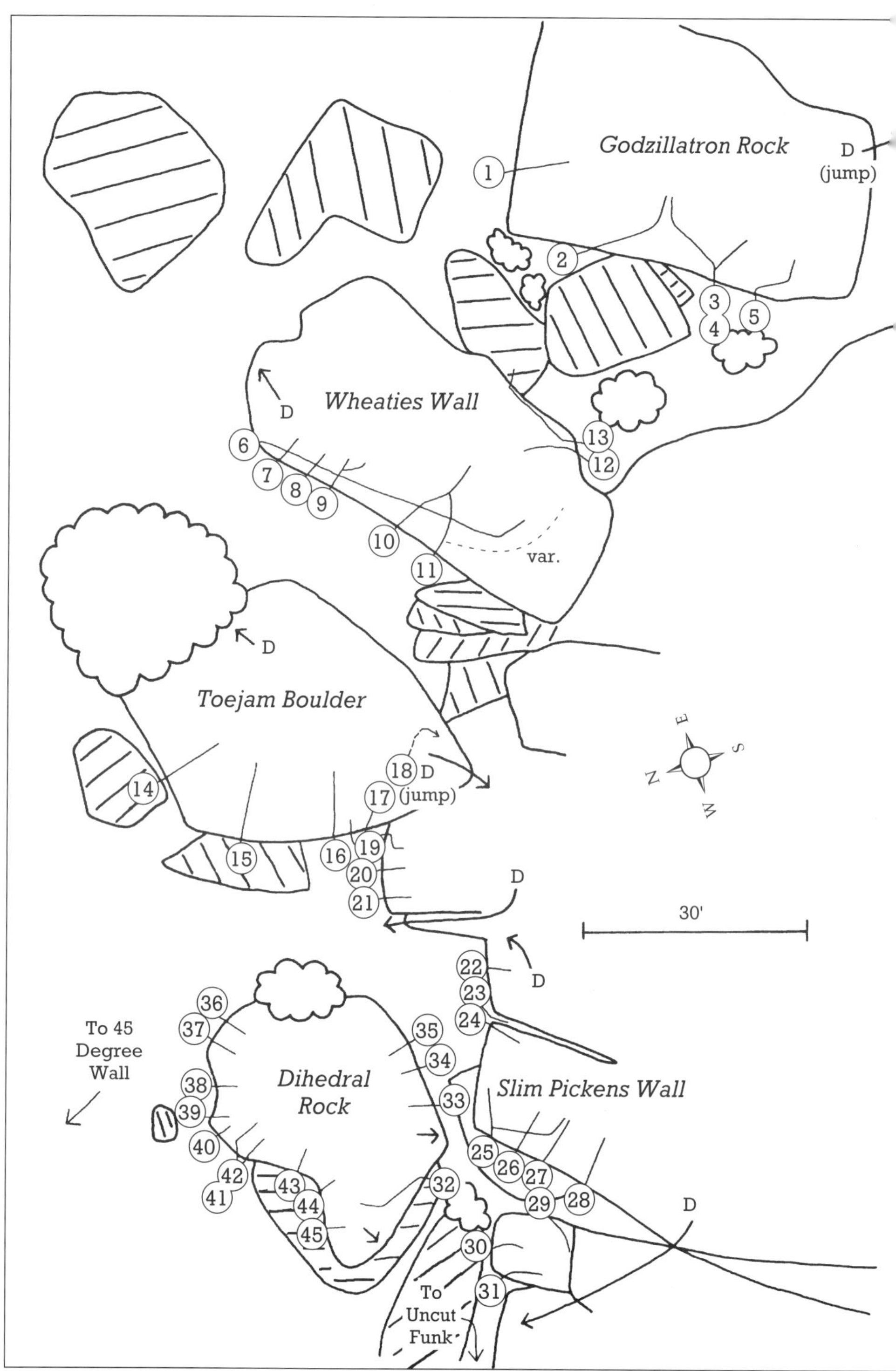

Godzillatron Rock
D (jump)
Wheaties Wall
D
var.
Toejam Boulder
D
D (jump)
D
D
30'
N
E
S
W
To 45 Degree Wall
Dihedral Rock
Slim Pickens Wall
D
To Uncut Funk
1
2
3
4
5
6
7
8
9
10
11
12
13
14
15
16
17
18
19
20
21
22
23
24
25
26
27
28
29
30
31
32
33
34
35
36
37
38
39
40
41
42
43
44
45

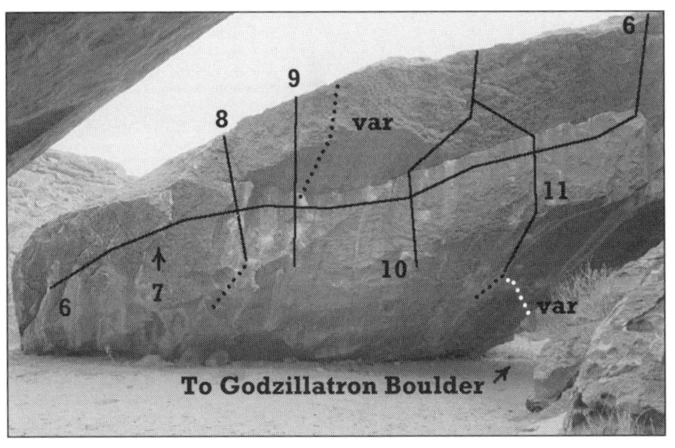

Wheaties Wall
6 *Torch Song 38 feet V5 ★★ SD*
7 *Garvey's Ghost 9 feet V0 ★*
8 *Burning Spear 12 feet V0+ ★*
9 *Point Blank 15 feet V1 ★* (var. is Point Blunk)
10 *Better Beat Your Sweeties V7 18 feet ★★*
11 *Better Eat Your Wheaties 20 feet V8 ★★* (right var. is *Crown of Aragorn*)

Wheaties Wall

6 *Torch Song 38 feet V5 ★★ SD*
Traverse right across the wall without using the lip.

7 *Garvey's Ghost 9 feet V0 ★*

8 *Burning Spear 12 feet V0+ ★*
Tack on a grade for a sit down start.

9 *Point Blank 15 feet V1 ★*
From a sit down start this is V3 ★
Variation: Point Blunk 16 feet V4 Move right from the flake to a two fingertip pocket at the overhang's lip. Crank off this pocket to the top.

East Spur Maze (topo at left)

1 *Thumpasaurus 25 feet V0+ scary*
2 *Jingus Bells 23 feet V5 ★★★*
3 *Slayride 20 feet V2 ★ BL*
4 *Funkicidal Vibrations 17 feet V2 BL scary loose*
5 *The Godzillatron Cush 14 feet V3 ★*
6 *Torch Song 38 feet V5 ★★ SD*
7 *Garvey's Ghost 9 feet V0 ★*
8 *Burning Spear 12 feet V0+ ★*
9 *Point Blank 15 feet V1 ★*
10 *Better Beat Your Sweeties V7 18 feet ★★*
11 *Better Eat Your Wheaties 20 feet V8 ★★*
12 *Trubblemaker 20 feet V4*
13 *Junior Varsity 12 feet V3*
14 *Odor Eater 17 feet V0 BL*
15 *Stinkfoot 20 feet V0 ★*
16 *Smegmatoesis 23 feet V5*
17 *Pugsley's Porch 33 feet V5*
18 *John Sherman Is Neither 12 feet V5*
19 *Ten Inch Plastic Boyfriend 10 feet V1 ★ SD*
20 *Udder Destruction 10 feet V0+ ★★ SD*
21 *Clumsy Plumber 10 feet V0 SD*
22 *Black And Blue 12 feet V1 ★★*
23 *Gangbanging That Wide Crack 13 feet V3*
24 *The Cowpuncher 13 feet V4 ★*
25 *Fats Domino 13 feet V0 or 20 feet V0+ ★★ BL*
26 *Chubby Checker 16 feet V0+ ★*
27 *Slim Pickins 17 feet V5 ★★*
28 *Slim Whitman 22 feet V1 ★ scary*
29 *Saab Story 24 feet V1 BL scary*
30 *Funk's Not Dead 13 feet V4 * BL*
31 *Wide Wedding 14 feet V2*
32 *The Jigsaw Puzzle 16 feet V5 ★★ BL*
33 *Sex With Oprah 11 feet V2*
34 *The Sizzler 12 feet V4*
35 *Horny 12 feet V1 ★*
36 *Bildo 11 feet V0*
37 *The Flexin' Texan 12 feet V0+*
38 *The Globetrotter 10 feet V1*
39 *Strip Show Faux Pas 10 feet V0+*
40 *The Lactator 9 feet V0 ★*
41 *The Dicktator 12 feet V0+ SD*
42 *The French Fry 10 feet V0+ SD*
43 *Italy Overthrown 9 feet V2*
44 *This Is Your Brain On Drugs 10 feet V2 ★ SD*
45 *Bilbo Gets Buggered 7 feet V2 ★ SD*

10 *Better Beat Your Sweeties V7 18 feet* ★★
6 feet above the ground is a flake incut deeply on it's left side. Start on this flake and climb to the roof via tiny razors, then go straight over the overhang to the top. Photo, page 295.

11 *Better Eat Your Wheaties 20 feet V8* ★★
Start 6 feet right of *Better Beat Your Sweeties* with your left fingers behind a thin incut flake 6 feet up, and the right hand on a flake just above the right side of a grey patch 5 feet up. V9 from a sit down start.
Variation: Crown of Aragorn 32 feet V13 ★★★ Starts at the far right end of the wall and traverses 12 feet left to finish up *Better Eat Your Wheaties.*

12 *Trubblemaker 20 feet V4*
Around the corner right of *Better Eat Your Wheaties* are the initials "JV" chiseled inside a football outline. Starting left of these initials, traverse right, round the lip of the overhang, then climb 10 feet of chossy ramp to the summit.
Variation: (Meatmaker V5) Starts sitting down at the right side of the scoop.

13 *Junior Varsity 12 feet V3*
From *Trubblemaker's* start, traverse the wall right; step off on the boulder to the right.

Toejam Boulder

Toejam Boulder is the 25 foot tall rock 6 yards north of Wheaties Wall. The 3 routes listed are on it's north face. To descend either downclimb the loose east face and the tree at it's base or do the toejamming jump off the west end.

14 *Odor Eater 17 feet V0 BL*
Start 11 feet right of the east face descent tree, on a well formed lip 3 feet right of a thick right-facing flake. You'll be standing on a boulder to start. Mantel the first lip to gain the next lip above. Marginal climbing leads to the top.

15 *Stinkfoot 20 feet V0* ★

16 *Smegmatoesis 23 feet V5*
Start 4 feet right of the Stinkfoot starting boulder.

17 *Pugsley's Porch 33 feet V5*
Start in the corridor right of *Smegmatoesis,* 4 moves back from the lip.

18 *John Sherman Is Neither 12 feet V5*
Start inside the corridor on the southwest side of Toejam Boulder where the corridor is the narrowest. Two finger flakes at 6.5 feet up are the first handholds. Traverse 12 feet up and right on slopers to a sloped finger scoop then give up. Really needs to continue up the big flake 4 feet right of the finish.

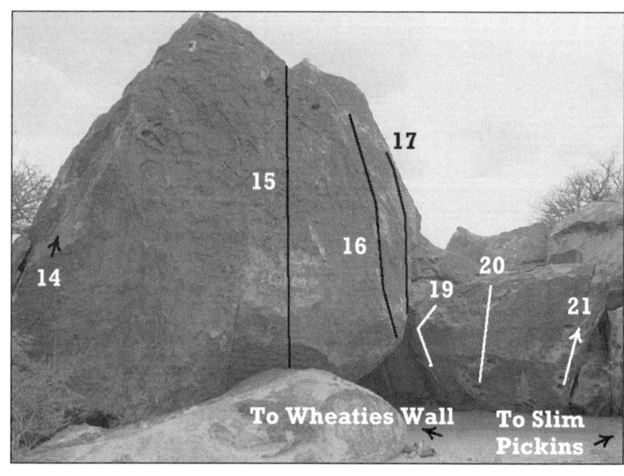

Toejam (left), Ten Foot Wall
14 *Odor Eater 17 feet V0 BL*
15 *Stinkfoot 20 feet V0* ★
16 *Smegmatoesis 23 feet V5*
17 *Pugsley's Porch 33 feet V5*
19 *Ten Inch Plastic Boyfriend 10 feet V1* ★ *SD*
20 *Udder Destruction 10 feet V0+* ★★ *SD*
21 *Clumsy Plumber 10 feet V0 SD*

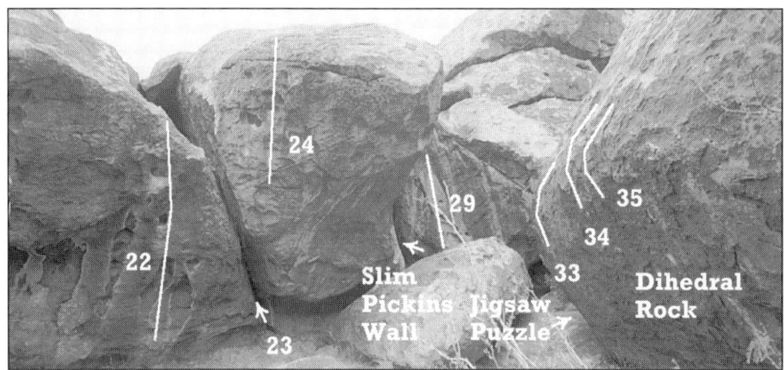

Ten Foot Wall, left, Slim Pickins Wall, Dihedral Rock

22 *Black And Blue 12 feet V1* ★★
23 *Gangbanging That Wide Crack 13 feet V3*
24 *The Cowpuncher 13 feet V4* ★
29 *Saab Story 24 feet V1 BL scary*
33 *Sex With Oprah 11 feet V2*
34 *The Sizzler 12 feet V4*
35 *Horny 12 feet V1* ★

Ten Foot Wall

Ten Foot Wall is the short overhung east facing wall immediately west of Toejam Boulder's north face.

19 *Ten Inch Plastic Boyfriend 10 feet V1* ★ *SD*
Climb the left edge of the east face. Toejam Boulder's proximity forces one right along the lip to top out.

20 *Udder Destruction 10 feet V0+* ★★ *SD*

21 *Clumsy Plumber 10 feet V0 SD*

22 *Black And Blue 12 feet V1* ★★
Start sitting or standing.

23 *Gangbanging That Wide Crack 13 feet V3*

Slim Pickins Face

Slim Pickins Face is the north-facing wall 12 feet around the corner right of *Black And Blue*. It contains one of the few hard slab problems at Hueco Tanks.

24 *The Cowpuncher 13 feet V4* ★
Start on the 2 foot tall bad landing boulder. Pinch tinies to slap the rough sloper above - an intimidating move. Big holds above.

25 *Fats Domino 13 feet V0 or 20 feet V0+* ★★ *BL*
A 20 foot variation goes up a move, then finger traverses the right angling seam line, topping out at the green lichen.

26 *Chubby Checker 16 feet V0+* ★

Slim Pickins Wall

25 *Fats Domino 13 feet V0 or 20 feet V0+* ★★ *BL*
26 *Chubby Checker 16 feet V0+* ★
27 *Slim Pickins 17 feet V5* ★★
28 *Slim Whitman 22 feet V1* ★ *scary*

27 Slim Pickins 17 feet V5 ★★
Possibly Hueco Tank's hardest slab problem. Bad landing if hit wrong.

28 Slim Whitman 22 feet V1 ★ scary
You'll be singing a sad tune if you fall off the crux on this one. Start on the ground. Scary, high crux.

Further right (west) on the *Slim Pickins* face, after walking through the chimney are many V0– possibilities not shown on the topo. If you follow the Slim Pickins Face to it's far west end, then take 2 more steps west you'll be at the base of a good V0 problem on another boulder (***Hefty 13 feet V0 ★★*** no topo). 6 feet left of this is a marginal 13 foot V0.

15 yards west of the Hefty boulder is a 16 foot tall boulder with 2 bushes flanking it's north face (cracked by a huge flake on it's left side). This is also not on a topo. The outside face of the flake starting midway between bushes is ***Glad Wrap 16 feet V0+*** (no topo).

29 Saab Story 24 feet V1 BL scary
The right-angling crack at the top is harder than it looks. Photo, page 297.

The following contrived problem is where the northern descent from *Slim Pickins* hops down from the lip of an overhung off-width.

Slip Pickins area
27 *Slim Pickins 17 feet V5 ★★*
30 *Funk's Not Dead 13 feet V4 ★ BL*
31 *Wide Wedding 14 feet V2*

Dihedral Rock
32 *The Jigsaw Puzzle 16 feet V5 ★★ BL*

30 *Funk's Not Dead 13 feet V4 ★ BL*
Start from a face level undercling (right hand) and a fingertip lip below "B 8-7."

31 ***Wide Wedding** 14 feet V2*
Climb the left wall of the off-width using holds inside the crack and huecos outside. Avoid the right wall. Bad landing.

32 *The Jigsaw Puzzle 16 feet V5 ★★ BL*
Start on the right side of the jigsaw hold face. Traverse left then angle up to top out halfway up the left arete.
Variation 1: starting at the left end of the traverse reduces it to V3.
Variation 2: going straight up (scary and loose) is V6.

Routes 33-35 are pictured on page 297.

33 *Sex With Oprah 11 feet V2*
Start just right of a foot tall slab at the left (west) end of the south face.

34 *The Sizzler 12 feet V4*
Turn the lip 3 feet left of *Horny.*

35 *Horny 12 feet V1 ★*
Surmount the highest point on the lip of the south face overhang. At this point, the lip is graced with several rounded horns.

Dihedral Rock

36 *Bildo 11 feet V0*
Climb the east bulge, starting 3 feet right of a bush. Watch for loose holds up high. Photo, page 300.

37 *The Flexin' Texan 12 feet V0+*
The line 5 feet right of the bush using the big flexing flake 9 feet up. Photos below and on page 300.

38 *The Globetrotter 10 feet V1*
Way easier since some stud retrochiseled it (V0+). Photos right and on page 300.

39 *Strip Show Faux Pas 10 feet V0+*

East Spur Maze West, approaches to Uncut Funk Area

36 *Bildo 11 feet V0*
37 *The Flexin' Texan 12 feet V0+*
38 *The Globetrotter 10 feet V1*

Routes 40-45 are pictured on page 300.

40 *The Lactator 9 feet V0 ★*

41 *The Dicktator 12 feet V0+ SD*

42 *The French Fry 10 feet V0+ SD*

43 *Italy Overthrown 9 feet V2*
Start with fingers on a flake 5 feet up. This flake looks like an upside-down map of Italy.

44 *This Is Your Brain On Drugs 10 feet V2 ★ SD*
Start on flakes 4½ feet up.

45 *Bilbo Gets Buggered 7 feet V2 ★ SD*
Climb the right wall of the dihedral from a sit down start.

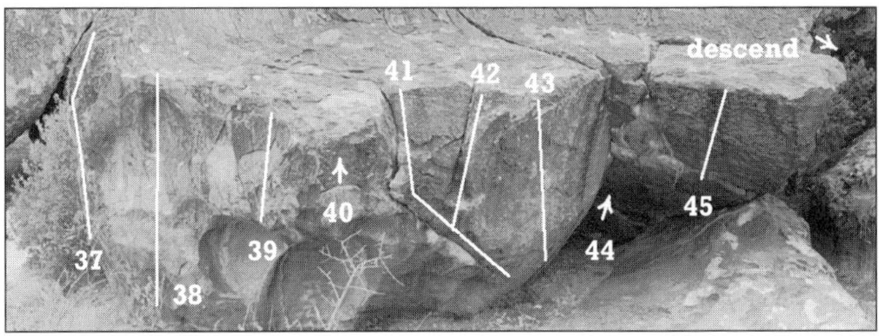

Dihedral Rock

37 *The Flexin' Texan 12 feet V0+*
38 *The Globetrotter 10 feet V1*
39 *Strip Show Faux Pas 10 feet V0+*
40 *The Lactator 9 feet V0 ★*
41 *The Dicktator 12 feet V0+ SD*
42 *The French Fry 10 feet V0+ SD*
43 *Italy Overthrown 9 feet V2*
44 *This Is Your Brain On Drugs 10 feet V2 ★ SD*
45 *Bilbo Gets Buggered 7 feet V2 ★ SD*

UNCUT FUNK AREA (AKA THE OFFICE)

The following boulder problems are in the corridor on the southwest side of The Bomb boulder. The southeast end of this corridor extends all the way to *Wide Wedding* (problem 31). Enter the corridor at the south end of The Bomb boulder (see photo on page 299). *All Purpose Grind* and *Average* are found in the corridor near the south end of The Bomb Boulder. *Uncut Funk* is another 10 yards to the northwest. *Uncut Funk* can also be reached by scrambling around the northwest end of The Bomb Boulder, but is harder to find this way.

46 *All Purpose Grind 11 feet V5*
Start on grainy slopers 3 feet below the lip. Murder on the tips.

47 *Average 12 feet V4*
Start on sharp flakes next to "Tommy."

Uncut Funk Area

46 *All Purpose Grind 11 feet V5*
47 *Average 12 feet V4*

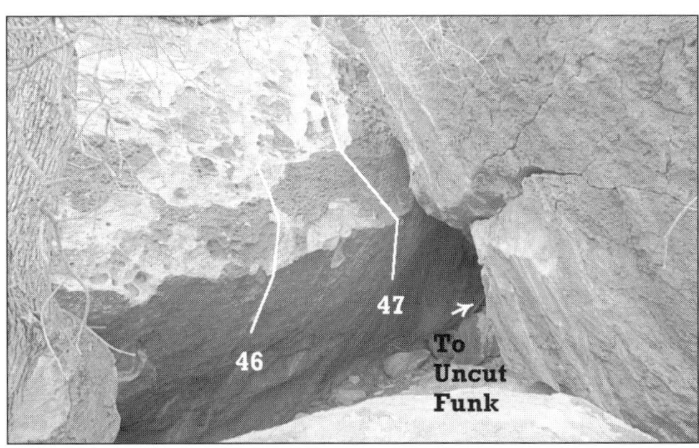

48 *Nobody 10 feet V6 ★*
Low start in sloping scoop.
Variation: Funky Ring-Eye V9 starts sitting down beneath *Uncut Funk*, moves left to the scoop, and finishes up Nobody.

49 *Nobody's Funky 15 feet V7 ★*
Start as for Nobody, finish up the top of *Uncut Funk.*

50 *Nobody's Ugly After Two AM 13 feet V10 ★*
Start on *Nobody,* climb to the lip of *Uncut Funk,* downclimb the crux bulge of *Uncut Funk,* then traverse right to finish up a 4-inch wide left-facing corner.

51 *Uncut Funk 13 feet V7 ★★*
Start with both hands underclinging the melon. From the sit down start this is V8.

52 *Shazam 12 feet V5 SD*
The sit down sloper problem on the east-facing wall two steps west of *Uncut Funk.*

53 *The Bomb 20 feet V1 BL scary loose*
7 feet east of *Uncut Funk* is a 20 foot prow. Climb it's right side. The sit down start, coming in from the left, is V4.

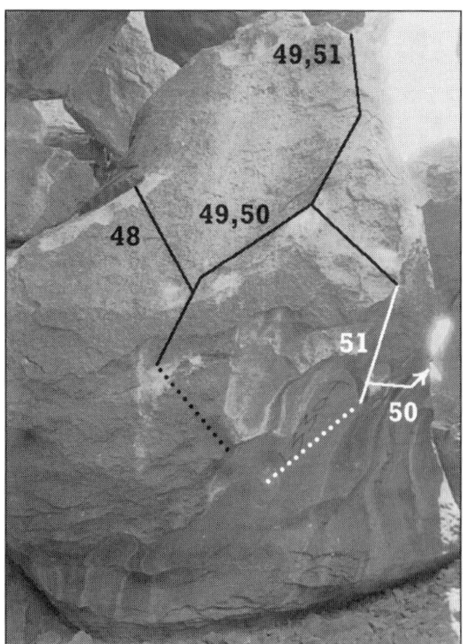

Uncut Funk Area

48 *Nobody 10 feet V6 ★*
49 *Nobody's Funky 15 feet V7 ★*
50 *Nodody's Ugly... 13 feet V10 ★*
51 *Uncut Funk 13 feet V7 ★★*

German Photo Route

The following problems are in the dark coridor underneath the southeast end of the *German Photo Route* boulder.

54 *The Dark Flower length and grade variable ★*
The overhanging handcrack is V0+ if started high (in the handjams), or as hard as you want it to be if you start further and further back in the offwidth sit down start. This crack splits the boulder and is actually *The Handcuff Trick* where it cleaves the west face.

55 *Glas Roof 15 feet V9 ★★ SD*
Unbeknownst to the first ascensionist, the fingertip pocket over the lip was chiseled by another suitor prior to the first ascent. Due to heavy chalk build-up he didn't know this and used the pocket. This climb will go without the doctored pocket (the moves have been done, but not linked from the start), hence I have included it in the book.

German Photo Rte. Boulder
(photo of corridor beneath boulder)

54 *The Dark Flower length and grade variable ★*
55 *Glas Roof 15 feet V9 ★★ SD*

Blockbuster boulder

(Southeast end of corridor below German Photo Route boulder)

56 *Blockbuster 10 feet V2 ★ SD*

57 *Flabio 14 feet V3 BL*

58 *True Romance 15 feet V2*

56 *Blockbuster 10 feet V2 ★ SD*

57 *Flabio 14 feet V3 BL*

58 *True Romance 15 feet V2*

German Photo Route (aka Klingon Warship) 40 feet 2nd class

Absurdly contrived, tremendously stupid, stupendously photogenic, 100% Euro. This climbs the 40 foot tongue of rock thrusting eastward over the low boulders 20 yards north of the East Spur Maze. Walk up the tongue to the lip, taking care not to trip over two bolts on the way (empty sleeves at presstime).

Variation: (5.11) Instead of walking to the top, hand traverse rotting flakes across the southern edge of the tongue.

THE SAUSAGE FACTORY

The Sausage Factory is the group of boulders north of Big Brother Boulder. To get there, walk 45 yards southeast of the East Spur Maze on the 7 foot wide trail (former dirt road). At this point the trail forks to meet the dirt service road in a triangle junction. At the north end if this triangle junction is another wide trail heading northeast. Take this trail 75 yards to Big Brother Boulder, the 40-foot tall perched boulder with the very overhung south face. Walk underneath its east side to enter the Sausage Factory. Photos, pp. 304-306.

The Sausage Factory

1 *Big Brother's Been Bolting 30 feet 5.11+*

2 *Blind Eel Fury 12 feet V1*

3 *The Weenie Roast 12 feet V0+*

4 *Huevos Y Chorozo 12 feet V0 ★*

5 *The Edge Of Jing 15 feet V4 SD*

6 *The Cheese Dog 10 feet V2*

7 *That Slab There 14 feet V5*

8 *Wurst Case Scenario 30 feet V4 ★★*

9 *Glass Ass Crack. 13 feet V9 ★★*

10 *Smokin' Sausage 30 feet V4 ★★★ SD*

11 *The Give 13 feet V3 ★★ SD*

12 *The Hot Link 38 feet V5 SD*

13 *Member's Only 13 feet V5 ★ SD*

14 *The Long Haul 18 feet V8 ★★ SD*

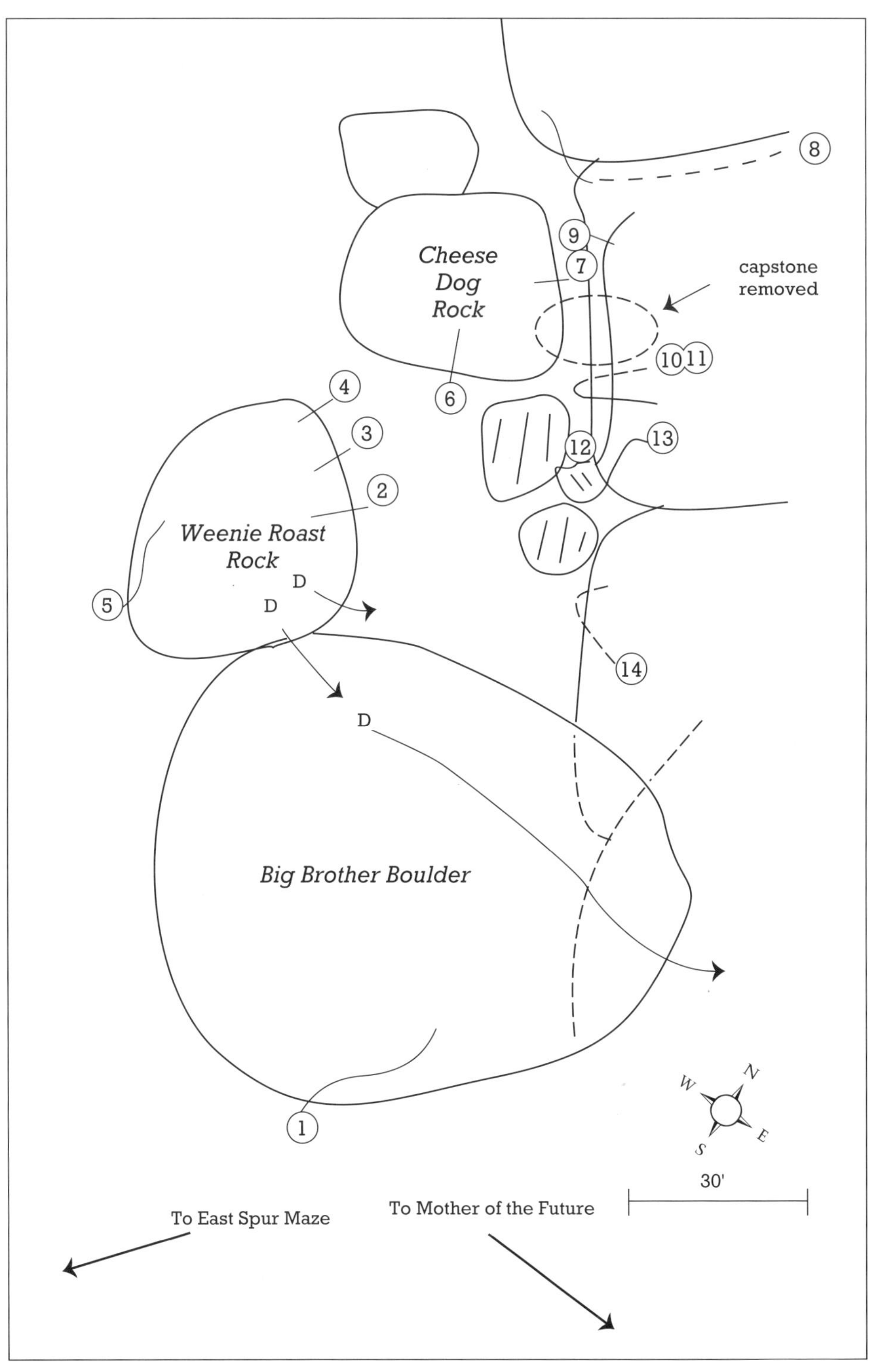
8
9
7
Cheese
Dog
Rock
capstone
removed
10 11
6
4
3
12
13
2
Weenie Roast
Rock
5
D
D
14
D
Big Brother Boulder
1
N
W
E
S
30'
To East Spur Maze
To Mother of the Future

The Sausage Factory area

From south of East Spur Maze.

The Sausage Factory

1 *Big Brother's Been Bolting 30 feet 5.11+*

The Sausage Factory

2 *Blind Eel Fury 12 feet V1*
3 *The Weenie Roast 12 feet V0+*
4 *Huevos Y Chorozo 12 feet V0* ★

---

1 *Big Brother's Been Bolting 30 feet 5.11+*

2 *Blind Eel Fury 12 feet V1*
V5 from a sitdown start.

3 *The Weenie Roast 12 feet V0+*
V4 from a sit down start.

4 *Huevos Y Chorozo 12 feet V0* ★

5 *The Edge Of Jing 15 feet V4 SD*
On the boulder's southwest face, traverse from right to left topping out on loose jugs.

6 *The Cheese Dog 10 feet V2*
Start 4 feet up on an obvious flake just right of center on the south face.

7 *That Slab There 14 feet V5*
Inside the corridor, the undercut slab on the northeast face.

The Sausage Factory
8 *Wurst Case Scenario 30 feet V4 ★★*
9 *Glass Ass Crack. 13 feet V9 ★★*

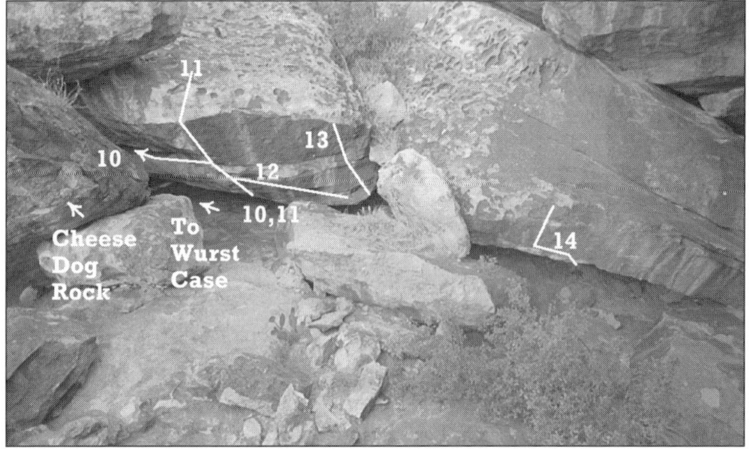

The Sausage Factory
10 *Smokin' Sausage 30 feet V4 ★★★ SD*
11 *The Give 13 feet V3 ★★ SD*
12 *The Hot Link 38 feet V5 SD*
13 *Member's Only 13 feet V5 ★ SD*
14 *The Long Haul 18 feet V8 ★★ SD*

8 *Wurst Case Scenario 30 feet V4 ★★*
The long wrist-torquing undercling jam.

9 *Glass Ass Crack. 13 feet V9 ★★*
Start from two seperate underclings under the roof. Slap up to the polished seam, then right to join the end of Smokin' Sausage.

10 *Smokin' Sausage 30 feet V4 ★★★ SD*
Climb the first half of *The Give,* then traverse the long shelf left until holds lead up and left to top out.

11 *The Give 13 feet V3 ★★ SD*
Watch your head when manteling the lip.

12 *The Hot Link 38 feet V5 SD*
A variant start to *Smokin' Sausage,* beginning at the right end of the wall. Nearly impossible not to brush against the boulder to the west during the first 10 feet.

13 *Member's Only 13 feet V5 ★ SD*

14 *The Long Haul 18 feet V8 ★★ SD*
Start underneath the roof.

Stage Dive Wall

To get to Stage Dive Wall, hike up to the *Mother Of The Future* cave then traverse slabs 100 yards left (northwest), gaining only slight elevation. Stage Dive is in a deep, angled slot. To descend, downclimb to the lip right of Stage Dive and jump off. Overview, p. 304.

1 *Stage Dive 20 feet V7 ★★★ BL*
Start down in the chimney, grabbing the two-hand jug at the top of the thick flake.

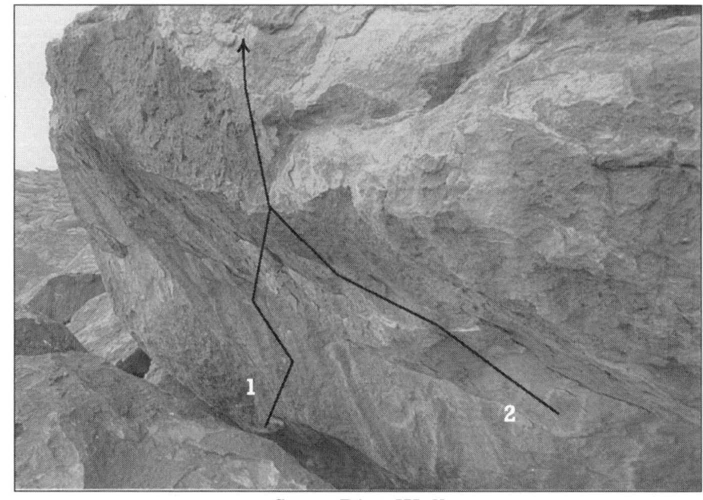

Stage Dive Wall
1 *Stage Dive 20 feet V7 ★★★ BL*
2 *Old School Retrogrind Crunch Funk 15 feet V4 ★*

2 *Old School Retrogrind Crunch Funk 15 feet V4 ★*
Start with left hand on good flake and right hand in horizontal crack. Climb out left to meet Stage Dive, trying to avoid as many loose flakes as you can in the process.

An unnamed spooky route with big loose holds ascends the right end of this wall (V1).

Mother Of The Future 50 feet V9 ★★★
Makes the Morgue look like a playpen. Start at the back of the roof crack done 30 feet from the lip. Desperate finger jamming above uncomfortable blocks gets one past the initial 12 foot crux section and established on the end of a flake. Relatively simple jamming leads to a second, easier, crux at the lip. An enjoyable 20 foot hand crack solo over the lip finishes it. (Variation: starting on the end of the flake, avoiding the first 12 feet of crux jamming, is called ***Morgue's Mother 38 feet V4 ★***). Bad landing in places. Overview photo, p. 304.

Rubberband Man 40 feet 5.12
30 yards right of *Mother Of The Future* is a 70 foot wide grey wall capped by a prominent roof. Climb up the left side of the wall then follow an arcing crack right out the roof. This crack eventually parallels the lip. Pull up to a second crack paralleling the lip , then turn the lip at a small right facing corner. Overview photo, p. 304.
Variation: (35 feet 5.11) Instead of following the arcing roof crack, surmount the roof on its narrower left side.

Mother's Cookie

1 *Lovin' In The Oven 15 feet V0+*
2 *Chocolate Chip 17 feet V0*
3 *Cookie Cutter 17 feet V0 ★*
4 *Nookie Butter 16 feet V0– ★★*
5 *Lick Bush 15 feet V0*
6 *Bushman 15 feet V0 ★*
7 *Home Cooking 15 feet V1 ★*
8 *Apple Pie Arete 15 feet V2*

Mother's Cookie

Mother's Cookie is the big boulder at the hillside's base, 20 yards south of Big Brother Boulder. Its northeast face has several good easy routes.

1 *Lovin' In The Oven 15 feet V0+*

2 *Chocolate Chip 17 feet V0*
6 feet left of *Cookie Cutter.*

3 *Cookie Cutter 17 feet V0 ★*

4 *Nookie Butter 16 feet V0– ★★*

5 *Lick Bush 15 feet V0*

6 *Bushman 15 feet V0 ★*

7 *Home Cooking 15 feet V1 ★*
The wall left of the northwest arete. The arete is not used.

8 *Apple Pie Arete 15 feet V2*

CONFIDENCE SCHEME AREA

Confidence Scheme Wall lies 215 yards southeast of the East Spur Maze. It's on the northwest side of a long rib of rock whose southwest end reaches the ground 30 yards from the dirt service road. Overview photo, p. 310.

1 *Eurofools 10 feet V1*
The left side (4 feet right of the left end) of the short wall facing Confidence Scheme Wall.

2 *Best Supporting Cougar 11 feet V1*
Start 7 feet left of Rent-A-Rattler.

3 *Rent-A-Rattler 12 feet V3 BL*
The shallow 1 inch crack on the right side of the wall. Harder than it looks.

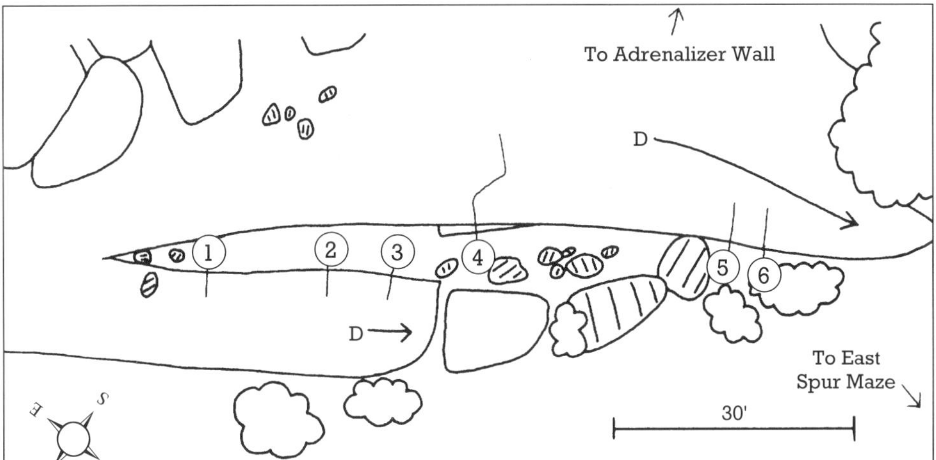

To Adrenalizer Wall

To East Spur Maze

30'

Confidence Scheme Area

1 *Eurofools 10 feet V1*
2 *Best Supporting Cougar 11 feet V1*
3 *Rent-A-Rattler 12 feet V3 BL*
4 *Confidence Scheme 25 feet V1 ★★★ BL*
5 *Texas Crude 17 feet V3*
6 *Repeat Offender 14 feet V2*

4 *Confidence Scheme 25 feet V1 ★★★ BL*
Start on the huge incut flake 5 feet up. Climb straight up between black streaks (the left black streak is mottled with yellow lichen) to the lip. A long crank is involved. At the lip move right, crossing the top of the right hand black streak, to sink fingers into a welcome pocket 3 feet above the lip. Easy moves past some loose flakes follow. Good health insurance a must.

5 *Texas Crude 17 feet V3*
Start 3 feet right of a boulder leaning against the wall. Huecos and fingertip edges (some of which might blow) lead straight to the top. An unusually soft landing if you don't spill back into the bushes.

6 *Repeat Offender 14 feet V2*
Climb the wall next to the tree trunk, brushing through the branches.

Confidence Scheme
From atop *Rent-a-Rattler*
4 *Confidence Scheme 25 feet V1 ★★★ BL*

Flake
Community
College
Adrenalizer
Confidence Scheme
Ostrich Egg
To East
Spur Maze

Flake Community College, left, and Adrenalizer Wall

1 *Flake Community College 45 feet 5.9*
2 *The Exposure Meter 22 feet V1 ★★ BL*
3 *The Adrenalizer 20 feet V4 ★★★ BL scary*

Flake Community College

This is on the northwest-facing wall between Confidence Scheme and The Adrenalizer Wall.

1 *Flake Community College 45 feet 5.9*
Climb the right facing flakes, big and loose to a small roof 25 feet up. Turn this roof on the right, enter a right-facing dihedral, then turn the final roof on its right.
Variation: (45 feet 5.12–) At the top of the loose flakes, climb directly over the first roof then straight to the top.

ADRENALIZER WALL

This wall is 75 yards southeast of Confidence Scheme Wall. It's a bulging, west-facing wall starting 20 feet above ground level atop slabs. The wall is divided into two 20 foot tall sections. Together the sections measure 100 feet long. The left side of the left section is capped by a 15 foot tall by 40 foot wide boulder. The Adrenalizer is the seam running straight up to the middle of this caprock.

Left side of Adrenalizer Wall

2 *The Exposure Meter 22 feet V1 ★★ BL*
Start 10 feet left of the *Adrenalizer* at a V-slot hueco 7 feet up. Follow the hueco line up and right to the top of the *Adrenalizer*. Escape right, under the caprock.

3 *The Adrenalizer 20 feet V4 ★★★ BL scary*
Climb the thin crack/seam. Traverse right along the base of the caprock to escape.

Right side of Adrenalizer Wall

4 *Look Ma, Just One Cavity 16 feet V4 BL*
5 *Full Mettle Junket 21 feet V4 ★★ BL*
6 *Risky Business 21 feet V1 BL*
Directly above the tree, climb big holds avoiding the loose stuff.
7 *Ground Zero 18 feet V0 BL loose*

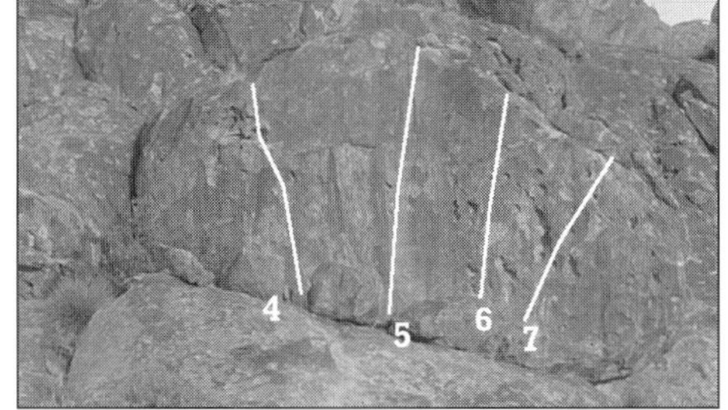

Right side of Adrenalizer Wall

4 *Look Ma, Just One Cavity 16 feet V4 BL*
5 *Full Mettle Junket 21 feet V4 ★★ BL*
6 *Risky Business 21 feet V1 BL*
7 *Ground Zero 18 feet V0 BL loose*

SOUTHERN EAST SPUR

The Ostrich Egg (aka East Spur Boulder)

100 yards from the south end of the East Spur are two large boulders (25 and 35 feet tall) standing away from the main cliff. Overview photo, p. 310.

The service road passes within 5 yards of them.

In general the climbing on these is disappointing. The bigger one is The Ostrich Egg and has many toprope possibilities.

A 5.12 toprope has been done on the west face, starting 10 feet right of a bush beneath a series of small right-facing corners.

On the spur itself

The Face Off 50 feet 5.10

Directly east of The Ostrich Egg is a steep brown north-facing wall at the top of the Spur. A wide left-angling crack pierces its left side. Climb on thin holds right of the crack for 50 feet.

Weakend 65 feet 5.9+

Start at the base of a crack which goes through three overlaps 40 yards north of the Sand Master boulder. Climb the first steep crack to the second overlap, then traverse 35 feet left around a corner to a ledge.

The Sand Master Boulder

At the south tip of the East Spur is this 50 foot tall boulder with severely overhanging east, north and west faces.

1 *The Sand Master 60 feet 5.12* ★★

On the west face, climb from a hueco on the north end, right to the hanging flake. Undercling this right and lieback up past another big flake to 2 bolts. From the second bolt, traverse the horizontal crack right past a pin to the exit ledge at the crack's end.

Straight up from the second bolt on *Sand Master* is a third bolt and sometimes a fixed wired. Too bad two of the holds were beat into shape before the claimed first ascent. It's been written that this line was "retro-chipped by a climber of lesser talent" than the "first ascensionist." Could such a person exist? If so, then the route has been doctored at least twice.

The Sand Master Boulder

1 *The Sand Master 60 feet 5.12* ★★

Sand Master Boulder
2 *The Warning 40 feet 5.11*
3 *The Wizard 45 feet 5.12+ ★*

2 *The Warning 40 feet 5.11*

3 *The Wizard 45 feet 5.12+ ★*

Step off a boulder then climb past 4 bolts to the top. (At presstime the first bolt is hangerless and the second an empty hole.)

Toss The Dice 50 feet 5.10

This route is in the canyon that runs east-west past the north face of Sand Master boulder. This route is 30 yards east of Sand Master Boulder, faces south, and climbs a thin crack past a 6 inch wide slot in the middle and a foot-wide V groove at the top.

EAST SIDE OF EAST SPUR

Old Chef Boulder

This is the only worthwhile boulder on the east side of East Spur. It is located 350 yards from the south end of East Spur (distance along the trail from *Sandmaster* Boulder, the southwest tip of East Spur, to Old Chef). The footpath along the east side of East Spur goes through a miniature pass (between the East Spur and a low lying 100 yard long northeast-southwest band of rocks to the east) 130 yards to the southeast of Old Chef Boulder. The boulder is squat, 20 feet tall by 70 feet wide. A shortcut to get to Old Chef Boulder (if you've already on the west side of East Spur) is to cross the top of East Spur above the Adrenalizer Wall then head southeast to Old Chef Boulder. Depending on where you cross the top of East Spur, the boulder will be 100-150 yards to the southeast. Overview photo, p. 314.

1 *Old Chef 20 feet V4 ★★*

Start in the narrow grassy gully just above the catclaw trunk. Grab the left end of the 5 foot long flake-ledge then yard to the lip, risking a fall into the catclaw below. Dice over the lip to reach stimulating looseness above.

The East Side of East Spur (looking south from two-thirds of the way down the spur)

Old Chef Boulder

1 *Old Chef 20 feet V4 ★★*
2 *Last Of The Red Hot Levers 20 feet V7 ★★*
3 *Acme Roof 24 feet V8 ★★★ SD*

---

2 *Last Of The Red Hot Levers 20 feet V7 ★★*
Start on the slab at the right end of the Old Chef flake/ledge. False grip the pointed flake to the right and beast a lever move to grab the distant lip. Reel 4 feet left along the lip to a 2 inch deep, 3 foot long finger crack. Rock over the lip here and join *Old Chef* to finish.

3 *Acme Roof 24 feet V8 ★★★ SD*
Start deep under the roof. The crux is not brushing the slab below when negotiating the bulging lip. Could be easier if you're short.

Raindance
Cilleypotamia
3 Lobe Buttress
Great White Book
The Eagle
Dam Rock
Adventureland
main dam
Natural Buttress
Devil's Butthole
Dockyard

WEST MOUNTAIN

Descriptions for West Mountain go counterclockwise around the mountain starting at the southwest end of the Main Dam. The parking area closest to West Mountain is at the end loop of the Frontside road.

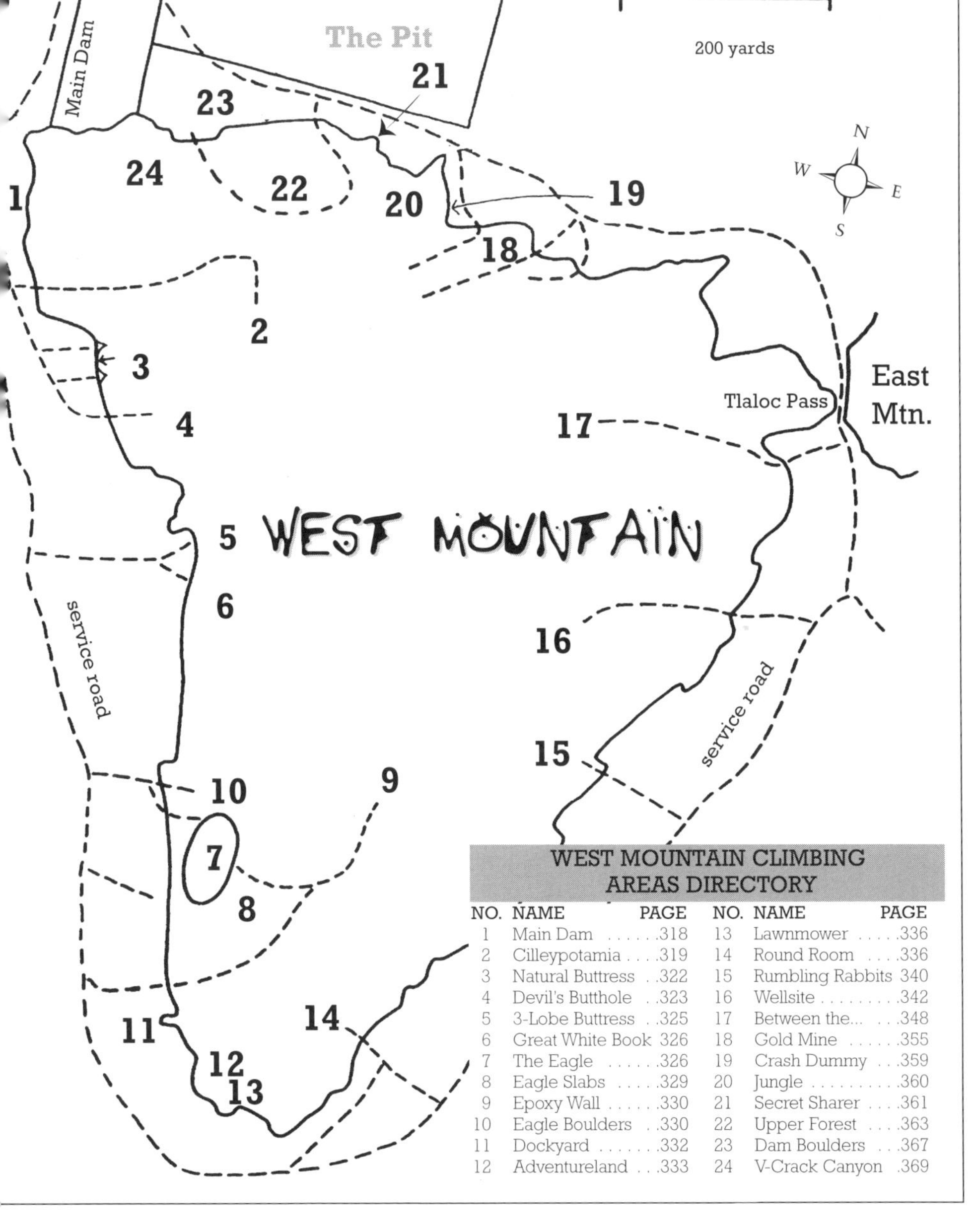

WEST MOUNTAIN CLIMBING AREAS DIRECTORY

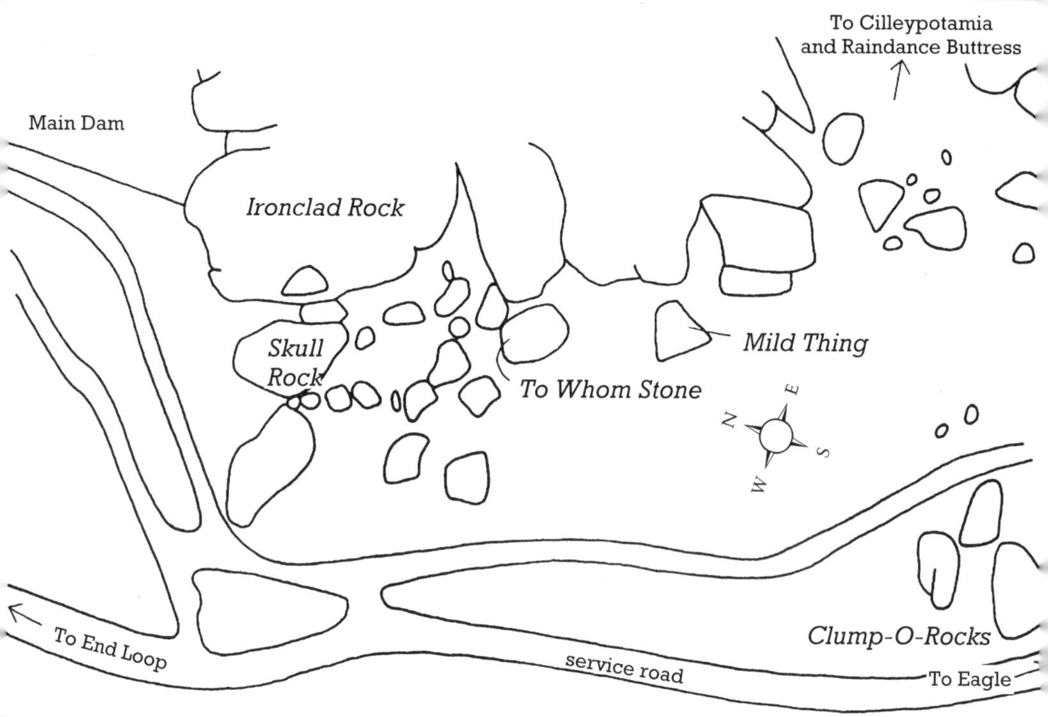

To Cilleypotamia and Raindance Buttress
Main Dam
Ironclad Rock
Skull Rock
Mild Thing
To Whom Stone
N E S W
To End Loop
service road
Clump-O-Rocks
To Eagle

MAIN DAM TO CLUMP-O-ROCKS

1 *Ironclad 26 feet 5.13 TR* ★★

At the south end of the main dam, on its western flank, is a buttress with a prominent overhanging north-facing prow.

This buttress is 25 yards west of Dam Rock. The northeast face, left of the prow, is beautiful ironrock.

The route ascends the center of the northeast face, starting with hands on the right end of a 5 foot long incut horizontal flake. Easier lines on either side of this have since been done.

Skull rock has several 10-foot beginner problems across its northwest face. Look for the skull-shaped hueco. Also look for an overhanging 14-foot hand-crack in the bushy notch east of Skull Rock.

Located 33 yards south of Skull Rock and 100 yards north of Clump-O-Rocks is To Whom Stone. ***To Whom It May Concern, (19 feet V3*** ★), ascends thin ironrock flakes on its northwest face. Obscure, but worth finding.

Mild Thing Boulder, 70 yards north-northeast of Clump-O-Rocks, appears low angle and worthless

South end of the main dam

1 *Ironclad 26 feet 5.13 TR* ★★

when viewed from Clump-O-Rocks. The best problems are on the north face and get harder from left to right (V0-V1); the best ascends the center of the face , 4 feet right of a small left-facing corner. Potential for a finger scorching traverse exists. Clump-O-Rocks, the cluster of three large boulders between the dirt service road and the trail, features problems on the northmost boulder of the three. The north side problems are easy, but tall and feature a cactus landing. Scary for beginners. The south face is composed of great rock. The crux is reaching the base through the bushes.

CILLEYPOTAMIA

To get to Cilleypotamia, hike to the summit ridge of East Mountain via the gully east of Clump-O-Rocks. An imposing 40 foot tall west facing overhang marks the top of this gully. Halfway up the left (north) side of the gully is Raindance Buttress. From the top of this gully walk south along the summit ridge, threading your way between boulders, for 50 yards to Cilleypotamia. The Cilleypotamia wall is on the ridge, is north facing, and has a prominent left angling 3 foot long slash near it's left side Overview photo, p. 316.

Raindance 80 feet 5.11+
Start in the middle of the south face of Raindance Buttress, at a 30 foot long left-facing dihedral. Climb to the top of the dihedral then angle left up big huecos to a headwall with 4 bolts. 2 bolt anchor. See photos, pp. 316, 323..

Cilleypotamia

1 *Ulcerific 22 feet V2 ★ SD*
Start sitting down at a left hand horizontal incut and a right hand hueco. Don't bump into the boulder behind you. Either step off or climb easy jugs right to the top.

Cilleypotamia

1 *Ulcerific 22 feet V2 ★ SD*
2 *Duodenum 20 feet V1 ★★★*
3 *Maalox Moments 22 feet V1 ★★★*
4 *Boop 18 feet V3 ★★★*
5 *Poop 11 feet V0*
6 *Cilleypotamia 50 feet V3 ★★*

2 *Duodenum 20 feet V1 ★★★*
Same sit down start as *Ulcerific*, but follows direct line to the top. Classic.

3 *Maalox Moments 22 feet V1 ★★★*
The same top out as *Duodenum*, but starting to the right and using the big diagonal incut. This has been climbed straight up with a top rope (5.12).

4 *Boop 18 feet V3 ★★★*

5 *Poop 11 feet V0*
Start off the low rock at the base, on a big chest level flake.

6 *Cilleypotamia 50 feet V3 ★★*
Traverse the wall from far right to far left using the lip for the first 8 feet then dropping down and eventually finishing up *Ulcerific*. Great jug hauling.

Problems 7 and 8 serve as their own or each other's descent.

7 *Grunge 16 feet V0+ loose*

8 *Kurt Nobrain 15 feet V0+ loose*

Zeist Boulder

The Zeist Boulder is located 100 rugged yards east of *Cilleypotamia*.

1 *The Planet Zeist 20 feet V6 ★★★ SD BL*
Start in the corridor, at the lowest hueco on the south face.

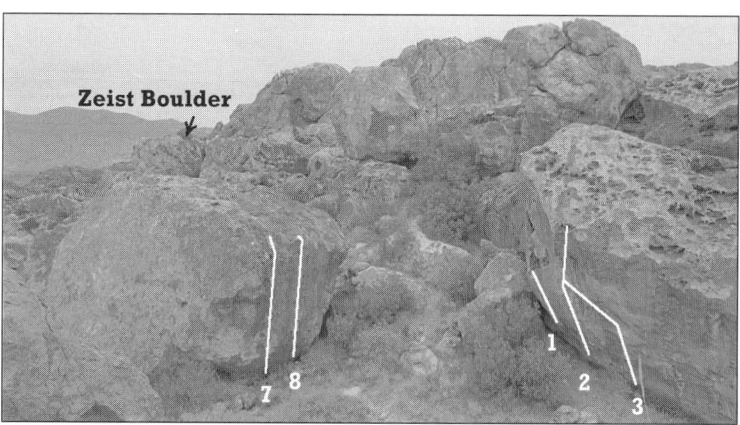

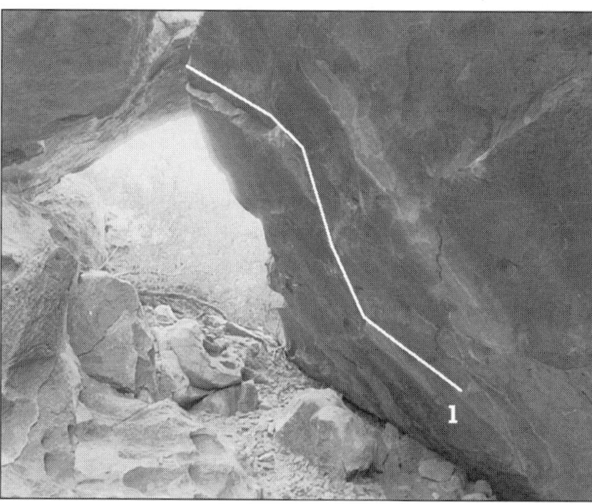

Cilleypotamia (above)
As seen from atop slab to west.

1 *Ulcerific 22 feet V2 ★ SD*
2 *Duodenum 20 feet V1 ★★★*
3 *Maalox Moments 22 feet V1 ★★★*
7 *Grunge 16 feet V0+ loose*
8 *Kurt Nobrain 15 feet V0+ loose*

Zeist Boulder (left)

1 *The Planet Zeist 20 feet V6 ★★★ SD BL*

Between the Sheets

Natural Buttress (foreground), Great White Book

1 *All Natural*
2 *Supernatural Anesthetist*
3 *Mr. Natural*
A *Moon Light Drive 100 feet 5.8*
B *The Great White Book 150 feet 5.10*
C *Cosmic Stupidity 180 feet 5.9*

AREA 3 MAP, P. 317

NATURAL BUTTRESS

Walk 350 yards south from the Main Dam, along the western flank of West Mountain, to a steep north-facing wall. The Natural Buttress is flanked to the north by a shallow canyon with a big roof block capping the rear of the canyon. The descent off the top is tricky and hard to find. Walk east off the top, then turn south and scramble down the first canyon south of Natural Buttress.

1 *All Natural 35 feet 5.8*
This route climbs the short wall to the large sloping ledge below *Supernatural Anesthetist*. It follows an ancient hangerless bolt ladder.

2 *Supernatural Anesthetist 150 feet 5.12* ★★
Belay in the wide spot 20 feet over the roof. The second pitch climbs up the thin crack to a left-facing dihedral, (5.10).
Variation: Climb up buckets up and right after the roof.

3 *Mr. Natural 75 feet 5.11* ★
Four bolts; at presstime, the first two were hangerless, as were the belay bolts on top. It should be noted that most of the missing hangers at Hueco were stolen by souvenir-collecting rappelers, not by fueding bolt warriors.

4 *Iron Man 130 feet 5.10*

5 *Sunny Side Up 60 feet 5.12* ★
Five bolts, two-bolt anchor.

6 *Max Headroom 110 feet 5.11*
Climb the first 40 feet of *Ramp To Hell,* stopping 15 feet above a console TV size block wedged against the ramp. Follow huecos and six bolts straight to the top and a two bolt anchor.

7 *Ramp To Hell 150 feet 5.10*
Climb up the obvious right-angling, left-facing corner/ramp on the south side of the Natural Buttress. Finish via a luscious off-width at the top.

Natural Buttress

4	*Iron Man*	6	*Max Headroom*
5	*Sunny Side Up*	7	*Ramp To Hell*

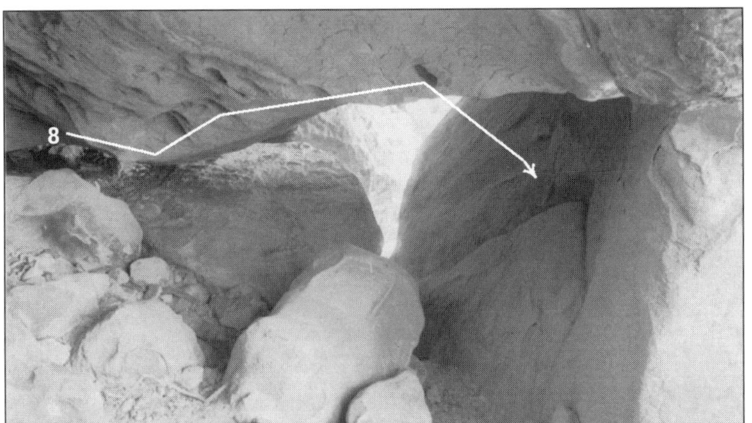

Whine Celler

8 *The Whine Cellar*

---

8 *The Whine Cellar 20 feet V6 ★ SD*
This problem is underneath the huge boulder at the base of *Sunny Side Up* and always stays dry. Sit down on the boulder to start. Finish with a wild dismount onto the face of the boulder to the northwest.

THE DEVIL'S BUTTHOLE

The Devil's Butthole climbs the underside of a 60-foot diameter boulder 180 yards southeast of Clump-O-Rocks. Sunnyside Up (a popular south facing lead on Supernatural Buttress) is 50 yards to it's north. The Devil's Butthole Boulder is perched 30 feet above ground level at the right edge of the toe of a 100 foot long, 60 foot wide, tan, rounded buttress. A big overhang dominates the south face of the boulder. Below this overhang, at ground level, is a northwest facing ironrock face with a 20 foot diameter boulder leaning against its left side. This face is the Don't Mess wall. See overview photo, p. 316.

1 *Don't Mess 25 feet V3 ★★ BL scary*
Start below the big chockstone, then exit left.

2 *Buster 28 feet V3 ★★ scary+*
Finish up the wall 5 feet right of the big chockstone. Continuous.

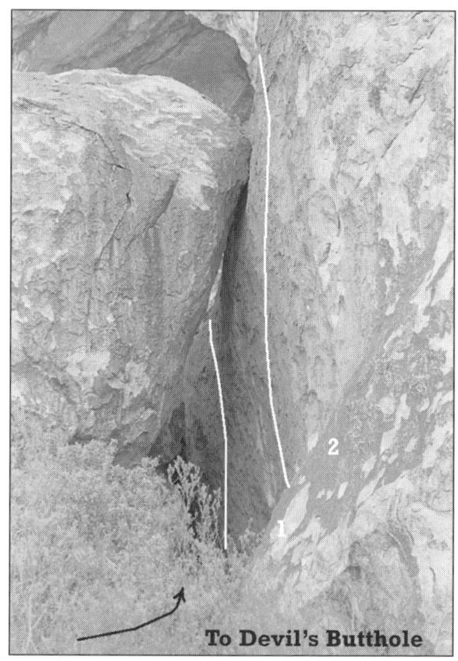

Don't Mess Wall
1 *Don't Mess 25 feet V3 ★★ BL scary*
2 *Buster 28 feet V3 ★★ scary+*

To get to the Devil's Butthole, first find Don't Mess Wall. From the start of *Don't Mess,* walk 30 feet uphill, ducking under some rocks, until you're under the overhang on the south face of the Devil's Butthole Boulder. Skirt the boulder on it's right (east) side to get to its uphill (north) side. Crawl in left under the overhang on the uphill side. You should be able to see all the way underneath the boulder to an exit (or entrance) under its west face.

Devil's Butthole 36 feet V6 ★★★ (no topo)
The problem starts near the west face exit on a big hanging flake the size of an ice chest top. Climb up and out 36 feet of big hold bonanza roofing and turn the lip on the north face. The roof is never more than 5 feet off the ground. Halfway across the problem is the infamous Devil's Butthole, most likely the deepest hueco in Hueco Tanks. So deep you can rest in it. In fact you can chimney up it in the darkness for how far I won't tell. You must experience that ritual for yourself. Flashlights are off-route.

Devil's Butthole

The Jungle Gym

100 yards south of Natural Buttress is a wide boulder strewn gully leading up to a low point in the crest of West Mountain. The Jungle Gym is located 100 yards northeast of the low spot or pass. It is a big roof even in elevation with the level of the pass. The approach involves 3rd classing up licheny slabs. The climbing at the Jungle Gym is similar to Bucket Roof, but the rock quality is poorer. The two lines done over the lip are exceedingly grainy at the lip, but the climbing under the roof is powerful fun. Photo, p. 353.

AREA 5

MAP, P. 317

THREE-LOBE BUTTRESS

100 yards south of Natural Buttress is a wide boulder-strewn gully leading up to a low point in the crest of West Mountain. 30 yards right (south) of this low point is a three-lobed buttress. The right hand (southern) lobe has a 115 degree south face with the following two routes. The Great White Book is 50 yards south of Three-Lobe Buttress. See overview photo, p. 316.

1 *Natural Mystic 85 feet 5.11* ★

2 *Huecool 80 feet 5.12 TR* ★★★
5 bolts + 2 at anchor. This route has been given an undeserved horror-show reputation for the "runout" up to the first bolt. The first clip is well protected if you place your own gear. Bring nuts.

Three-Lobe Buttress

1 *Natural Mystic 85 feet 5.11* ★

2 *Huecool 80 feet 5.12 TR* ★★★

GREAT WHITE BOOK AREA

At the top of the west side of West Mountain is a buttress with a large white dihedral on its northwest face.

This buttress is 150 yards north of The Eagle. The summit of this buttress is also the highest point in Hueco Tanks.

See photos, pp. 316, 322.

A *Moon Light Drive 100 feet 5.8*

20 yards to the left of *The Great White Book* is this line of huecos on a 100-foot tall northwest-facing buttress.

B *The Great White Book 150 feet 5.10*

Stem and lie-back up the large white dihedral for two pitches.

C *Cosmic Stupidity 180 feet 5.9*

Climb the pillar 20 feet to the right of the base of the large white dihedral, to the large huecos. Follow these huecos up and left following the arching buttress to a huge white hueco and a belay. The more stupid the way taken, the more cosmic. Continue traversing left above the dihedral to an excellent iron rock wall with fun huecos. Climb to the top on nice holds after traversing most of the wall, and belay on the summit of Hueco Tanks.

THE EAGLE

The Eagle is located on the south end of The West Side of West Mountain and is visible from the road leading to Hueco Tanks. This impressive piece of free-standing rock has several wildly overhanging routes. See overview photo, p. 316. The descent is simple - scramble down easy rock on the east side of The Eagle.

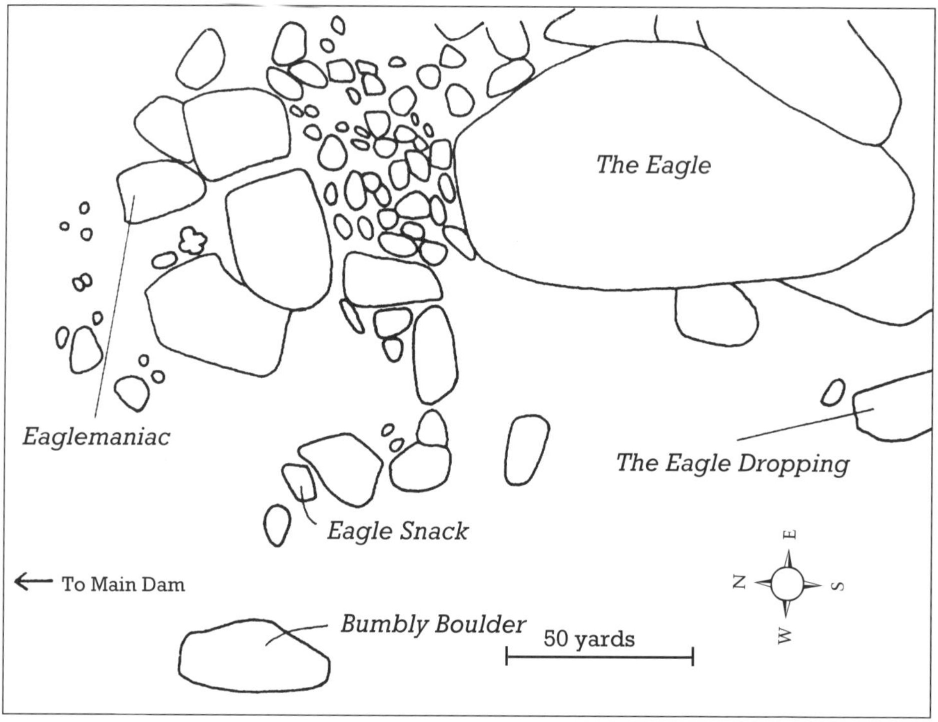

The Eagle
Eaglemaniac
The Eagle Dropping
Eagle Snack
← To Main Dam
Bumbly Boulder
50 yards
N E S W

Eagle Areas

- 2 *When Legends Die 75 feet 5.13* ★★★
- 3 *Road To Nowhere 45 feet 5.11+* ★★
- 4 *Electric Hueco Land 140 feet 5.11* ★★
- 5 *Through the Looking Glass 200 feet 5.11+* ★
- 6 *New Wave 85 feet 5.10–*
- 7 *Blood Stained Highway 120 feet 5.10 R*
- 8 *Scurvy Dogs 80 feet 5.8*
- 9 *Dumbfighter 80 feet 5.5*

1 *The Gunfighter 100 feet 5.13–* ★★

Variation: After pulling the bulge, follow the right leaning crack 20 feet then belay. For the second pitch, exit the right- leaning crack on its left and follow a striking 5.11+ thin crack straight up the northeast face to the top of the Eagle.

2 *When Legends Die 75 feet 5.13* ★★★

Seven bolts, two-bolt anchor.. Beware the premeditated runout at the top.

3 *Road To Nowhere 45 feet 5.11+* ★★

Climb the steep rock on the corner until the crack is reached. Climb the severely overhanging crack until it ends, then lower off the anchors.

4 *Electric Hueco Land 140 feet 5.11* ★★

From the belay ledge on *Through The Looking Glass,* climb the wild overhanging rock, via huecos, a pin and a bolt, to a belay over the lip (1 bolt, back it up with nuts in the horizontal crack below the bolt). Finish up *Through The Looking Glass.* Approach *Electric Hueco Land* by climbing the dirty first pitch of *Through The Looking Glass,* or by rappeling down to the belay ledge.

The Eagle

1 *The Gunfighter 100 feet 5.13–* ★★
2 *When Legends Die 75 feet 5.13* ★★★
3 *Road To Nowhere 45 feet 5.11+* ★★

5 *Through the Looking Glass 200 feet 5.11+* ★

Traverse left, following the left-leaning crack under the roof, to a wide crack that cleaves the roof. Climb the roof on huge jugs, via the wide crack, to a small ledge. Step up right to the next ledge and belay. The next section can be done as one or two pitches. Climb off the right end of the belay ledge, (5.10-), to easier ground. Continue up and left to a black water streak near the top, and traverse left to good holds on friable rock. Climb straight up to the top (5.8).

Mechanical Rape 90 feet 5.11 A0

This route ascends from inside the deep chimney system on the southeast side of The Eagle following a large conspicuous flake. Start on a large chockstone below the flake and aid two moves to attain a stance. Step left to a left-leaning crack and climb to the top.

Hand Job 55 feet 5.7

In the same chimney system as *Mechanical Rape*, but on the wall facing west, is a left-leaning crack. Start above a chimney and climb the crack to the top.

SOUTHWEST END OF WEST MOUNTAIN

These three route are on walls right (south) of the Eagle.

6 *New Wave 85 feet 5.10–*

On the face 30 yards south from The Eagle, climb 10 to 15 feet right of the obvious crack past two bolts.

7 *Blood Stained Highway 120 feet 5.10 R*
70 yards right (south) of The Eagle, climb a long ramp system to the base of a right-leaning arch (5.7). Several light brown streaks descend from the arch. Undercling right under the arch (5.10). Finish up the right-facing corner above.

8 *Scurvy Dogs 80 feet 5.8*
This steep route is located on the southwest-facing buttress to the right of *Blood-Stained Highway's* first pitch. Climb hidden holds for 80 feet to a rap anchor. 2 bolts, 2 bolt anchor.

EAGLE SLABS

Eagle Slabs, the large expanse of rock to the south of the Great White Book buttress and northeast from The Eagle, contains numerous routes that range from 5.4 to 5.11. This area is largely undeveloped and hard to approach, but there are many moderate routes with clean protection. The top of Eagle Slabs forms part of the crest of West Mountain. Epoxy Wall faces southeast and lies on the other side of the crest from Eagle Slabs. It is easily seen when driving into the park from Pete's. To approach Western Playland and Epoxy Wall, climb up the 3rd class gully east of the Eagle (much route finding involved), or go up the ramps beneath Blood Stained Highway (also some 3rd class). Either approach takes one to the crest of West Mountain which is then followed north to the routes. Epoxy Wall may also be approached by climbing up the slabs above the Round Room (some 3rd class). Regardless of which way you take, the approach is the longest in Hueco Tanks – nearly 30 minutes from ground level.

9 *Dumbfighter 80 feet 5.5*
50 yards north of The Eagle is a 40 foot wide, 80 foot tall, low angle slab with a thin crack splitting its upper left side. The crack passes over a small roof 30 feet below the top. Fire it.

10 *Western Playland 50 feet 5.11+ ★★*
This route is on the crest of West Mountain 75 yards east of the Eagle and 50 yards southwest of Epoxy Wall. Climb south-facing, grey rock up a triangular face at the top of Eagle Slabs. The rock this route is on can be seen from The Eagle, but the route itself cannot be seen until one is atop the approach gully on the crest of the mountain.

Western Playland

10 *Western Playland 50 feet 5.11+ ★★*

Epoxy Wall

11 Wise To The Future 40 feet 5.12+
12 No Future 40 feet 5.13–
13 Bicepian Traverse 75 feet V4

EPOXY WALL

Due to its steepness and southern exposure, this wall looks enticing from a distance. The rock, however, is poor. See overview on page 337.

11 Wise To The Future 40 feet 5.12+

12 No Future 40 feet 5.13–

13 Bicepian Traverse 75 feet V4

Traverse the base of Epoxy Wall. Crumbly at the right end.

EAGLE BOULDERS

The Eagle is surrounded by boulders of which the four located on the map below have seen development. Further development is sure to occur here, likely with the assurance of topropes. The potential is great. Photo, p. 327; map, p. 326.

Eaglemaniac Stone

This huge boulder is located amongst 4 other enormous rocks on the hillside 75 yards north of The Eagle. Great toprope potential exists amongst these five rocks.

Fairy Canary 15 feet V0– ★★
Climb the shallow dihedral 17 feet left of the northeast arete, meeting that slab 9 feet up.

Buzzard's Delight 19 feet V0 ★
Climb the strangely pocketed face 7 left of the northeast arete topping out next to the hanging summit block. Start off a boulder. Bad landing.

1 *Eaglemaniac 20 feet V2 ★★ BL*
Starting on the ground, climb the northeast arete. It finally lets up two-thirds of the way up.

2 *Bald Eagle 28 feet 5.12- TR ★★*
Could possibly be led with micronuts.

3 *Think Light 28 feet 5.11+ TR ★★*

4 *Ban Lite 29 feet 5.12 TR loose*
Not as good as it looks.

Eaglemaniac Stone

1 *Eaglemaniac 20 feet V2* ★★ *BL*
2 *Bald Eagle 28 feet 5.12- TR* ★★
3 *Think Light 28 feet 5.11+ TR* ★★
4 *Ban Lite 29 feet 5.12 TR loose*
5 *Super Eagle 28 feet 5.12 TR* ★
6 *Eagle Trip 30 feet V0* ★★★ *BL scary*

5 *Super Eagle 28 feet 5.12 TR* ★
6 *Eagle Trip 30 feet V0* ★★★ *BL scary*
Huecos you could toss basketballs into. Climb the center of the overhanging west face starting on or just left of the 3 foot tall rocks where the slope rises. Continuous, with a high crux and very bad landing. Only those with aerial confidence and a good ability to judge the soundness of holds should attempt this ropeless.

The Bumbly Boulder

This great beginner's rock is found at ground level 100 yards northwest of The Eagle.

Bumbly's Challenge 17 feet V0– ★
Climb the east face 10 feet left of the northeast arete.

Crumbly Bumbly 17 feet V0
The face 3-4 feet left of the northeast arete.

Bumbly Buster 19 feet V0+ ★
Climb the center of the slightly overhung north face above "E".

Wall Of Horrors 10-14 feet V0- ★★
The west face is climbable anywhere at V0-. It has a sand landing friendly to beginners.

Eagle Snack Rock

Eagle Snack Rock is 25 yards east and slightly uphill from Bumbly Boulder. It's a small boulder (14 feet tall) just northwest of a much larger rock.

7 *Milk Bone 14 feet V1*
8 *Eagle Snack 13 feet V1* ★

Eagle Snack Rock

7 *Milk Bone 14 feet V1* 8 *Eagle Snack 13 feet V1* ★

The Eagle Dropping
9 *Mantel As Anything 8 feet V0+ ★*
10 *Cat Scratch Fever 8 feet V0+*
11 *Shove It 9 feet V2 ★ SD*
12 *Mantle City Madhouse 12 feet V3*

The Eagle Dropping

The Eagle Dropping is 20 feet west of the major diagonal crack at the base of the Eagle's west face (this crack is the first pitch of *Through The Looking Glass*).

9 *Mantel As Anything 8 feet V0+ ★*
Mantel the lip.

10 *Cat Scratch Fever 8 feet V0+*
Start with hands 2 feet below the lip.

11 *Shove It 9 feet V2 ★ SD*
The lip that is. Sit down start at the low left-facing corner 4 feet right of the northeast prow. Straight up to yet another mantel.

12 *Mantle City Madhouse 12 feet V3*
Same start as Shove It, but follows flakes up and right to the lip. One of the key flakes sounds hollow.

MAP, P. 317

THE DOCK YARD

This group of large boulders is 65 to 100 yards south of The Eagle and contains numerous topropes and boulder problems. Overview photo, p. 316.

Ship Rock

This is the large boulder 65 yards south of The Eagle. It roughly resembles a ship, or the state of Texas. This description depends on your vantage point and imagination.

Seasick 29 feet V0–
Climb up the middle of the back (east side) of Ship Rock.

1 *The Bilge Pump 29 feet V0+*
Start on a bulge on the northeast corner and climb to the top.

2 *Ship Side 28 feet 5.10– TR*

3 *Time Dwarfs 29 feet 5.10+ ★★*
This amazing problem climbs the overhanging northeast corner of the large boulder 25 yards southeast of Ship Rock. Climb good holds 4 feet left of the northeast arete and 10 feet right of a cat claw tree. Descend by walking to the south end of the boulder and scrambling down the west face. Originally soloed, but a competent leader could protect this with tiny wireds.

The Dockyard

1 *The Bilge Pump 29 feet VO+*
2 *Ship Side 28 feet 5.10- TR*
3 *Time Dwarfs 29feet 5.10+ ★★*

ADVENTURELAND

This is the place to get the feel for the Hueco Experience as it used to be – no numbers, no stars, no led-by-the-hand approach. Just cool problems waiting to be judged on their own merits, not an assigned reputation.

This area was listed in the last guide as a boulderfield that would probably see a lot of toprope development. So far all the routes have been put up cordless. I have left it up to you to judge whether the rock is loose, the crux high, the landing bad, the moves scary, your ability adequate. Many routes not listed here have also been done. You're on your own. Have a good adventure. Overview photo, p. 316.

1 ***The Downer*** ***14 feet***
Also the descent for this boulder.

2 ***Tough Love*** ***26 feet***

3 ***Pleasure Revenge*** ***25 feet***
Same start hold as *Tough Love*. Go right.

A 16 foot left to right undercling is under the northeast side of the boulder from which *The Downer* starts. A 14 foot ironrock face climb is just right of the undercling's finish.

4 ***Chicken In A Casket*** ***33 feet***
Mantel start at low level.

5 ***The Broomsticker*** ***23 feet***

6 ***Uncle Drunkie*** ***24 feet***

The wall left of *Uncle Drunkie* has several lines exiting left of the boulder contacting the face. Facing this wall is an 11 foot problem starting 2 feet left of a white paint stripe on the slab at the base.

Adventureland

From halfway up the approach to *Best of the Best.*

1 *The Downer 14 feet*
2 *Tough Love 26 feet*
3 *Pleasure Revenge 25 feet*
4 *Chicken In A Casket 33 feet*
5 *The Broomsticker 23 feet*
6 *Uncle Drunkie 24 feet*

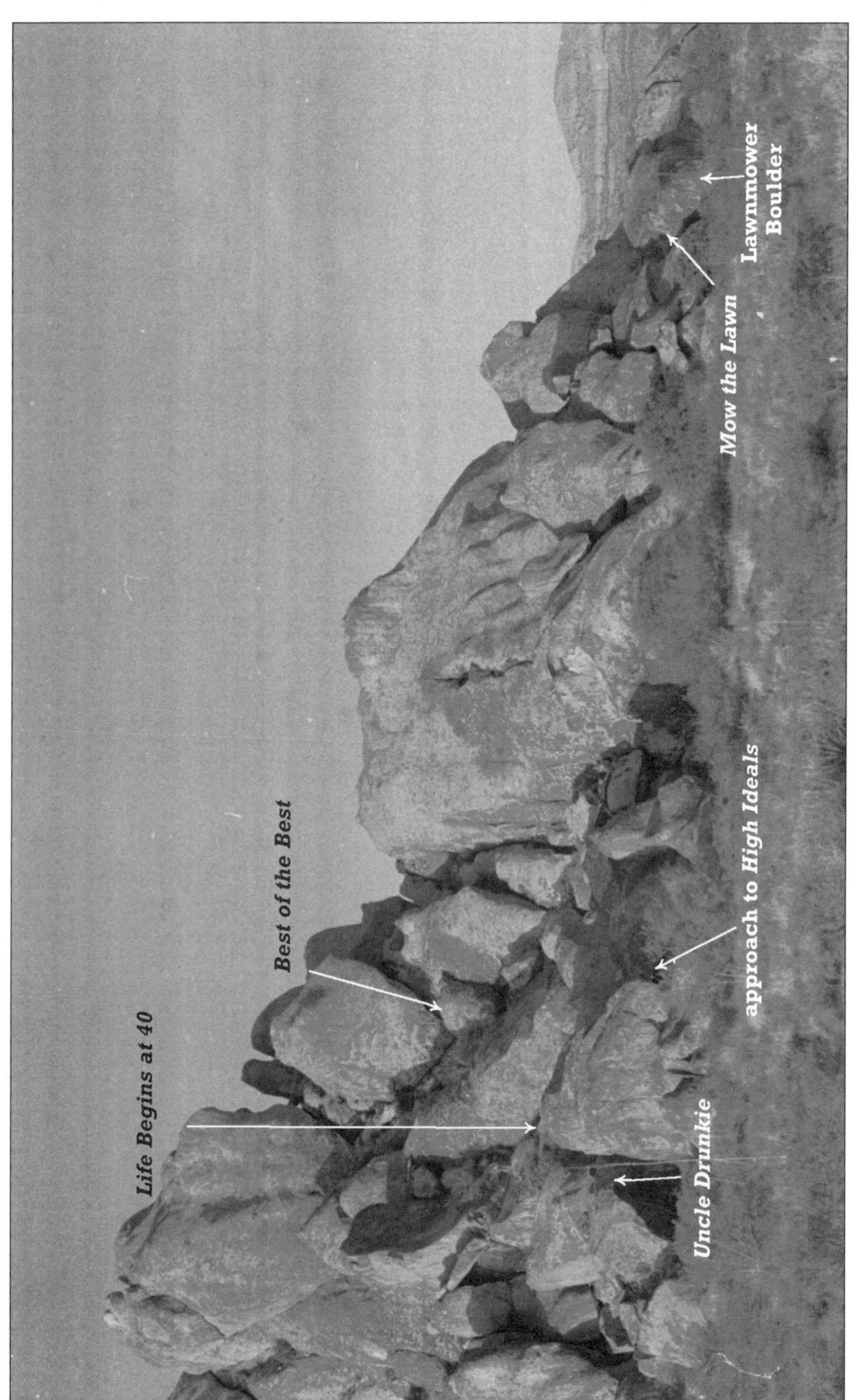

Adventureland

7 *Crunch Time 13 feet*
8 *Low Morals 24 feet*
Start with a mantel of the undercut bulge.
9 *High Ideals 21 feet*
10 *Life Begins At Forty 40 feet*
Well hidden. Many variations/link-ups.
11 *Best Of The Best 31 feet*

Adventureland
Top:
7 *Crunch Time 13 feet*
8 *Low Morals 24 feet*
Middle
10 *Life Begins At Forty 40 feet*
Bottom Left:
9 *High Ideals 21 feet*
Bottom Right:
11 *Best Of The Best 31 feet*

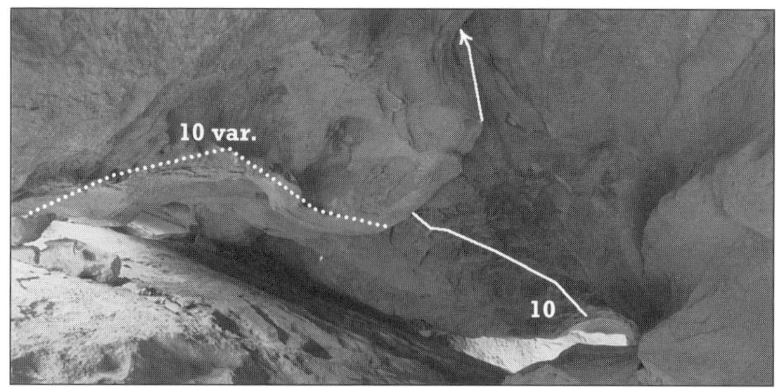

The Lawnmower Boulder
1 *Mow The Lawn 22 feet V5 ★★*

THE LAWNMOWER BOULDER

Photo, p. 334.

1 *Mow The Lawn 22 feet V5 ★★*
2 *Trim The Hedge 14 feet V0+*

Around the corner right of *Mow The Lawn*, start halfway up the diagonal crack and climb straight up the face above.

North of Mow The Lawn is a 20 foot slab with many good V0 lines.

THE SOUTHEAST SIDE OF WEST MOUNTAIN

The areas on the Southeast Side of West Mountain are spread out. Because most of them aren't visible from ground level they can be hard to find.

THE ROUND ROOM

This is one of the more difficult to find bouldering spots in Hueco Tanks. Several possible approaches are given. Walk to the far south end of West Mountain (the end closest to Pete's). From the southernmost end of West Mountain's southernmost boulder walk 165 yards northeast along the wide dirt trail on West Mountain's southeast side. 105 yards along this trail, to your left, is a 20 foot tall boulder that one woman claimed when viewed from the south "looks like a penis." Perhaps her boyfriend should see a doctor. An alternate entrance to the Round Room involves scrambling up the gully to this boulder's northwest, hooking a right at the first chimney (Chez Peron, a big thumb shaped pinnacle, rises above this chimney's southeast side) and following the chimney north until is deposits you in the Round Room. Fatsos might not manage the last squeeze this way.

Back to the easier way. After walking 165 yards from West Mountain's end (count your paces) turn left and walk 25 yards to meet the rocks. At this point a large oak tree grows in a corner in the rocks. The corner faces north, so you won't see it until you're even with it. Even then it's indistinct. 15 feet left of this oak is a small ailing oak at the toe of a 24 foot tall buttress (marked "Marcy, Pete" 5 feet above the base). If you've found yourself now, simply scramble up the vine covered slab to your west, (just right of the big healthy oak), past one 3rd class move, until you're in the Round Room (you'll gain 25 feet elevation). If you haven't found the approach slab yet try finding the 30 foot tall, 3 foot wide black water streak to it's right. This streak disappears into a group of trees at it's base. 28 yards left of the streak is the toe of the approach slab. The 17 foot overhanging wall at ground level on the right of the approach slab has been toproped (5.12).

The third way to find the Round Room, and perhaps the easiest way, is to stay on the dirt service road that loops around West Mountain's south end. This road is more distant from the mountain than the trails mentioned above. From the point on this road 30 yards south of West Mountain's southernmost boulder, walk east, then northeast on this road. A wash will be to your left. After 175 yards you should see a pile of dozens of football to basketball size rocks on your left (northwest) placed there to prevent the road from eroding into the wash. 15 feet west of this pile is a 10 foot tall mesquite on the northwest side of the road. Behind the pile of rocks is an 8 foot wide notch dropping into the wash. Directly across the wash

West Mountain from the East Spur Maze

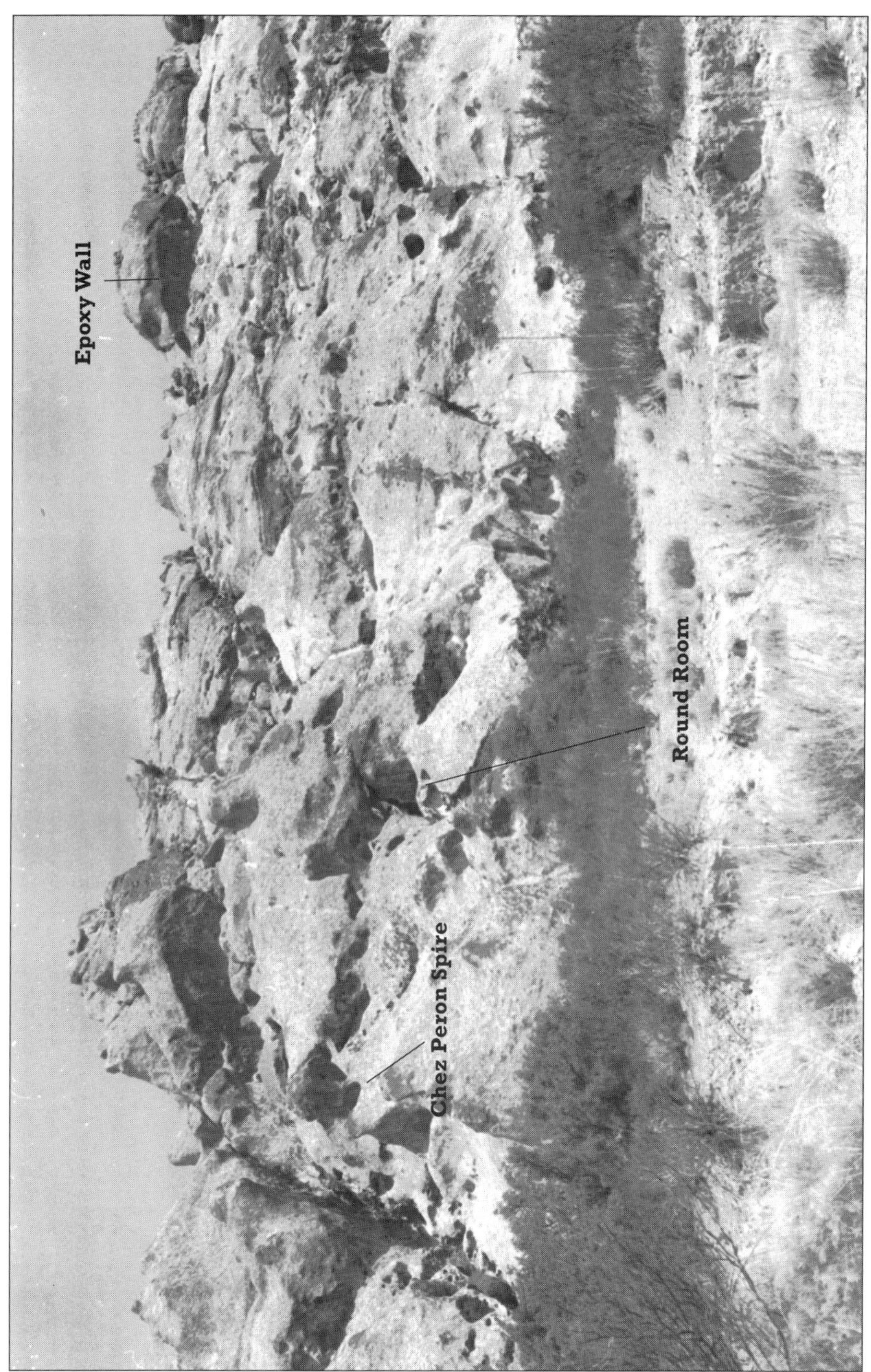
Epoxy Wall
Round Room
Chez Peron Spire

from this notch is an 8 foot wide trail (formerly a dirt road) that leads to the approach slab (the black water streak mentioned above can be seen at the northwest end of this wide trail).

Chez Peron Spire 20 feet 5.10
The thumb-shaped pinnacle 50 feet south of the Round Room. Either solo the east face to the top or toss a rope over the summit to top rope it (hoping the rope doesn't slide off the top, risky at best). The favored descent is the exceedingly dangerous *Big Daddy Jump* over the chasm to the west (★★★). The landing slab is scaly and loose and a botched attempt could prove fatal. Nevertheless, it has been done several times. If not up to the jump, use a rope to descend.

1 *The Round Room Traverse 100 feet V0– ★★★*
Only in Hueco Tanks. Traverse the entire room in either direction.
Variation 1: Pursuit Race 2 climbers start on opposite sides and chase each other until one is caught or someone falls. A mega-pump with evenly matched competitors. I once participated in a pursuit that lasted 20 laps - 2000 feet of skin-torching jug moves with no stop.
Variation 2: Time Trial Record attempts are timed starting on the right side of the slabby South Face wall and ending 100 feet later at the same point. For years Blazin' Bill Hoadley held the record of 42 seconds. He used EB's and it was thought that sticky rubber technology was slowing everyone else down. Unfortunately records are made to be broken and I've heard claims of the 40 second barrier being broken.
Variation 3: Tag Play tag, but stay on the walls.
WARNING: PARTIERS SOMETIMES THROW BOTTLES AGAINST THE WALLS. LOOK OUT FOR GLASS IN THE HUECOS.

2 *Pizza Face 24 feet V2 ★ BL*
Instead of pulling the hideously loose lip off, stem behind you at the top to back off.

3 *FTC 30 feet 5.10+ ★*
Offwidth until you can squeeze through the chimney at the top.

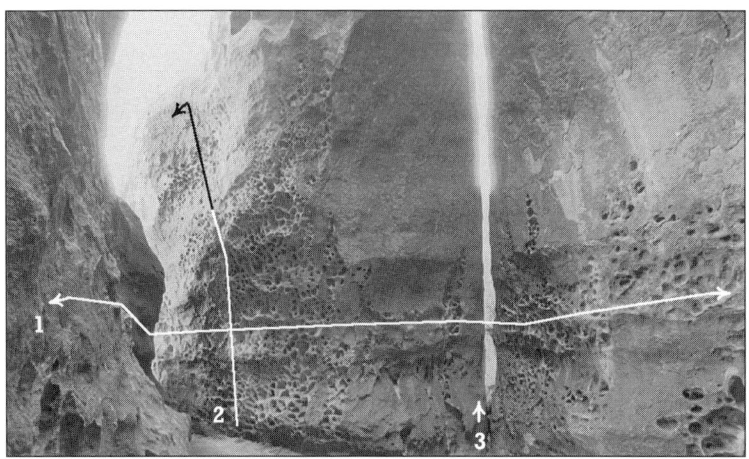

The Round Room

Standard entrance on left, alternate entrance (and approach to *Chez Peron Spire*) through squeeze chimney on right.

1 *The Round Room Traverse 100 feet V0– ★★★*
2 *Pizza Face 24 feet V2 ★ BL*
3 *FTC 30 feet 5.10+ ★*

The Round Room

1 *The Round Room Traverse 100 feet V0– ★★★*
4 *The Unnameable 25 feet V3 ★★ scary*
5 *Loose Screw 24 feet V1 ★ BL scary loose*
6 *STB 20 feet V0+*

4 *The Unnameable 25 feet V3 ★★ scary*

5 *Loose Screw 24 feet V1 ★ BL scary loose*

The last 6 feet are the crux. There's a ¼ inch stud above the lip on this. A bad landing if one doesn't fall far enough out from the wall to miss the base.

6 *STB 20 feet V0+*

Avoid an early exit to the right.

MAP, P. 317

THE WALL OF THE RUMBLING RABBITS

This wall is also well hidden, but not as hard to find as the Wellsite or the Round Room. From the northernmost curve in the dirt service road (the same spot near the trash can mentioned in the Wellsite approach directions) walk south on the service road for 300 yards. At this point there is a T intersection with another road (or wide trail if you will, a 10 foot tall banana yucca is on the northwest corner of this intersec-

Entrance to the Wall of the Rumbling Rabbits

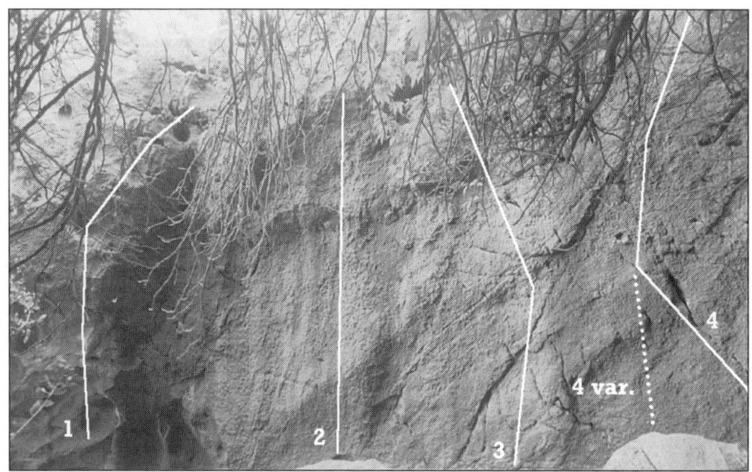

Wall of the Rumbling Rabbits

1 *Spotty's Mean Streak 18 feet V4 ee BL*
2 *Spotty In A Rage 13 feet V1 ★ BL*
3 *Rabbit Stew 20 feet V3 ★★ BL*
4 *Rabbit-Fu 25 feet V3 ★★ BL*

tion). This other road heads northwest for 110 yards to the base of West Mountain. Sighting along this road, you should see some 25 foot tall boulders at the base of the mountain. They may at first appear to be part of the mountain. There's an oak tree in the gap between these rocks and more oaks to their right (north). The Rabbit Rumble Wall is on the back of the boulder bounding the south side of this gap. Overview photo, p. 337.

1 ***Spotty's Mean Streak 18 feet V4 ★★ BL***

2 ***Spotty In A Rage 13 feet V1 ★ BL***
Starts off the boulder.

3 ***Rabbit Stew 20 feet V3 ★★ BL***
From a swinging start between the two boulders at the base, continue straight up 2 slots, a layaway flake, then knobs to the top.

4 ***Rabbit-Fu 25 feet V3 ★★ BL***
Start 3 feet right of the taller boulder of the two mentioned above. Traverse left above this boulder until you can go straight up and exit just left of the contact with the giant chockstone above. Starting from the boulder makes it 21 feet V2 ★. Either way it's a bad landing. Photos above and on page 342.

5 ***Hoppity Spills His Guts 20 feet V0+ ★★★ BL***
Poor Hoppity. Start in virtually the same place as *Rabbit-Fu* at a 2 hand pocket 5 1/2 feet up. Angle up and right on well spaced holds, exiting to the right of the giant chockstone. Possibly the best problem of it's grade at Hueco Tanks. Scary if V0+ is your limit. Photo, page 342.

6 ***The Hutch Hussy 20 feet V2 ★★★***
After an undercut start with feet on a watermelon size knob 3½ feet up, parallel *Hoppity Spills His Guts* 3 feet to it's right. The holds on *Hoppity Spills His Guts* are off-route. Photo, page 342.

7 ***The Hitch 18 feet V2 ★★ BL***
Start off the 2 foot tall boulder just right of *The Hutch Hussy's* start. A funky trailer hitch ball hold 8 feet up and a flake just left of it are the first holds. A 5 foot pull gets one to a hold 18 inches up and left of the white stained undercling scoop above. From there it's easy to the top. Photo, page 342.

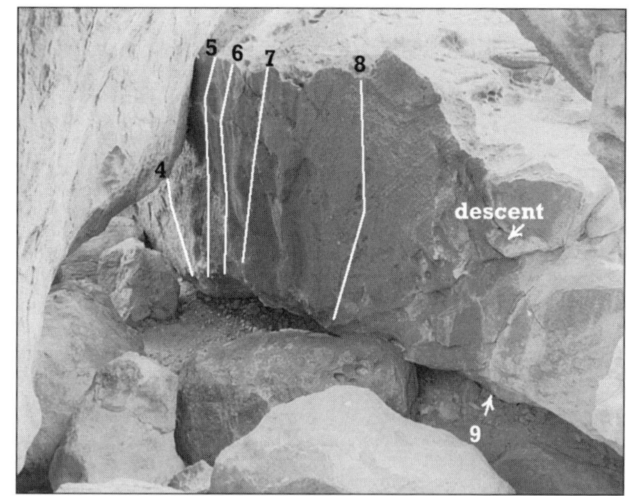

Wall of Rumbling Rabbits

4 *Rabbit-Fu 25 feet V3 ★★ BL*

5 *Hoppity Spills His Guts 20 feet V0+ ★★★ BL*

6 *The Hutch Hussy 20 feet V2 ★★★*

7 *The Hitch 18 feet V2 ★★ BL*

8 *The Unlucky Rabbit's Foot 12 feet V0–*

9 *Pindejo 16 feet V5*

8 *The Unlucky Rabbit's Foot 12 feet V0–*

9 *Pindejo 16 feet V5*
Start from the ground and climb the fingercrack.

AREA 16 MAP, P. 317

WELLSITE (AKA THE WATER CONTROL SYSTEM)

The Wellsite is, like most areas on West Mountain's southeast side, quite challenging to find. If the photos on pages 337 and 343 don't locate it for you, try these directions.

From the pass between East and West Mountains (you can actually straddle the pass, the mountains are so close together) walk south for 180 yards along the 6 foot wide trail until you meet the curve in the dirt service road (more like a sand road at this point) that winds between East Spur and West Mountain. (15 yards north of this curve should be a rusted white trash barrel.) From the northernmost point in this curve (closest point to the trash barrel), walk 100 yards south along the side of West Mountain.

You should end up at two large oak trees (one live, one dead) with much mistletoe in their branches. Behind these oaks is an 18 foot high boulder with "Joe y Norma 78" spray painted in red on it's northwest overhanging face. This point where Joe and Norma fucked up the rock marks the base of the approach slabs. Start scrambling west up the slabs. An enormous overhanging boulder should be to your left 20-40 yards up the slab (a distinct 6 inch wide hueco at the top of a 3 foot diameter white patch can be seen on it's north face 20 feet from it's left end). Continue up the slabs keeping this boulder to your left (south).

When you pass the boulder, another north-facing overhanging wall can be seen in front and to the left. An oak tree separates the boulder you've just walked past from the base of this wall. A one to two foot wide fissure angles along this wall's base. To the north, this fissure system becomes The Wellsite. Follow the fissure for 100 yards where it meets a northeast/southwest trending bush-filled fissure system. At this point it opens wide enough to drop into The Wellsite. Topo, page 344.

Wellsite approach

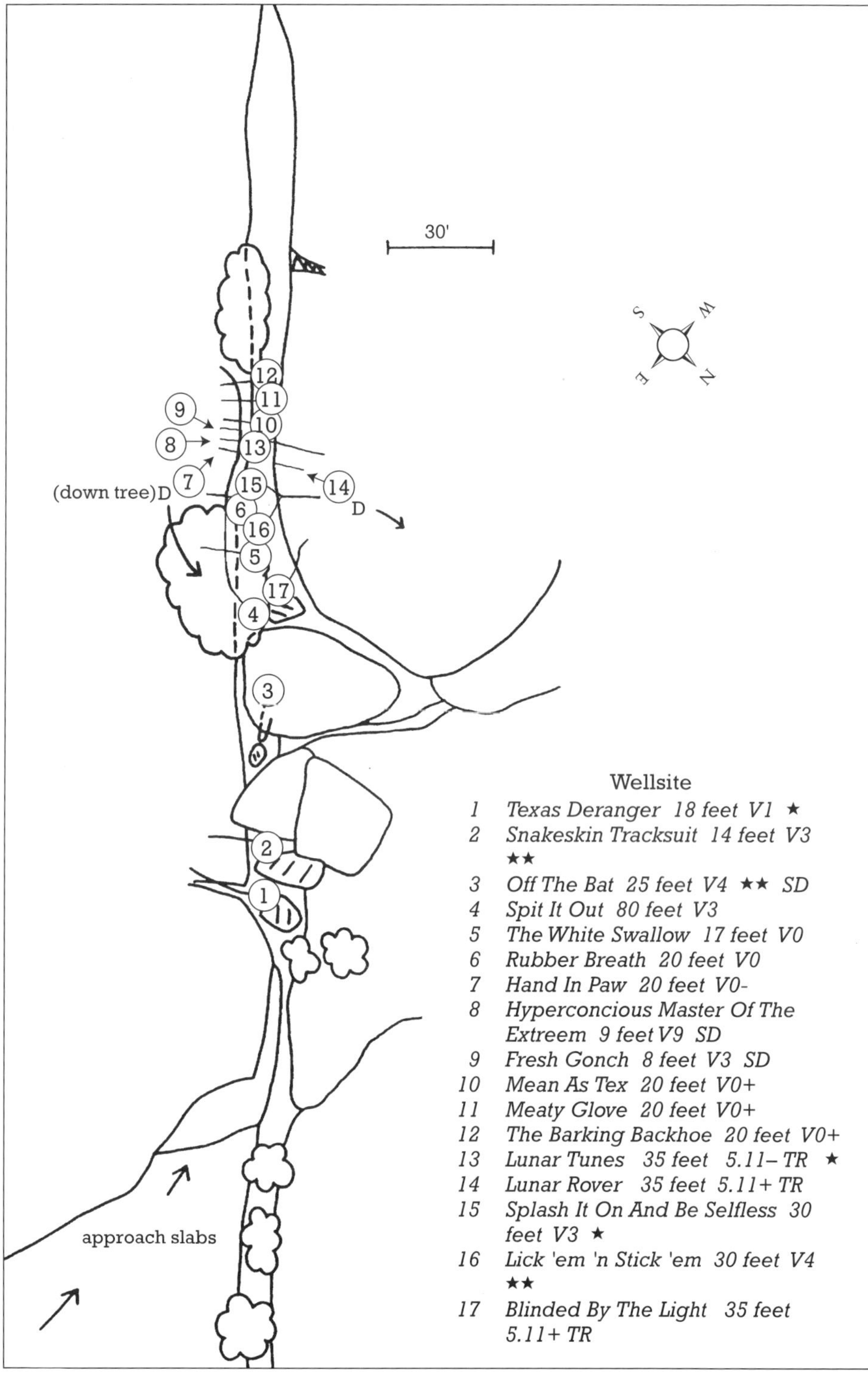

Wellsite

1 *Texas Deranger 18 feet V1* ★
2 *Snakeskin Tracksuit 14 feet V3* ★★
3 *Off The Bat 25 feet V4* ★★ *SD*
4 *Spit It Out 80 feet V3*
5 *The White Swallow 17 feet V0*
6 *Rubber Breath 20 feet V0*
7 *Hand In Paw 20 feet V0-*
8 *Hyperconcious Master Of The Extreem 9 feet V9 SD*
9 *Fresh Gonch 8 feet V3 SD*
10 *Mean As Tex 20 feet V0+*
11 *Meaty Glove 20 feet V0+*
12 *The Barking Backhoe 20 feet V0+*
13 *Lunar Tunes 35 feet 5.11– TR* ★
14 *Lunar Rover 35 feet 5.11+ TR*
15 *Splash It On And Be Selfless 30 feet V3* ★
16 *Lick 'em 'n Stick 'em 30 feet V4* ★★
17 *Blinded By The Light 35 feet 5.11+ TR*

1 *Texas Deranger 18 feet V1* ★
Immediately upon dropping into the wellsite fissure, one is greeted by this 55 degree overhanging off width. Too bad jamming it isn't necessary as hidden holds abound and up high it's possible to reach all the way through. Start sitting down with hands on a diagonal flake between the crack walls.

2 *Snakeskin Tracksuit 14 feet V3* ★★
Climb the huecoed wall 27 feet right of *Texas Deranger.* Don't touch the big chock block on the right when topping out.

3 *Off The Bat 25 feet V4* ★★ *SD*
Start sitting down 20 feet back from the lip, at the base of the keel between the A- frames. Keeping your butt and feet from touching the ground is the crux. One of Hueco Tank's most classic butt drags. Check for bats in the huecos before grabbing them.

4 *Spit It Out 80 feet V3*
Start just past the southwest end of *Off The Bat Rock.* Traverse the northwest facing wall from left to right for 80 feet ending where dead branches hang down over the face. This traverse crosses the following eight routes. Photos, page 346.

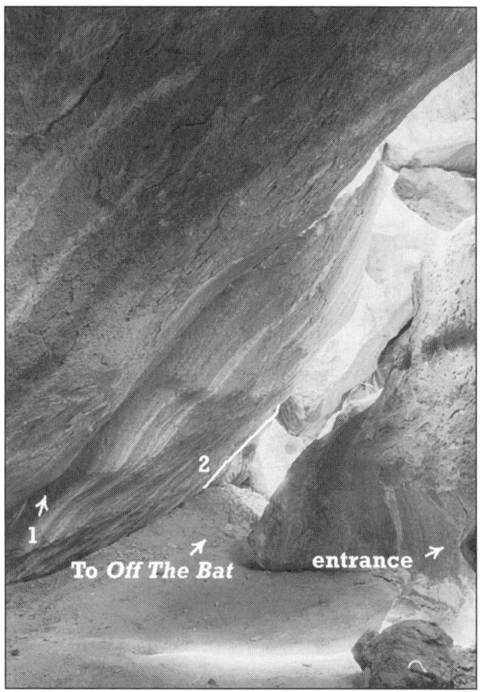

Wellsite
1 *Texas Deranger 18 feet V1* ★
2 *Snakeskin Tracksuit 14 feet V3* ★★

Wellsite
3 *Off The Bat 25 feet V4* ★★ *SD*

5 *The White Swallow 17 feet V0*
The wall 3 feet right of the big oak tree. This tree is used for descents.

Routes 6-12 are pictured on page 346.

6 *Rubber Breath 20 feet V0*

7 *Hand In Paw 20 feet V0-*
This route can be used as a descent instead of the tree. Photo, page 346.

8 *Hyperconcious Master Of The Extreem 9 feet V5 SD*

9 *Fresh Gonch 8 feet V3 SD*

10 *Mean As Tex 20 feet V0+*
The big brown bowl 8 feet up and 3 feet to the left is off-route.

11 *Meaty Glove 20 feet V0+*

12 *The Barking Backhoe 20 feet V0+*

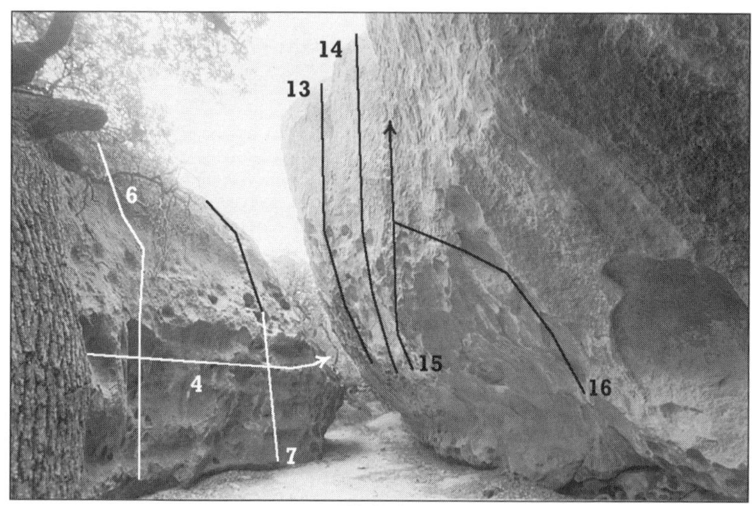

Wellsite

4 *Spit It Out 80 feet V3*
6 *Rubber Breath 20 feet V0*
7 *Hand In Paw 20 feet V0-*
13 *Lunar Tunes 35 feet 5.11– TR ★*
14 *Lunar Rover 35 feet 5.11+ TR*
15 *Splash It On And Be Selfless 30 feet V3 ★*
16 *Lick 'em 'n Stick 'em 30 feet V4 ★★*

13 *Lunar Tunes 35 feet 5.11– TR ★*

14 *Lunar Rover 35 feet 5.11+ TR*
This is the squeezed line on the face between the black streaks.

15 *Splash It On And Be Selfless 30 feet V3 ★*
Licheny and scary up high.
The undone 150-foot left to right traverse of the southeast face, finishing up *Splash It On...* will make traversing the Gymnasium wall feel like a day in Romper Room.

16 *Lick 'em 'n Stick 'em 30 feet V4 ★★*

17 *Blinded By The Light 35 feet 5.11+ TR*
Start off the boulder at the right end of the south-facing wall. Angle up the wall to the left, topping out left of the tree branch.

Wellsite

4 *Spit It Out 80 feet V3*
8 *Hyperconcious Master Of The Extreem 9 feet V5 SD*
9 *Fresh Gonch 8 feet V3 SD*
10 *Mean As Tex 20 feet V0+*
11 *Meaty Glove 20 feet V0+*
12 *The Barking Backhoe 20 feet V0+*

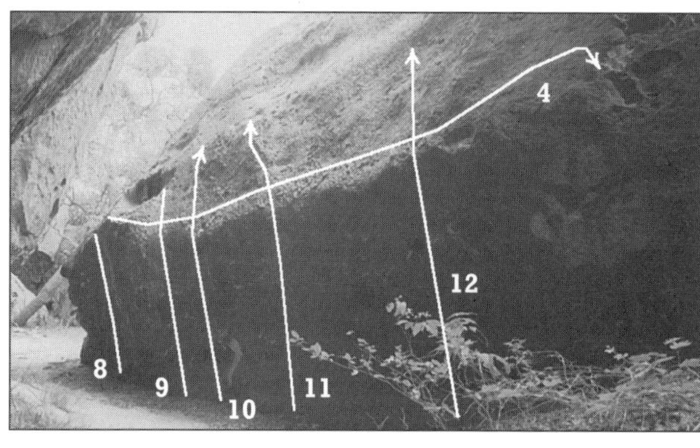

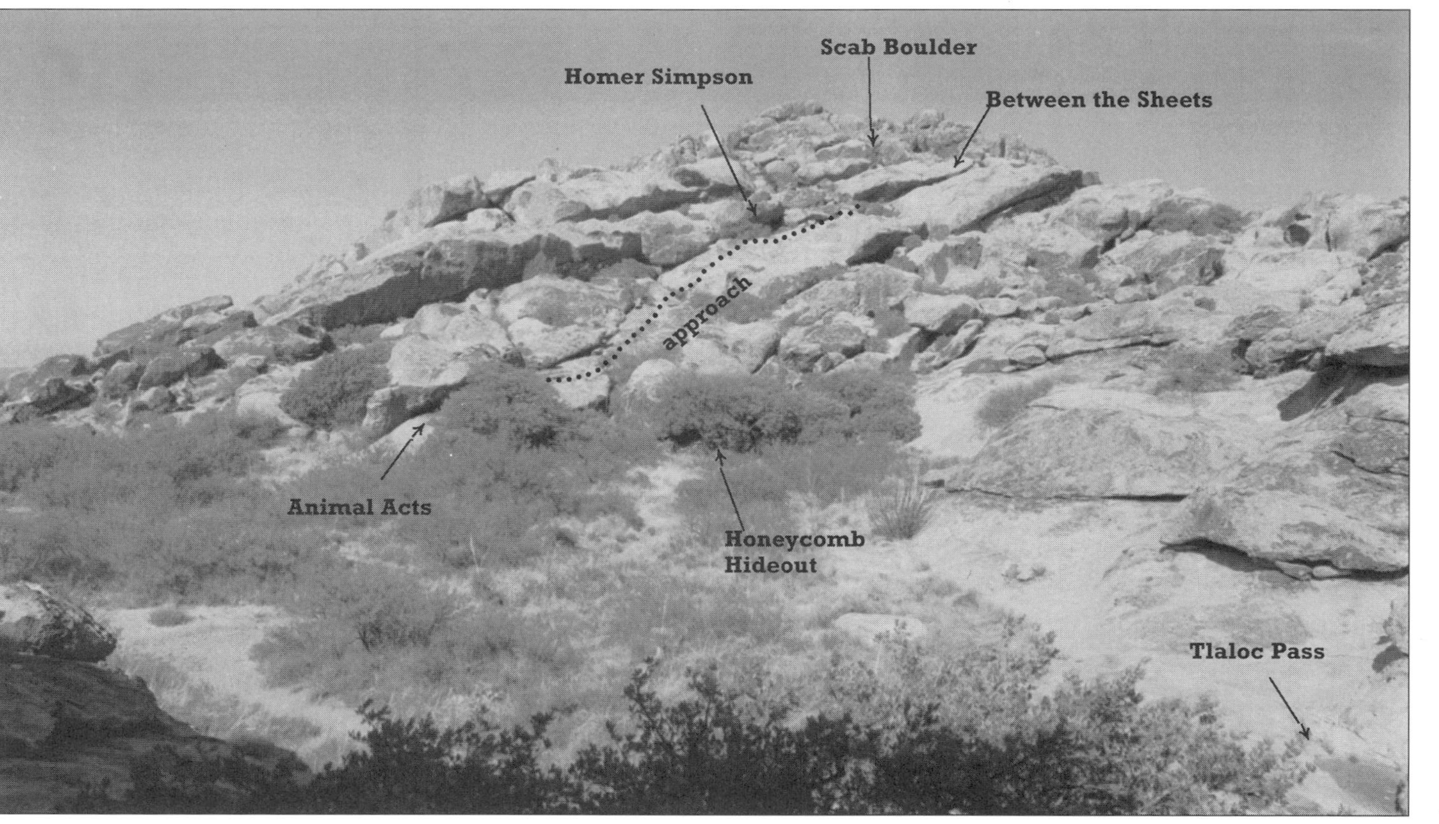

Between the Sheets approach

BETWEEN THE SHEETS AND SCAB WALL

The photo on page 347 shows the approach to the following problems. The approach starts on the first major tongue of rock 75 yards southwest of Tlaloc Pass (the pass between East and West Mountains). A major fissure system runs 270 yards up this tongue to *Between The Sheets* (BTS). Down low on the tongue, this fissure system forms a long north-facing overhang with several loose hold, bad landing problems of less popularity than even the Scab Wall problems. At *Between The Sheets,* the fissure is parallel sided and only 3 to 4 feet wide. The Scab Wall lies on the terrace above *Between The Sheets. Bodysnatcher* is on the level above the Scab Wall. Problems 1 and 2 are near ground level (see photo, page 349).

1 *Animal Acts 16 feet V6 ★*
Start low and traverse right and up, omitting the big jug at the right end 3 feet left of the crack. There are numerous other problems and variants on this wall.

Between The Sheets, Scab Wall

4 *Max Bedroom 13 feet V0+ SD*
5 *The Umbra Of Discontent 18 feet V4 SD*
6 *Between The Cheeks 25 feet V7 ★★★ SD*
7 *Between The Sheets 20 feet V4 ★★★ SD*
8 *Between The Puffs 19 feet V5 ★★ SD*
9 *Carkles And Bits 17 feet V2 SD*
10 *Three Sheets To The Wind 13 feet V2 SD*
11 *Under The Covers 12 feet V2 SD*
12 *The Comforter 15 feet V0+*
13 *The Dipstik Of Exstasy 24 feet V1 SD*
14 *Death By Mambo 15 feet V3*
15 *Rubbing Uglies 18 feet V0–*
16 *Feline Therapy 9 feet V3 SD*
17 *Pick It 16 feet V4 BL*
18 *Williams Dihedral 15 feet V1 ★ SD*
19 *Chicken Lickin' 20 feet V1*
20 *On The Loose 20 feet V0+*
21 *Scab 20 feet V1*
22 *Union Buster 20 feet V1 ★*
23 *Bodysnatcher 17 feet V4 ★*

Above the Scab Wall

Scab Wall

30'

2 *Honeycomb Hideout 25 feet V5 ★ BL*
This problem is at ground level and hidden behind a big oak tree. Start back and left under the roof at a 4-inch tall, 24-inch wide, 6-inch deep eel-shaped hueco. Loose lip.

3 *Homer Simpson 30 feet V3 ★*
This problem is hard to see when approaching until one is almost past it. Traverse honeycombed rock in from the left, then loop either direction around the lip of the huge hueco.

Rocks along Between the Sheets approach

Top:
1 *Animal Acts 16 feet V6 ★*

Middle:
2 *Honeycomb Hideout 25 feet V5 ★ BL*

Bottom:
3 *Homer Simpson 30 feet V3 ★*

Between The Sheets area

4 *Max Bedroom 13 feet V0+ SD*

5 *The Umbra Of Discontent 18 feet V4 SD*

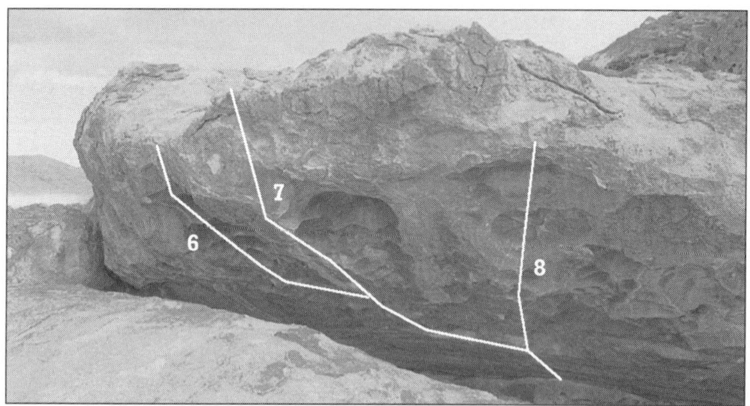

Between The Sheets area

6 *Between The Cheeks 25 feet V7 ★★★ SD*

7 *Between The Sheets 20 feet V4 ★★★ SD*

8 *Between The Puffs 19 feet V5 ★★ SD*

---

4 *Max Bedroom 13 feet V0+ SD*

5 *The Umbra Of Discontent 18 feet V4 SD*
Several different sit down starts.

6 *Between The Cheeks 25 feet V7 ★★★ SD*
Same start as Between The Sheets.

7 *Between The Sheets 20 feet V4 ★★★ SD*
Start crouched down with both hands jammed in the horizontal crack at the roof's base.

8 *Between The Puffs 19 feet V5 ★★ SD*

9 *Carkles And Bits 17 feet V2 SD*
Left finish is also V2.

10 *Three Sheets To The Wind 13 feet V2 SD*

11 *Under The Covers 12 feet V2 SD*

12 *The Comforter 15 feet V0+*

Between The Sheets area

8 *Between The Puffs 19 feet V5 ★★ SD*
9 *Carkles And Bits 17 feet V2 SD*
10 *Three Sheets To The Wind 13 feet V2 SD*
11 *Under The Covers 12 feet V2 SD*
12 *The Comforter 15 feet V0+*

---

13 *The Dipstik Of Exstasy 24 feet V1 SD*
Low traverse starting right of the tree and finishing up around the corner to the right.

14 *Death By Mambo 15 feet V3*
This is located next to the squat juniper 90 feet up the fissure system from *Between The Sheets*. Loose looking, but seemingly sound jug/flakes lead out the roof from right to left. Move right on the lip for the gruesome mantel.

Scab Wall

ALL SCAB WALL PROBLEMS MAY BE LOOSE ON TOP. These are only recommended for those with much experience in Hueco Tank's rock quality.

15 *Rubbing Uglies 18 feet V0–*
16 *Feline Therapy 9 feet V3 SD*

Left of Scab Wall

15 *Rubbing Uglies 18 feet V0–* 16 *Feline Therapy 9 feet V3 SD*

Scab Wall

17 *Pick It 16 feet V4 BL*
18 *Williams Dihedral 15 feet V1 ★ SD*
19 *Chicken Lickin' 20 feet V1*
20 *On The Loose 20 feet V0+*
21 *Scab 20 feet V1*
22 *Union Buster 20 feet V1 ★*

17 *Pick It 16 feet V4 BL*
Start 6 feet under lip of roof.

18 *Williams Dihedral 15 feet V1 ★ SD*
The best top out is left of the dihedral's top.

19 *Chicken Lickin' 20 feet V1*

20 *On The Loose 20 feet V0+ BL scary*
Start 3 feet right of *Chicken Lickin'. Jughaul* up to the same chicken size hueco 11 feet up. Top out on the loose hanging flakes above. Not for family men.

21 *Scab 20 feet V1*
Start 7 feet right of a sotol at a downward pointing sharkstooth flake 7 feet up. Straight up.

22 *Union Buster 20 feet V1 ★ BL scary*
The line 6 feet right of Scab, following the right margin of the black staining.

Above the Scab Wall

23 *Bodysnatcher 17 feet V4 ★*
This is the best of many problems to be found on the level above the Scab Wall. It's located in an arching roof pod 37 yards uphill (southwest) of the right end of the Scab Wall. Start in an undercling at the base of the left side of the roof pod. Cross the roof turning the lip on its right side. Some chossy rock.

Above the Scab Wall

23 *Bodysnatcher 17 feet V4 ★*

North Side of West Mountain

A Jungle Gym, p. 325
B *Quest for Huecos*, p. 360
C *Texas Radio,* p. 364
D *Scepter,* p. 364
E Sheep Buttress, p. 370
F Dog Wall, p. 371
G South Gold Mine, p. 355
H Middle Gold Mine, p. 357
I North Gold Mine, p. 358
J *Crash Dummy,* p. 359
K Pit Boulder, p. 360
L *Lord of the Flies,* p. 360
M Rockslide Wall, p. 360
N Lost Canyon, p. 361
O Biko Rock, p. 361
P Secret Sharer, p. 362
Q Pit Roof, p. 367
R Cream Rock, p. 369
S Dam Boulders, p. 367-369
T Dam Rock, p. 371

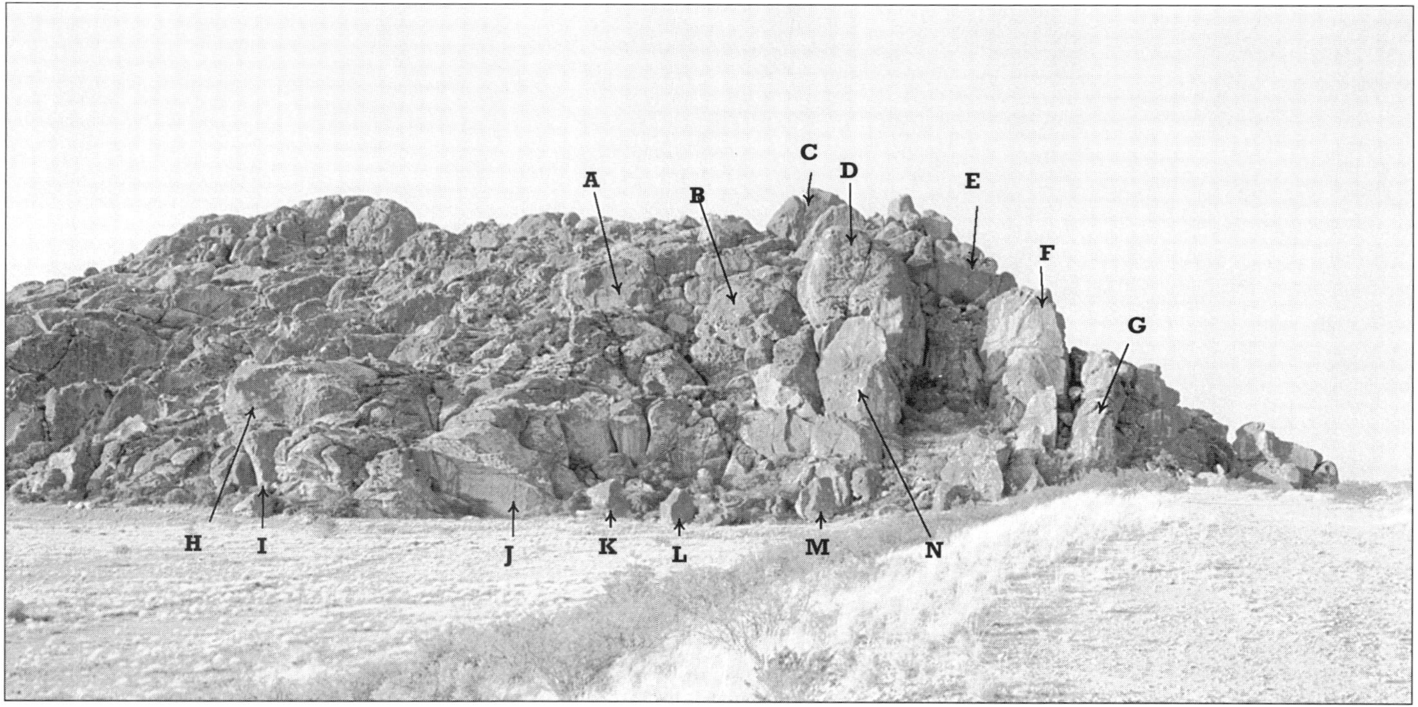

North Side of West Mountain from Main Dam

A Texas Radio Wall, p. 364
B *The Fundamentalist,* p. 364
C *The Scepter,* p. 364
D Sheep Buttress, p. 370
E V-Cracks, p. 370
F Dog Wall, p. 371
G Dam Rock, p. 371
H Biko Rock, p. 361
I Secret Sharer, p. 362
J Pit Roof, p. 367
K Horsehoe Boulder, p. 368
L Caca Boulder, p. 368
M Ferrodactyl Boulder, p. 369
N Cream Rock, p. 369

Looking toward *Star Power* and South Mine from the east.

NORTHEAST SIDE OF WEST MOUNTAIN

Star Power 40 feet V5 ★★★ SD

This is found under the south end (uphill side) of the boulder pictured above. 36 feet of moderate jug hauling leads out the 60-degree overhang to a loose lip encounter. Without the lip, this is only V3. Start as low down in the cave as possible.

Locals Only 30 feet V7 ★★★

The thin flake line paralleling *Star Power* to the left. *Star Power* holds are off route until the big jugs 3 feet below the lower lip. Join Star Power here to top out.

THE GOLD MINE

The Gold Mine is a series of three parallel canyons trending east to west: one small box canyon and two large canyons. Looking south from the southeast corner of The Pit, a small natural bridge or window is visible atop a rib of rock. The entrance to the North Mine is a narrow chimney on the north side of the natural arch. The Middle Mine is immediately south, behind the natural arch. The South Mine, or smaller box canyon, is the next canyon south.

South Mine

The South Mine is a small box canyon immediately south of the Middle Mine. There are several fine routes in this area.

1 *Custom Fit 25 feet 5.10*

2 *Austin City Limits 60 feet 5.10–*

Start on the 9 foot tall boulder right of the tree and climb huecos to the top. Descend by scrambling down the next canyon to the south. A hangerless bolt is near the top.

3 *Nuclear Fallout 35 feet 5.11 TR*

Toprope the overhanging rock that blocks the end of the canyon.

South Mine

1 *Custom Fit 25 feet 5.10*

2 *Austin City Limits 60 feet 5.10–*

3 *Nuclear Fallout 35 feet 5.11 TR*

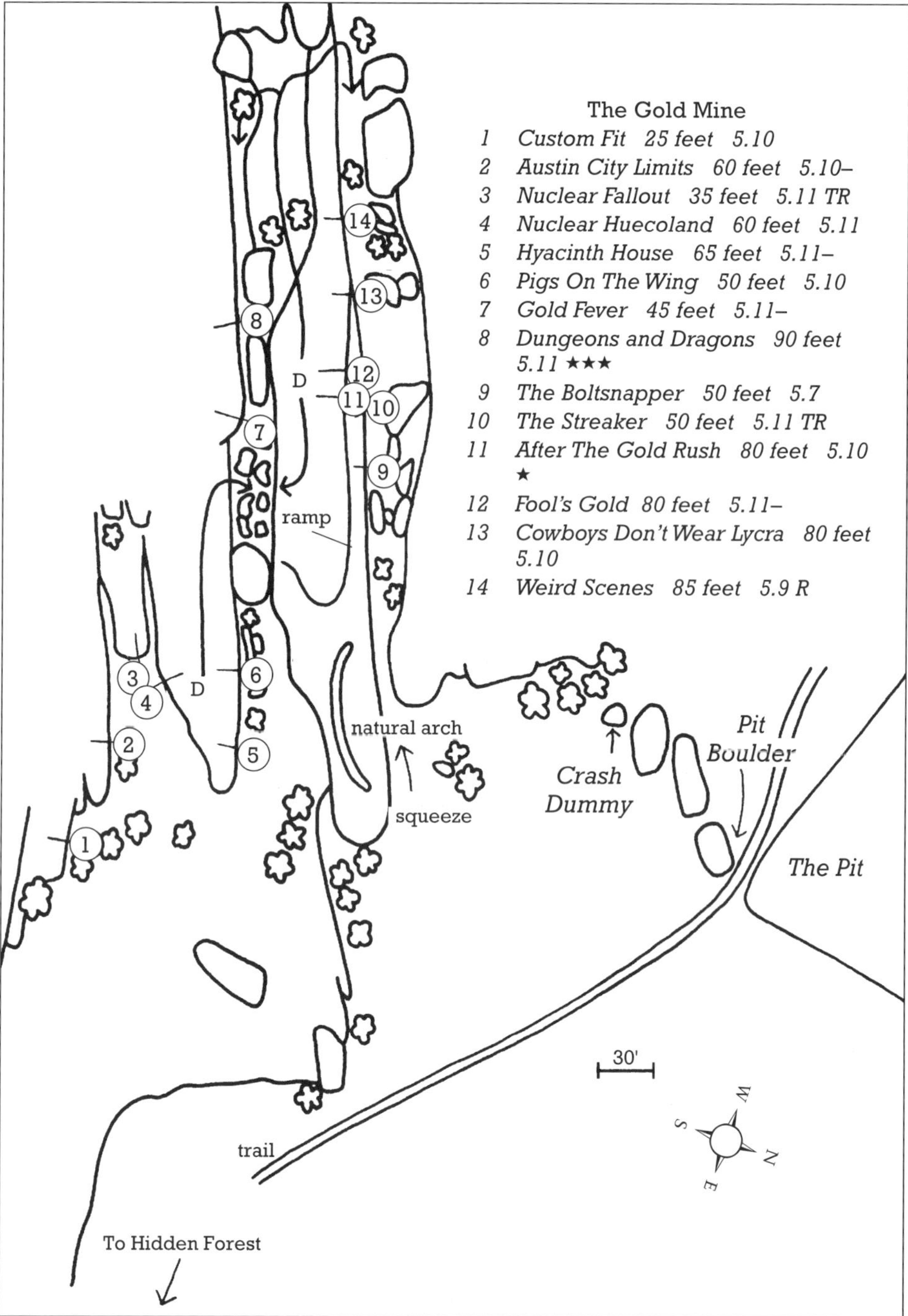
The Gold Mine
1 Custom Fit 25 feet 5.10
2 Austin City Limits 60 feet 5.10–
3 Nuclear Fallout 35 feet 5.11 TR
4 Nuclear Huecoland 60 feet 5.11
5 Hyacinth House 65 feet 5.11–
6 Pigs On The Wing 50 feet 5.10
7 Gold Fever 45 feet 5.11–
8 Dungeons and Dragons 90 feet 5.11 ★★★
9 The Boltsnapper 50 feet 5.7
10 The Streaker 50 feet 5.11 TR
11 After The Gold Rush 80 feet 5.10 ★
12 Fool's Gold 80 feet 5.11–
13 Cowboys Don't Wear Lycra 80 feet 5.10
14 Weird Scenes 85 feet 5.9 R
D
ramp
natural arch
squeeze
Crash Dummy
Pit Boulder
The Pit
30'
trail
To Hidden Forest
W
S
N
E

4 *Nuclear Huecoland 60 feet 5.11*
Climb the center overhanging right (south-facing) wall of the canyon past 4 bolts and many huecos to a steep, rotten face at the top. To descend, walk west until you can escape right and scramble down The Middle Mine.

Middle Mine

The Middle Mine is the first canyon located on the south side of the natural arch. This canyon has several fine climbs, some of which are hidden. Descend by walking west until you can exit down right. From here walk east down the canyon. The Middle Mine is choked with large chockstones that form several large steps. If you cannot find the routes, remember that all of the Middle Mine routes are on the same wall, but they are on different levels because of the huge chockstones that choke the canyon. *Dungeons and Dragons* is halfway up the mountain.

5 *Hyacinth House 65 feet 5.11–*
One bolt, no hanger at presstime.

6 *Pigs On The Wing 50 feet 5.10*

Middle Mine
5 *Hyacinth House 65 feet 5.11–*
6 *Pigs On The Wing 50 feet 5.10*

Middle Mine
7 *Gold Fever 45 feet 5.11–*
8 *Dungeons And Dragons 90 feet 5.11* ★★★

7 *Gold Fever 45 feet 5.11–*
20 yards west of *Pigs On The Wing* the canyon apparently ends where it is choked by huge chockstones. Above this, however, the canyon continues. Scramble over and under the chockstones until you get above them. On the north-facing wall to your left is an obvious 45 foot tall, left-facing, arching dihedral. Start 15 feet to the right of the dihedral on thin holds which lead to a line of huecos. 2 bolts. Photo, page 357.

8 *Dungeons and Dragons 90 feet 5.11* ★★★
This well-hidden route is on the same wall as *Gold Fever,* but is located 50 feet to the right, down in the chimney west of the big boulder blocking the canyon. From Gold Fever squeeze under the gap between the north-facing wall and the big boulder. The route starts off a boulder in the bottom of the chimney and climbs gently overhanging rock up and past two bolts, several nut and Friend slots,, and a loopable horn. A third bolt protects the last 16 feet. Photo, page 357.
Variation: More Power In The Shower 5.12– Toprope up *Dungeons and Dragons* to the second piece of protection. Traverse right 13 feet and continue straight up.

North Mine

The entrance to the North Mine is a shoulder-width chimney hidden behind trees north of the natural arch. This chimney leads 20 yards west to a grove of small trees. After the grove, huge boulders fill the canyon. Left of the boulders is is 10 foot tall "hueco staircase" that allows access past the boulders to the routes in the canyon above. This "hueco staircase" is 50 yards from the canyon's chimney entrance and is the first spot one will be tempted to scramble up the left (north-facing) wall to progress up the canyon. "JR" is in blue paint 12 feet right of the "hueco staircase."

The first two routes listed start below the "hueco staircase" and finish on an angling ledge that's right end meets the ground immediately left of the "hueco staircase." This ledge, entitled Gold Rush Ledge, is the descent route for routes 9 and 10, and the approach route for routes 11 and 12.

9 *The Boltsnapper 50 feet 5.7*
Start 75 feet left of the "hueco staircase." Climb the continuous hueco line to Gold Rush Ledge. If one looks carefully, they might find a ¼ inch buttonhead stud near the top. The hanger on this snapped as it was being clipped. The force on it was only a pound or two. One should not put their trust in a single piece of gear.

10 *The Streaker 50 feet 5.11 TR*

11 *After The Gold Rush 80 feet 5.10* ★
Belay at a horizontal crack 15 feet above the second white stain. From here, traverse the crack left. The descent is simple: walk west to the end of The North Mine and scramble down ramps into the the upper end

North Mine

10 *The Streaker 50 feet 5.11 TR*
11 *After The Gold Rush 80 feet 5.10* ★
12 *Fool's Gold 80 feet 5.11–*
13 *Cowboys Don't ... 80 feet 5.10*
14 *Weird Scenes 85 feet 5.9 R*

of The North Mine. *After The Gold Rush* and *Fools Gold* share the same upper belay and descent.

12 ***Fool's Gold* 80 feet 5.11–**
Go to the same horizontal belay crack as *After The Gold Rush.*

13 ***Cowboys Don't Wear Lycra* 80 feet 5.10**

14 ***Weird Scenes* 85 feet 5.9 R**

AREA 19

MAP, P. 269

CRASH DUMMY AND THE PIT BOULDER

Crash Dummy Rock

To find *Crash Dummy* (no simple task) start atop the southeast corner of the Pit (the huge depression between north and west mountains where the dirt was excavated to make the Main Dam). Crash Dummy is 50 yards to the south, on what looks like a small boulder (bushes and other rocks obscure it's entirety). A 30 foot tall by 30 foot wide boulder is 10 yards to it's north. Both boulders are on the right (northwest) side of a recess in the mountain. The Gold Mine entrance is also in this recess, 45 yards southeast of *Crash Dummy.*

1 ***Hellcat On The Loose* 12 feet V0+**

2 ***Crash Dummy* 17 feet V7 ★★★ BL**
Start beneath the east facing overhang on an undercling 3 feet southeast of a volley-ball size hueco used for the feet. The shelf under this hueco is off-route. A tricky sequence leads out the overhang at one point risking a bad landing on the edge of the platform behind.

3 ***Complete Dummy* 20 feet V9 ★★★ BL+**
Start as for *Crash Dummy* but after two moves (to the 3-finger hueco) reach up to the upside-down horizontal fingerjam slot. From here blast out right. The diagonal seam and everything to the left of it are off route.

Crash Dummy

1 *Hellcat On The Loose* 12 feet V0+
2 *Crash Dummy* 17 feet V7 ★★★ BL
3 *Complete Dummy* 20 feet V9 ★★★ BL+

The Pit Boulder

The Pit Boulder is 10 yards west of the southeast corner of The Pit. Jim, Chuck, and Paul have painted their names on the left side of it's northwest face. Also on the northwest face are several V0- to V0 20 foot jughauls.

THE JUNGLE

The Jungle consists of the canyons between The Gold Mine and Biko Rock/Green Blanket Buttress.

As the name implies, the approaches require some thrashing through dense vegetation.

1 *Lord of the Flies 50 feet 5.11–*

2 *Quest For Huecos 50 feet 5.11–* ★★

This climbs the continuous line of huecos on the left side of the north face of a buttress two canyons to the south of Lost Canyon. The wall is nearly halfway up the side of the mountain. Approach by thrashing up the gullies west of the Pit Boulder. The first bolt is in a small white scar 12 feet above the ledge at the base. Up and right 6 feet is another bolt. Keep going up and right until you reach a pin in a horizontal crack. Finish straight up.

Rockslide Wall

This is the north-facing wall in the canyon between Lost Canyon and Quest For Huecos canyon.

3 *But Crack 40 feet 5.10–*

4 *Pox 45 feet 5.10–*

Thrash through some branches to get started, then angle slightly right to the top.

The Jungle
Right:
1 *Lord of the Flies*
Below:
2 *Quest For Huecos*
3 *But Crack*
4 *Pox*

Lost Canyon

The Lost Canyon is directly behind (south of) Biko Rock and contains several fine routes. The canyon can be identified by the stack of blocks choking the passage. These routes share virtually the same start from the top of the blocks and ascend the north-facing wall.

5 *Left Out 55 feet 5.11–*
To the bolt on *Curse Of The Lefties,* then traverse left to the next hueco line.

6 *Curse Of The Lefties 50 feet 5.11–*
Climb up and left 20 feet to a small roof with a bolt at its right end. Pull over and continue up a steep wall following huecos. Beneath the start is a thin left-leaning crack that could provide an alternate start.

7 *Middle Of The Road 45 feet 5.10*
Climb straight up, on huecos, from the blocks in the canyon. 2 bolts, the first hangerless at presstime, the second is 5 feet right of the bolt on *Curse Of The Lefties.*

8 *Righthand Man 50 feet 5.9*
Start as for *Middle Of The Road,* or 12 feet to the right. Traverse up and right to an obvious line of huecos which lead to the top.

Lost Canyon
5 *Left Out 55 feet 5.11-*
6 *Curse Of The Lefties 50 feet 5.11–*
7 *Middle Of The Road 45 feet 5.10*
8 *Righthand Man 50 feet 5.9*

SECRET SHARER AREA

Biko Rock

This is the 50 foot tall, roof-capped north-facing rock directly above Green Blanket Buttress (Secret Sharer). The easiest approach is to walk up a hidden ramp system to the right of The Pit Roof. Diagonal left up this ramp over the top of The Pit Roof, threading your way through boulders and trees to the base of Biko Rock. Alternately, approach up easy 5th class terrain left of Green Blanket Buttress.

Biko Rock (top), Green Blanket
1 *Creatures of the New Left*
2 *Biko Roof*
3 *Wet Blanket Face 40 feet 5.10– TR* ★
4 *Green Blanket Crack 40 feet 5.10–*
5 *The Secret Sharer 45 feet 5.12–* ★★★

1 *Creatures of the New Left 55 feet 5.10* ★★★
1 bolt.

2 *Biko Roof 45 feet 5.12*
4 bolts.

Green Blanket Buttress

This 45-foot ship's prow buttress is located at ground level below Biko Rock, on the south side of The Pit, 185 yards east from the south end of the main dam. Photo, page 361.

3 *Wet Blanket Face 40 feet 5.10– TR* ★
The face 7 feet left of *Green Blanket Crack.*

4 *Green Blanket Crack 40 feet 5.10–*

5 *The Secret Sharer 45 feet 5.12–* ★★★
4 bolts, 2 bolt anchor.
Variation: From half height move right and finish up left side of arete (5.12 TR).

SS Boulder

The SS Boulder is located 10 yards northwest of Secret Sharer. The problems on the SS Boulder are closely spaced.

6 *It's A Gas 15 feet V1*

7 *The Final Solution 16 feet V2*
Start in rotten, hollow undercling just right of the bulge. Up to a crescent then left to join It's A Gas at the jugs.

8 *SS Atrocities 17 feet V3*
The same rotten undercling start as *The Final Solution,* but off-routes jugs to the left by grabbing the crescent with the left hand then going straight up.

9 *To Strengthen The Strain 15 feet V3*
The huecos to the right are off-route.

10 *Stukas Over Disneyland 15 feet V1 loosc*
Start in the obvious hueco.

SS Boulder

6 *It's A Gas 15 feet V1*
7 *The Final Solution 16 feet V2*
8 *SS Atrocities 17 feet V3*
9 *To Strengthen The Strain 15 feet V3*
10 *Stukas Over Disneyland 15 feet V1*
11 *Ilsa Applies The Jumper Cables 14 feet V4* ★
12 *Ilsa, She Wolf Of The SS 13 feet V3* ★★
13 *Dachaucabana 13 feet V0*

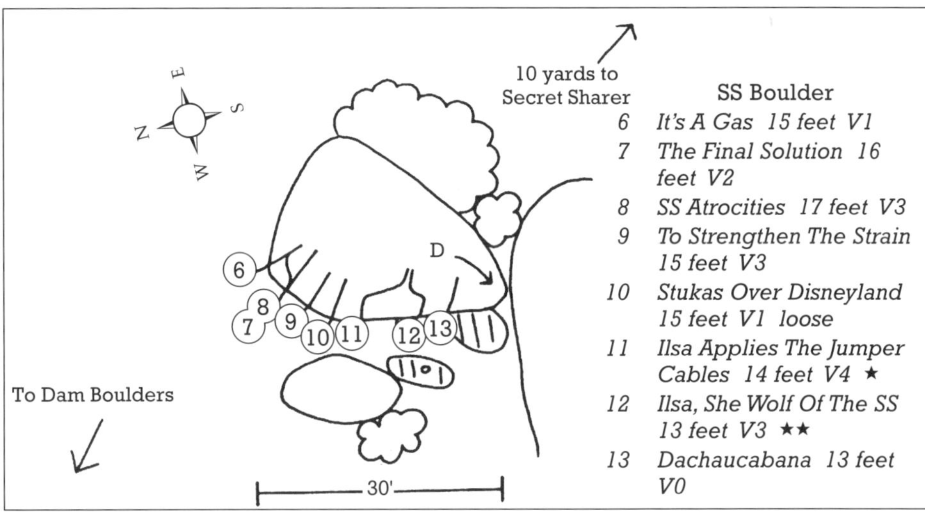

11 *Ilsa Applies The Jumper Cables 14 feet V4* ★

12 *Ilsa, She Wolf Of The SS 13 feet V3* ★★
Start on the low rock next to a small hueco at thigh level.

13 *Dachaucabana 13 feet V0*
Start on the next low rock right of *Ilsa, She Wolf Of The SS.*

THE UPPER FOREST

This area is the jumble of rocks directly behind and above The Pit Roof. Descriptions start at Biko Rock and progress right.

The Upper Forest Walls

These walls are located high on the north side of West Mountain. From the right side of Biko Rock, walk up a ramp system to a series of steep north-facing walls. The first of The Upper Forest Walls, Texas Radio Wall can be identified by a horizontal crack which cuts across the face to an obvious finger-sized crack on the right side of the wall.

1 *Rebel Chef 50 feet 5.11+* ★
This is on the north-facing wall 40 feet around the corner left (east) from *Texas Radio.* On the left side of the wall, climb pockets to a lesser overhanging dark brown face with many horizontal seams. All clean pro.

The Upper Forest Walls

1 *Rebel Chef*
4 *Texas Radio 50 feet 5.10* ★
5 *Tiny Rubber Love 60 feet 5.12–*
6 *Pazuzu 55 feet 5.11* ★
7 *Padudu 50 feet 5.11 TR*

The Upper Forest Walls

9 *Abortion Stories*

2 *R.B. Is A Homo Commie Wimp 20 feet 5.9*
From the top of *Texas Radio,* walk down towards the left to the top of an overhanging rock. Bridge across the chimney and climb straight up the steep brown wall on mostly good holds.

3 *Mariachi Man 25 feet 5.11*
From a cave directly below *Texas Radio,* climb up the left side of an overhanging, east-facing, hueco covered wall. A VW Bug size block is wedged directly above the route.

Routes 4-7 are pictured on page 363.

4 *Texas Radio 50 feet 5.10 ★*
Start at the left side of Texas Radio Wall, off the top of a 10 foot boulder. 1 pin, 1 bolt.

5 *Tiny Rubber Love 60 feet 5.12–*
3 bolts with a sporty stretch after the second.

6 *Pazuzu 55 feet 5.11 ★*
2 bolts, the second being superfluous.

7 *Padudu 50 feet 5.11 TR*
Toprope the hueco line 5 feet right of *Pazuzu.*

8 *Rites of Pazuzu 50 feet 5.10*
Climb the huecos up and right from the start of *Pazuzu* to a long reach for a ledge. Climb over a bulge and continue to the top via perfect huecos.

9 *Abortion Stories 45 feet 5.9*
This remarkable hueco wall is 20 yards west (right) of Texas Radio Wall along a broken ledge system. The route is characterized by a large number of huecos in a short headwall. Every part of this wall is climbable (5.7 to 5.9).

10 *The Fundamentalist 60 feet 5.10–*
This route is on the 60-foot northeast-facing wall directly below *Abortion Stories.* The wall can be identified by the green-lichened ramp that runs along the undercut base. Start midway along the ledge/ramp. Climb big huecos on overhanging rock to a steep headwall.

The Scepter 50 feet 5.10 ★
50 yards south along the crest of West Mountain from Sheep Buttress is a slightly overhanging north face cleft by a crack. *The Scepter* varies from a finger crack at the start to an off-width crack at the top.

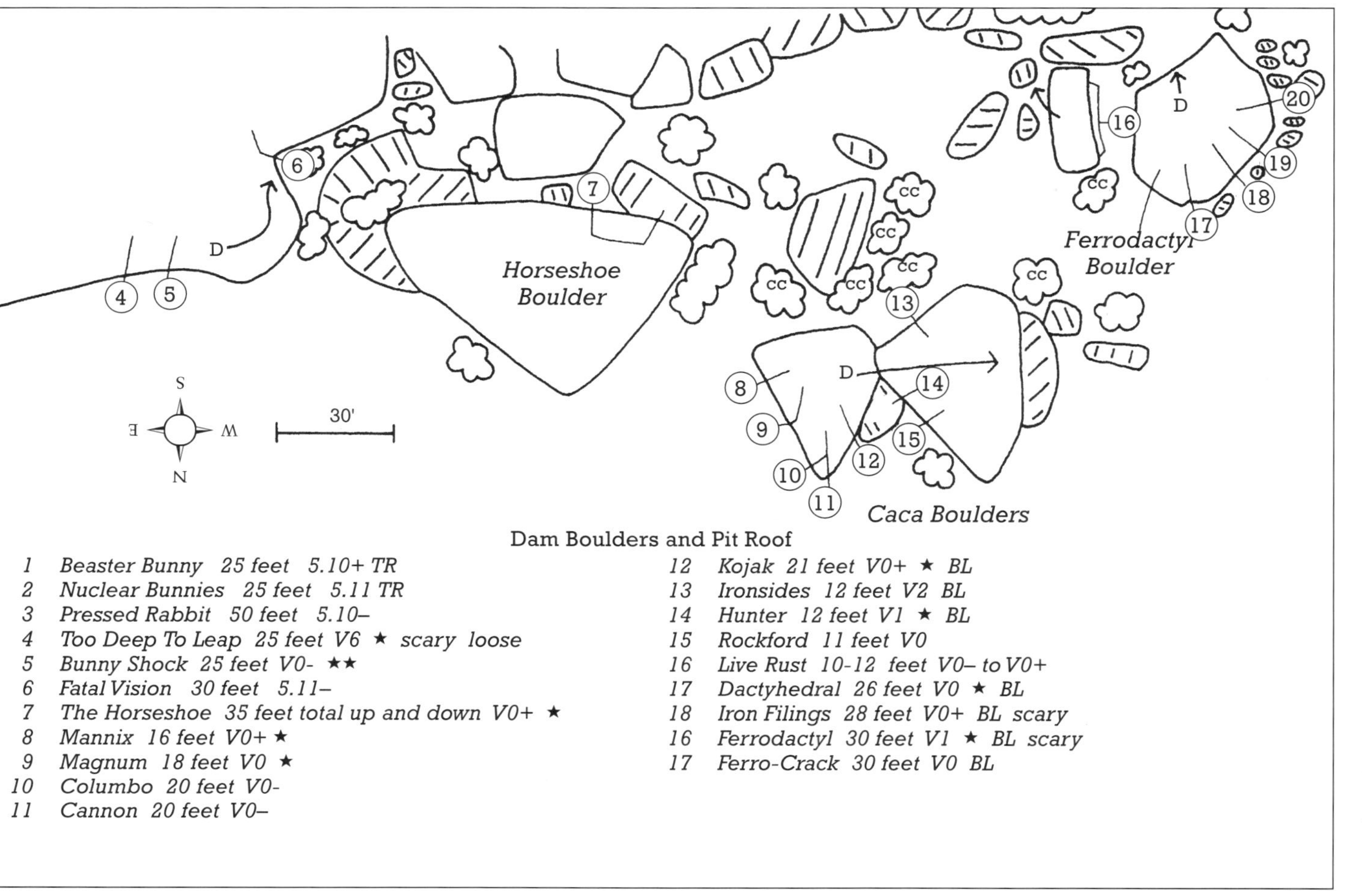
Horseshoe Boulder
Caca Boulders
Ferrodactyl Boulder
30'
S
W
N
E
D
cc
Dam Boulders and Pit Roof
1 Beaster Bunny 25 feet 5.10+ TR
2 Nuclear Bunnies 25 feet 5.11 TR
3 Pressed Rabbit 50 feet 5.10–
4 Too Deep To Leap 25 feet V6 ★ scary loose
5 Bunny Shock 25 feet V0- ★★
6 Fatal Vision 30 feet 5.11–
7 The Horseshoe 35 feet total up and down V0+ ★
8 Mannix 16 feet V0+ ★
9 Magnum 18 feet V0 ★
10 Columbo 20 feet V0-
11 Cannon 20 feet V0–
12 Kojak 21 feet V0+ ★ BL
13 Ironsides 12 feet V2 BL
14 Hunter 12 feet V1 ★ BL
15 Rockford 11 feet V0
16 Live Rust 10-12 feet V0– to V0+
17 Dactyhedral 26 feet V0 ★ BL
18 Iron Filings 28 feet V0+ BL scary
16 Ferrodactyl 30 feet V1 ★ BL scary
17 Ferro-Crack 30 feet V0 BL

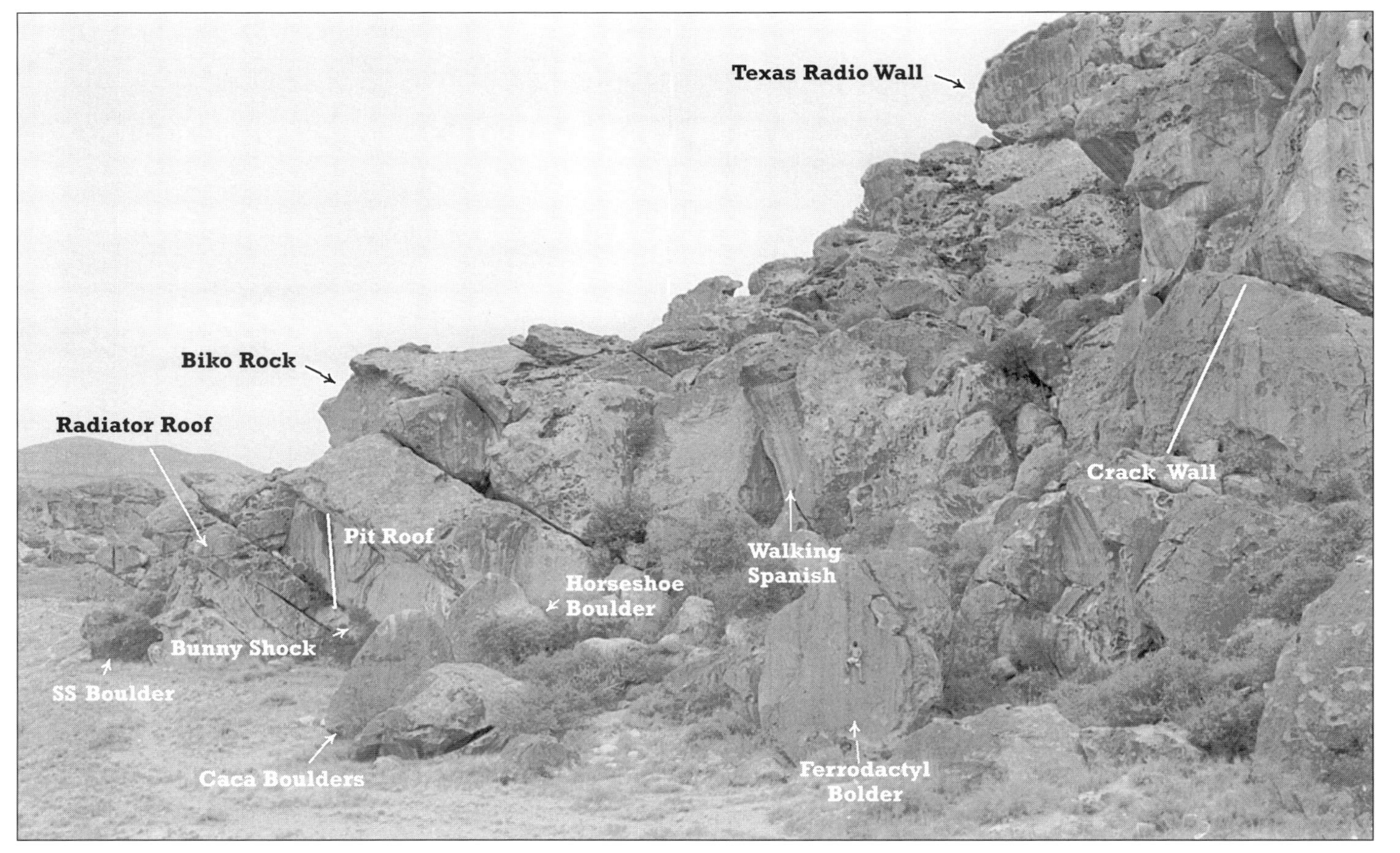

Dam Boulders

Pit Roof

1 *Beaster Bunny 25 feet 5.10+ TR*
2 *Nuclear Bunnies 25 feet 5.11 TR*
3 *Pressed Rabbit 50 feet 5.10–*
4 *Too Deep To Leap 25 feet V6 ★*
5 *Bunny Shock 25 feet V0- ★★*
6 *Fatal Vision 30 feet 5.11–*

DAM BOULDERS AND PIT ROOF

This section covers the rocks along the base of the north side of West Mountain, from the base of the Main Dam to a distance 75 yards east of the dam. Pit Roof is the 40 foot roof towering over The Pit (the large excavated depression between North and West Mountains, on the east side of the Main Dam). Pit Roof is 50 yards east of the dam. An overview photo is on page 366.

Radiation Roof

This 10-foot roof is 10 yards to the left of The Pit Roof. Radiation Roof is above a large ledge 20 feet off the ground, and is crossed by two toprope routes.

1 *Beaster Bunny 25 feet 5.10+ TR*
Begin at Nuclear Bunnies and climb left on good huecos.

2 *Nuclear Bunnies 25 feet 5.11 TR*
From an obvious pony keg size hueco in the center of the roof, climb right on rounded huecos to a desperate lip move.

Pit Roof

3 *Pressed Rabbit 50 feet 5.10–*
4 *Too Deep To Leap 25 feet V6 ★ scary loose*
5 *Bunny Shock 25 feet V0– ★★*
Descend the ramp to the right.
6 *Fatal Vision 30 feet 5.11–*

Horseshoe Rock

7 *The Horseshoe*

Caca Boulder (left), Mini-Caca Boulder

8	*Mannix 16 feet V0+ ★*	12	*Kojak 21 feet V0+ ★ BL*
9	*Magnum 18 feet V0 ★*	13	*Ironsides 12 feet V2 BL*
10	*Columbo 20 feet V0-*	14	*Hunter 12 feet V1 ★ BL*
11	*Cannon 20 feet V0–*	15	*Rockford 11 feet V0*

Horseshoe Rock

7 *The Horseshoe 35 feet total up and down V0+ ★*

To the right of the *Bunny Shock* descent is a large boulder, overhung on it's south side. On the left side of the south face there is a line of huecos rising out of a pit often filled with tumbleweeds. Climb the huecos, then instead of a loose top out (which has been done) swing left on jugs and downclimb the hueco line 6 feet to the left. This can be done in the opposite direction or back and forth. This would get an extra star if it weren't for all the dirt in the huecos.

Caca Boulder

8 *Mannix 16 feet V0+ ★*

9 *Magnum 18 feet V0 ★*

10 *Columbo 20 feet V0–*

Climb the face 5 feet right of the dihedral ending up on the arete.

11 *Cannon 20 feet V0–*

12 *Kojak 21 feet V0+ ★ BL*

Mini-Caca Boulder

13 *Ironsides 12 feet V2 BL*

Climb the thin southeast face of the descent boulder shooting for a jagged seam dropping 2 feet from the lip.

14 *Hunter 12 feet V1 ★ BL*

Start in close quarters between the east face and a small boulder behind it. A long crank from an incut flake 6 ½ feet up earns a sturdy press at the lip.

15 *Rockford 11 feet V0*

Lieback the big face level hueco.

Rusty Rock

This is the small rock immediately east of Ferrodactyl Boulder.

16 *Live Rust 10-12 feet V0– to V0+*

The west face is climbable anywhere. It gets harder towards the left (V0+). The best line starts at a 15 inch diameter, shallow circular indent.

Ferrodactyl Boulder

This boulder is distinguished by it's nearly vertical, very flat, northwest face. A prominent ramp/corner runs up the left side of this face.

17 Dactyhedral 26 feet V0 ★ BL

18 Iron Filings 28 feet V0+ BL scary
Dactyhedral's ramp to the left is off-route.

19 Ferrodactyl 30 feet V1 ★ BL scary
Start just right of the tiny, thin tree and climb straight up to the highest point. This route is thin, fragile, and ultra-continuous. Don't expect it to ease up until the last move. Ususally toproped.

20 Ferro-Crack 30 feet V0 BL
Climb the crack just 2 feet around the corner from the northwest face.

Ferrodactyl Boulder, Cream Rock, etc.

17 Dactyhedral 26 feet V0 ★ BL
18 Iron Filings 28 feet V0+ BL scary
19 Ferrodactyl 30 feet V1 ★ BL scary
21 Crump Dihedral 30 feet 5.7
22 Crack Walk 25 feet 5.8
23 Cream 60 feet 5.9 ★
24 Peaches And Cream 35 feet 5.8
25 Rest And Relaxation 55 feet 5.10+ R ★
27 Surprising Sheep 120 feet 5.9 ★★★

V-CRACK CANYON

This area is comprised of Cream Rock, Sheep Buttress, V-Crack Wall, Dog Wall, Dam Rock and all the other rocks between the Dam Boulders and the Upper Forest Walls. These rocks are all above ground level and are south or southeast of the main dam. With the exception of the first four routes, all of the routes are accessible from V-Crack canyon, the steep north-south trending canyon south of the dam.

Funky Wall 30 feet 5.4
This boring hidden wall is 20 yards to the left of the Upper Forest Access at the same level. Funky Wall is north-facing and low angle. Climb the huecos.

Upper Forest Access 30 feet 5.4
20 yards uphill from the Caca Boulders, and to the left of *Crump Dihedral* is a short, low angle wall that leads to the Upper Forest. Start on a boulder and climb up left to easy rock.

21 Crump Dihedral 30 feet 5.7

22 Crack Walk 25 feet 5.8

Cream Rock

23 Cream 60 feet 5.9 ★
From the left end of the approach ramp, climb fourth-class to a large sloping belay ledge (top of *Rest And Relaxation*). Start by traversing down and left 20 feet to a stance below the shallow scooped dihedral. Continuc on cxccllcnt rock with small holds to the top. 3 bolts.

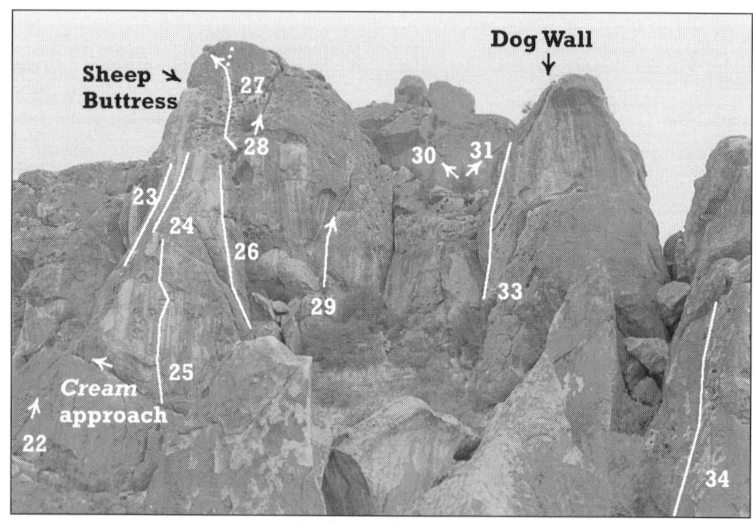

V-Crack Canyon

22 *Crack Walk 25 feet 5.8*
23 *Cream 60 feet 5.9 e*
24 *Peaches And Cream 35 feet 5.8*
25 *Rest And Relaxation 55 feet 5.10+ R ★*
27 *Surprising Sheep 120 feet 5.9 ★★★*
28 *JAM 120 feet 5.7*
29 *Lords and the New Creatures 100 feet 5.11 ★★*
30 *Left Mother's V 50 feet 5.11+ ★*
31 *Right Mother's V 50 feet 5.11– ★*
33 *Yllabian Dogfight 100 feet 5.8 R ★*
34 *Tunnel Vision 50 feet 5.7*

---

24 *Peaches And Cream 35 feet 5.8*

25 *Rest And Relaxation 55 feet 5.10+ R ★*
2 bolts.

26 *A Feast Of Toads 55 feet 5.8 R*
Around the corner, uphill and right from *Rest...* are two left-leaning cracks. Climb the right hand crack for 15 feet, then continue up to a vertical crack at the top.

Sheep Buttress

The two routes on Sheep Buttress can be accessed either by a desperate 5.7 chimney pitch (the lower part of the *JAM* crack) or by tunneling through the *JAM* crack from the back of the buttress, emerging above the top of the 5.7 chimney approach.

27 *Surprising Sheep 120 feet 5.9 ★★★*
Clean pro can be dicked into the huecos and a few horizontal cracks. A tricky lead or stimulating solo.
Variation: Continue straight up from the start of the left-leaning crack instead of climbing left out the crack.

28 *JAM 120 feet 5.7*

29 *Lords and the New Creatures 100 feet 5.11 ★★*

V-Crack Wall

This north-facing wall at the top of the canyon is characterized by the obvious "V-shaped" crack, and is visible from any where on the Main Dam. The approach up the canyon ascends some 3rd class rock.

30 *Left Mother's V 50 feet 5.11+ ★*

31 *Right Mother's V 50 feet 5.11–* ★
Climb the right-hand V-crack on the wall.
Variation: (5.11) Toprope the face to the right of *Right Mother's V* route.

32 *Lowercase 30 feet 5.9* ★
20 feet to the right of the "V-shaped" crack, climb a short right-angling hand crack.

Dog Wall

33 *Yllabian Dogfight 100 feet 5.8 R* ★
Start on the ground by a tree at the base of the V-Crack Wall approach ramp. Climb an easy, right-leaning wide crack to a large sloping ledge 20 feet up. From the ledge step left and climb up staying 15 to 20 feet from the left edge of the wall.
Variation 1: (5.10–) Start on *Yllabian Dog fight,* and climb to a horizontal crack 70 feet up. This crack leads to a left-facing dihedral. Traverse right following the crack for 15 feet. Continue straight up on good rock 10 feet left of the dihedral.
Variation: (5.10–) Instead of climbing straight up, like the first variation, keep traversing right to the left-facing dihedral and climb it to the top.

Dam Rock

34 *Tunnel Vision 50 feet 5.7* 35 *Dam Huecos 45 feet 5.9–*

Dam Rock

Dam Rock is the first rock south of the Main Dam. This fin's base touches the south end of the dam.

34 *Tunnel Vision 50 feet 5.7*

35 *Dam Huecos 45 feet 5.9–*
Variation: (5.10–) This variation joins *Dam Huecos* at the small roof at the top of the west face on Dam Rock.

RATING INDEX

5.7

5.8

5.9

5.10–

5.10

5.10+

5.11–

5.11

5.11 (cont.)

- ☐ Goodhueco Variation ★ (73)
- ☐ Horse Latitudes ★★★ (243)
- ☐ Krispy Kritters (177)
- ☐ Lizard King ★★ (244)
- ☐ Lords and the New Creatures (370)
- ☐ Luther ★ (66)
- ☐ Maidenhead (217)
- ☐ Mariachi Man (364)
- ☐ Max Headroom (322)
- ☐ Memorial (75)
- ☐ Mojo Risin' ★★ (49)
- ☐ Monkey Man ★ (135)
- ☐ Mr. Natural (322)
- ☐ My Captain ★ (244)
- ☐ Natural Mystic ★ (325)
- ☐ Nautilus, The ★★ (137)
- ☐ Nuclear Bunnies (367)
- ☐ Nuclear Fallout (355)
- ☐ Nuclear Huecoland (357)
- ☐ Padudu (364)
- ☐ Pazuzu ★ (364)
- ☐ Plastic Fantastic ★★★ (238)
- ☐ Prostate (105)
- ☐ Rainbow Bridge (79)
- ☐ Streaker, The (358)
- ☐ Stress Fracture (244)
- ☐ Strong Arm (135)
- ☐ Tailfeather (48)
- ☐ Upwind (242)
- ☐ Waiting For The Sun ★★ (243)
- ☐ Warning, The (313)
- ☐ Wasp Warrior ★ (240)
- ☐ Watchtower (244)
- ☐ Windy Days (51)
- ☐ Zombi (49)
- ☐ Zumi (49)

5.11+

- ☐ Amplified Heat ★★ (79)
- ☐ Battle Star (49)
- ☐ Big Brother's Been Bolting (305)
- ☐ Blinded By The Light (346)
- ☐ Bob's Day off (174)
- ☐ Central Latitudes ★★★ (243)
- ☐ Crunchy Toad Ten ★★ (202)
- ☐ Danger Bird ★ (177)
- ☐ Empire of The Senseless ★★ (202)
- ☐ Eternal Apples ★★ (76)
- ☐ Final Stone ★★ (73)
- ☐ Geek Stop (73)
- ☐ Hairy Chingadera (137)
- ☐ Icarus ★★ (117)
- ☐ Keelhauler, The (e (290)
- ☐ Left Hand Perverts ★ (67)
- ☐ Lunar Rover (346)
- ☐ Mechan's Cracked ★ (248)
- ☐ Montana Crack ★ (52)
- ☐ Mother's V, Left ★ (370)
- ☐ Mumblety-peg (173)
- ☐ Optical Promise ★★★ (80)
- ☐ Paddled Severely During Sorority Initiation ★ (290)
- ☐ Pervert's Delight ★ (67)
- ☐ Pink Adrenaline ★★★ (80)
- ☐ Plastic Surgery ★★ (238)
- ☐ Raindance (319)
- ☐ Ranger Turd (177)
- ☐ Rebel Chef ★ (363)
- ☐ Road To Nowhere ★★ (328)
- ☐ Skidmark, The (177)
- ☐ Think Light ★★ (330)
- ☐ Through the Looking Glass ★ (328)
- ☐ Western Playland ★★ (329)

5.12–

- ☐ Bald Eagle ★★ (330)
- ☐ Blue Balls ★★ (34)
- ☐ Deliverance ★★ (80)
- ☐ Dos Equis or Double Cross ★★ (75)
- ☐ F.H.I.T.A. (243)
- ☐ Fred's Toprope (76)
- ☐ Lunar Abstract ★ (75)
- ☐ M & M Sex Toy ★ (76)
- ☐ Maidenform ★★ (217)
- ☐ Mexican Toprope (32)
- ☐ More Power In The Shower (358)
- ☐ No Fear of Flying ★★ (75)
- ☐ Now It's Dark (244)
- ☐ Right Hand Perverts ★ (67)
- ☐ Rock Hard Nipples (129)
- ☐ Secret Sharer, The ★★★ (362)
- ☐ Tiny Rubber Love (364)
- ☐ Tlaloc ★★ (177)
- ☐ Wild, Wild, West, The ★ (243)
- ☐ Wyoming Cowgirl (103)

5.12

5.12+

5.13–

5.13

5.13+

V0–

V0–

V0

V0 (cont.)

- ☐ Fats Domino ★★ (297)
- ☐ Feces of The Ages (89)
- ☐ Ferro-Crack (369)
- ☐ Finders Keepers (126)
- ☐ Frankenstem ★★★ (134)
- ☐ Freddy's Facials (159)
- ☐ Free Salathe, The (111)
- ☐ Free The Gerbils (218)
- ☐ Frisco Thin Crack ★ (53)
- ☐ Gangrene Seam (122)
- ☐ Garvey's Ghost ★ (295)
- ☐ Groove Thang ★ (106)
- ☐ Ground Zero (311)
- ☐ Have It Your Way ★ (117)
- ☐ Hector (114)
- ☐ Hefty (298)
- ☐ Hide Pounds Fast (263)
- ☐ High and Mighty ★★★ (137)
- ☐ High Protein Snack ★ (101)
- ☐ Ho Ho Ho ★★ (254)
- ☐ Holey Shit (190)
- ☐ Honey Hole, The (133)
- ☐ Horst Scale, The ★ (183)
- ☐ Hueco-Fu Right ★ (195)
- ☐ Huevos Y Chorozo ★ (305)
- ☐ Hug-A-Jug Wall (189)
- ☐ I Saw Mommy Frenching Santa Claus ★ (254)
- ☐ IM Force (34)
- ☐ In Like Flint (237)
- ☐ Inchworm (271)
- ☐ Infield Single (207)
- ☐ Iron Maiden ★ (159)
- ☐ Iron Rich ★ (289)
- ☐ It's Not The Heat (261)
- ☐ Jason The Mongolard (196)
- ☐ Jimmy Hats On Parade ★★ (139)
- ☐ Jugular ★ (57)
- ☐ Juvenile offender (185)
- ☐ Karnivore (196)
- ☐ Lactator, The ★ (299)
- ☐ Laughing Sutra, The ★ (59)
- ☐ Least of Your Problems ★ (189)
- ☐ Left Groove ★ (109)
- ☐ Leftover, The (172)
- ☐ Leggo My Egg Hole (233)
- ☐ Lick Bush (308)
- ☐ Little Head (109)
- ☐ Little Spermaid, The (179)
- ☐ Lizard Face ★ (179)
- ☐ Loaf 'N Jug (52)
- ☐ Lost Souls (123)
- ☐ Maggie's Nightmare (206)
- ☐ Magnum ★ (368)
- ☐ Maple's Syrup (131)
- ☐ Melon Patch, The ★★★ (90)
- ☐ Melonhead, The (195)
- ☐ Men In Chains (131)
- ☐ Midriff Bulge (36)
- ☐ Mom Sells Kidney To Buy Furniture ★★ (263)
- ☐ Monkey Business (282)
- ☐ Monster Slab, The ★★ (173)
- ☐ Moonwalk ★ (209)
- ☐ Mud Flaps (109)
- ☐ Mud Shark (44)
- ☐ Mushroom Boulder, East Face ★★ (93)
- ☐ N.A.M.B.L.A. Hoedown, The (276)
- ☐ Odor Eater (296)
- ☐ Old Spice (156)
- ☐ Onky On A Donkey ★ (259)
- ☐ Otimojoginkbrute (223)
- ☐ Pacific Sock Exchange (166)
- ☐ Pancake Batter (129)
- ☐ Peeler, The (134)
- ☐ Pistons of Flesh (168)
- ☐ Plate Job (277)
- ☐ Playtex Husband (40)
- ☐ Poop (320)
- ☐ Puppy Chow ★ (275)
- ☐ Pushy, Pushy (174)
- ☐ Real Bruce Lee, The ★★★ (195)
- ☐ Return Business ★★★ (140)
- ☐ Rip Van Winkle (233)
- ☐ Rockford (368)
- ☐ Rubber Breath (345)
- ☐ Rumble In The Jungle (42)
- ☐ Savage With A Cinder (224)
- ☐ Saxon Tactics (88)
- ☐ Scarlett Unleashed ★ (179)
- ☐ Seagram's VO (274)
- ☐ Short Leash (212)
- ☐ Sidewall Blowout ★★ (237)
- ☐ Slam Dip (103)
- ☐ Solid Pleasure ★★ (139)
- ☐ Son of Funkenstone (206)
- ☐ Sphincter, The (89)
- ☐ Split Crack ★★★ (85)
- ☐ Split Ends (85)
- ☐ Split Shift (85)
- ☐ Splitting Hairs (83)
- ☐ Stinkfoot ★ (296)
- ☐ Stretch and Fetch ★ (57)
- ☐ Surf and Slam (220)
- ☐ Tension Deficit Disorder (122)
- ☐ Tobacco-chewing Gut-chomping Kinfolk From Hell (87)
- ☐ Tongue-In-Groove ★★★ (106)
- ☐ Training Bra, The (129)
- ☐ Tralfaz (36)
- ☐ Trivial Pursuit (218)
- ☐ True Grot (287)
- ☐ Truth Or Consequences ★ (113)
- ☐ Unconditional Love (232)
- ☐ Urge To Purge, The (180)
- ☐ UTEP Two Step ★ (282)
- ☐ White Swallow, The (345)
- ☐ Why? (48)

V0 (cont.)

V0+

VO+ (cont.)

V1

V1 (cont.)

V1 (cont.)

V2

V2 (cont.)

V3

V3 (cont.)

V4

V4 (cont.)

- ☐ Pearl Necklace ★ (36)
- ☐ Pick It (352)
- ☐ Picking Straws (126)
- ☐ Plunger, The (283)
- ☐ Point Blunk (295)
- ☐ Politics Or Pontiacs ★ (208)
- ☐ Pounding System ★★ (45)
- ☐ Rattlesnake Left ★ (118)
- ☐ Rembrandt Pussyhorse (185)
- ☐ Ricardo Cracker ★★ (82)
- ☐ Right Fluff, The ★ (288)
- ☐ Robocock (272)
- ☐ Saint Vitus' Dance (271)
- ☐ Serious Attitude Problem ★ (152)
- ☐ Sign of the Choss ★ (32)
- ☐ Silly Goose ★ (273)
- ☐ Sinful Longings ★★ (149)
- ☐ Sizzler, The (299)
- ☐ Slash, The ★ (40)
- ☐ Slippery Little Devil ★ (206)
- ☐ Smokin' Sausage ★★★ (306)
- ☐ Snappy Tom (179)
- ☐ Sound of Power, The ★ (255)
- ☐ Spotty's Mean Streak ★★ (341)
- ☐ Squirm (54)
- ☐ T-Bone Shuffle ★ (40)
- ☐ Tall Stack ★ (147)
- ☐ Thingfish (65)
- ☐ Tri Hard ★ (174)
- ☐ Trubblemaker (296)
- ☐ Umbra of Discontent, The (350)
- ☐ What's Left of Les Left ★★ (94)
- ☐ Whatsa Matter Baby (31)
- ☐ When Legends Lie ★ (53)
- ☐ William's Lectric Shave (207)
- ☐ Woman's Place, A ★ (27)
- ☐ Wurst Case Scenario ★★ (306)
- ☐ Young Guns (187)

V5

- ☐ 45 Degree Wall, The ★★★★ (286)
- ☐ All Purpose Grind (300)
- ☐ Amazing Little Halfboy ★ (266)
- ☐ Another Dick Face (62)
- ☐ Assault of The Killer Bimbos ★ (182)
- ☐ Between The Puffs ★★ (350)
- ☐ Brutus (174)
- ☐ Bulb of Percussion, The ★★ (238)
- ☐ Bulbicide Traverse ★ (224)
- ☐ Buttcracker (259)
- ☐ Camel's Back (167)
- ☐ Chemical Warfare ★ (148)
- ☐ Coffee Achiever ★★ (62)
- ☐ Dead Legends ★★ (278)
- ☐ Dentugrip ★ (31)
- ☐ Devastating Mic Control ★★ (278)
- ☐ Dick Almighty ★ (101)
- ☐ Dogmatics ★★★ (183)
- ☐ Donkey Show, Left ★★★ (259)
- ☐ Donkey Show, Right (259)
- ☐ Dragonfly ★★★ (183)
- ☐ El Mussy ★ (101)
- ☐ Elements of Style, The ★★★ (230)
- ☐ Fistfucker (127)
- ☐ Girls of Texas (126)
- ☐ Gravy Train Tryout ★ (276)
- ☐ Gulp 'n Blow ★ (27)
- ☐ Gutbuster Plus (220)
- ☐ Hey, Hey, Hey We're The Monkees ★★ (282)
- ☐ Hillary In A Blender ★ (206)
- ☐ Hobbit In A Blender ★★★ (174)
- ☐ Honeycomb Hideout ★ (349)
- ☐ Hot Link, The (307)
- ☐ Howler, The ★ (251)
- ☐ Hyperconcious Master of The Extreem (345)
- ☐ Instant Expert (274)
- ☐ Jigsaw Puzzle, The ★★ (299)
- ☐ Jingus Bells ★★★ (293)
- ☐ John Sherman Is Neither (296)
- ☐ Leapin' Lizards ★ (140)
- ☐ Legless Little Hero (265)
- ☐ Lip Traverse ★ (97)
- ☐ Long Term Memory Loss ★ (252)
- ☐ Member's Only ★ (307)
- ☐ Moonshine Roof Right ★★★ (256)
- ☐ Morgue, The ★★★ (40)
- ☐ Mow The Lawn (336)
- ☐ Nice Girls Do ★★ (41)
- ☐ No Place Like Home ★★ (205)
- ☐ Pimpin' ★ (111)
- ☐ Pindejo (342)
- ☐ Pirelli (289)
- ☐ Pugsley's Porch (296)
- ☐ Rattlesnake Right (118)
- ☐ Red (180)
- ☐ Robospot ★ (272)
- ☐ Schadenfraud ★ (127)
- ☐ Shazam (301)
- ☐ Slick Watts ★ (62)
- ☐ Slim Pickins ★★ (298)
- ☐ Smegmatoesis (296)
- ☐ So Damn Insane (173)
- ☐ Springtime for Hitler (31)
- ☐ Star Power ★★★ (355)
- ☐ Straight Outta Conway ★ (278)
- ☐ Tall People In A Blender (167)

V5 (cont.)

V6

V7

V8

V9

V10

V11

V12

V13

ROUTE INDEX

C

D

E

F

G

H

I

J

K

L

Q

R

S

T

X

Y

Z

Access: It's everybody's concern

The Access Fund, a national, non-profit climbers' organization, is working to keep you climbing. The Access Fund helps preserve access and protect the environment by providing funds for land acquisitions and climber support facilities, financing scientific studies, publishing educational materials promoting low-impact climbing, and providing start-up money, legal counsel and other resources to local climbers' coalitions.

Climbers can help preserve access by being responsible users of climbing areas. Here are some practical ways to support climbing:

- COMMIT YOURSELF TO "LEAVING NO TRACE." Pick up litter around campgrounds and the crags. Let your actions inspire others.
- DISPOSE OF HUMAN WASTE PROPERLY. Use toilets whenever possible. If none are available, choose a spot at least 50 meters from any water source. Dig a hole 6 inches (15 cm) deep, and bury your waste in it. *Always pack out toilet paper* in a "Ziploc"-type bag.
- UTILIZE EXISTING TRAILS. Avoid cutting switchbacks and trampling vegetation.
- USE DISCRETION WHEN PLACING BOLTS AND OTHER "FIXED" PROTECTION. Camouflage all anchors with rock-colored paint. Use chains for rappel stations, or leave rock-colored webbing.
- RESPECT RESTRICTIONS that protect natural resources and cultural artifacts . Appropriate restrictions can include prohibition of climbing around Indian rock art, pioneer inscriptions, and on certain formations during raptor nesting season. Power drills are illegal in wilderness areas. *Never chisel or sculpt holds in rock on public lands, unless it is expressly allowed* – no other practice so seriously threatens our sport.
- PARK IN DESIGNATED AREAS, not in undeveloped, vegetated areas. Carpool to the crags!
- MAINTAIN A LOW PROFILE. Other people have the same right to undisturbed enjoyment of natural areas as do you.
- RESPECT PRIVATE PROPERTY. Don't trespass in order to climb.
- JOIN OR FORM A GROUP to deal with access issues in your area. Consider clean-ups, trail building or maintenance, or other "goodwill" projects.
- JOIN THE ACCESS FUND. To become a member, *simply make a donation (tax-deductable) of any amount.* Only by working together can we preserve the diverse American climbing experience.

The Access Fund. Preserving America's diverse climbing resources.

The Access Fund • P.O. Box 17010 • Boulder, CO 80308